Lives and Times

Lives and Times

Individuals and Issues in American History

Since 1865

Blaine T. Browne and Robert C. Cottrell

ROWMAN & LITTLEFIELD PUBLISHERS, INC.
Lanham • Boulder • New York • Toronto • Plymouth, UK

Published by Rowman & Littlefield Publishers, Inc.
A wholly owned subsidiary of The Rowman & Littlefield Publishing Group, Inc.
4501 Forbes Boulevard, Suite 200, Lanham, Maryland 20706
http://www.rowmanlittlefield.com

Estover Road, Plymouth PL6 7PY, United Kingdom

British Library Cataloguing in Publication Information Available

Library of Congress Cataloging-in-Publication Data

Browne, Blaine T. (Blaine Terry)
  Lives and times : individuals and issues in American history / Blaine T. Browne and
Robert C. Cottrell.
     p. cm.
  Includes bibliographical references and index.
  ISBN 978-0-7425-6193-9 (v. 2 : cloth : alk. paper) — ISBN 978-0-7425-6194-6
(v. 2 : pbk. : alk. paper) — ISBN 978-1-4422-0060-9 (v. 2 : electronic)
  1. United States—Biography. 2. United States—History. I. Cottrell, Robert C., 1950–
II. Title.
  CT211.B76 2010
  973—dc22

                                                                              2009032103

Printed in the United States of America

~

Contents

~

Preface

"Read no history: nothing but biography, for that is life without theory." So wrote the British man of letters and Conservative politician Benjamin Disraeli in his 1832 novel *Contarini Fleming*. His contemporary, English historian Thomas Carlyle, offered a somewhat different perspective on the relationship between history and biography when he stated, "History is the essence of innumerable biographies." Modern historians generally agree that biography can stand alone as a worthy genre as well as complement history. This reader was developed with the idea that biography imbedded within a historical context can be an effective means of teaching history, engaging readers with compelling narratives of the lives of individuals who decisively shaped their times. Too often, primary texts, due to editorial constraints, devote relatively little coverage to the lives of even prominent individuals who reshape history. Many of those texts offering some biographical information excise it from the main narrative and relegate it to a sidebar, thereby inviting readers to consider it to be optional information. This text was conceived to fill an often discernible gap in many primary texts.

As this volume was conceived chiefly as a supplement to primary survey texts in American history, much consideration has been given to the chronological and thematic design of individual chapters. We have striven to include an array of individuals from a multitude of social, economic, ethnic, and religious backgrounds. Some were born to affluence and wielded considerable power and influence; others came from society's lower orders, in certain cases from outside the bounds of the majority society altogether, and spent much of their lives struggling against considerable odds.

The usual editorial constraints preclude a comprehensive examination of all the major issues in American history of this period, so this text is necessarily selective regarding those issues that are included. In each of the thirteen chapters in this volume, the lives of two individuals are examined within the context of an issue of their time and in relation to one or more other issues. Our intent has not been to structure this text exclusively around a "contrasting visions" approach, though some chapters are so designed. Elsewhere, the chapters jointly examine two individuals whose lives illuminate an issue, though they may not have been on opposing sides of it. Readers will find that each chapter opens with an introduction of the issue and the two individuals to be profiled. Using a narrative approach complemented with analysis, the lives and times of each figure are examined, and then a summary conclusion is presented. Each chapter concludes with a list of suggested study questions and a selected bibliography.

The authors express their deep appreciation to their wives, Marian Browne and Sue Cottrell, for the usual patience and support that they unhesitatingly offered throughout the course of this project.

~

Introduction

The American Civil War, which began nearly a century and half ago, laid the foundations for a republic rapidly transformed beyond any expectations of the founding generation. The war helped to redefine the meaning of freedom, with a new stress on the importance of liberty and equality. For American ethnic minorities, especially African Americans, this was an ongoing struggle, marked by both advance and setback, which has continued into the twenty-first century. One cannot help but marvel at the changes that have transpired between the 1860 election of Abraham Lincoln and that of Barack Obama, the first African American president, in 2008. Ironically, for Native Americans, the continent's indigenous people, the relentless advance of the American nation in the nineteenth century meant the inevitable near extinction of their civilization.

The Civil War also marked the advent of an industrial revolution that forever changed the nation, spawning new economic elites with unprecedented financial power together with a working class that was compelled to fight for decades to ensure recognition of its basic rights. Broader concerns for social and economic justice became paramount during the Progressive Era of the early twentieth century, but the progressive reformers proved divided as to the nature of the nation's new role in the world as of World War I. The postwar era saw a relaxation of both the reform impulse and internationalist policies, as the American people, still divided by economic, ethnic, and religious barriers, nevertheless came together to celebrate an increasingly vibrant popular culture. The Depression decade of the 1930s brought challenges, while affording opportunities for reform and a fundamental transformation of national politics as President Franklin Roosevelt and other reformers responded energetically to the social and economic ills ravaging the nation.

Those same years compelled Americans to address their place in the wider world, as crises threatened in both Europe and Asia. Some advocated isolation in the face of the mounting totalitarian threat from abroad, while others recognized it as a challenge to the American way of life and acted to combat the menace. Rapidly changing international circumstances from the 1930s through the 1950s paralleled shifting conceptions of how one defined loyalty, and many fell victim to the shifts in public opinion. Recognizing the benefits to be reaped from popular fears of subversives, whether they were Nazis or communists, astute politicians constructed political careers at the expense of countrymen who failed to conform to ideological conventions.

The turbulent years after World War II nevertheless brought opportunities to address lingering inequities in American society. Activists took up a multitude of causes, including environmentalism, racial justice, women's rights, and opposition to what many saw as an immoral war in Vietnam. These movements in turn sparked changes that produced a conservative reaction. By the 1980s, the liberal political mode that had shaped national politics since the 1930s gave way to an ascendant conservatism that defined liberty as necessitating less government intervention at home and an aggressive anticommunist foreign policy abroad. The neoconservative advocates of American world hegemony, encouraged by the collapse of the Soviet empire in the early 1990s, found little public support for their outlook through that generally prosperous and peaceful decade, but the terrorist attacks of September 11, 2001, convinced the recently elected Republican president George W. Bush that the security of the United States required a radical departure from the policy of containment in favor of a new unilateralism and doctrine of preemption.

The American electorate, politically polarized since the 1990s, remained so throughout the first six years of the presidency of George W. Bush, who sought to implement a strongly conservative domestic agenda despite his controversial electoral victory in 2000. But within several years there were growing indications that public support for the Bush administration and Republican policies was flagging. Bush's controversial decision to invade Iraq in 2003 ultimately proved disastrous for his presidency, as casualties mounted, the rationale for the invasion proved flawed, and no viable exit strategy emerged. Though Bush won reelection in 2004, stressing national security issues, his administration's general competency to govern was widely questioned as early as 2005, in the aftermath of the Hurricane Katrina fiasco. The Democrats' recapture of Congress in 2006 signaled growing dissatisfaction with the Iraq War and Republican economic and social policies. The collapse of financial markets and institutions during the presidential election campaign of 2008 afforded Illinois senator Barack Obama, virtually unknown four years earlier, with his promise of transformational change, to prevail easily. The twentieth-century political paradigm, it appeared, had been eclipsed, as new demographics and expectations laid the ground for new approaches to both domestic and international issues in the twenty-first century.

CHAPTER ONE

~

A New Birth of Freedom Deferred

During the Civil War, President Abraham Lincoln demonstrated his rhetorical eloquence on numerous occasions, but perhaps none was as memorable as the dedication of the military cemetery at Gettysburg, Pennsylvania, on November 19, 1863, where he delivered a surprisingly brief address before a restless crowd. The president seized the occasion to present to a war-weary nation the deeper meaning of the terrible conflict, the cost of which had already reached into many American homes, both North and South. Lincoln reminded his audience of the historical purpose and promise of their nation, which, he proclaimed, had been "conceived in liberty, and dedicated to the proposition that all men are created equal." Acknowledging the "unfinished work" that lay ahead, Lincoln spoke of "the great task remaining before us . . . that this nation, under God, shall have a new birth of freedom." That last phrase, together with the president's earlier reference to Jefferson's dictum about the equality of all men, hinted at a more inclusive definition of freedom, one that would encompass African Americans. Lincoln had already begun formulating policies for the reconstruction of those Confederate states occupied by federal forces, and the issue of the postwar status of freed slaves grew increasingly urgent. The president himself had only gradually begun to reconsider his previous beliefs about the unworkability of a biracial society and colonizing freed blacks abroad. Within his Gettysburg Address could be seen a glimmer of a more enlightened conception of race relations and the meaning of freedom. Though Lincoln would not live to see it, his own Republican Party would seek to realize this vision during the era of Reconstruction.

Congressional or Radical Reconstruction effectively began in early 1867 with the passage of the Military Reconstruction Act, which imposed military government on the former Confederate states. Under the protection of the U.S. Army, new Republican-led state governments took power with the broad support of recently enfranchised freedmen. Undertaking diverse political, social, and economic reforms, these Reconstruction governments initially gave promise of realizing Lincoln's "new birth of freedom," but such hopes dimmed after 1870, the year that the last former Confederate state was readmitted to the Union. The attentions of Congress and the Northern public to Southern affairs began to wane even as white southern Democrats began the process of "Redemption," wresting political control of their states from Republicans. Any pretense of pursuing the idealistic vision of Congressional reconstruction ended with the Compromise of 1877, which resolved a disputed presidential election in favor of Republican Rutherford B. Hayes in return for his party's agreement to end Reconstruction. This marked the beginning of a new era that saw Lincoln's lofty goals deferred for nearly a century. The Redeemers reestablished white supremacy in the South through black disfranchisement and a system of legal racial segregation marking the beginning of a nightmarish era for many African Americans. Choices were stark: one could submit to the dictates of white supremacy and all of its attendant humiliations, or one could challenge the system and run the very real risk of retaliation, which often meant impoverishment, physical injury, or death.

One of those who struggled to redeem his state from "carpetbag" government and to establish a white supremacist regime was South Carolinian Benjamin R. Tillman, who served two terms as governor and four terms as a U.S. senator. Known as "Pitchfork Ben" because of his championing of farmers, Governor Tillman built his political career on his defense of white supremacy and attacks on the "aristocrats" who profited at the expense of the working man. Renowned for the vulgarity and violence of his language, Tillman gained infamy as an advocate of lynch law, once proclaiming that he would "willingly lead a mob in lynching a Negro who had committed an assault upon a white woman." As a freshman U.S. senator in 1895, Tillman brought his raw language to the Senate floor, where he drew huge galleries with his rhetorical crudities in defense of the "Southern perspective" on race. The South Carolinian was not alone in his views; he was one of a number of Southern demagogues who came to power in the post-Reconstruction period advocating white supremacy. Though some political figures and editors denounced the New South racists, beleaguered black Americans had no effective voice in the national political system and were left to their own devices.

These depressing circumstances posed major dilemmas for African Americans, especially those living in the Southern states where politicians such as Tillman seemed to encourage violence against blacks. Some saw logic in former slave Booker T. Washington's perspective—blacks should "accommodate" themselves to the realities of the New South and forgo pressing for civil rights in favor of hard work and productivity. Other African Americans saw only degradation and submission in Washington's accommodationist outlook and concluded that racial injustices had to be confronted boldly. Ida B. Wells, born to a slave family in Mississippi in 1862, actively opposed white supremacy even as racists such as Ben Tillman were striving to institutionalize it. As a young adult, Wells personally challenged Jim Crow laws and turned her writing talents to journalistic use, attacking the myriad injustices endured by African Americans. Her greatest crusade was in opposition to lynching, which reached epidemic proportions in the 1890s. Torture, mutilation, and death through mob action was one of the most horrific means by which white supremacy was maintained, and Wells sought not only to awaken the nation to the extent of these horrendous crimes but to analyze the lynchers' motives and expose the disingenuousness of the rationales offered by Tillman and other Southern demagogues. In an era in which some sought to ensure that African Americans should not experience a new birth of freedom, Wells struggled against great odds to see that vision fulfilled.

～ BENJAMIN R. TILLMAN ～

As soon as he had begun his maiden speech before the U.S. Senate on January 29, 1895, it was clear that South Carolina Democrat Benjamin Tillman intended to establish a reputation as an outspoken maverick who cared little for the traditions of decorum within that usually staid body; he was willing to employ any rhetorical excess in defense of his region, his state, and the working-class whites he professed to represent. His physical appearance, many contemporaries noted, reinforced the blunt impact of his words. One observer remarked that Tillman, who had lost one eye to an adolescent infection, had a face that "would compel attention in any gathering of distinguished men," and another commented, "Above this gigantic man there gleams the fiercest face ever seen on a public man." Known for a dramatic speaking style replete with violent gestures, contorted facial expressions, and exaggerated intonations, Tillman on this occasion stunned many in his own party with a withering assault on Democratic President Grover Cleveland, whom he had denounced during the previous year's campaign as "an old bag of beef." It was then that Tillman had vowed to "go to Washington with a pitchfork and prod him in his old fat ribs." Now on the Senate floor, Pitchfork Ben proceeded to do just that, assailing the corpulent Cleveland as a hopelessly conservative "Bourbon" Democrat who conspired with the "money-changers" of Wall Street

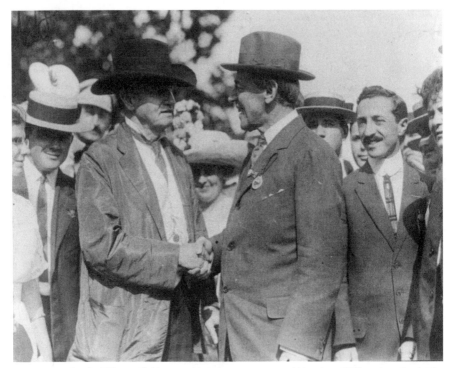

Senator Benjamin Tillman (left) greets New Jersey governor Woodrow Wilson (no date). The South Carolina Democrat and the Virginia-born Wilson shared segregationist sentiments, though Tillman's rhetoric was considerably less restrained than that of the professorial Wilson. As both a governor and a senator, Tillman was infamous for his advocacy of violence in defense of white supremacy. As president from 1913 to 1921, Wilson sought to segregate the federal civil service, restricting black employees to menial positions and dismissing them where possible. (Library of Congress, LC-USZ62-68424)

to reduce the nation's working classes to "a hopeless existence of toil year in and year out." Leveling such harsh allegations against a president from one's own party was deemed outrageous. Senatorial colleagues refused to offer Tillman the usual postspeech congratulations, and numerous newspapers denounced the South Carolinian in unequivocal terms. The *New York Times* dismissed Tillman as "a filthy baboon, accidentally seated in the Senate chamber." The *Springfield Republican* was equally condemnatory, calling the senator "a slang-whanging buffoon and demagogue." The Philadelphia *Record* described the South Carolinian as representative of the "ignorance, intolerance and violence of the state's mean white trash."

Tillman's inaugural speech prefigured a senatorial career built around the intentional cultivation of controversy through hyperbolic rhetoric. Though his speeches touched on a number of contemporary issues, he was best known for his persistent defense of the Southern perspective on Reconstruction, race relations, and the necessity of violence to preserve the Southern social order from black "outrages." In an infamous March 23, 1900, Senate speech, Tillman responded to Wisconsin Senator John Spooner's allegations of Democratic misdeeds during Reconstruction with a reiteration of the classic Southern account of that era. Republicans had not given blacks the franchise as a means of self-defense, Tillman charged, but rather "because the Republicans of that day, led by Thad[deus] Stevens, wanted to put white necks under black heels and to get revenge." Those same Republicans had "propped your carpetbag Negro government with bayonets." Proclaiming his desire that "the country get the full view of the southern side of this question and the justification for anything we did," Tillman asserted that "we did not disfranchise the Negroes until 1895" and then only to ensure social order in the state. "The negro is as contented and prosperous and as well protected in South Carolina today as in any state of the Union south of the Potomac," Tillman declared. "He is not meddling with politics, for he found that the more he meddled with them the worse off he got." In a characteristically defiant tone, Tillman continued:

> As to his "rights"—I will not discuss them now. We of the South have never recognized the right of the Negro to govern white men, and we never will. We never believed him to be equal to the white man, and we will not submit to gratifying his lust on our wives and daughters without lynching him. I would to God the last one of them was in Africa and that none of them had ever been brought to our shores.

Tillman's sentiments shocked many outside the South, but his equation of African American equality with black sexual predation was a commonplace component of white Southern thought, which rationalized lynching as a necessary weapon against black men who sought to assert their equality through sexual violence against white women. This concept was central to the poisonous mind-set of white supremacy that pervaded much of the post-Reconstruction South, and Ben Tillman sought to establish himself as its most able defender.

The Edgefield district of South Carolina, where Benjamin Ryan Tillman was born on August 11, 1847, had a special reputation for lawlessness in a state that some saw as defined by the two corollaries of personal violence and radical sentiments. The Palmetto State's political representatives were renowned for behavior and rhetoric that were equally rash long before the Civil War. Two of the state's most famous native sons, John C. Calhoun and Preston Brookes, owed their fame respectively to provocative rhetoric and a ready resort to violence. Few could have been surprised that the South Carolina legislature was the first among the Southern states to proclaim its secession from the Union in late 1860, or that the war's first shots were fired at Charleston harbor. At the onset of the conflict, James Petigru, one of South Carolina's few Unionists, memorably characterized his state as "too small for a republic, but too large for a lunatic asylum." A legacy of rash action and violence also ran through the Tillman family. The senior Benjamin R. Tillman, given to gambling and religiosity, killed a man in 1847 but went unpunished, dying of typhoid fever two years later and leaving his young son Ben in the care of his mother, Sophia Ann Hancock. Over the next two decades, five of her seven sons died, four through violence. These incidents all occurred within the broader context of a slave society that routinely utilized violence as a means of disciplining and controlling black slaves.

Though widowed for many years, Sophia successfully built up the family's resources to include some 3,500 acres and eighty-six slaves by 1860. Prior to the Civil War, Ben's childhood was typical for those of his race and class in the South Carolina backcountry, including the many outdoor pursuits that led Tillman to recall later, "I grew up wild as a jimpson weed." Young Ben unquestionably embraced prevailing concepts about slavery and the nature of African Americans, telling his mother that they were "the most miserable lot of human beings—the nearest to the missing link with the monkey—I have ever put eyes on." Ben typified the sons of the planter class in other regards, however. One frequently voiced rationale for black slavery was that it was a system of labor that freed whites for intellectual pursuits. As a private school student, Ben was a voracious reader who developed an early and extensive acquaintance with classic literature. In the summer of 1864, Ben left preparatory school to join the Confederate army but was felled by a serious eye infection. After months of agony, he underwent the extraction of his left eye and was left with an empty socket that forever marked his countenance. Only months later, the Civil War ended and Ben Tillman confronted jarring new political and racial realities. In 1868, after a brief unsuccessful effort to establish a farm in Marion County, Florida, Ben returned to Edgefield, where he married Sallie Starke. Sophia provided the couple with 430 acres, and Ben struggled to establish himself as a farmer, sometimes frustrated by the need to rely upon paid African American labor. "You cannot work free Negroes," Tillman complained, "without cussing." By 1874, however, Tillman's success at farming compelled the hiring of one white and twenty black laborers. He was one of Edgefield County's leading citizens when the transformative events of 1876 took place.

Like many white Southerners, Ben Tillman saw myriad injustices in the Republican reconstruction policies that had been underway since 1867. Slavery, the chief institutional base of white supremacy, had been abolished, and the Fourteenth and Fifteenth Amendments to the Constitution had established the political equality of the freedmen. Slavery could never be restored, but by the late 1870s, many Southern whites saw an opportunity to restore their political dominance as a first step toward reestablishing white supremacy. In Edgefield, former Confederate generals Matthew C. Butler and Martin W. Gary schemed to drive blacks out of politics through intimidation and violence. Variously known as the Edgefield or "Shotgun" policy, the plan required the organization of white military companies to confront black Republican militias. Once blacks were disarmed, whites could control the polls. During the summer of 1876, armed white bands, some calling themselves "Redshirts," clashed with black militias on several occasions. Tillman, a leading participant in these activities, was present at the Hamburg Massacre on July 8, when Redshirts executed seven captured black militiamen. Tillman later described the episode as a "firebell in the night" summoning white men to "make one desperate fight to gain their lost liberties." The suppression of black voting in the subsequent elections sealed the doom of the state's Republican government and brought Democrat Wade Hampton, an ex-Confederate general and avid supporter of the Edgefield policy, to the governor's office in 1877. The first step toward the reestablishment of white supremacy had been completed. In subsequent years, Ben Tillman emerged as the chief advocate of a new social order in South Carolina, one in which conservative Democrats were castigated as thoroughly as were Republicans and blacks.

The roots of Ben Tillman's agrarian radicalism may be found in the 1880s, when personal economic reverses compelled him to examine the causes of his state's agricultural woes. Inefficient farming was partly to blame, he believed, chiefly the fault of ignorant whites and lazy blacks. But beyond the problems that agricultural education might remedy, Tillman noted the pernicious effects of an alliance of conservative Democrats and monied interests. This cabal of professional office seekers and greedy businessmen, he was convinced, were content to see hardworking farmers locked into a pernicious credit system that reduced them to poverty and hopelessness. By the mid-1880s, Tillman and like-minded allies were making frequent appeals to farm organizations as part of a strategy to gain influence in the state's Democratic Party. In 1886, Tillman's support for a new agricultural college (later Clemson University) bolstered his standing among farmers, and he was well positioned to seek the governor's office as an agrarian reformer in 1890. Tillman defeated conservative Democrat Alexander Haskell, who disdained Tillman's populist rhetoric, and took the oath of office on December 4. In his inaugural address, he was forthright about what his victory meant: "The triumph of democracy and white supremacy over mongrelism and anarchy, of civilization over barbarism, has been most complete." He was correspondingly frank about what this meant for the state's African Americans. "The whites have absolute control of the state government," he proclaimed, "and we intend at any and all costs to retain it. The intelligent exercise of the right to vote . . . is as yet beyond the capacity of the vast majority of colored men. We deny, without regard to color, that 'all men are created equal'; it is not true now, and was not true when Jefferson wrote it." The new governor tempered these remarks with a plea that responsible whites treat blacks decently and asked that lynching be abolished so as to improve the state's image.

During his first term, Governor Tillman attempted to make good on his promise to end lynching, unsuccessfully urging the legislature to grant him the authority to remove sheriffs who failed to protect prisoners from mobs. Tillman, a firm believer in the need for social order, saw lynching as an assault on law, and during his first year as governor there were no lynchings in the state. When a lynching did occur the following year, Tillman reprimanded the sheriff involved. His relatively progressive stance on this issue was not matched elsewhere. A dedicated social conservative, Tillman believed that white male supremacy could be maintained only if blacks and women were kept in their respective places. For the former, that meant tightening the Jim Crow racial segregation laws; for women, it meant reinforcement of traditional social and economic roles. To this latter end, in 1891 Tillman was instrumental in founding Winthrop College, which offered appropriate education and vocational training to white women. Tillman told a dedication day audience that the college's mission was to instill "self-confidence" in women without their becoming "unsexed." Women who strove for equality with men lost their respectability, he declared, becoming "strong-minded, bold, brazen, pert, self-asserting." Women, like blacks, also had no place in politics, as far as the governor was concerned. They were unsuited by nature, and politics was a degrading field that could potentially besmirch the moral purity of white women. The need to preserve the purity of women had long been a cardinal tenet of Southern thought and could be used to justify restricting women's roles as well as a rationale for lynching blacks who perpetrated "outrages" against white women.

"Tillmanism," a combined appeal to class as well as racial biases, was dynamic enough to return Tillman to the governership in 1892, after which he abandoned his earlier position on lynching. Blacks who continued to insist on exercising the franchise threatened Tillman's political power, and the governor grasped the usefulness of lynching as an instrument of terror against "uppity" blacks, though he took care to specify that it was appropriate only in specific circumstances. As early as the 1892 campaign, he had proclaimed, "There is only one crime that warrants lynching, and Governor as I am, I would lead a mob to lynch the Negro who ravishes a white woman." Subsequently, when John Peterson, a black resident of Barnwell County, was accused of raping a fourteen-year-old white girl, Tillman notified a Barnwell sheriff that "the villain deserves lynching," and warned that the chief concern was to "preserve the proprieties." In the future, Tillman rarely equivocated about the practice that he had once condemned, and the number of lynchings began to rise in South Carolina, paralleling a general trend throughout the region. Tillman also sought to ensure that the growing populist movement did not draw voters away from Tillmanism. Both movements grew out of agrarian and working-class resentments of privilege and power, and Tillman adroitly protected his electoral base by having the state's Democratic Party adopt the Ocala Demands, the platform that populists had agreed to at a Florida meeting that year. He was outspoken in his disdain for North Carolina populists who sought black support. "Be a white man or be a nigger," he declared. "You have got to make your choice."

Even as the state legislature affirmed his elevation to the U.S. Senate in December 1894, Tillman worked to call a state constitutional convention, which met in 1895. Here, Tillman's supporters introduced suffrage qualifications that would ensure the participation of almost all whites while excluding most blacks. Residency and literacy requirements, along with poll taxes, proved to be highly effective in limiting black voting. The new constitution also enumerated a variety of disqualifying petty crimes that blacks were believed to commonly commit. After the prescribed voter reregistration of 1896, only 5,500 blacks qualified, as opposed to 50,000 whites. The more challenging controversy grew out of the reconsideration of the state's laws prohibiting interracial marriage. A potentially embarrassing debate over legal definitions of race provided an opportunity for the few black delegates at the convention to introduce a proposal requiring that any white man cohabiting with a woman of more than "one-eighth Negro blood" be barred from public office. As a professed defender of racial purity, Tillman was placed in the uncomfortable position of conceding the logic of the proposal. Like many of his cohorts, Tillman did not accord to black women the same native morality that they beheld in white women. Tillman had once informed a correspondent that "as far as sexual relations" went, African American women were "little more than animals." Such beliefs determined Tillman's reluctance to raise the state's legal age of consent, which, set at ten, was considered by many South Carolinians to be a national embarrassment. Tillman feared that lascivious black adolescent girls might conceivably entrap and ruin incautious white men. Convention delegates ultimately agreed to raise the age of consent to fourteen.

The South Carolina Constitutional Convention revealed the often bizarre complexities of political, racial, and gender relations in the New South, and as a U.S. senator, Ben Tillman was quick to defend his region's perspective before a national audience. He unflinchingly reiterated the racist perspectives on which white supremacy was grounded, once asserting that African Americans were "so near akin to the monkey that scientists are as yet looking for the missing link." He likewise defended the violence and illegalities inherent in establishing white domination, proudly proclaiming "in 1876 we shot Negroes and stuffed ballot boxes." Before a variety of audiences, Tillman argued that racism was merely a manifestation of a natural instinct to "race preservation" innate in all races. In the American South, he argued, naive Reconstructionists had fed blacks the dangerous notion of equality, which had led to years of black misgovernment, followed by a wave of black sexual predation that threatened racial purity. "The poor African became a fiend," he claimed, "a wild beast . . . lurking around to see if some helpless white woman [could] be murdered or brutalized." President Theodore Roosevelt's White House meeting with Booker T. Washington provoked Tillman's dire prediction that Roosevelt's action "in entertaining that nigger will necessitate our killing a thousand niggers in the South before they will learn their place again."

Tillman delighted in reminding audiences that antiblack prejudice was as widespread in the North as it was in his own region. "Northern people," he sneered, "have no more use for the colored man at close quarters than we have. . . . They love him according to the square of the distance [from him]." The South Carolinian likewise proclaimed that Northern outrage over Southern lynching was hypocritical. Arguing that Northerners indiscriminately brutalized blacks, Tillman noted, "In the South, on the other hand, the mob hunts down the man who is guilty or supposed to be guilty, and innocent Negroes are not molested." Tillman was especially ardent in defending the lynching of rapists, once telling astounded senators that, as governor of South Carolina, he had promised to "lead a mob to lynch any man, black or white, who ravished a woman, black or white." Despite his professed commitment to equal mob justice, Tillman's characteristically Southern obsession with the threat of black rapists was evident in an oft-quoted assertion: "I have three daughters but, so help me God, I would rather find either one of them [sic] killed by a tiger or a bear . . . than to have her crawl to me and tell me the horrid story that she had been robbed of the jewel of her womanhood by a black fiend." He professed fears that, were his message about the dangers of black equality and race mixing disregarded, the nation would face serious peril within a century: "All over the North, big buck Negroes marrying white women and no law to prevent it!"

As a senator, Tillman did engage other issues. He was an outspoken opponent of imperialism in the aftermath of the Spanish-American War, worrying that imperial acquisitions would only benefit the capitalist elite and that colonial expansion would lead to an influx of "Negroes . . . Malays, Negritos, Japanese and Chinese [and] mongrels of Spanish blood." Tillman did support the rapid naval expansion of the Roosevelt years, largely because of the expected benefit to South Carolina's ports. He favored some progressive causes, most notably the railway regulation acts that often came before the Senate, to which he was returned in 1901, 1907, and 1913. An ardent supporter of fellow

Southerner Woodrow Wilson, who as president resegregated the federal civil service, Tillman likewise endorsed Wilson's intervention in the European war in 1917. Suffering a number of strokes late in his senatorial career, Benjamin Tillman died in the nation's capital on July 3, 1918.

Ben Tillman would long be remembered not only as the "wild man of the senate" but as one of the most ardent proponents of white supremacy in the postwar South. He was among the first of a long succession of Southern demagogues who established white supremacist regimes, making race the crux of Southern politics. Georgia's Thomas Watson, Mississippi's James K. Vardaman, and Tillman's gubernatorial successor Cole Blease were among others who proved willing to take the rhetoric of racial hatred to new depths. For African Americans living in the Southern states, these were grim decades, during which the freedoms that Reconstruction had promised often seemed impossibly distant.

~ IDA B. WELLS ~

In a decade that saw lynchings of African Americans reach a historic high, the murder of Sam Hose on April 23, 1899, was especially barbaric. Hose, a laborer in rural Georgia, was alleged to have murdered his employer, a white farmer, before raping the man's wife and inflicting serious physical injuries on her infant. This version of events, circulating quickly among the white residents of the nearby town of Palmetto, contained all the classic elements of what was known as a black "outrage," replete with callous murder, interracial rape, and savage cruelty. In hundreds of like episodes in previous years, similar accusations had presaged vicious mob actions and by 1899, many lynchings had evolved into carefully choreographed public spectacles meant to reaffirm white supremacy through terror. Prior to the actual lynching, some 2,000 people, described in the *Atlantic Constitution* as including "lawyers, doctors, merchant farmers . . . from half a dozen counties" gathered in the small town, about two-thirds having arrived on special trains commissioned for the event. That afternoon, the spectacle began as the nude victim, tied to a tree, was methodically mutilated: his fingers were cut off and his face was skinned before he was emasculated. Next, Hose was soaked in oil and burned alive. At one point, as the writhing victim seemed on the verge of slipping his bonds, his tormentors temporarily doused the flames and secured him more firmly before reigniting the pyre. When the flames died out, some in the mob dissected the corpse and sold the body parts as souvenirs. One man was said to have taken a slice of Hose's heart to Atlanta to present to the governor.

Ida B. Wells, a thirty-seven-year-old African American activist and journalist, had dedicated her life to fighting lynching in 1892, when several acquaintances were murdered by a white mob. She believed that only through careful

Ida B. Wells, as she appeared in an illustration in The African American Press and Its Editors *in 1891. Reaching early adulthood during Reconstruction, Wells was determined to assert her equal rights as a citizen, despite white resistance and federal inaction. Much of her adult life was dedicated to a campaign against lynching, an act of terrorist intimidation against blacks that peaked in the 1890s. (Library of Congress, LC-USZ62-107756)*

documentation and analysis could the extent and purpose of lynching be made known to the American people; only then would effective political action to halt the practice have any chance of success. Wells had on numerous past occasions penned an article or editorial in reaction to such horrors, but the lynching of Sam Hose was so ghastly that it demanded a more substantial response. To research the pamphlet that would be published as *Lynch Law in Georgia*, Wells collected around 500 news articles about the Hose lynching so as to analyze the narrative that they presented. All the national news reports, she discovered, reiterated the same locally generated unsubstantiated accusations against the "black fiend" and provided morbidly detailed accounts of the victim's tortures and agony—a vicarious indulgence that one later scholar would deem "folk pornography." Wells also dispatched a white Chicago private detective to Georgia to gather information that would not be available to her. His findings revealed that Hose, whose name was actually Wilkes, had thrown an ax at his employer when the white farmer drew a gun on him. The allegations of rape and the attack on the child were completely without substance. No member of the mob that killed Wilkes had been arrested, much less prosecuted. In her introduction to *Lynch Law*, Wells proclaimed that her objective was "to give the public facts, in the belief that there is still a sense of justice in the American people and that it will yet assert itself in the condemnation of outlawry and in defense of oppressed and persecuted humanity." Given the events of previous decades these hopes seemed far-fetched, but Ida Wells established early in her life a fierce determination to see justice served regardless of the odds.

Ida Wells was born into slavery in Holly Springs, Mississippi, on July 16, 1862. Her father, James Wells, was a carpenter, while her mother, Elizabeth, was renowned as a cook. When Union forces under General Ulysses S. Grant pushed into Marshall County that fall, the Wells family experienced freedom for the first time. James Wells quickly became active in local civic affairs and like many freedmen was a dedicated Republican. Ida, with few memories of slavery, pursued reading avidly and eventually attended Shaw University, a Methodist institution that framed its academic curriculum in a context of Christian morality. Her life changed dramatically in 1878 when both her parents and a brother died of yellow fever. Determined to keep the remnants of the family together, she gained certification as a teacher and taught at a local black school. In 1881, with three of her siblings old enough to fend for themselves, Ida and her two younger sisters moved to Memphis, Tennessee, to live with an aunt. It was there, while working again as a teacher, that Ida made her first public commitment to the struggle for racial justice.

As Wells worked at a school in Woodstock, a dozen miles from Memphis, she relied on rail travel on a daily basis. The Chesapeake, Ohio and Southwestern Railroad (C&O), like many throughout the South, had formulated regulations that enabled the company to segregate black and white passengers, and a Tennessee law of 1875 gave businesses the right to provide separate and equal facilities to customers and to refuse service to any individual for any reason. Women who sought first-class travel could utilize the "ladie's car," a safe oasis from the often crude male behaviors that prevailed in the "smoker" car. While a separate ladies' car was provided for black women, its sanctity was not assured—white men could enter the car to smoke and drink, activities forbidden in the white ladies' car. Such were the circumstances on September 15, 1883, when Wells sought seating in the white ladies' car to escape an inebriated white smoker in the Jim Crow car. When the conductor ordered her out, Wells refused and a struggle ensued, in which the man tore the sleeve from her dress. Biting and scratching, Ida was hauled from the car with the help of several white passengers as the other whites in the car applauded. Refusing seating in the "colored" car, Ida chose instead to get off at the next stop. She quickly filed a suit against the railway, asserting that the C&O had failed to provide equal facilities. Despite two monetary judgments against the railroad by a state court judge, the rulings were overturned in 1887 by the state's supreme court, which branded Wells an agitator who had sued only to harass.

Wells may not have gained justice with her railroad suit, but the event did garner considerable coverage in the nation's growing African American press, which included some 1,800 newspapers prior to 1915. The episode also brought the young schoolteacher to the attention of several individuals in positions to further her ambition for writing. She was asked to write an article on the railroad suit for the Memphis *Living Way*, and its publication drew her into a network of African American journalists and newspapers, resulting in requests for more articles and essays. Though Wells had found a teaching job in Memphis in 1884, she forsook it in 1886 when her aunt persuaded her to accompany her to California. However, she found little in the Golden State to keep her there. Shortly after returning to Memphis, she was invited to attend the convention of the National Colored Press Association in Louisville, Kentucky, an event that ensured her broader ingress into journalism. Now writing under the pen name Iola, Wells addressed a broader variety of racial justice issues in her articles and was acknowledged by another black female journalist as the "Princess of the Press" in 1889. That same year, Ida became a co-owner of the Memphis *Free Speech and Headlight*, from which forum she launched an editorial assault on the all-white Memphis school board for its neglect of black educational facilities, also accusing board members of offering black women teaching jobs in return for sexual favors. As she discovered, any suggestion that white men or women were willingly engaging in interracial sex was potentially dangerous, as it threatened the precepts of white supremacy, one of which held that unrestrained sexuality was an innate African American trait. Oft-repeated warnings about the dangers of miscegenation stemmed from this premise, as did one of the chief professed rationales for lynching. Such beliefs were not confined to uneducated whites— pseudoscientific Darwinian and "racialist" theories pervaded academia in the late nineteenth century, both in Europe and in the United States. In 1890, Yale graduate Daniel G. Brinton, a University of Pennsylvania professor, declared that African Americans as a race were "midway between the Orang-utang and the European white." Renowned sociologist Lester Frank Ward maintained that "the imperious voice of nature" drove the black man to rape white women to "raise his race to a little higher level." With even eminent academics lending their support to popular notions of black sexual depravity, any effort to challenge prevailing notions or expose white hypocrisy was inevitably rebuked. For her impertinence, Wells was dismissed from her teaching job, though she remained unbowed. Her writings were now eagerly sought by such publications as the *New York Age*, the *Indianapolis World*, the *Gate City Press*, and the *Little Rock Sun*.

Though lynching was among the topics that she addressed, it did not become the focus of her life's work until 1892.

Ida was on business in Mississippi when the event that changed the course of her life occurred in her hometown of Memphis. Racial tensions in the city had been rising in early 1892, due in part to white resentments over the improved economic status of some of the city's black residents. The lynching of black businessmen Thomas Moss, Calvin McDowell, and Henry Stewart, owners of the People's Grocery, followed several days of racial confrontations near the store, which brought threats against the owners. On March 5, the three opened fire on a trio of whites who invaded the store, killing all three of them. Moss, McDowell, and Stewart were arrested and jailed, but days later were given over to a mob by their guards. Taken to a field outside town, the three black men were riddled with bullets and buckshot. The *Memphis Appeal-Avalanche* praised the lynching as "one of the most orderly of its kind ever conducted." The Memphis lynching galvanized the black press and provoked an outpouring of outrage and despair. Writing in *Free Speech*, Wells suggested that blacks abandon the Southern towns that would not protect them and move west, perhaps to the Oklahoma Territory, where she had recently visited all-black Langston City. Black residents of Kingfisher had successfully fended off white violence by organizing an armed militia. Wells soon recognized that rather than seeking to flee the horrors of lynching, she could best combat it by first understanding the motivations behind it. She soon discovered that the white press was more frequently citing rape as the justification for the rising number of lynchings. The *Memphis Appeal* was typical when it argued that black rapists were more active because the post-Reconstruction generation had "lost in large measure the traditional and wholesome awe of the white race which kept Negroes in subjection." Even lynching, the paper feared, was no longer an adequate deterrent. "The facts of the crime," the paper noted, "appear to appeal more to the Negro's lustful imagination than the facts of the punishment do to his fears." A writer for the *Memphis Daily Commercial* seconded these notions and warned that the ostensible wave of rapes was the result of a "devilish purpose," a premeditated campaign of sexual terror and degradation aimed at despoiling the moral purity of white women. Outraged at such inanities and well aware that the recent People's Grocery lynching had nothing to do with rape, Wells realized that fantasies about the sexual purity of white women and the "brute nature" of African Americans were a construct formulated for the purpose of maintaining white supremacy in the face of rising black accomplishments and aspirations. Speaking out in a *Free Speech* article that was published after she left for a visit to New York, Wells warned that, in their obsession with interracial rape and white purity, Southern white men would "overreach themselves" and "a conclusion will then be reached which is very damaging to the moral reputation of their women." It was a risky, provocative argument that struck directly at the heart of white supremacist mythology, and her opponents responded with all the expected fury. Threatening editorials filled the Memphis newspapers, innocent blacks were beaten, and in late May, the *Free Speech* offices were torched. Ida was not intimidated but rather was more determined than ever to resist injustice. She had already purchased a pistol and later recalled, "I had already determined to sell my life as dearly as possible if attacked. I felt if I could take one lyncher with me, this would even up the score a bit."

Barred from returning to Memphis by the climate of violence there, Wells remained briefly in New York, where she poured her analytical talents into "The Truth about Lynching," a lengthy article for the *New York Age*. Addressing the volatile issue of interracial sex, Wells offered an observation that was sure to provoke white rage: "White men lynch the offending African-American not because he is a despoiler of virtue, but because he succumbs to the smiles of a white woman." To refute the "blacks as rapists" charge, she offered numerous examples of white women attracted to black men and enumerated incidents of white men raping black women. Statistics, she noted, did not support current claims of increasing incidents of rape—of the 728 lynchings in the previous eight years, only one-third of the victims were accused of rape. Clearly, the myth of the black rapist was a fiction intended to justify the most savage means of controlling the New South's ambitious black population. Wells concluded with a call for civil disobedience to protest racial injustice and armed self-defense in the face of white violence. Experiences such as those in Oklahoma confirmed the utility of fighting back. "The lesson this teaches," she wrote, "and which every Afro-American should ponder well, is that a Winchester rifle should have a place of honor in every black home." Having found her voice and identified her cause, Wells quickly became the moving force in a growing antilynching campaign, traveling cross-country on a speaking tour to educate the public about lynching and traveling to Great Britain on two occasions to speak on the subject. Meanwhile, her *New York Age* article was published in book form as *Southern Horrors* and in 1895 she published *Red Record*, which addressed the issue again with an analysis of the most recent statistics. There were some signs of progress; several religious organizations approved antilynching resolutions, and legislatures in several Southern states passed statutes aimed at suppressing lynching. Such laws were often aimed more at improving the South's public image than at stopping the violence, and there was little effective enforcement.

In 1893, having moved to Chicago, Wells married Ferdinand Barnett, an attorney and newspaper owner. The couple eventually had four children despite their mutually frenetic schedules. The second half of the decade brought a succession of new challenges for Wells. She bristled at much of Booker T. Washington's 1895 Atlanta speech, in which the famous educator described blacks as an "ignorant" and "childish" race and insisted that black lynching victims were "invariably vagrants, men without property or standing." Her dispute with Washington and others who seemed to apologize for their race would never be reconciled. Then, 1896 proved a momentous year, as the U.S. Supreme Court upheld racial segregation in the *Plessy v. Ferguson* decision. Determined to continue the struggle against such inequities, Wells was among a number of activists who organized the National Association of Colored Women that same year. Meanwhile, the election of Republican President William McKinley gave hope to some African Americans, as the Ohioan appointed unprecedented numbers of blacks to federal positions, but Southern blacks remained especially vulnerable to racist violence. In February 1898, even as the nation stood on the verge of a war against Spain over inhumanities in Cuba, a South Carolina mob gunned down Frazier Baker, a local black postmaster, together with his entire family. "If this thing had happened in Cuba," Wells charged at a protest meeting, "the country would have wrung with indignation for weeks." Subsequently, Wells was among a group of black representatives granted a meeting with McKinley, to whom she passionately made her case for justice. Clearly sympathetic, the president promised to investigate the Baker lynching, though the events of the next several months undoubtedly claimed most of his attention. That fall, even as Americans indulged in a self-congratulatory celebration of their nation's triumph over inhumane Spanish rule in Cuba, white supremacist Democrats in North Carolina terrorized the black population during the fall elections in a campaign to oust the more racially tolerant populists. The following spring, the horrendous Sam Hose lynching occurred. As the decade came to an end, statistics revealed that over 1,200 African Americans had died at the hands of lynch mobs.

In his 1905 work *The Souls of Black Folk*, W. E. B. DuBois trenchantly observed, "The problem of the twentieth century is the problem of the color line." The early years of the new century confirmed DuBois's contention, as issues growing out of the "color line" often dominated the national dialogue. Perhaps most controversial was the Brownsville Incident of 1904, in which black soldiers serving near the Texas town, weary of racist insults, armed themselves and shot it out with local whites. President Theodore Roosevelt, considered generally liberal in racial matters because of his meetings with Washington, outraged black opinion when he approved the mass dishonorable discharge of 167 Brownsville soldiers, six of whom were Medal of Honor winners, because of the inability of the War Department to specifically identify guilty individuals. Roosevelt's decision, the *New York World* declared, was akin to "executive lynch law." Wells and other increasingly energetic activists were convinced that racial justice could be achieved only through more effective organization and agitation. Lynchings had increased for several years when Wells attended the first meeting of the Niagara Movement in 1905. There she, DuBois, and others formulated strategies for challenging segregation, disfranchisement, and Washington's accommodationist policies. In 1909, the membership of the Niagara Movement would join with white progressives to form the National Association for the Advancement of Colored People. The daunting challenges that the activists faced were highlighted that year by two horrific lynchings, the first in Livermore, Kentucky, where the lynchers sold admission tickets to see the black victim shot to death on the stage of the town's opera house. In Coatsville, Pennsylvania, a black prisoner chained to a hospital bed was rolled into the street and slowly roasted to death, as lynchers pushed the bed in and out of a bonfire. Wells struggled to divide her energies between the antilynching crusade and local activities, such as the establishment of a Negro Fellowship Reading Room and Social League in Chicago and her founding of the Alpha Suffrage Club for black women. She discovered to her chagrin that even at the famous 1913 suffrage parade in Washington, DC, the African American women were expected to march separately.

Hopes for racial progress at the national level received a major setback with the 1912 election of Democratic President Woodrow Wilson. Though an accomplished progressive, Wilson held traditional Southern attitudes about race, a depressing reality evidenced in his endorsement of D. W. Griffith's feature-length film about the Reconstruction, *Birth of a Nation*. Based on Thomas Dixon's popular novel *The Clansman*, the film portrayed a heroic Ku Klux Klan defending virtuous white women against the depredations of sex-crazed black men. Like many African Americans, Wells was troubled by the resurgence of racial animosities during the Wilson years, brought on by the migration of Southern blacks into northern cities and exacerbated by wartime tensions after U.S. intervention in World War I in 1917. That year, whites in East St. Louis, Illinois, launched a veritable war against the city's black population. Wells described the two days of arson, beatings, and murder in *The East St. Louis Massacre: The Greatest Outrage of the Century*, estimating that 150 blacks had died. Only weeks later, black soldiers based near Houston, Texas, and local whites got into a deadly firefight growing out of racial animosities; fifteen whites and six blacks died. Of the sixty-three black soldiers charged with mutiny, thirteen were peremptorily hanged, while the others received life prison terms. Wells, organizing a protest, was informed that doing so would violate the Espionage Act, a wartime statute aimed at suppressing dissent. The War Department's Military Intelligence Division, which had organized a "Negro Subversion" unit, deemed Wells "a far more dangerous agitator than Marcus Garvey." Wells had met with the Jamaican immigrant, whose Universal Negro Improvement Association promulgated a black nationalist message that worried authorities. Garvey's *Messenger* had once editorialized that making "Georgia safe for the

Negro" was a more fitting goal for blacks than dying in Mr. Wilson's crusade abroad. Government authorities sought to discourage any wartime discussion of racial issues; activists planning for a series of "race congresses" were warned that their efforts could aid the German cause.

When the United States entered the Great War, W. E. B. DuBois was among those black activists who urged blacks to openly demonstrate their patriotism, in hopes that this might help lead to improved postwar race relations. By 1919 it was clear that such hopes would not be met. Lingering wartime tensions, a Red Scare, serious economic dislocations, and public embitterment all combined to create a volatile atmosphere in which racial hatreds soon exploded during what activist James Weldon Johnson termed the Red Summer of 1919. The year saw twenty-five major race riots, and lynchings rose from sixty in 1918 to seventy-six in 1919. Despite these postwar horrors, Wells's long antilynching crusade seemed on the verge of success in April 1921, when a Republican-dominated U.S. Congress gave consideration to the Dyer Bill. The antilynching measure passed in the House only to die in a Senate committee. It was a tantalizing glimpse of victory that fell short. It was a disappointment only partly compensated for by the recent ratification of the Nineteenth Amendment, a triumph that longtime suffragists like Wells could legitimately celebrate.

The 1920s were years of both promise and disappointment for Wells and other civil rights activists. This was the decade of the "New Negro," confident, proud, and increasingly defiant. The Harlem Renaissance produced an abundance of African American literary talent while the growing popularity of jazz ensured a new preeminence for black musicians. Yet the limits of progress were always self-evident; black Americans remained politically powerless and socially isolated in a predominantly white Anglo-Saxon society that was increasingly defensive and conservative in the postwar years. The advent of the Great Depression after 1929 exacerbated existing social and economic tensions, making any advances in race relations highly problematic for the foreseeable future. Wells focused her attentions on local issues, working as an advocate for African Americans caught up in the injustices of the Illinois criminal justice system. In 1930 she ran unsuccessfully for the office of state senator as an independent candidate. The defeat did not diminish her enthusiasm for activism and despite the continued lack of federal antilynching legislation, the direction of events offered encouragement. While lynchings had averaged sixty-two a year between 1910 and 1919, there was a noticeable decline after 1923. During the 1930s, the number of lynchings fell to about three per year. Some of the decline has been attributed to growing opposition on the part of Southern elites, especially businessmen and women. In late 1930, for example, white activists established the Association of Southern Women for the Prevention of Lynching. Ida Wells's long crusade was beginning to bear discernible fruit when she died of uremia on March 25, 1931. Though seven presidents urged Congress to end lynching and nearly 200 antilynching bills were introduced during the first half of the century, none made it through the Senate. In June 2005, the Senate endorsed a resolution apologizing for its failure to act.

Conclusion

Benjamin Tillman and Ida Wells were born into a world that was swept away by the hurricane of civil war and both were drawn into the struggle to shape the postwar South. For Tillman, born into a family of South Carolina planters, the reestablishment of white supremacy was requisite to the maintenance of a stable social order in which white males held predominance. Strictly defined racial and gender roles could be effectively enforced, Tillman understood, through the construction of countervailing myths of white female purity and black male depravity. Tillman openly endorsed lynching in selected circumstances, legitimizing it as an instrument of terror and control. His legacy, both immediate and long-term, was a tradition of Southern political demagoguery that thrived on racial invective and implicitly sanctioned extralegal violence against blacks. Race remained the crux of Southern politics well into the second half of the century. Ida B. Wells, born into slavery, observed the promise of Reconstruction as a young adult, only to see the promised freedoms deferred as Republican rule in the South gave way to the Redeemers. She was the driving force in the organization of the antilynching campaign and skillfully analyzed the phenomenon of lynching as she publicized its horrors. In publicly challenging the professed rationale for lynching, she exposed white hypocrisy about interracial sexual relations, refuted allegations of black sexual depravity, and demonstrated that lynching was primarily an instrument of racial terror. A major contributor to the organization of the civil rights movement during the Progressive Era, Wells continued her struggle to end lynching and achieve racial justice to the end of her life.

Study Questions

1. To what degree was Benjamin Tillman's adult perspective shaped by his early life in South Carolina up to the 1880s?
2. Why did Southern lynchings of African Americans rise so dramatically during the last two decades of the nineteenth century?
3. What freedoms did Ida Wells find denied to her as an African American in the post-Reconstruction South?
4. How did Tillman, as a U.S. senator, defend his region's treatment of African Americans before a national audience?
5. As no federal antilynching law was ever passed, how would you evaluate Wells's long crusade against lynching?

Selected Bibliography

Brown, Mary Jane. *Eradicating the Evil: Women in the American Anti-Lynching Movement, 1892–1940*. New York: Routledge, 2000.

Burton, Orville V. *In My House Are Many Mansions: Family and Community in Edgefield, South Carolina*. Chapel Hill: University of North Carolina Press, 1985.

Davidson, James West. *"They Say": Ida B. Wells and the Reconstruction of Race*. New York: Oxford University Press, 2007.

Duster, Alfreda M., ed. *Crusade for Justice: The Autobiography of Ida B. Wells*. Chicago: University of Chicago Press, 1970.

Edgar, Walter. *South Carolina: A History*. Columbia: University of South Carolina Press, 1998.

Friedman, Lawrence J. *The White Savage: Racial Fantasies in the Postbellum South*. Englewood Cliffs, NJ: Prentice Hall, 1970.

Giddings, Paula J. *Ida: A Sword among Lions*. New York: Amistad, 2008.

Kantrowitz, Stephen. *Ben Tillman and the Reconstruction of White Supremacy*. Chapel Hill: University of North Carolina Press, 2000.

Key, V. O. *Southern Politics in State and Nation*. New York: Vintage, 1969.

Litwack, Leon. *Trouble in Mind: Black Southerners in the Age of Jim Crow*. New York: Alfred A. Knopf, 1998.

Logan, Rayford W. *The Betrayal of the Negro, from Rutherford B. Hayes to Woodrow Wilson*. New York: Da Capo, 1997.

McMurry, Linda O. *To Keep the Waters Troubled: The Life of Ida B. Wells*. New York: Oxford University Press, 1998.

Nolen, Claude H. *The Negro's Image in the South: The Anatomy of White Supremacy*. Lexington: University of Kentucky Press, 1968.

Royster, Jacqueline Jones. *Southern Horrors and Other Writings: The Anti-Lynching Campaign of Ida B. Wells, 1892–1900*. Boston: Bedford Books, 1997.

Simkins, Francis Butler. *Pitchfork Ben Tillman: South Carolinian*. Baton Rouge: Louisiana State University, 1967.

CHAPTER TWO

~

Final Frontiers, Vanishing Americans

On July 12, 1893, Frederick Jackson Turner, a history professor at the University of Wisconsin, stood before members of the American Historical Association in a Chicago hall to deliver an address called "The Significance of the Frontier in American History." The setting itself was remarkable enough—the city was the site of the World Columbian Exposition, an ambitious fair organized to celebrate the 400th anniversary of the European "discovery" of the Americas, an event that could be accurately described as one of history's most important turning points. During the subsequent four centuries, the New World had been fundamentally transformed, as vast and shifting frontiers delineated the sweep of European conquest and settlement across American landscapes. Turner's address focused more specifically on the significance of this transient boundary to the social, political, and economic development of the United States, and to the character of the American people. The topic was more than academic; only three years earlier, the U.S. Census Bureau had proclaimed that, demographically, a contiguous frontier no longer existed. To a people for whom the frontier had long before taken on mythic significance, this was a potentially troubling development.

Before the assembled historians, Turner contended that "the existence of an area of free land, its continuous recession and the advance of American settlement explain American development." He characterized the frontier as "the meeting point between savagery and civilization," where a developmental process "begins with the Indian and the hunter and goes on with the disintegration of savagery" through the passing of successive stages, culminating in "the manufacturing organization with the city and the factory system." The character of those successive generations of Americans who embraced the challenges of life on a continually moving frontier was inevitably shaped by that environment. "The frontier," Turner proclaimed, "is the line of most rapid Americanization," fostering all the commendable traits so crucial to individualism and to democratic habits of mind and practice. Turner's "frontier thesis" offered a bold and controversial explanation for the uniquely democratic character of American civilization that many found appealing, but it also posited troublesome uncertainties in the future. "The frontier has gone," the tall, mustachioed professor acknowledged, "and with its going has closed the first period of American history." In the years to come, some would propose that an overseas empire might substitute for the American frontier, thus perpetuating the regenerative process deemed so crucial to the national character and democracy itself.

In his 1893 address, Turner failed to speak to what the frontier's disappearance meant for those indigenous peoples who were swept aside in the relentless westward press of the traders, farmers, ranchers, and businessmen whom he identified as the advance agents of civilization. The historian casually equated "Indians and hunters" with a state of "savagery" and had posited as a premise of his thesis "the existence of an area of free land." When Turner presented his theory of American development, the last of the Indian wars of the late nineteenth century was over, the U.S. Army having finally subdued even the fiercest of Native American resistance. The army's massacre of more than 300 Ogallala Sioux at Wounded Knee, South Dakota, in December 1890 was a tragic and needless act that signaled the last major action in a decades-long military campaign against Native Americans. According to historian Arrell Gibson, this effort was begun in 1845 and culminated in 1886 with the subjugation of the Apaches of the Southwest. After the Civil War, military action was the force behind a policy of increasingly restrictive concentration, as Indians were driven out of desirable areas and onto reservations. The last phase of this effort, from 1866 to 1886, ended with once extensive Native American civilizations reduced to isolated remnants.

This was an era in which the figure of the "Noble Red Man," introduced earlier in the century in the novels of James Fenimore Cooper, gave way to an overwhelmingly negative stereotype of a barbaric savage whose base nature was untempered by any humane instinct, a feral being who had not produced anything deserving of the characterization "civilized." Such attitudes transected class and region. In his 1870 essay "The Noble Red Man," Mark Twain, destined to become one of the most perceptive critics of American prejudices, was unequivocal in rejecting Cooper's Indian. In his own experience in the West, Twain found Indians to be "little, and scrawny and dirty . . . thoroughly pitiful and contemptible." The "Red Man" was, Twain averred, nothing but "a poor, filthy, naked scurvy vagabond, who to exterminate were a charity to the Creator's worthier insects and reptiles, which he oppresses." Even worse, this unredeemable aborigine was innately dangerous. "His heart is a cesspool of falsehood, of treachery and of low and devilish instincts," the Missourian wrote. Confirming a widely held view, Twain declared that "the Red Man is a skulking coward and windy braggart who strikes without warning . . . kills helpless women and little children and massacres the men in their beds." In his popular 1872 work *Roughing It*, Twain pronounced the Goshoot (Paiute) Indians "inferior to all races of savages on our continent" who had no concept of a "Great Spirit" other than whiskey. "The [African] Bushmen and our Goshoots," he wrote, "are manifestly descended from the self-same gorilla or kangaroo or Norway rat, whichever Adam-animal the Darwinians trace them to." Harvard-educated Theodore Roosevelt revealed a similar prejudice in an oft-quoted remark: "I am not one to say that the only good Indian is a dead Indian, but I would say that nine out of ten are, and I wouldn't be too sure about the tenth." Like many of his contemporaries, Roosevelt also believed that Native American civilization was destined to vanish even if the Indian was guaranteed land, as he, like the hunters and trappers of an earlier age who depended on wild game for survival, would refuse to work and would "perish from the face of the earth which he encumbers." A January 1874 editorial in the *New York World* expressed a similar outlook, declaring, "The Indians have their choice of incorporation with the general mass of the population and a life of civilized industry . . . or of betaking themselves to such regions as are not needed for the maintenance of civilized men." Those who refused, the editorial warned, "must be punished with death if no less penalty avails. The country is not yet so crowded that the Indian must be told to work or die; but it is so crowded that he must be told to behave himself or die." Having inspected a Native American exhibit at the 1876 Philadelphia Exhibition, the urbane William Dean Howells, novelist and editor of the *Atlantic Monthly*, concluded, "The red man, as he appears in effigy and in photographs in this collection, is a hideous demon, whose malign traits can hardly inspire any emotions softer than abhorrence." The Indian, Howells declared, was destined for "extinction."

Faced with the alternatives of assimilation, concentration under degrading circumstances, or annihilation, many Native Americans chose to resist. With the tribes of the Pacific coastal states largely subdued prior to the Civil War and those of the Great Basin sorely pressed during that conflict, the focus of military action shifted to the Great Plains at war's end. The Plains Indian Wars contributed heavily to the burgeoning mythology of the frontier, familiarizing the public with the names of Indian fighters such as George Armstrong Custer, Philip Sheridan, and George Crook, as well as the more memorable names of their opponents, Sitting Bull, Crazy Horse, Black Kettle, Chief Joseph, and scores of lesser figures. Few Indian warriors, however, attained the notoriety that surrounded Geronimo, a Chiricahua Apache whose name was by the 1880s synonymous with courage, ferocity, cruelty, and a seemingly inexhaustible determination to resist efforts to confine his people, the Bedonkohé, on an Arizona reservation. Though Geronimo, whose Bedonkohé name was Goyahkla, reserved his most intense hatred for the Mexican soldiers who massacred his family in the 1850s, he proved equally committed to fighting those Americans who threatened his people's way of life in the desert Southwest. Though never a chief, Geronimo exercised considerable influence as a proven warrior and a powerful medicine man who over the span of several decades led Apache bands of various sizes in raids that terrorized whites in southern Arizona and New Mexico. Those who pursued him grudgingly acknowledged his mastery of guerrilla warfare, even if they despised him as a mercurial and untrustworthy man who rarely felt bound to keep agreements made with white authorities. Prior to his capture in 1886, Geronimo was for many Americans the personification of the merciless "red devil," who had to be subdued or exterminated.

Given the pervasive influence of racist thought and social Darwinism in late-nineteenth-century America, few white Americans spoke out or acted in defense of Native Americans. Those who did often had roots in the abolitionist or feminist movements; Lydia Maria Child, Wendell Phillips, and Harriet Beecher Stowe all advocated humane treatment of Indians and the reform of federal Indian policy. The individual who most effectively drew public attention to the plight of Native Americans did not, however, fall into those categories. Born in Massachusetts in 1830, Helen Hunt Jackson grew up in a region fired with reformist zeal, but led an unexceptional middle-class life. She married and then was widowed in her early thirties, when she turned her energies toward writing. Though she traveled extensively in the Rocky Mountain West in the 1870s, she evinced no special interest in Indians until 1879, when she attended a Boston lecture by Chief Standing Bear, a Ponca. Moved at his recounting of the forcible removal of his tribe from its Nebraska reservation, she dedicated her life to activism on behalf of Native Americans. Her work, which began with fund-raising, letter writing, and petition drives, grew more ambitious in 1881 when she published A Century of Dishonor, a scathing indictment of federal Indian policy. Undeterred by the absence of any congressional action, she turned to fiction to publicize the plight of Native Americans. Her novel Ramona was intended to depict the travails of Indian life as effectively as Stowe's Uncle Tom's Cabin had shown the life of Southern slaves. Confronted with seemingly intransigent public attitudes and a reluctant Congress, Jackson's crusade to gain justice for Native Americans seemed as unlikely to succeed as did Apache resistance in the

Southwest, but she proved as stubborn in pursuit of her goal as did Geronimo. She died the year before the Chiricahua warrior's capture, but left behind a legacy that outlived her.

⁓ GERONIMO (GOYAHKLA) ⁓

Though the vast majority of Americans came to know him as Geronimo, the Chiricahua Apache warrior who came to personify the "Indian menace" in the late nineteenth century was known only as Goyahkla, "He Who Yawns," until the 1850s, when a devastating personal loss compelled him to commit himself to a lifetime of resistance against those who threatened his people's way of life. The year of the event that changed Goyahkla's life is still uncertain. Though historian David Roberts placed "the most important event in Geronimo's life" in March 1851, other writers have dated it as late as the summer of 1858. The

Chiricahua Apache warrior and medicine man Geronimo at the time of his surrender to General Crook's troops in March 1886. Perhaps the best-known leader among the resistant southwestern tribes in the post–Civil War years, Geronimo fought against Mexican as well as U.S. military forces, and was seen by many Americans as the personification of Native American cunning and savagery. (Library of Congress, LC-USZ62-46637)

Janos Massacre occurred in northern Mexico, where relations between the Apaches and Mexican authorities had been problematic for decades. The Mexican government blamed the Apaches for numerous depredations against ranchers and soldiers and in the 1830s, when Goyahkla was still a child, the northern Mexican states of Sonora and Chihuahua had offered a $100 bounty for the scalps of Apache warriors, with smaller amounts for women and children. In 1837, American scalp hunters lured several hundred Mimbreño Apache to a purported feast, then fired on the group with a hidden howitzer. Some twenty Indians were killed and scalped. Ironically, scalping was broadly and inaccurately depicted as a characteristic Indian practice.

Goyahkla's tribe—the Bedonkohé—was familiar with the brutal policies and deceits of Mexican authorities, so when the group camped near the Chihuahuan town of Janos that March, a number of warriors were left behind with the women and children when the men went into town to trade. On the afternoon of March 5, a detachment of 400 Mexican soldiers under the command of Colonel Jose Carrasco descended on the camp. "My duty," Carrasco later remarked, "was to destroy the enemy wherever I could find him." Carrasco claimed to have killed 130 Indians in the subsequent battle; the 90 who were captured were sold into slavery. A small number who escaped the slaughter related news of the disaster to Goyahkla and other returning warriors, and the band fled to a prearranged safe haven. Devastated to learn that his mother, wife, and three children were among the dead, Goyahkla later recounted, "I had no purpose left." He numbly followed Chihenne chief Mangas Colorados and the remnants of the group back to their settlement on the Gila River. There, in accordance with custom, Goyahkla burned the remaining material possessions of his dead family—they would not be spoken of again. During this period of mourning, Goyahkla had an experience acknowledged in Apache tradition—a voice spoke his name and assured him, "No gun can ever kill you." This "power" was one that strengthened his determination to wreak revenge on those who had destroyed his family. In subsequent years, his power expanded to include healing, and the man who would be known to whites as Geronimo was famed among his people as a medicine man as well as a warrior. By his later years, his body was scarred by numerous knife and bullet wounds, which Geronimo displayed as evidence of his invulnerability.

The opportunity for revenge came in summer 1859, when an Apache force of 200 warriors under the leadership of chiefs Mangas, Cochise, and Juh assembled at the Mexican border before heading south along the Sierra Madre Mountains. Crossing the Sonora River, the war party halted outside the town of Arispe. Their intent was soon made clear; eight Mexicans who rode out under a white flag to parley were summarily killed and scalped. For the following two days, the Apaches fought pitched battles with companies of Mexican cavalry and infantry. Believing these to be the soldiers who had slaughtered his family, Goyahkla fought fiercely, killing and wounding many. His fearlessness in attacking his enemies was said to have unnerved many of the Mexican soldiers, who shouted, "¡*Cuidado!* [Watch out!] Geronimo!" Biographer Angie Debo speculates that the soldiers were invoking St. Jerome's name; others suggest that perhaps the battle occurred on the saint's feast day. Regardless, the famous name has its origins in what one historian termed "one of the greatest Apache victories of the nineteenth century." The Mexicans abandoned the battlefield and fled the area. Geronimo's desire for revenge was unabated, however, and in subsequent months he continued to lead further raids into Mexico. Gernonimo's name became familiar to most Americans only during the two decades of the Indian wars that followed the Civil War, but in that span of time, his name became synonymous with the ferocity, cunning, and brutality that were held to be the cardinal qualities of the Apache. A government census taker at Arizona's San Carlos reservation captured the prevailing view of Geronimo in the 1880s when he described the Apache warrior as "sly and vicious," a "schemer" who was responsible for "the wrecking of countless homes; the pillage and plunder of ranches; the making of widows and orphans; the cause of carnage and torture; the mutilation of surprised victims." In an 1886 assessment, the *New York Times* described Geronimo as "The Cruelest of Our Indians." Journalist Charles F. Lummis saw the Chiricahua warrior's character written in his physical appearance:

> He was a compactly built, dark-faced man of one hundred and seventy pounds, and about five feet eight inches in height. The man who once saw his face will never forget it. Crueler features were never cut. The nose was broad and heavy, the forehead low and wrinkled, the chin full and strong, the eyes like two bits of obsidian, with a light behind them. The mouth was the most notable feature—a sharp straight, thin-lipped gash of generous length without one softening curve.

The uncertainty of memory precludes a dependably accurate dating of the chief events of Geronimo's life, but he placed his birth in June 1829 along the Gila River in the Mogollon Mountains, whether in modern-day Arizona or New Mexico remains unclear. His father was known as Taklishim (the Gray One), while his mother was named Juana. Geronimo's grandfather Mahko had been a famous Bedonkohé chief. The Bedonkohé were a subgroup of the Chiricahua, one of seven Apache tribal groups situated primarily in eastern Arizona and western New Mexico, both of which were part of northern Mexico at the time of Geronimo's birth. As a hunting and gathering people living in an austere environment, the Apache had to effectively utilize extremely sparse food and water resources, which required intimate familiarity with the land and the ability to endure the privations that it imposed. Apaches held that a sacred power derived from the ground itself and believed that select individuals were granted special powers, often discerned through visions. Their relatively small numbers compelled their often furtive way of warfare, which was dependent on stealth, strategic retreats, and unorthodox tactics. The Chiricahua likely first encountered Europeans in the sixteenth century when Spanish conquistadores ventured north, and they quickly established an enduring reputation for ferocity. One Spanish missionary, writing in 1660, observed, "They hurl themselves at danger like a people who know no God nor that there is any hell." Unlike other Native American tribes, the Apaches did not initially integrate Spanish-introduced horses into their lifestyle, though they later earned a reputation as first-rate horsemen. Generally, the Apache were dependent on periodic trading with or raids on Spanish settlements.

During Goyahkla's adolescence and young adulthood, Apache relations with newly independent Mexico were problematic, especially when miners infiltrated Apache lands. With the end of the Mexican War in 1848, many traditional Apache lands fell under the jurisdiction of the United States, and the American government pledged to halt Apache raids into Mexico. Geronimo's determination to exact ongoing vengeance on the Mexicans led to sporadic forays into Mexico during the 1850s. During the same decade, Americans traveling the California Trail encroached on Apache territory, which was a cause for Apache concern, though not necessarily hostility. In 1858, Cochise, at a meeting with representatives of the Butterfield Overland Mail, agreed to the construction of a stage station in southeastern Arizona, and Geronimo, also present, posed no objection. This period of relative harmony came to abrupt end in 1861, when a U.S. Army officer seized Cochise and unjustly accused him of kidnapping a young boy from a local ranch. The Mimbreño Apache escaped and, together with Geronimo, mounted a series of attacks on the Butterfield Mail station and killed several white hostages. Army troops responded by capturing and hanging Cochise's brother and two nephews. Subsequently, as Geronimo was to later recall, "After this trouble all of the Indians agreed not to be friendly with the white men any more." Complicating matters, the nation was engulfed in the Civil War in early 1861, and that conflict, according to historian Arrell Gibson, "produced a thorough militarization of the West which had a dreadful effect upon the Indian nations." When the U.S. government briefly pulled troops from the Southwest, John Robert Baylor, the newly appointed Confederate governor of the New Mexico territory, ordered Confederate officers to "use all means to persuade the Apaches or any other tribe to come in for the purpose of making peace, and when you get them together, kill all the grown Indians and take the children prisoners and sell them to defray the expense of killing the Indians." Confederate President Jefferson Davis soon removed Baylor from office and Confederate forces proved incapable of holding the region. In 1862, General James H. Carleton, the new U.S. commander of the Department of New Mexico, implemented an equally horrific policy toward the Mescalero Apache: "All Indian men of that tribe are to be killed wherever you find them." Carleton also introduced a policy of "concentrating" Indians in camps where many died from disease and exposure. An event that ensured the bitter resentment of all Apaches was the murder of the elderly chief Mangas in January 1863. Battle-scarred and weary, Mangas met with a group of miners at Pinos Altos to work out some means of ending the incessant conflict between whites and Indians. He was treacherously seized and turned over to nearby army troops, who cruelly tortured and then shot the old chief to death. Mangas was scalped and decapitated, his head sent to an eastern phrenologist for measurement and display at the Smithsonian Institute. The mutilation was especially appalling for the Apache people, as they believed that it condemned Mangas to enter the afterlife headless. Geronimo later characterized this betrayal and callous disrespect as "perhaps the greatest wrong ever done to the Indians."

Geronimo's precise activities throughout the Civil War years are difficult to chronicle, though it is known that the Bedonkohé supported the Apache resistance, clashed with army troops, and endured great privation. In May 1865, General Carleton ordered that the remaining at-large Apache bands should settle at the inhospitable camp at Bosque Redondo. Mangas's successor, Victorio, refused and resumed raiding, as did Geronimo and Cochise. The U.S. government, however, was on the verge of implementing policies that would mark the beginning of the final phase of the military conquest of Native American tribes. In 1867, the congressional Doolittle Committee issued its *Report on the Condition of the Indian Tribes*. Its seven members, having toured the West in 1865, had seen the terrible impact of the Civil War on Native Americans, whose societies were already stressed by years of conflict with miners, settlers, and Mexican forces. The committee concluded that the nomadic lifestyle of the Apaches and others was no longer feasible, and that Indians must reconcile themselves to reservation life. It also criticized the use of military force to implement policy, instead endorsing a "peace policy" aimed at transforming Indians into "civilized" people, largely through instruction by religiously affiliated agents. Though the peace policy gained the support of President Ulysses S. Grant, beginning in 1869, it was widely disparaged by advocates of a "force policy," including General William T. Sherman, an ardent proponent of the concept of "Americanization at the point of a bayonet." The antagonisms between supporters of the two policies further complicated federal policy during the final two decades of the Indian wars.

The weakened condition of Native Americans and the increased military powers of the national government after the Civil War favored the latter. In the Southwest, statistics provided stark evidence of the enfeebled position of the Indians. As the white population of the newly designated Arizona Territory grew to over 9,600 by 1870, the number of Apaches was estimated to be 6,000 to 8,000. Chiricahuas probably accounted for 1,000 to 2,000 of that number. In September 1871, Vincent Colyer, secretary of the Board of Peace Indian Commissioners, traveled to the Southwest to establish four reservations for the Apaches, three in Arizona and one in New Mexico. From his office at Arizona's Fort Apache, Colyer assigned the Chiricahuas to the San Carlos Reservation on the Gila River and began efforts to contact free-roving bands with instructions to come in to their reservations. As of October, Colyer had designated five additional temporary reservations and induced 4,000 Apaches to settle on them. Like most whites, however, Colyer, despite his desire to treat the Apaches justly, failed to understand crucial aspects of Native American culture, notably the importance that Apache groups attached to living in specific locales. Thus when he assigned Victorio's Chihenne Apache to an area around the Tularosa River, disregarding their insistence on being settled near their traditional homeland at Ojo Caliente (Warm Springs) in New Mexico, he unwittingly ensured that there would be problems in the near future when the Chihenne balked at settling on the barren land on the Tularosa. Ultimately, about a thousand Apache fled their home at Warm Springs rather than be removed to the designated reservation. Though those in Washington who favored the peace policy often lauded Colyer, he proved to be a controversial figure. A New York City Quaker and artist, Colyer had been a dedicated abolitionist, commanding a black Union regiment during the Civil War. He perceived the Apaches as having been wronged by avaricious and brutal whites, observing that "the peaceable relations of the Apaches with the Americans continued until the latter adopted the Mexican theory of 'extermination' and by acts of inhuman treachery and cruelty made them our implacable foes."

One of Colyer's most outspoken detractors was General George Crook, who was assigned command of the Department of Arizona the same year that Colyer arrived. A West Point graduate and career army officer, Crook's experience in fighting Indians began in California in 1857 and was interrupted briefly by the Civil War. He enhanced his military reputation in the postwar years, earning the nickname "the Gray Wolf" in the course of subduing the Paiute in Oregon. Crook characterized Indians as "filthy, odoriferous, treacherous, ungrateful, pitiless, cruel and lazy," seeming to embrace the common viewpoint of most whites. Yet while fighting the Shasta Indians in California, he came to believe that they had been greatly abused by whites and conceded his admiration of the Native American ability to wrest a living from often unforgiving environments. Arriving in Arizona, with orders to enforce the reservation policy, Crook disdained Colyer's policies as naive. Committed to a military solution, Crook was determined to compel the Apaches to settle on the reservations. Long a believer in the dictum that extensive knowledge of an enemy was a first step toward his defeat, Crook sought out all available local information about the Apaches, with the intent of developing a strategy for their subjugation. Much of what he discovered was alarming. The Apaches were clever, courageous, and tenacious, characteristics that later led even General Sherman to despair that Arizona would have to be conceded to the fierce tribe. Crook came to believe, however, that through mobility, speed, and the judicious use of Indian scouts, some of whom were Apache, victory was possible. Over the next dozen years, the lives of Crook and Geronimo would intermittently intersect as the general was ordered to apprehend and confine the unpredictable Apaches.

Surprisingly, by the time Crook was transferred to head the Department of the Platte in 1875, Arizona seemed to have been pacified. After a few confrontations with the army, Victorio reluctantly brought his people to the Tularosa reservation and in the fall of 1872, General Oliver Howard had made his way to Cochise's mountain stronghold to convince the Apache chief to accept life on the Chiricahua reservation in southeastern Arizona, which roughly conformed to their traditional homeland. Geronimo, who was present at the meeting, was also amenable to a treaty. Subsequently, as Crook mounted a campaign to subdue the few renegade Apaches in the mountains of northern Arizona in late 1872, and as most stragglers were brought onto the reservations, Geronimo disappeared from the historical record for several years. Cochise died in 1874 and in early 1875, Arizona governor Anson Safford, addressing the legislature, proclaimed, "Comparative peace now reigns throughout the territory, with almost a certainty that no general Indian war will ever occur again." His optimism proved premature. Though Geronimo had seemingly acquiesced to reservation life in 1872, his innate distrust of government promises, combined with his mercurial temperament and the often egregiously inept management of the Apache reservations, led to a dozen years of unrest in the Southwest as the last phase of the Apache wars took shape.

Several events provoked Geronimo's first breakout from the reservation. At the San Carlos reservation, agent John Clum's efforts to impose his idea of discipline on the Apaches provoked dangerous resentments. Likewise, the Indian Bureau belatedly acknowledged the unworkability of the Tularosa Agency and ordered its inhabitants to new locales. Geronimo then chose to return to raiding into New Mexico, which posed problems for Mexican-American relations. These events prefigured the Indian Bureau's decision to implement a policy of concentration, requiring that disparate Apache bands settle at San Carlos. The Chiricahua reservation was to be returned to the public domain. In June 1876, Clum led a company of the Indian Police that he had organized to gather up errant Apaches. He returned to San Carlos to discover that Victorio's band had left for Warm Springs, and that Geronimo had fled with a number of war-riors to Mexico. Victorio's band rampaged across the territory for the next two years, killing more than 175 whites before fleeing into Mexico, where Victorio died in an 1879 battle with Mexican troops. Geronimo reappeared at Warm Springs in March 1877, driving a large herd of stolen livestock and planning to reprovision. Informed of his presence, Clum traveled to the Warm Springs Agency with two companies of Indian Police and announced that he desired to confer with the Chiricahua warrior. At the subsequent meeting, Geronimo was seized at a prearranged signal, shackled, and taken back to San Carlos. Seeming to accept his new status in subsequent months, Geronimo behaved passively enough that he was named "captain" of the Warm Springs Apache. In April 1878, however, a sequence of events provoked Geronimo to flee again. After a drunken quarrel with his nephew, who later killed himself, Geronimo, accom-panied by the Nednhi chief Juh, headed for Mexico's Sierra Nevada, attacking a wagon train and engaging U.S. Army troops just north of the border. Geronimo and his followers returned to San Carlos in December 1879. White authorities believed that the Chiricahua warrior cynically exploited circumstances, raiding when possible and feigning submission whenever his band grew weary or short of provisions. Meanwhile, the Chihenne chief Nana led his band in continuing raids through 1881.

The event that precipitated Geronimo's final and arguably most famous breakout, which signaled the final five years of the Chiricahuas' resistance, was the execution of the Apache medicine man Nochedelklinne, who began proph-esying an Indian resurgence in the summer of 1881. Nochedelklinne did not advocate rebellion but rather patience, as he foresaw the white man's disappear-ance and the return of the great chiefs. White authorities inevitably perceived dangers in his group dances and visions, and the prophet was murdered while in the custody of army troops at Cibecue Creek, Arizona. Enraged Apaches im-mediately attacked the soldiers and later besieged their camp at Fort Apache. Ominously, many of the Apache scouts so vaunted by General Crook had mu-tinied and gone over to their Apache brethren after Nochedelklinne's death. Alarmed at the unwarranted killing of the medicine man and at the sudden ap-pearance of troops at San Carlos, Geronimo, again joined by Juh, led some 700 Apaches toward Mexico. In nearby Tombstone, word of the breakout produced near panic, but the Apaches headed for the safety of the "stronghold" in the northern Sierra, where the Chihenne chief Nana joined them. Together, they comprised the largest Apache force since the legendary Cochise had terrorized the region. In April 1882, refreshed and emboldened, Geronimo and a group of warriors audaciously made their way back to San Carlos and compelled several hundred Mimbreño under Loco to join them. With U.S. troops in pursuit, the band headed for Mexico, where they suffered considerable casualties, mainly women and children, in battle with Mexican troops. Despite their losses, they reveled in their newfound freedom, convinced that they were safe in the wild mountains of northern Mexico.

President Chester A. Arthur was sufficiently alarmed at the situation in Arizona to restore Crook to his former command in the Southwest in 1882. Having further strengthened his Indian-fighting credentials on the Great Plains, Crook arrived in Arizona determined to restore peace, but also willing to consider events from the Apache perspective, an approach that quickly revealed that Apache hostility was largely the product of numerous perceived injustices. He was unequivocal about the renegades in the Sierra Madre. "They are an incorrigible lot," he wrote to the secretary of the interior, "the worst band of Indians in America." Crook's strategy for bringing an end to the Apache insurgency was twofold: to address legitimate Apache grievances with reforms on the reservation and to use the necessary military force to drive the renegades back to the reservation. A Chiricahua raid into Mexico provided Crook with the necessary pretext to lead his troops across the border, beginning a long series of intermittent clashes with fast-moving Apache bands. In May 1883, Geronimo, repeating a well-established pattern, agreed to return to San Carlos after Crook contrived to have himself captured in order to persuade the Apache warrior to give up. In hopes of reconciling the Chiricahua to a settled existence, Crook arranged for a new reservation at Turkey Creek on the Black River, some forty miles from San Carlos. The tenuous tranquility there collapsed in May 1884, when Geronimo and other Apache warriors led about 200 Indians off the reservation following a dispute over the recent arrests of two Apache men. As the Apaches, feuding among themselves, broke into small bands and headed for the Mexican border, over 4,000 troops were mobilized to deal with the crisis. Geronimo's name may have been largely responsible for the terror that gripped whites in the region, but the Apache warriors Chihuahua, Nana, Naiche, and Ulzana all contributed to a growing litany of atrocities reported in the newspapers. Through the summer of 1885, army units pursued the Apaches across northern Mexico, confronted with all of the challenges of countering what would at century's end be termed guerrilla warfare. Eventually worn down by relentless pursuit even in their Mexican refuge, short of ammunition and food, the Apache bands confronted the inevitability of surrender. In March 1886, Geronimo and other Chiricahua leaders met with Crook at the Canyon of the Funnels in northern Mexico. Though Geronimo agreed to surrender, he evidently changed his mind subsequent to drinking large quantities of mescal during a celebration, and together with Naiche and twenty warriors, fled again. Geronimo's small band continued raiding through the summer, leaving a trail of American and Mexican bodies in its path. Crook, rebuked for having agreed to a conditional Apache surrender, resigned his command and was replaced by General Nelson Miles, who deployed over 5,000 soldiers, 600 Apache and Navajo scouts, and thousands of civilian militia in a determined effort to corner the wily Chiricahua. In early September, Miles induced Geronimo to meet again, this time at Skeleton Canyon in southeastern Arizona. Accepting that he would be exiled to Florida, Geronimo agreed to return to Fort Bowie in the Chiricahua Mountains. He soon learned, once again, that the white man's word was often broken.

Unbeknownst to Geronimo, Miles had already decided on a mass removal of the Chiricahua to Fort Marion, Florida. Even as the negotiations at Skeleton Canyon were underway, over 400 Chiricahua, together with 1,200 horses and an estimated 3,000 dogs, were making the difficult trek to Holbrook, where they had been led to believe that they would board a train to take them to visit the "Great Father" in Washington, DC. Arriving back at Fort Bowie with Geronimo's band under escort, Miles, in an exchange of telegrams, only with some difficulty convinced President Grover Cleveland to honor the general's promise that the sixty-three-year-old warrior and his followers be deported rather than hanged, as Cleveland had urged. Geronimo was unaware that the deportation to Florida was to be permanent, and on September 8, 1886, boarded a sealed passenger car for the long journey into exile. With the dreaded Geronimo in captivity, the Apache wars ended.

The journey to Florida was interrupted by a lengthy pause in San Antonio, Texas, as bureaucrats squabbled over the fate of the four dozen detainees. To his chagrin, Geronimo learned that the "dangerous" warriors were to be separated from their families and held at Fort Pickens, which was situated on a sandy offshore Florida island. There, they were displayed as curiosities to tourists and journalists. Meanwhile, as the internees at Fort Marion were ravaged by disease, the post's army commander decided that all of the older children were to be removed from their families and sent to the Carlisle Indian School in Pennsylvania, where they could be educated in the white man's ways. Many were soon infected with tuberculosis. In April 1887, the Fort Marion group was transferred to Mount Vernon Barracks in Alabama; as the infected Carlisle students arrived, they spread the disease further. About a year later, Geronimo's group was allowed to join them. When General Crook visited the Alabama camp, the Apaches unsuccessfully implored him to allow them to return to Arizona. Crook died only months later, leading Geronimo to comment that his death was divine retribution for the "evil deeds he committed." In October 1894, with over a hundred of their number dead of disease and malnutrition, the Chiricahuas learned that they would be resettled at Fort Sill in the Oklahoma Territory.

In captivity, Geronimo's celebrity grew enormously. The old warrior was the embodiment of the frontier subdued, and was in increasing demand as an attraction and performer in Wild West shows such as that organized by Pawnee Bill. In 1904, Geronimo was the star attraction of the Apache Village at the St. Louis World's Fair, where the eighty-one-year-old warrior rode a Ferris wheel, watched a puppet show, and demonstrated particular interest in magic acts. The following year, even as Geronimo consented to have educator Stephen M. Barrett write his autobiography, he was invited to head up Theodore Roosevelt's inaugural parade and later met with the president. Though he made an impassioned plea for freedom, Roosevelt, citing white resentments, responded, "It is best that you stay where you are." Geronimo privately pursued an ongoing spiritual quest, even studying Christianity in an effort to understand what had befallen him and his people. He died of pneumonia on February 17, 1909, and was buried at Fort Sill cemetery in what is now designated as the Apache POW (Prisoner of War) Cemetery. In 1913, when the Chiricahua were granted their freedom, only 261 remained of the tribe that numbered some 1,200 during Cochise's heyday.

They shared the fate of other Native American tribes, subdued, reduced in number, relegated to reservations, destined to witness the extinction of their traditional way of life as the frontier itself was rapidly subsumed by the relentless advance of an alien civilization.

ᜪ   HELEN HUNT JACKSON   ᜪ

As she sat in the audience at Boston's Horticultural Hall on October 29, 1879, Helen Hunt Jackson was at a turning point in her life. The forty-nine-year-old New Englander, though born into a stable, middle-class family, had endured more than her share of personal tragedy in the course of an increasingly rootless life. Her firstborn son, Murray, had died in 1854 of a brain disease. In 1863, her first husband, army officer Edward B. Hunt, died in an accident. Diphtheria claimed her second son, Rennie, in 1864. In the face of these losses, she had worked diligently to establish herself as a writer, composing poetry, short stories, and novels as well as essays chronicling her frequent travels. Marrying again in 1875 to William Jackson, she was increasingly plagued by doubts as to the importance of literature that did not address relevant social issues. The product of a region steeped in reformist zeal and the daughter of a minister who stressed the primacy of Christian morality, Jackson was quickly captivated by the story related by that evening's featured speaker, Ponca chief Standing Bear. The Ponca leader, aided by Omaha interpreter Suzette La Flesche (Inshta Theumba, "Bright Eyes"), was on a six-month speaking tour through the East to publicize the injustices that his people suffered in the course of a congressionally mandated relocation from Nebraska to the Indian Territory. During that

Though she initially aspired to a literary career, Helen Hunt Jackson became an influential advocate for humane treatment of Native Americans after hearing a lecture by Ponca chief Standing Bear in 1879. During an era when the vast majority of Americans dismissed Indians as ignorant and degraded savages, Hunt turned her literary talents to exposing the shameful record of federal ineptitude and corruption in Indian affairs, publishing A Century of Dishonor *in 1881. (Library of Congress, LC-USZ62-38827)*

difficult journey, Standing Bear's young son died, and the chief, together with some thirty warriors, broke off to return the child's body to their ancestral land. The small band of grieving Indians alarmed settlers, and a cavalry force under George Crook arrested Standing Bear's party and jailed them in Omaha. The Ponca chief stood before his Boston audience in October only because sympathetic whites in Omaha had provided his group with legal counsel, sought a writ of habeas corpus, and gained a ruling from a district court judge that Indians were persons and as such entitled to the protection of the Constitution.

Standing Bear's account of the plight of the Poncas moved Hunt, whose personal losses and incessant wanderings may have compelled immediate sympathy for the beleaguered, homeless tribe. Touched by the dignified charisma of Standing Bear, Hunt quickly turned her literary talents toward the Ponca cause. On November 20, her essay "Standing Bear and Bright Eyes" appeared in the New York *Independent*, noting the "unutterable sadness" in Standing Bear's countenance and praising his interpreter as "a well educated, graceful, winning, lovely girl" who "speaks English so quaint, so simple, and yet so stately in its very simplicity, that one is lost in wonder." Such positive characterizations of Indians were rare only three years after the Lakotas' annihilation of George Custer's Seventh Cavalry command at the 1876 Battle of the Little Big Horn. Hunt's intent, however, was not to offer a sentimental, romanticized picture of Native Americans, but rather to acknowledge the basic humanity that many denied them. Further, she was increasingly convinced that establishing the legal rights of Indians was the key to reforming Indian policy. In early 1880, she made clear her enthusiasm for the new cause in a letter to her mentor, Massachusetts writer and reformer Thomas Wentworth Higginson. "I have become what I have said a thousand times was the most odious thing in life, 'a woman with a hobby,'" she wrote. "But I cannot help it. I think I feel as you must have in the old abolition days. I cannot think of anything else." Helen Hunt Jackson could not know that she had only a half dozen years left at that point, but in that short span of time, she established herself as the nation's most prominent voice in defense of Indian rights and left an enduring legacy of social reform literature.

Born in Amherst, Massachusetts, on October 14, 1830, Helen Maria Fiske was inevitably shaped by the cultural milieu of a region with a long tradition of religious fervor and a crusading spirit. Born to Calvinist minister Nathan Welby Fiske and an equally devout mother, Deborah Vinal Fiske, Helen grew up in the midst of the Second Great Awakening, as New England's clergy committed themselves to saving souls and fighting moral evils ranging from alcohol to slavery. Passing her youth in a loving but strict Calvinist household, Helen confronted illness and death early, losing her year-old brother in 1833 and then watching her mother slowly weakened by tuberculosis prior to her death in 1844. Her father, similarly afflicted, sought to renew his health by traveling to Palestine, but died there in 1847, leaving Helen and her sister Ann orphaned. Helen, already used to separation from family through long years of boarding school, was placed under the guardianship of a Boston lawyer, who provided guidance and financial support as she returned to her studies at the Abbott Institute in New York City. John Abbott was one of several ministers who supervised and encouraged Helen's budding interest in literature. Like her father, Abbott stressed the importance of Christian submission, but also urged that she develop and use the literary talents that God had given her. Helen, now living with the family of minister Ray Palmer, taught for a little over a year at the Abbott Institute as she pondered her future. She read widely in both classical and contemporary literature and was drawn to the works of transcendentalist sage Ralph Waldo Emerson, whose perspective she described as "thrilling and awakening, even though it does not always prove . . . practical."

The uncertainties in Helen's life were somewhat reduced when she married Edward Hunt in October 1852. A West Point graduate, Hunt was often away on duty assignments with the Corps of Engineers, affording his wife the opportunity to pursue her literary studies. A son, Murray, was born to the couple in 1853 but died within a year, a not uncommon occurrence in the nineteenth century. Struggling with grief, Helen discovered a new interest when she was greatly moved by Harriet Beecher Stowe's controversial antislavery novel *Uncle Tom's Cabin* the following year. Though her conservative husband disapproved of abolitionism, Helen developed a friendship with the radical abolitionist clergyman Moncure Conway, who argued that writers were obligated to use literature as a positive moral instrument. Under Conway's influence, Helen gradually discarded the orthodox Calvinism of her father in favor of Unitarianism, which emphasized the importance of social reform. Like Conway, she was drawn to Emerson's transcendentalist teachings, especially his essay *Nature*, which stressed the spiritual character of art as well as nature. The same year, however, Edward was posted to Key West, Florida, beginning a series of assignments that took him away from his family in New York until 1862 when, in the midst of the Civil War, he died as a result of an accident at the Brooklyn Navy Yard. Only eighteen months later, as the Civil War came to an end in April 1865, Helen's nine-year-old son Rennie died. Now alone, Hunt turned to travel and writing to regain her bearings.

In early 1866, Hunt took up residence in Newport, Rhode Island, where she began to hone her writing skills. The town's large seasonal artistic community included Thomas Wentworth Higginson, former radical abolitionist, transcendentalist, and ex–Union army officer, who mentored and encouraged the young widow in subsequent years. Hunt soon established her reputation as a poet, earning praise from Emerson who, questioned as to whether Hunt was the best woman poet in North America, responded, "Perhaps we might as well omit the *woman*." By 1870, Hunt's stature was such that she was aiding Emily Dickinson's efforts to find a publisher. Hunt also capitalized on her extensive European travels, begun in 1868, with a series of travel essays complementing those she wrote about New England. An emergent theme in these essays was her concern regarding the consequences of the rapid industrialization of the nation, which she feared was destructive of the genteel culture that she had been born into, as well as of the natural environment. Her writings amplified the latter theme after she moved to Colorado Springs in the mid-1870s. Here she met and married William Sharpless Jackson, a wealthy banker and railroad executive. Her efforts now turned to short fiction and novels, as she published the somewhat autobiographical *Mercy Philbrick* in 1876. Her reputation as one of America's leading poets and her successful career as a novelist left Helen Hunt Jackson unfulfilled, however, and she had yet to identify her true ambition when she heard Standing Bear's plea in 1879.

Jackson was not a complete social radical. Indeed, among her writings are several articles that broadly condemned the women's rights movement of her day and argued against woman suffrage. Likewise, much of her poetry focused on the spiritual dimension of domestic duties. The injustices suffered by the Poncas, however, aroused her social conscience, and in late 1879, she embarked on the first phase of her Indian reform crusade. The diminutive, stout Jackson, who stood only five feet three inches, was highly energized by this new undertaking and was instrumental in founding the Boston Indian Citizenship Committee as well as working with the Women's National Indian Association and organizing petition drives. Her chief efforts on behalf of the Poncas, however, were through her writings. She sought to enlist numerous influential writers and newspaper editors to publicize the issue, contributing numerous editorials of her own. Jackson also engaged in a contentious exchange of letters with Secretary of the Interior Carl Schurz, whom she accused of blocking efforts to bring the issue of Indian citizenship before the U.S. Supreme Court. In early 1880, Jackson took up the cause of Colorado's White River Utes, who were being denied rations because of the murder of an Indian agent. Stressing the injustice of such collective punishment, she was soon engaged in a highly publicized and bitter editorial debate with William Byers, editor of the *Rocky Mountain News*, who had defended the infamous 1864 Sand Creek Massacre. Having hopefully sparked public interest in the issue, Jackson moved to New York City in early 1880 to begin research for the book that she hoped would bring a seismic shift of public opinion.

A Century of Dishonor grew out of Jackson's intention to awaken the public through a book that was "simply & curtly a record of our broken treaties." There was to be "no sentiment—no prattle of suggestion" but rather "a bare record of facts in the fewest possible words." Though her husband, who believed Indians to be lazy and dishonest, offered little support, Jackson finished the book in early May and Harper and Brothers brought it out in 1881. Jackson's study began with an effort to establish the legal basis for Native American land rights, then moved on to examine federal relations with seven tribes, including the Poncas, chronicling the mistreatment and injustices suffered by Native Americans. One chapter dealt with white massacres of Indians, presenting graphic details of atrocities in official records, while the conclusion cited the findings of the 1869 Grant Commission, which included a damning indictment of white aggressions. In October 1880, Jackson attended congressional hearings on the Ponca issue and distributed copies of her newly published book to every member of Congress. In March 1881, Congress approved $165,000 in reparations for the Ponca removal and agreed to permit the tribe to select their own reservation land. A *Century of Dishonor* provoked generally positive reviews, including one from historian Francis Parkman, who termed it "an honest and valuable record of a scandalous and shameful page in the history of the American people." Sadly, Jackson soon realized that the book was read largely by those who were already sympathetic and was not reaching the audience she hoped to affect. "I confess that I am greatly disheartened by the entire failure of my book," she wrote to a friend. "It has not sold 2000 copies, outside of those I bought myself."

Though disappointed, Jackson soon discovered a new direction for her campaign when she traveled to southern California to gather material for a series of travel essays. Though her initial interest was in exploring the survival of traditional ways of life in a rapidly modernizing state, she found herself drawn to the plight of the "Mission" Indians, who had fallen victim to massive land dispossessions as more whites moved to California. When Jackson arrived there, fewer than 4,000 Mission Indians survived, reduced in number from about 15,000 in 1852 after they lost the protection that earlier Mexican land grants had afforded. Before returning to Colorado Springs, Jackson arranged to be named as an official commissioner to the Mission Indians, hoping to serve as their advocate. She completed the essays to be published in *Century* magazine in 1883, addressing the impact of "civilization" in southern California, the Spanish legacy, and the current status of the Mission Indians. Jackson found much to admire in the Franciscan missionaries' treatment of Indians, which she contrasted unfavorably with American practices, for the Indians' lives had been better under Spanish and then Mexican rule. "The combination of cruelty and unprincipled greed on the part of the American settlers," she concluded, "with culpable ignorance, indifference and neglect on the part of the Government at Washington has resulted in an aggregate of monstrous injustice." Traveling to Los Angeles in February 1883 in her new official capacity, Jackson found her initial conclusions about the mistreatment of Indians confirmed by additional evidence. Shortly afterward, she confided in a letter to an editor acquaintance, "My opinion of human nature has gone down 100 per ct. in the last thirty days. Such heart sickening fraud, violence, cruelty as we have unearthed here—I did not believe could exist in civilized communities." In her subsequent official report, Jackson proposed eleven recommendations that could ensure Indian rights "to remain where they are."

Once again, Jackson found that her efforts did little to affect either government policy or public opinion. Increasingly, she gave consideration to turning fiction to her cause and in May 1883 told magazine editor Thomas Aldrich, "If I could write a story that would do for the Indian a thousandth part of what *Uncle Tom's Cabin* did for the Negro, I would be thankful for the rest of my life." Later that year, she wrote Aldrich, "My story is all planned. . . . It is chiefly Indian—but the scene is in southern California, and the Mexican life will enter it largely. I hope it will be a telling book—and will reach people who would not read my *Century of Dishonor*." The novel *Ramona* was completed in only three months and was published in November 1884. Set in midcentury southern California, the novel centers on the travails of a half-Indian, half-Scottish orphan girl, who experiences numerous personal tragedies in the broader context of the white dispossession of the Mission Indians—her baby dies after a white doctor refuses medical treatment; her husband goes insane as a result, and is murdered by a white man who is never brought to justice. Ultimately, Ramona finds refuge in Mexico, having found life in southern California unendurable due to white greed and racism. Though the novel garnered generally positive reviews, it failed to achieve Jackson's objective. Most readers evidently embraced the book for its romantic themes and its nostalgic depiction of old Spanish California. The idealized tone of the novel tended to mask its reform message, and though *Ramona* endured as a popular favorite, it never had the catalytic impact that Stowe's famous work did.

Shortly after *Ramona* was published, Jackson was seriously injured in a fall that presaged the rapid decline of her health but did not diminish her commitment to the Native American cause. Appalled at the continued mistreatment and neglect of Indians, some of whom were starving to death even as record wheat crops were harvested, she wrote Moncure Conway in 1884, declaring, "If I were the Lord I'd rain fire & brimstone on these United States." Disillusioned by the lack of a sense of moral duty and social conscience among adults, she gave thought to raising the consciousness of the younger generation by writing an "Indian (& Mexican) story" for a popular children's publication. Though illness precluded this ambitious project, Jackson did complete several shorter children's stories, some of which addressed the issues that were dear to her. By 1885, however, it was evident that she suffered from stomach cancer, and the disease gradually wore her down. One of her last letters was addressed to President Grover Cleveland, imploring him to read *A Century of Dishonor* and asking that he redress "the wrongs of the Indian race." Helen Hunt Jackson died on August 12, 1885, and was buried in a Colorado mountain gravesite according to her wish.

Conclusion

Jackson won broad posthumous praise for her literary accomplishments, but her efforts on behalf of Native Americans failed to produce the national response that she sought. In 1887, Congress approved the Dawes Act, which largely defined federal Indian policy until 1934. The act granted 160-acre allotments to Indian families, but the resulting individual holdings were rarely economically viable. The legislation, which had the intent of compelling the assimilation of Indians into mainstream society, had the effect of further eroding tribal communities and lifestyles. Passed the year after Geronimo's final surrender, the Dawes Act was in effect a legislative requiem for Native American civilization in the United States, which most white Americans had long considered in irrevocable eclipse. Jackson's campaign for the Mission Indians did produce a California act that set aside lands for the hard-pressed southern California tribes, but the benefits were enjoyed only by a small remnant. The crusade for Native American rights lay largely dormant for eight decades, to be revived in the 1960s as a new debate on minority rights reshaped society.

Geronimo was fated to spend his final years in relative obscurity, though he proved a popular attraction at Wild West shows and fairs. Feared and despised when he roamed free, he and other Indian warriors were widely celebrated in fiction, biography, and film after they were rendered harmless. Ironically, many Americans saw in the Chiricahua warrior traits that had traditionally been held in high esteem in American culture, such as courage and tenacity in the face of overwhelming odds. Even as many Americans indulged in celebrating the "Lost Cause" of the Confederate South, they could likewise admire those Native Americans who resisted the enormous military and historical forces arrayed against them. Tragedy is commonly defined as a drama grounded in the conflict between a protagonist and a superior force such as destiny or fate, having a sorrowful conclusion that provokes pity or terror. The American West provided an immense stage for such a tragedy during the last third of the nineteenth century, and the closing of that frontier left an enduring mythology that has since shaped the American perspective.

Study Questions

1. How did the majority of white Americans view Indians during the late nineteenth century? How would you explain this perspective?
2. Discuss Frederick Jackson Turner's frontier thesis. Is it a convincing explanation for the development of American democracy?
3. What drew Helen Hunt Jackson into the campaign for the reform of Indian policy? Were her proposals realistic?
4. What did Geronimo and other Apaches find so objectionable about reservation life?
5. Was the reduction and concentration of Native Americans an inevitable consequence of westward settlement, or was some other outcome possible?

Selected Bibliography

Barrett, S. M., ed. *Geronimo: His Own Story*. New York: Ballantine Books, 1971.
Debo, Angie. *Geronimo: The Man, His Time, His Place*. Norman: University of Oklahoma Press, 1976.

Faulk, Odie B. *The Geronimo Campaign*. New York: Oxford University Press, 1969.

Gibson, Arrell Morgan. *The American Indian*. New York: D.C. Heath, 1980.

Hook, Jason. *American Indian Warrior Chiefs*. New York: Firebird Books, 1989.

Limerick, Patricia Nelson. *The Legacy of Conquest: The Unbroken Past of the American West*. New York: W.W. Norton, 1987.

Reedstrom, E. Lisle. *Apache Wars: An Illustrated Battle History*. New York: Sterling, 1990.

Roberts, David. *Once They Moved Like the Wind: Cochise, Geronimo and the Apache Wars*. New York: Simon and Schuster, 1993.

Slotkin, Richard. *The Fatal Environment: The Myth of the Frontier in the Age of Industrialization, 1800–1890*. New York: Atheneum, 1985.

———. *Gunfighter Nation: The Myth of the Frontier in Twentieth-Century America*. New York: Atheneum, 1992.

Thrapp, Dan L. *The Conquest of Apacheria*. Norman: University of Oklahoma Press, 1979.

~

CHAPTER THREE

Wealth and Social Justice
in Industrial America

The Industrial Revolution that swept across America in the decades following the Civil War was everything the phrase implies. In less than half a century, vast and unpredictable economic forces thoroughly transformed the nation, replacing the predominantly rural and agricultural society of the antebellum years with a dynamic urban, industrial society. In economic as well as political revolutions, traditional institutions and relationships give way to new forms and patterns, and America's Industrial Revolution brought new types of manufacturing, corporate structures, and labor-management relations. In overthrowing the old economic order, the Industrial Revolution brought immense power, privilege, and wealth to those individuals who proved most capable of anticipating, adjusting, and adapting to a rapidly changing capitalist economy. Success, despite the claims of some industrialists, had little relationship to good intentions or morality. While empowering an elite few, the Industrial Revolution also reordered the world of working men and women, often leaving them in a weakened position, lacking any significant leverage in negotiating their wages and working conditions and often condemned to lead degraded and hopeless lives. Rarely in the nation's history have the disparities between rich and poor been as glaring or as seemingly intractable as they were during those decades. Given the gross inequities in power and prosperity, an intellectual climate that deemed natural law to be the only legitimate agency of change, and the determination of powerful industrialists to impose their vision of order on the industrial landscape, conflict between management and labor was almost preordained.

This was a violent era in the history of industrial relations, as some American workers sought to organize to improve their lot, and managers used every possible means, legal and otherwise, to defeat those efforts. Conservative courts, ever ready to issue injunctions, as well as corrupt politicians often served the industrialists' cause, as did state militias and federal troops employed to squelch protests and break strikes. In the absence of these forces, wealthy businessmen hired private armies to intimidate labor organizers and fight strikers. The legal process itself was at times perverted to allow the arrest and jailing of labor activists, while turning a blind eye to illegal activities undertaken by corporations. Violence was the inevitable consequence of the clash between these two intractable forces. Major strikes in 1877, 1892, and 1894 all featured bloody confrontations between workers and authorities, as did the deadly Haymarket Square riot in 1886. The twentieth century brought no respite from the violence, which moved from heavy industry and railroads to the mining industry in Appalachia and the Rocky Mountain West. In 1914, on the eve of World War I, Colorado state militia and sheriff's deputies wantonly fired on the families of striking coal miners in Ludlow, resulting in several dozen deaths. Clashes between labor and management did not end with the Ludlow Massacre, but the event did compel a national debate about the issue.

Andrew Carnegie's name was virtually synonymous with industrial wealth and power in the late nineteenth century, and the former bobbin boy could legitimately claim that his eventual status as the richest man in the world came as a result of personal diligence coupled with an acute business acumen and the unique economic conditions of late-nineteenth-century America. Getting his start in the railroad industry, Carnegie invested wisely and regularly demonstrated an ability to anticipate the direction of the nation's industrial economy, making him a leader in the iron and steel industry from the 1870s to the turn of the century. However improbably, he saw himself as a friend of the working man, convinced that his employees were the beneficiaries of his benevolent policies. Not even strikes and violence at his plants convinced him otherwise, as he inevitably dismissed such occurrences as the work of a disgruntled few. Immensely wealthy at a young age, Carnegie believed that the only defensible rationale for seeking wealth was to give it away so as to benefit society. He unquestionably lived up to his professed creed, and his philanthropic activities remain his greatest legacy. Carnegie also sought recognition as a man of letters, publishing several books, expounding on his "Gospel of Wealth" and seeking to establish a reputation as an acknowledged public voice on almost any contemporary subject of importance. The latter ambition figured in his prominent role in the anti-imperialist movement that emerged after the Spanish-American War and his involvement in the campaign for international peace in the years before World War I.

Mary Harris "Mother" Jones was, like Carnegie, an immigrant, arriving in the United States from Ireland the same year that Carnegie's family came over from

Scotland. Like Carnegie, she knew privation in her early years and grew up in a working-class family. The persona of the labor activist Mother Jones did not evolve until after a relatively unremarkable young adulthood, which brought marriage and four children. Jones's transformation began in the years after her personal tragedies of 1867, when she lost her husband and four children to a yellow fever epidemic. After losing her dressmaking business as a result of the Great Chicago Fire of 1871, Jones embraced the labor movement as her new family, working as an organizer for groups as diverse as the Knights of Labor, the United Mine Workers, and the Socialist Party of America. She also was instrumental in founding the radical Industrial Workers of the World in 1905. She was valued for her speaking abilities, which were deemed crucial to maintaining worker morale in numerous strikes and demonstrations, as well as serving as a labor educator. She managed to play a role in many of the era's most famous labor disputes and was frequently at the center of contentious and even dangerous confrontations. Her fiery rhetoric and personal courage endeared her to many working men and women, though she often embellished accounts of her exploits, either from design or because of poor memory—she was unclear as to her own birth date, and often claimed a more advanced age than records substantiate.

Whatever her personal foibles, Mother Jones earned considerable stature in the labor movement of the late nineteenth and early twentieth centuries. Perhaps the best testament to her notoriety came during a 1902 coal strike when West Virginia District Attorney Reese Blizzard denounced Mother Jones as "the most dangerous woman in America." Despite her long affiliation with labor causes, she never adhered to any specific ideology, and much of her contention with the Socialist Party grew out of her disdain for arcane doctrinal disputes. Much of the popular reverence that she enjoyed stemmed from her willingness to literally dedicate her life to her cause, sharing all of the hardships and privations that befell those for whom she fought, and going to jail for the principles for which she stood. Such dedication and determination led radical organizer Elizabeth Gurley Flynn to proclaim Jones "the greatest woman agitator of our times." Socialist activist Kate Richards O'Hare offered a more poetic tribute after hearing Jones speak for the first time: "Here was one woman in a million, a personality that was fire-tempered, a soul that had been purified in world travail, a voice whose call I could follow to the end of the road." Only during the last decade of her life did Jones's fame diminish, as the intensity of labor conflict waned temporarily after 1920. During the prosperous, conservative 1920s, businessmen prophesied the end of significant labor-management disputes as "welfare capitalism," which promised worker benefits provided by benevolent corporations, would resolve the disputatious issues that had erupted during the Industrial Revolution. Mother Jones died largely forgotten in 1930, shortly after celebrating a dubious 100th birthday.

⌒ ANDREW CARNEGIE ⌒

In some respects, the careers of Andrew Carnegie and J. Pierpont Morgan roughly paralleled one another. Born within a couple of years of one another in the 1830s, both had established business empires during the four decades following the end of the Civil War, as the American economy rapidly industrialized. Both were adroit risk takers who were quick to perceive financial opportunities in a rapidly shifting, dynamic capitalist economy, and both had an almost preternatural ability to foresee the industrial landscape beyond the visible horizon. Beyond those similarities, however, there were few commonalities. Morgan had the advantage of being born into a wealthy family that was well established in banking. Carnegie had arrived in the United States in 1848 as the son of a struggling Scottish weaver and began his working life as a bobbin boy in a textile factory, building his industrial empire only through years of diligence and hard work. As their lives intersected in 1900, the two men did not much like

Industrialist and philanthropist Andrew Carnegie seated in his study around 1913, a dozen years after his sale of Carnegie Steel Corporation to J. P. Morgan. A classic rags-to-riches life made the Scottish immigrant one of the wealthiest men in the world during America's Industrial Revolution. Though he considered himself enlightened in his dealings with labor, Carnegie proved willing to resort to violence to subdue restive workers. (Library of Congress, LC-USZ62-44165)

one another. Ruthless in his determination to exert control over vast sectors of industry and finance, the imperious Morgan disdained the white-bearded, gnomish Scotsman as an old-fashioned entrepreneur who celebrated competition and was altogether too unpredictable. Carnegie, who had often made public his disapproval of those like Morgan who had gained much of their wealth through stock and bond speculation, had additional reasons for disliking the man whose fortune was so vast that in 1895 he loaned the U.S. government the money necessary to preserve the gold standard in the midst of a devastating depression. The morally conventional owner of Carnegie Steel was appalled at rumors of Morgan's alleged sexual excesses. The founder of the House of Morgan was said to keep multiple mistresses, and to have provided the funds for a New York City women's hospital that accommodated those who became pregnant.

Whatever their mutual animosities, the two giants of industry and finance were brought together in 1901 by respective ambitions that conveniently dovetailed. Carnegie had reached the point in his life where divesting himself of his iron and steel empire made considerable sense, given his age and his commitment to his Gospel of Wealth, an outlook holding that those blessed with riches were obliged to put them to the best use. Retirement would afford Carnegie the opportunity to devote his energies full time to giving away his immense fortune. Morgan shared neither Carnegie's desire to retire from active life nor his philanthropic outlook. Intent on consolidating his industrial holdings, Morgan had been working with Elbert "Judge" Gary to construct a vertically integrated steel trust that would undoubtedly provoke a conflict with Carnegie, who had just committed to constructing a new tube works on Lake Erie. A corporate war between the two tycoons would be costly, so at a New York City dinner gathering for Carnegie Steel president Charles Schwab in December 1900, Morgan took Schwab aside and proposed buying out Carnegie, who owned over 50 percent of the company's stock. The two men worked out the details in following weeks and in early February Schwab, acting on the advice of Carnegie's wife Louise, brought up the proposal during a game of golf, telling Carnegie that Morgan had asked that he name his price. The following day, Carnegie did so—he wanted $480 million for the company that bore his name. When Schwab presented the offer to Morgan, he glanced only briefly at the amount and said simply, "I accept this price." Days later, as Morgan ended a visit with Carnegie at the Scotsman's Fifty-first Street home, the powerful financier shook the former bobbin boy's hand, saying, "Mr. Carnegie, I want to congratulate you on being the richest man in the world." Morgan's energies were soon directed toward the formation of United States Steel, the first corporation with a capitalization over $1 billion.

The remaining years of Carnegie's life would be dedicated in large part to giving away as much as possible of his fortune, which in 1901 was estimated at $225 million. He had risen from factory hand to successful entrepreneur within two decades of his arrival in the United States in 1848, an achievement made possible not only by his ambition and business acumen but by the exceptional circumstances in which America's Industrial Revolution unfolded. In an age in which the regulatory state was little more than hypothetical, those with fore-sight and daring could turn unprecedented opportunities for investment and profit into sprawling industrial empires and vast personal fortunes. Carnegie enjoyed the challenges involved in doing so and was counted among the chief industrial giants of the age, celebrated by many Americans for his achievements as well as his sunny disposition. In an era in which relations between manage-ment and labor were often contentious at best and violent at worst, Carnegie differed from many industrialists in that he publicly professed concern for his workers and was convinced that his personal solicitude was manifested in the policies governing his mills. Though a self-professed disciple of social Darwinist Herbert Spencer, Carnegie thought himself a benevolent employer who treated his employees justly. His mill workers found reason to disagree, however, and the 1892 strike at Carnegie's Homestead plant was one of the most violent in American labor history. Afterward, Carnegie, unwilling to reconsider his views on labor-management relations, purged his plants of labor union activity with no evident pangs of conscience. Once divested of any ownership responsibili-ties in 1901, Carnegie dedicated himself not only to his massive philanthropic undertakings but also to offering his services as unofficial adviser on almost any issue to any public officeholder or head of state willing to listen. Carnegie was also a dedicated opponent of the expanding American empire and later joined the campaign to halt the world's drift into war. He died in 1919, as the first stage of America's industrial economy reached maturity and the world into which he had been born was swept away by the relentless forces unleashed by the world war.

The first son of Scottish weaver William Carnegie, Andrew faced uncertain prospects when he was born in the small town of Dunfermline on November 25, 1835. The Industrial Revolution was rapidly transforming society and economy in the British Isles, spawning growing working-class unrest that drew William into the Chartist movement, which advocated democratic constitutional re-forms in a society still very much stratified by class. Andrew's mother, Margaret, maintained the family's two-room, two-story cottage, which housed William's loom on the first floor. During the first decade of his life, as his father struggled to make a living, Andrew excelled as a student, convincing many of the towns-people that great things awaited him. However, the advent of the power loom and an economic downturn in the late 1840s ended William's hopes for sup-porting his family in Scotland, so the dejected weaver gathered up his family and sailed for America in May 1848, a year in which revolutions swept across most of continental Europe.

Andrew was twelve when the family settled among other Scottish immigrants at Allegheny City, later absorbed into Pittsburgh. The economic destinies of father and son soon diverged, as William failed to discover a craft that was reliably profitable and worked less regularly, while Andrew demonstrated an uncanny ability to seize the opportunities that a vibrant capitalist economy in an expanding nation offered. Working briefly as a bobbin boy in a cotton factory for $1.20 a week, Carnegie moved on to the job of messenger for the Ohio Telegraph Company, where he soon caught the eye of Thomas Scott, superintendent of the Pennsylvania Railroad Company. Hired as Scott's private secretary in 1853, the young Scotsman was positioned to advance rapidly in an industry that was crucial to the nation's burgeoning economy. Even as William died in 1855, his son's rise proved meteoric. Appointed as superintendent of the Pittsburgh division, Carnegie earned an extraordinary annual salary of $50,000 and was already building an impressive investment portfolio with Scott's advice, putting money into iron, steel, construction, and railroad locomotives and sleeping cars. The Civil War brought new opportunities in 1861 and Scott, now an assistant secretary of war, named Carnegie superintendent of military railways and federal telegraph lines in the East. As the conflict settled into a stalemate in 1862, Carnegie and his family undertook a triumphant return to Dunfermline, which Andrew found depressing. Returning to the United States that fall, Carnegie discovered that the war's growing carnage made him increasingly vulnerable to conscription. In early 1864, summoned for duty, Carnegie worked through a draft broker to find and pay a substitute $850 to take his place in the Union ranks. That same year, again demonstrating an eye for future markets, Carnegie invested $40,000 in a Pennsylvania oil field. All his investments to date were adroitly placed to take advantage of a rapidly industrializing economy spurred by war.

As the Civil War ended, Carnegie resigned his railway position, placed his investments in the care of his younger brother, and headed off on a year-long tour of Europe, where he both took in the sights and toured iron mills. It was becoming clear to him that, as profitable as railroads were, they were only one of many industries with a seemingly insatiable need for iron and steel. In 1867 he organized Freedom Iron and Steel in Lewistown, Pennsylvania, marking his entry into that industry. In the early 1870s, he developed the Keystone Bridge Works and the Union Iron Works, both in Pittsburgh, capitalizing on his railroad industry connections to sell iron railway bridges. In 1873, he became a partner in the Edgar Thompson Steel Works, named after the influential railroad industrialist and Carnegie acquaintance. The E.T. works utilized the new process developed by Englishman Henry Bessemer, which more effectively removed impurities from molten pig iron, producing a higher grade of steel. Industrial expansion was pulled up short, however, by the panic of 1873, which was precipitated by the collapse that September of Jay Cooke and Company, a major banking establishment. Carnegie, who had moved his family to New York City's elegant St. Nicholas Hotel several years earlier, was better positioned than most to ride out the crisis, which brought a lengthy economic downturn replete with numerous bankruptcies, rising unemployment, and labor unrest. Financial panics and economic slumps were a characteristic of the era's dynamic, rapidly expanding industrial economy, and industrial titans as well as factory hands were affected. Carnegie was compelled to cease investments, husband his existing capital reserve, and secure loans if necessary to meet payrolls. Though the crisis badly dented his investment portfolio, his lifestyle, unlike that of laid-off workers, remained unaffected. In 1874, his family moved to the more luxurious Windsor Hotel, even as the economic downturn led managers at the Union Iron Mills to impose lower wages on some of the workers. Then as later, Carnegie seemed oblivious to the calamitous impact of wage reductions, believing that both management and labor must necessarily equally bear the consequences of economic slowdowns.

Carnegie's mills rode out the erratic economic fluctuations during the next two decades not by cutting production and worker hours, as did most of his competitors, but by keeping his plants up and producing regardless of the price of steel. Carnegie thereby kept his workforce intact and kept buyers supplied, thus ensuring the loyalty of both. He also realized, as did many of the great industrialists of his age, that private control of an often chaotic marketplace was key to ensuring profits. Though Carnegie and his fellow tycoons paid frequent homage to the importance of competition as a regulating mechanism in a free market economy, they often privately determined who got what share of the marketplace. In the steel industry, productive capacity determined market shares, effectively ensuring that Carnegie and others who operated at industrial economies of scale always took home the lion's share of the market. Market forces also did not always determine prices, which were sometimes set instead by informal agreements within an industry. Further, mutual agreements among the ten steel manufacturers who shared and licensed basic patents such as the Bessemer process ensured rapid concentration in the steel industry. Those who dominated the industry effectively controlled competition within it, and there was little inducement to encourage newcomers. Carnegie also began to formalize his philosophy of labor-management relations during this period, though he seemed to take little direct interest in his own workers or their activities during the 1870s. He assigned no special importance to the labor component of manufacturing, evidently viewing workers as little more than an item of outlay in his company ledgers. He endorsed the industry-wide practice of sliding scales for wages, which tied worker pay to company profits. If steel prices fell, the sliding scale required that worker wages decrease. This practice failed to take into account that hard times meant decreased profits for management, but personal privation and suffering for workers. The inequities inherent in this system of compensation would play a major role in the events of 1892.

As the American economy stabilized somewhat, Carnegie began a round-the-world trip in 1878, both to relax and to educate himself about the wider world. He had once remarked that once he had achieved an annual income of $50,000, he would make no further efforts to increase his fortune, but would "spend the surplus each year for benevolent purposes" and "cast business aside" in favor of education and "making the acquaintance of literary men." His global journey was the first of several foreign excursions, most to Britain, aimed at least indirectly at establishing a literary career and a circle of literary and intellectual acquaintances. His travel diary was published as *Notes on a Trip Round the World* (1879) and drew a generally positive reaction. Clearly delighted at the forum that a published work afforded, and easily embracing the role of successful businessman turned commentator, Carnegie soon returned to Britain for a lengthy "coaching" tour of the island. Left behind was Louise Whitfield, whom the very eligible bachelor had begun courting in previous months. Though years were to elapse before the couple married, Louise became a permanent if irregular companion. The two-month-long excursion provided Carnegie with material for another book, in which the now leisurely industrialist indulgently pontificated on a number of subjects, notably the pointlessness of moneygrubbing and the importance of relaxation. "Among the saddest of all spectacles to me," the industrialist wrote, "is that of an elderly man occupying his last years grasping for more dollars." Breaking with the long-standing American celebration of the value of hard work and sacrifice, Carnegie preached the benefits of idleness and leisure. Americans worked too hard and long, he opined, evidently forgetting his role in assigning lengthy working hours to his employees. Before returning, the Scottish immigrant again visited his hometown of Dunfermline, where he laid the cornerstone of a free library that he had funded.

Carnegie returned to the United States to growing renown in both business and social circles, though his most immediate concern was the reorganization of his immensely successful steel mills, which were consolidated in April 1881 as Carnegie Brothers and Company. Later that year, Carnegie bought into the H.C. Frick Coke Company to ensure a ready supply of the high-grade fuel required for his blast furnaces; by 1888, Carnegie owned a 74 percent interest in Frick. He also acceded to the unionization of the E.T. Steel Works and agreed to a higher wage scale for some of the employees to maintain production in a tight market. Concern over labor relations and steel prices could not distract him from the impulse to travel, however, and he returned to Britain in 1882, this time making the acquaintance of such notables as Prime Minister William Gladstone, poet Matthew Arnold, and, perhaps most important, Herbert Spencer. Unsociable to the point of wearing earplugs to block unwanted conversations, the renowned philosopher was perhaps the most articulate proponent of social Darwinism, a theory which held that natural laws governed human social evolution, ensuring the "survival of the fittest." Those who failed to triumph in life's competition, Spencer had argued, were weeded out through natural selection. "If the poor are not sufficiently complete to survive," he had written in an especially brutal maxim, "they die, and it is best that they should die." What led Carnegie to embrace Spencer's philosophy was not its callousness toward the "unfit." For Carnegie, Spencer's synthetic philosophy, incorporating recent discoveries in psychology and biology, supplanted the grim Calvinism of his youth. Having long since rejected Christian "superstition," Carnegie later recalled, "At this period of my life, I was all at sea. No creed, no system reached me. All was chaos." Spencer's philosophy posited a universe governed by natural laws that ensured human social progress. Better yet, Spencer defined progress in moral as well as material terms. Natural moral laws need only be discerned and acted on for the individual, as well as society, to prosper. Carnegie later claimed that his conversion to social Darwinism took place subsequent to an epiphany that he experienced while reading Spencer's works: "Suddenly the light came in as a flood, and all was made clear." Spencerian philosophy, which hailed the industrial age as the latest stage in human evolution, enabled Carnegie to view himself and the great industrialists of the age as material and moral agents of inevitable progress. It was a gratifying assertion, readily endorsed by many of those at the apex of the nation's industrial economy. Though the misanthropic Spencer regularly dodged Carnegie's suggestion that they meet, the industrialist remained reverential toward the Englishman for the rest of his life. Carnegie was more successful in cultivating a friendship with Matthew Arnold, hosting receptions and dinners for the writer during a stateside tour in 1883. Determined to establish a reputation as an unofficial international ambassador at large, Carnegie traveled to England yet again in 1884, a decision that caused the long-suffering Louise to suspend their previously announced engagement. This coaching tour brought Carnegie much publicity, not all of which was positive, as many in England concluded that the brash Scotsman, who publicly voiced his disdain for Britain's "antiquated institutions and abuses," had become a typically arrogant and self-righteous American, lacking in manners and reserve.

Back in the United States, Carnegie launched his philanthropic career with a $50,000 donation toward building New York City's Bellevue Hospital while struggling to repair relations with Louise. Determined to establish his role as a commentator on contemporary issues, Carnegie astounded New York City's Nineteenth Century Club with a defense of socialism. In a subsequent interview in the *New York Times*, Carnegie seemed to take labor's side: "Labor is all that the working man has to sell, and he cannot be expected to take kindly to reductions in wages, even when such are necessary in order that he may have any work at all." He also declared that "socialism is the grandest theory ever presented, and I am sure that some day it will rule the world. Then we will have obtained the millennium." It was not a viewpoint that would be embraced in many corporate boardrooms, but it was a testament to Carnegie's unique perspective, which seemed to defy categorization. He had recently compelled the workers at the E.T. works to accept a reinstatement of the twelve-hour work day, a physically debilitating schedule. Oblivious to these baffling contradictions, he began work on *Triumphant Democracy* (1886), a paean to America's republican institutions, replete with statistics purporting to demonstrate that American civilization had surpassed that of Great Britain in every category. Though the public response was mixed, the steel magnate gloried in his new reputation as an established man of letters.

However, 1886 brought events that shook Carnegie's insulated world, as his sunny prediction of industrial harmony in an April magazine article proved overly optimistic. A massive railroad strike spread across the Southwest and in early May violence swept Chicago's Haymarket Square when a bomb detonated during a labor rally. Despite the subsequent national hysteria over the specter of labor radicalism, Carnegie retained his conviction that industrial relations would soon revert to a natural peaceful state. The more immediate tragedies for the middle-aged Scot, who had only recently sought U.S. citizenship, were personal. His brother Thomas grew ill and died in October, and his mother, Margaret, died only weeks later. Stunned by the deaths, he reluctantly agreed to marry Louise. Before the April 1887 wedding, Carnegie had his fiancée sign a prenuptial agreement, guaranteeing her a $20,000 annual income. His fortune, he was determined, would be given away. His previously optimistic disposition seemed dimmed by the rush of events in the late 1880s. In another speech to the Nineteenth Century Club, Carnegie was relentless in his criticisms of those who failed to appreciate the promise of America and pronounced the end of socialism in the face of triumphant democracy. "It received its lesson at Chicago," he warned. "If you want to live in this country you must be quiet citizens or quiet corpses." To those who failed to heed the warning, he declared, "we will hang more of you." Labor radicals, he continued, "are mostly foreigners, the scum and dregs . . . the idle ne'er-do-well and dissipated." For those who proposed radical alternatives to just American institutions, Carnegie had a simple prescription: "Shoot him on the spot." These surprisingly harsh judgments sprang from Carnegie's deeply held belief that "triumphant democracy" provided the solutions to all reasonable grievances in American society; anyone who believed that social injustice was rooted in basic American institutions was a hopeless crank undeserving of even being heard.

This new intolerance was voiced even as a new era of intensified labor conflict was on the horizon in the late 1880s. With steel prices falling, Carnegie insisted his employees accept a sliding scale of wages, which meant reductions. He also proved willing in 1887 to employ the notorious Pinkerton Agency to resolve a strike at the E.T. steel mill. It was a given among workers that the appearance of the "Pinkertons," nominally employees of a detective agency but operating as corporate mercenaries, signaled management's willingness to resort to violence, and the strike ended with the workers compelled to accept a twelve-hour day and no minimum rate. The workers, Carnegie insisted with twisted logic, had no one to blame but their own unions, which had failed to compel Carnegie's competitors to maintain the eight-hour day; he could not be expected to unilaterally allow his workers shorter work days. Oblivious to the contradictions in his views, Carnegie increasingly promoted himself a social philosopher, most notably with the publication of "Wealth" in the June 1889 issue of *North American Review*. In this explication of his social philosophy, Carnegie maintained that contemporary inequities in wealth were natural and inevitable, and that men of great organizational ability such as himself deserved great recompense because they were in short supply. He further explained that the successful industrialist should first strive to accumulate wealth, and then distribute it to benefit society. This self-serving Gospel of Wealth celebrated the moral worthiness of the wealthy industrialists and proclaimed the absurdity of leveling schemes. The article drew praise from Carnegie's friend Gladstone and others but also provoked pointed criticism. Methodist bishop Hugh Price Hughes conceded that Carnegie was an "estimable and generous man," but given his effective endorsement of inequality, nonetheless found the industrialist to be "an anti-Christian phenomenon, a social monstrosity, and a grave political peril." Carnegie partly blunted such criticism with a frenzy of philanthropic activity, including the building of Pittsburgh's Carnegie Library and a music hall in New York City. However generous these gestures, the events of 1892 undid whatever goodwill they generated.

Carnegie acquired the Homestead Steel Works in 1883, and its workers, organized by the Amalgamated Association of Iron and Steel Workers (AAISW), demonstrated their determination to fight for their interests in July 1889 when they turned back a trainload of strikebreakers headed for the plant. Days later, the townspeople faced down a sheriff with 125 deputies, ensuring the union's victory. Henry Clay Frick, chairman of Carnegie Brothers since 1888, blamed the union for slowing production and was determined to break it. When the AAISW's three-year contract expired in late June 1892, Frick proposed a 22 percent wage reduction and announced a deadline for concluding negotiations. If there was no agreement by that time, the union would no longer be recognized. Carnegie, overseas as the crisis unfolded, approved of Frick's strategy. On

June 28, Frick locked the workers out of several plants and began preparations for a major confrontation. Barbed wire fences, sniper towers, and high-pressure hoses were installed to protect the mills and furnace buildings. Observing the construction of "Fort Frick," workers prepared to prevent the company from reopening the plant with strikebreakers, organizing in paramilitary fashion to establish defensive positions and acquiring boats to patrol the Monongahela River on which the Homestead works sat. On the night of July 5, 300 armed Pinkerton agents aboard two barges sought to surreptitiously land on the river-bank and secure the plant. Alerted, armed workers, cheered on by their families, confronted the Pinkertons. A ten-minute firefight broke out, followed by a lengthy standoff in which workers attempted unsuccessfully to sink the barges with cannon fire, dynamite charges, and flaming oil dispersed on the river. In nearby Pittsburgh, thousands of angry steelworkers set out to aid their comrades at Homestead, arriving as the battle ended in late afternoon. Two workers and two Pinkertons had died in the shootout. The besieged Pinkertons were allowed to come ashore and be escorted out of the area, but only after running a gauntlet of enraged workers, who enthusiastically beat and stoned them. The company regained control only on July 12, when 4,000 state militia arrived by train and occupied the plant. Strikebreakers were brought in, the union leaders arrested, and the town placed under martial law. On July 23, with tensions high, Alexander Berkman, a young anarchist, confronted Frick in his office and shot him twice in the neck before stabbing him. Frick survived his wounds, and Berkman was later imprisoned. In late November, members of the Homestead chapter of AAISW, cold and hungry, voted narrowly to return to work, confirming the company's triumph, though it came at the cost of considerable unfavorable publicity for Carnegie Steel. In a statement to the *New York Times* in early 1893, Carnegie offered unconvincing rationales for his company's actions at Homestead and made clear his intent not to address the issue again, but public criticisms mounted. Carnegie increasingly seemed divorced from the daily realities that his workers confronted, preferring to cling to the dubious propositions that comprised his theories of wealth and industrial relations. Unwilling to question his most basic convictions, Carnegie set about enjoying a more leisurely life, spending the later years of the decade traveling with his wife and daughter Margaret, born in 1897. He began construction of Skibo, a Scottish castle near Dornoch, the same year.

One interest that consumed more of Carnegie's energy as the turn of the century neared was fledgling American imperialism, which was ignited after the swift U.S. victory in the Spanish-American War in 1898. Carnegie saw the creation of an American empire as fraught with dangers, and immediately lent his voice and pen to the growing anti-imperialist movement. He was especially appalled at the annexation of the Philippines, and his much-publicized opposition spawned the rumor that the industrialist had offered to buy the islands for $20 million and grant them independence. Even Carnegie lacked such an amount of ready capital, however, and he fought this battle with public statements and much unsolicited advice directed to American policymakers. He was distracted from this campaign by the need to address increasingly embittered relations with Henry Frick, who was driven out of the company's management in 1899 following years of disputes with Carnegie. The Carnegie Company, formed from the merger of Carnegie Steel and H.C. Frick Coke in April 1900, was not destined to long remain in the Scotsman's control. J. P. Morgan's purchase of the company in March 1901 transformed it into U.S. Steel, finally granting Carnegie the opportunity to pursue his oft-expressed ambition to give away his fortune.

An avid and eclectic reader since youth, Carnegie believed that libraries were a key to individual success, and so directed much of his money toward them. As of the early 1900s, he had donated library funds to thirty-seven cities; in his lifetime he provided $41 million to 1,689 libraries in the United States and its territories. An additional $15 million went to funding over 800 libraries around the world. Carnegie also gave away $6.25 million for pipe organs in churches, funding nearly 7,700 around the world. Other monies went to establish several institutes, such as California's Mount Wilson Observatory and the National Negro Business League. Finding that his annual income of $10–20 million still exceeded his giving, he also set up the Carnegie Hero Fund to reward heroic deeds. In addition to overseeing his donations, Carnegie strove to remain a presence in national life, offering frequent and sometimes ill-considered comments on prominent individuals, world events, and national affairs. As a self-appointed apostle of world peace, Carnegie annoyed presidents Theodore Roosevelt and William H. Taft with regular unwanted advice on foreign policy. An inveterate optimist, the now white-bearded Scotsman funded the Carnegie Endowment for International Peace. The outbreak of war in the summer of 1914 belied much of Carnegie's belief in human progress through social evolution, and he lapsed into depressed silence the following year, not to resume his public life until war's end in 1918. On August 11, 1919, Carnegie succumbed to pneumonia at his New York City home. His estate was valued at about $26 million, despite his giving away more than $350 million in his lifetime. "The sole purpose of being rich," Carnegie had once proclaimed, "is to give away money." The final decades of his life were largely dedicated to realizing that goal.

⌣ MARY HARRIS "MOTHER" JONES ⌣

West Virginia's Kanawha River valley appeared to be in a state nearing civil war in early 1913, as striking coal miners organized by the United Mine

President Calvin Coolidge, Mary Harris "Mother" Jones, Grace Coolidge, and Theodore Roosevelt Jr. pose on the White House lawn in September 1924. By the 1920s, Jones's reputation as a dangerous labor radical was considerably diminished, perhaps explaining her meeting with the very conservative Coolidge. During the late nineteenth century, however, Jones was renowned for her outspoken defiance of authority and personal courage in defense of the rights of laboring Americans. (Library of Congress, LC-USZ62-73975)

Workers (UMW) continued a work stoppage begun the previous March. The Carbon Coal Company had used all the means available to it to defeat the strike in the rugged hill country, including construction of concrete fortifications at mines and offices. These menacing blockhouses were equipped with machine guns and manned by notorious Baldwin-Felts guards, hired security men renowned for their ready resort to violence in defense of management objectives. The Baldwin-Felts men routinely harassed and threatened miners and their families on isolated roads in the back country. In self-defense, the miners at Paint Creek and Cabin Creek armed themselves. On July 26, 1912, miners and guards engaged in a bloody shootout at Mucklow, leaving sixteen dead. Governor William Glasscock deployed three companies of state militia to restore order in the area. It was not so much the miners who worried him, but rather the activities of labor organizer Mother Jones, who had been drawn to the strike like a moth to flame.

Some months before, the Republican governor had been invited to attend a labor rally that Mother Jones organized in the state capital and, when he failed to appear, Jones, according to a mine operator at the event, unleashed her rhetorical vitriol to stir up the assembled miners. Jones was said to have denounced the governor as "a goddamned dirty coward" and warned that "unless he rids Paint Creek and Cabin Creek of these goddamned Baldwin-Felts mine-guard thugs, there is going to be one hell of a lot of bloodletting." The mine owner reported that Jones then told the crowd, "Arm yourselves, return home and kill every goddamned mine-guard on the creeks, blow up the mines and drive the damned scabs out of the valley." The mine owner's account of Jones's rabble-rousing is problematic given his obvious bias, and no official record of the speech exists. Nonetheless, Jones's firebrand reputation gave credence to the account. In only marginally more ambiguous words, Jones did tell another audience, "I am not going to say to you don't molest the operators. It is they who hire the dogs who shoot you. I am not asking you to do it, but if he is going to oppress you, deal with him." Given Jones's established willingness to utilize incendiary rhetoric and her famously unshakeable determination once committed to a cause, Governor Glasscock saw her as a destabilizing influence in an already volatile situation. On September 2 he declared martial law and sent in 12,000 troops to suppress the "insurrection." He also authorized the military to court-martial civilians, a clearly unconstitutional act, leading to the conviction and jailing of sixty-six labor activists. Defiant in the face of the governor's repressive measures, Jones announced that she was coming to Charleston to present Glasscock with a petition. The *Charleston Daily Gazette* warned that the infamous radical was approaching with a mob of 500 along with plans to assassinate the governor. With the city alarm bell ringing and National Guard and police forces ringing the capitol, Mother Jones was arrested before she could confront Glasscock and was taken under military arrest to a prison in Pratt. Twenty-five others, mostly miners and labor organizers, also faced charges.

The trial of the seventy-six-year-old Irish immigrant, which began on March 7, 1913, was a national sensation. White-haired, pink-cheeked, and matronly, Jones was a grandmotherly figure whose appearance made it difficult to credit the infamies attributed to her. Nevertheless, she was charged with conspiracy resulting in murder and aiding the murderers to escape, both capital crimes. Jones refused to defend herself, and the court had little solid evidence to attribute the deaths directly to her incitements. A front-page story in the *New York Times* captured the manner in which the story was generally reported. Under the headline "Mother Jones Defiant," the newspaper quoted her as saying, "I am 80 years old and haven't long to live anyhow. Since I have to die, I would rather die for the cause to which I have given so much of my life." It was vintage Mother Jones, given the common inaccuracy about her own age together with a profession of self-denying commitment that was simultaneously self-serving. Though Jones's commitment was genuine, she commonly shaped her personal narrative with melodramatic exaggerations of events designed to affirm her public persona. She gave several interviews while imprisoned and sent letters to prominent individuals, always reiterating her undying determination to accept her fate and go out fighting. She gave her return address as "Military Bastille (In Russianized America)." Finally in early May, the new governor, Henry Hatfield, embarrassed by the publicity and hoping to defuse the situation in the Kanawha valley, ordered Mother Jones freed. Though the strike ended when the miners accepted a settlement imposed by the governor, the publicity surrounding her case prompted a U.S. Senate investigation of labor practices in West Virginia. Speaking in Pittsburgh, Jones remained defiant. "The governor wants your guns," she warned the miners. "Don't you dare give up any of them. If you are forced to use them, you use them." The trial and imprisonment of Mother Jones strengthened her already formidable legend. A writer for the *Christian Socialist* exuberantly described her as "God's great ministering angel, the incarnate spirit of motherhood, a mighty prophetess of the coming reign of justice, love and joy." This description comported closely to the image that Mother Jones had spent decades creating.

In her notoriously inaccurate and exaggerated autobiography, Mother Jones wrote, "I was born in the city of Cork, Ireland, in 1830." Contemporary scholars set the date in August 1837, but they do not dispute Jones's claim, "my people were poor." Writing her life story in 1923, Jones was far too dependent on unreliable memory, perhaps explaining why she devoted so few pages to her youngest years. Born to Richard and Ellen Cotter Harris, Mary was the second of five children and grew up in difficult circumstances in a country wracked by poverty and glaring economic inequities. There is little evidence for her later claim that her relatives were active in Irish secret societies in opposition to English policies, and her father, a laborer, likely immigrated to North America in 1847 because of a stagnant economy and the disastrous potato blight. Mary followed shortly along with the rest of the family. Settling first in Toronto, Canada, the Harrises, as Irish Catholics, faced considerable prejudice in a predominantly Protestant and English nation. Mary devotes little of her autobiography to these years, noting that she was active in her church and was educated as a teacher. In 1860, she moved to Monroe, Michigan, to teach at a Catholic academy, but stayed only briefly before heading for Chicago, where she worked as a dressmaker. Still restless, she moved south to Memphis, Tennessee, where she met and married ironworker George Jones. The couple produced four children before disaster struck in 1867. A yellow fever epidemic left Mary widowed and childless, and she moved to Chicago, where the Great Fire of 1871 left her penniless. Without a family of her own and desperate to give some meaning to her life, she began the pilgrimage that transformed her into Mother Jones, whose family was America's oppressed working class and downtrodden poor.

Mary Harris Jones had some acquaintance with the travails of the working class through her husband, a dedicated union member, but it remains unclear exactly when she identified with organized labor. Jones claimed that her class consciousness was raised when she did sewing for wealthy Chicagoans "who lived in magnificent houses on Lake Shore Drive" and who "seemed neither to notice nor to care" about the "poor, shivering wretches, jobless and hungry, walking alongside the frozen lakefront." For Jones as well as other working-class Americans, the 1870s was a decade of growing labor unrest fueled by economic decline. The Working-Men's Party was formed in Chicago in 1876, and the following year saw considerable violence during a rail strike. Jones later claimed to have witnessed the violent clashes in the Pittsburgh rail yards (biographers have not been able to verify her presence and note that Jones, especially in later life, often offered problematic or exaggerated accounts of her activities). The lessons of that year, she later wrote, were that "labor must bear the cross for others' sins, must be the vicarious sufferer for the wrongs of the world." Her growing sense of the value of martyrdom to a cause was enhanced in 1886 when the Haymarket Riot and its aftermath produced numerous martyrs, whom she termed "teachers of the new order." Some years later, she appropriated May 1, the day traditionally accorded to honor labor, as well as the day of the Haymarket affair, as her own birthday.

Part of the mystique of Mother Jones was that many of the events of her life before the 1890s were unknown or unverifiable, and accordingly Mary Harris Jones had considerable latitude in constructing the persona of Mother Jones to best suit herself and her cause. Her claims to have joined the Knights of Labor in the 1870s cannot be verified and the group was declining rapidly in the 1890s, the first point at which credible evidence of her activities may be found. Though she claimed to have initially established her name during the tumultuous events of 1877, the first recorded accounts of her activities are from 1894, when a depression stemming from a financial panic had created the worst economic conditions since the late 1830s. President Grover Cleveland, a conservative "Bourbon" Democrat whose governing philosophy did not allow for federal intervention in the economy, sat on his hands as the crisis worsened. The despair produced Coxey's Army, a protest movement that organized to march on the nation's capital demanding jobs. Mother Jones accompanied one group of marchers that made its way through Kansas City, where the local newspaper reported that she spoke and raised funds for the protestors. The progress of Jones's group was severely hampered when its leader absconded with funds intended to purchase boats for the journey down the Mississippi River. It is unknown whether Jones's group made it to Washington, but when the main band arrived in late April, Coxey and other leaders were arrested for walking on the White House grass, and the remaining demonstrators fled. It was an ignominious ending for Mother Jones's first crusade, and it marked the beginning of three decades of itinerant life, as she followed major labor developments around the country.

The rout of Coxey's Army did not deter laborers from other protests, however, and in April 1894 the UMW, with whom Jones was destined to work closely in future years, began a national coal strike. Even as it lost its momentum, the American Railway Union, led by Eugene Debs, launched a massive strike against the Pullman Company. Debs was jailed and federal troops broke the strike, which Jones observed in Alabama. When Debs was released in 1896, she organized a mass meeting in Birmingham to greet him and refused to allow authorities to prevent the event. Jones was already becoming aware that her gender and age brought some important advantages, as officials were sometimes hesitant to challenge or threaten an elderly woman. The fiery Irish immigrant impressed Debs, who described her as a "modern Joan of Arc." Jones evidently saw some promise in the populist movement, which demanded that government serve the interests of the people, rather than the powerful few. She attended the 1896 convention, where social critic Henry Demarest Lloyd confided to her that the party's decision to back Democrat William Jennings Bryan for the presidency effectively destroyed the populist movement. A more enduring influence in Jones's life was her friendship with Julius Wayland, publisher of the socialist newspaper *Appeal to Reason*. Published in Kansas, the paper became the nation's leading radical weekly by 1900 as American socialism entered its heyday. Jones's socialism was not dogmatic; she propounded economic transformation while preserving individual liberty and democracy. Though Jones helped found the Social Democratic Party in 1898 and the Industrial Workers of the World in 1905, she considered arcane doctrinal disputes of no interest and a distraction from the greater cause.

Beginning in the late 1890s, much of Mother Jones's energy was directed toward aiding coal miners. Coal was to turn-of-the-century America what petroleum would be a half century later—the nation's chief energy source. Nearly 680,000 Americans labored in the claustrophobic and dangerous mines in 1900. The mining industry had undergone the same concentration that shaped other major industries in the late nineteenth century. John D. Rockefeller monopolized most of the nation's petroleum through his Standard Oil Company; in Colorado, the Victor Coal Company and the Colorado Fuel and Iron Company controlled most of the coal. Mining companies often owned the towns that workers lived in, determining their rents, compelling them to buy from company stores, and dunning their paychecks for rent and food. In response to unjust policies and dangerous working conditions, the UMW organized in 1890.

Mother Jones quickly established a presence among the miners, as one UMW official remembered:

> She came into the mine one day and talked to us in our workplace in the vernacular of the mines. . . . She would take a drink with the boys and spoke their idiom, including some pretty rough language when she was talking about the bosses.

The same official recalled that "when she started to speak, she could carry an audience of miners with her every time. . . . She had a complete disregard for danger or hardship."

The exact moment of Jones's affiliation with UMW is unclear, but she played a major role in the Great Anthracite Strike of 1897, which grew out of efforts to organize miners in West Virginia's Central Competitive Field. Her activities in the area led to her arrest in 1902, when she and other organizers were accused of violating a court injunction against the strike. This trial led the district attorney to denounce her as "the most dangerous woman in America," but the judge freed her, explaining that he believed she was an unwitting dupe of "designing and reckless agitators." Jones responded with a denunciation of the judge as a scab. When the West Virginia strike was broken in 1903, Jones traveled to Colorado to support the UMW in a strike against the Rockefeller mines. A reporter for the *Denver Republican* marveled at the incongruity between "this eminently respectable and strictly conventional old lady" and "political doctrines, socialist propaganda, the labor movement, the teachings of Karl Marx, lockouts, black lists, riots." "What knowledge of these," wondered the writer, "belongs to this little old woman with the snowy hair and the soft pink cheeks?"

Mother Jones was in no way a "conventional old lady." Even as the UMW strike stalled, she turned to the cause of child labor in textile mills, organizing a "children's crusade" in 1903, enlisting several hundred New Jersey mill hands for the event. Demanding a meeting with President Theodore Roosevelt, she threatened to march on the president's Long Island home, Sagamore Hill. Though she and a few children managed to get to Roosevelt's house, he was absent, and the crusade fizzled. Jones subsequently urged working men not to vote for the president in 1904. Between 1904 and 1915, Jones worked primarily as an organizer and speaker for the Socialist Party, though she found time to travel extensively in support of brewery workers, copper miners, textile workers, telegraphers, garment workers, and even exiled Mexican revolutionaries. Her relationship with the socialists gradually deteriorated, however, as she viewed the party's interest in immigration, birth control, woman suffrage, and temperance as distractions from the central issue of justice for the working class. "We're not building a movement for free-lovers and job hunters," she huffed to socialist Thomas Morgan.

She left the socialists in 1911 in favor of the UMW and participated in the dramatic events of the 1913 West Virginia coal strike, which made her one of the most famous women in America. Later that year, she was drawn into the Colorado Coal War, a lengthy confrontation between miners and operators in which both sides were heavily armed, with violence expected. Arriving in Trinidad in early December, Jones urged the miners, who sought an eight-hour day and improved wages, to remain steadfast. When over 90 percent of the miners struck late in the month, their families were turned out of company housing by mine guards. Many of the displaced moved into tents at an encampment near Ludlow. Baldwin-Felts agents sought to terrorize them by bringing in machine guns, searchlights, and an armored automobile called the "Death Special." In October, guards fired over 400 rounds into one tent city, killing a miner. The arrival of Colorado National Guard troops failed to stem the accelerating violence, as miners killed four guards over the course of two weeks and Secretary of Labor William Wilson warned President Woodrow Wilson that "a condition of guerrilla warfare exist[ed]" because of the "feudal system" perpetuated by the operators, who refused to negotiate. When Jones left the state to raise funds back East, General John Chase prohibited her from returning, and when she arrived back in Trinidad in January 1914, she was arrested and detained at a nearby hospital for nine weeks. Mother Jones's arrest provoked widespread condemnation and a protest march in Trinidad, where 1,000 women and children demanded her release. Chase personally led the cavalry troops that broke up the march, injuring six women.

Freed prior to a hearing before the state supreme court and again warned to stay out of Trinidad, Jones defiantly boarded a train for that destination only to be arrested in Walsenburg and confined to the county courthouse there for nearly four weeks. Chase claimed that violence attendant to the strike was "inspired by this woman's incendiary utterances." Never charged with any crime, Jones was released before her pending court appearance and left the state to testify before a congressional committee about the situation in Colorado. In her absence on April 19, outright warfare between miners and company guards occurred. A day-long gun battle left twenty dead among the mine families, mostly women and children, while one guard died. Outraged local UMW officials issued a "call to rebellion" and state labor groups began handing out weapons. A week of running gun battles in the hills around Trinidad left over fifty dead. Mine operators blamed the violence on "ignorant, lawless and savage South-European peasants." As Mother Jones pleaded with the miners for moderation, President Wilson ordered federal troops into the coalfields. His proposed settlement, though it gave nothing to the miners and asked for a three-year moratorium on strikes, was rejected by the operators. Though Jones met with Wilson and pleaded for federal mediation, the president refused and the strike ended after fourteen months with no discernible gains for the miners.

The Ludlow Massacre did compel many Americans to acknowledge the egregious injustices suffered by many working men, largely due to the disproportionate and unfettered power and influence wielded by corporations. Though the Progressive reformers of the era sought to address the issue through legislation and regulation, their instruments were often blunt and ineffective. Progressives such as Theodore Roosevelt and Woodrow Wilson, while paying lip service to the need for a "square deal" for the working man, were unwilling to consider radical reforms that might alter the basic structure of existing socioeconomic relationships; the Progressive paradigm did not allow for it. At times Mother Jones seemed cognizant of the limitations of her times. In 1916, a presidential election year, she professed her belief in socialism before a Labor Day audience in Evansville, Indiana, but then announced her support for Woodrow Wilson. "Socialism is a long way off," she explained. "I want something right now!"

Now in her seventies, Jones continued to demonstrate zeal matched with energy. She supported the causes of dressmakers, streetcar workers, and labor organizer Thomas J. Mooney, who was unjustly sentenced to death for the terrorist bombing of a Preparedness Day parade in 1916. American entry into the European war in April 1917 put the UMW in an advantageous position, and Jones was at the forefront of efforts to secure better pay and conditions for the miners. In 1919, Jones took up the cause of organizing Pennsylvania steelworkers and, upon being arrested for speaking without a permit, famously informed the judge that she spoke on a permit issued by Patrick Henry, Thomas Jefferson, and John Adams. She also impressed a military intelligence agent who, having heard her speak in Chicago, described her words as "the foulest and most profane that can be imagined" in an address that "fairly teemed with ultra-radical suggestions." Despite her unflagging devotion to the cause, her talents failed her as she aged. Some listeners in 1919 detected a troubling incoherence in her speeches. In the winter of 1920, she suffered a rheumatic attack that slowed her considerably, though she journeyed into West Virginia in the early 1920s, where Baldwin-Felts mine guards had provoked a deadly gun battle in the coal town of Matewan. A veritable civil war followed, with army troops, including an air group, a chemical warfare unit, and a mortar squad, intervening to impose order. The episode, during which Jones had provided confusing and ill-considered leadership, was disastrous for the UMW, which was essentially driven out of the state. Increasingly restricted by physical ailments, Jones turned to writing her autobiography in mid-decade and fretted about personal finances. The book was a commercial failure, and Jones quickly faded from public view. Taken in by former Knights of Labor leader Terence Powderly, Jones ventured to Chicago in 1924 for her last public appearance in support of striking dressmakers. During her last half-dozen years, her activities were largely restricted to correspondence, and she died on November 30, 1930, as the nation slipped into its worst depression. Her physician explained that she was simply worn out. Father John Maguire, the priest who presided at her memorial, offered this eulogy: "She had a small frail body, but she had a great and indomitable spirit."

Conclusion

Andrew Carnegie and Mary Harris Jones shared common origins. They were children of struggling immigrant families that immigrated to the United States in the 1840s seeking a better future. However, their destinies ultimately diverged sharply. Carnegie, astute and ambitious, adroitly capitalized on the unique opportunities presented by America's Industrial Revolution to build a personal fortune and an industrial empire that made him one of the wealthiest men in the nation. Though he saw himself as a benevolent employer, he worked to crush the unions that sought to organize his workers. His greatest legacy was arguably his philanthropic empire, which has long outlived him. Mary Harris Jones, deprived of her family in terrible circumstances, essentially renounced the stable life of a housewife for a peripatetic existence as one of the nation's most colorful and persistent defenders of working-class Americans. Willingly enduring physical discomforts, the threat of physical violence, and multiple arrests and incarcerations on behalf of her cause, Mother Jones became the embodiment of labor activism for about three decades that coincided with the most turbulent era in the history of American labor relations. Though she was not always immediately victorious in these struggles, she gave both voice and heart to those who sought economic justice for America's working class.

Study Questions

1. How would you explain Andrew Carnegie's rapid rise to wealth and power?
2. How was it possible for Carnegie to embrace the seemingly incompatible doctrines of social Darwinism and his own Gospel of Wealth simultaneously?
3. What events transformed Mary Harris Jones into Mother Jones?
4. How would you explain the frequency of violence in labor disputes during this era?
5. Given that both Carnegie and Jones were immigrants from the United Kingdom, even arriving in the United States at about the same time, what do their divergent paths say about America during the Industrial Revolution?

Selected Bibliography

Adams, Graham, Jr. *The Age of Industrial Violence, 1910–1915.* New York: Columbia University Press, 1966.

Brody, David. *Steelworkers in America: The Nonunion Era.* New York: Harper, 1969.

Foote, Kenneth E. *Shadowed Ground: America's Landscape of Violence and Tragedy.* Austin: University of Texas Press, 1997.

Gitleman, Howard. *Legacy of the Ludlow Massacre: A Chapter in American Industrial Relations.* Philadelphia: University of Pennsylvania Press, 1988.

Gorn, Elliot J. *Mother Jones: The Most Dangerous Woman in America.* New York: Hill and Wang, 2002.

Hounshell, David. *From the American System to Mass Production, 1800–1932.* Baltimore, MD: Johns Hopkins University Press, 1994.

Kraus, Paul. *The Battle for Homestead, 1890–1892: Politics, Culture and Steel.* Pittsburgh, PA: University of Pittsburgh Press, 1992.

Montgomery, David. *The Fall of the House of Labor: The Workplace, the State and American Labor, 1850–1932.* Cambridge, MA: Harvard University Press, 1989.

Morris, Charles R. *The Tycoons: How Andrew Carnegie, John D. Rockefeller, Jay Gould and J. P. Morgan Invented the American Supereconomy.* New York: Owl Books, 2006.

Nasaw, David. *Andrew Carnegie.* New York: Penguin, 2006.

Werth, Barry. *Banquet at Delmonico's: Great Minds, the Gilded Age, and the Triumph of Evolution in America.* New York: Random House, 2009.

Wiebe, Robert. *The Search for Order, 1877–1920.* New York: Hill and Wang, 1968.

Zinn, Howard. *A People's History of the United States, 1492–Present.* New York: Perrenial, 1980.

CHAPTER FOUR

~

Progressive Americans and the World

During the 1890s, the United States became the leading manufacturer of industrial goods in the world and an economic power capable of competing with Great Britain. In that very decade, the nation nevertheless experienced a hitherto unprecedented economic calamity that crippled American cities and rural areas alike, with unemployment surpassing 18 percent by 1894 and remaining in double digits for six years. Beginning at the urban level, before expanding to state capitals and eventually Washington, DC, reformers attempted to tackle the dislocations caused by seemingly continuous boom-and-bust cycles. They favored various means to overcome American capitalism's erratic nature, with some championing a businesslike or professional approach to governance and others expressing more concern about social welfare considerations.

By the early stages of the twentieth century, this new vision, joined with contradictory ideas, strong personalities, and a host of movements—some clearly at odds with one another—dominated American politics. Referred to as progressivism, it involved, on the home front, an attempt to right some of the wrongs associated with industrial capitalism, which itself required, at a bare minimum, departure from the tenets of laissez-faire and social Darwinism. For some of its exponents, progressivism demanded similarly aggressive action in the field of international relations. However, Progressives argued among themselves, with more moderate elements largely accepting managerial capitalism but calling for addressing some of its most egregious abuses, while more radical forces proved willing to challenge capitalism altogether. They quarreled about foreign policy too, with presidents Theodore Roosevelt and Woodrow Wilson envisioning a more expansive role for the United States, and writers like Max Eastman and

Randolph Bourne questioning their nation's willingness to go to war on the side of imperialist states that, in certain instances, were scarcely democratic. The differences reflected a clash in world views, or, at a bare minimum, fractures within liberal ranks.

Associated with the Western Enlightenment, modern liberalism emerged during the eighteenth century, identified with challenges to government and religious authority. Challenging the theory of the divine right of kings and the sacrosanct nature of the Church, proponents of liberalism drew from the Renaissance and the Reformation, while propounding the need for the rule of law, a market economy, and transparent government. In the United States, liberalism became associated with constitutionalism, individual liberties, and, eventually, democracy. As both the positive and negative impacts of American industrialization became apparent, however, the clash between economic liberty and social equality—each linked to classical liberalism—became more obvious. More figures identifying with liberal ideals came to distance themselves from Adam Smith's classical economic theories involving laissez-faire. Rather, they argued that government had a role to play in preventing exploitation and helping to produce the good society. Others went further still, contending that capitalism itself was the problem, with some hearkening back to the exhortations of the biblical prophets and Jesus Christ or to the writings of utopian socialists or those of Karl Marx and Friedrich Engels. The contrasting perspectives of Woodrow Wilson and Randolph Bourne demonstrate this very chasm, with the nation's twenty-eighth president serving as the embodiment of early-twentieth-century liberalism and Bourne, one of his most scathing critics, demanding more radical solutions for domestic and international ills. This disagreement proved most pronounced following the U.S. entrance into World War I, with Wilson portraying it as a necessary crusade to foster democracy around the world and Bourne bemoaning the bloodletting on behalf of less than progressive forces and the repressive turn the American nation experienced.

⁓ WOODROW WILSON ⁓

The war in Europe was in its thirty-second month, with casualty figures already numbering in the millions. Trench warfare, poison gas, submarine assaults, and aerial bombardments characterized the first two and a half years of the conflict. Americans followed with horror and bewilderment the mass bloodletting, while politicians wrangled about whether the United States should enter the fray. The previous November, voters cast ballots to reelect as president the man who campaigned on the fact that he had kept America out of the cauldron.

President Woodrow Wilson asks a joint session of Congress for a declaration of war against Germany on April 2, 1917. After World War I broke out in August 1914, Wilson proclaimed U.S. neutrality, but eventually concluded that Germany's use of unrestricted submarine warfare demanded an American response. Though committed to "making the world safe for democracy," Wilson was willing to restrict constitutional rights to suppress domestic dissent. (Library of Congress, LC-USZC4-10297)

Now, less than six months later, Woodrow Wilson came before a joint special session of Congress seeking a declaration of war. The tall, bespectacled, austere-looking Wilson began his speech at 8:30 in the evening of April 2, 1917, recalling the address he had made to Congress two months earlier, during which he revealed that Germany had adopted a policy of unrestricted submarine warfare lacking "all restraints of law or of humanity." That had resulted in the severing of diplomatic relations with the Central European state. Now Wilson charged that Germany had "ruthlessly" fired on all kinds of ships, sinking them "without warning . . . or mercy." Germany had discarded "the humane practices of civilized nations," indeed "all scruples of humanity." The massive property damage hardly mattered most to Wilson, but rather "the wanton and wholesale destruction of . . . noncombatants, men, women, and children." Thus current German practices amounted to "warfare against mankind." The American nation itself had suffered, losing ships and lives, as had other neutral countries.

Wilson urged the nation's top legislators to respond judiciously, as befitting the American people who sought "only the vindication of right, of human right, of which we are only a single champion." No longer considering armed neutrality possible as he had previously, Wilson termed German submarines "outlaws" as they moved against commercial ships. As for his countrymen, Wilson pledged they would neither grovel nor allow the violation of their nation's "most sacred rights." He felt compelled to seek a congressional declaration of war so that the United States and the American people could more clearly defend themselves and bring an end to the war. This required providing Germany's foes with highly favorable financial terms and American industrial support, along with the strengthening of the U.S. military through universal service.

As America mobilized for the war, its policymakers, Wilson contended, had to underscore "our motives and . . . objects." The United States sought to sustain peace and justice while battling autocratic forces. It strove to establish unity of purpose between those who were "really free and self-governed." His own nation held no ill will toward the German people, viewing them sympathetically and with friendship, Wilson insisted. By contrast, the German government had sought to foster anti-American sentiment, sending the Zimmerman telegram offering the return of former Mexican territory if the United States lost the war.

Eloquently, Wilson affirmed, "The world must be made safe for democracy" and peace "planted upon the tested foundations of political liberty." His own nation, Wilson professed, possessed no selfish designs, no desire for control or financial recompense, regardless of its sacrifices. Admittedly difficult times threatened as the United States entered "the most terrible and disastrous of all wars," with "civilization itself seeming to be in the balance." Nevertheless "right [was] more precious than peace," and the American people stood ready to champion democracy, self-determination for all states, and an international confederation to sustain peace and freedom.

Wilson was born on December 28, 1856, in Staunton, Virginia, to Dr. Joseph Ruggles Wilson, a slaveholding Presbyterian minister, and Janet "Jessie" Woodrow Wilson, both possessing Scottish roots. Thomas Woodrow Wilson was the third of four children, raised in Augusta, Georgia, where the family moved when he was still a baby. Wilson witnessed the devastation of the South and Union soldiers marching through his hometown, as well as the ensuing period of Reconstruction. During the early 1870s, the family lived in Columbia, the state capital of South Carolina, as Joseph served as a professor at Presbyterian Theological Seminary. Possibly afflicted with dyslexia, young Woodrow was tutored by his parents and educated at private schools. In 1873 Wilson enrolled at Davidson College, performing well but departing at the close of his freshman year because of illness. The following year he entered the College of New Jersey (later Princeton University), graduating in 1879, having studied English literature and politics. There he helped to establish the Liberal Debating Club to explore "political questions of the present century." The politically ambitious Wilson attended the University of Virginia Law School, opening a practice in Atlanta in 1882. Within a year, Wilson, disillusioned with the law, enrolled as a graduate student in political science at Johns Hopkins University, completing his doctorate in 1886. By that point he was already a published author, having written *Congressional Government* (1885), which lauded the British parliamentary system and decried the American system of checks and balances. He also married Ellen Louise Axson from Savannah, Georgia, whose father was also a Presbyterian minister, and the two eventually had three daughters.

Following a three-year stint teaching political economy and law at Bryn Mawr College, located outside Philadelphia, Wilson became a professor of history and political economy at Wesleyan University in Middletown, Connecticut. He also offered regular lectures at Johns Hopkins University. In 1889 he published *The State: Elements of Historical and Practical Politics*. The next year found him back at his alma mater, where he acquired a reputation as one of the nation's foremost social scientists. This was the period when the American university underwent considerable transformation, caught up in the culture of professionalism that other institutions experienced. For many educated Americans, the university served as a fount of knowledge as well as a laboratory where ideas could be explored and solutions to society's problems devised. The seeds of the Progressive movement were already being planted as the nineteenth century neared its end, nurtured by that culture of professionalism and the belief in the university's potential for pragmatic engagement. In the meantime, Wilson, offering classes on jurisprudence and economics, was acclaimed the most popular professor at recently renamed Princeton University in 1896. By 1902 Wilson completed his five-volume *A History of the American People* and began his eight-year tenure as president of Princeton, whose earlier leaders included Jonathan Edwards and Aaron Burr Sr. Wilson sought and garnered a nearly twenty-five-fold increase in university expenditures to allow for a large expansion of the faculty. In 1908 Wilson published *Constitutional Government of the United States*, which envisioned a presidency "as big as and as influential as the man who occupies it."

Throughout his academic career, Wilson reflected on the possibility of entering the political arena. That opportunity arose in 1910, when the Progressive movement was ascendant. Beginning in urban centers during the later stages of the nineteenth century and soon extending to the state and federal levels, the movement began to dominate American politics. An attempt by opponents of laissez-faire and social Darwinism to ameliorate the worst aspects of industrial capitalism, progressivism had champions in both the Republican and Democratic parties. Encouraged by George Harvey, who ran the *North American*

Review, and by political bosses, Wilson entered the New Jersey gubernatorial race. Elected in 1911, Wilson proved to be his own man, supporting a strong Progressive agenda. Running as a Progressive the following year, Wilson captured the Democratic Party nomination for the presidency on the forty-sixth ballot. In a hotly contested four-way race, which included President Howard Taft, former president Teddy Roosevelt, and Socialist Party candidate Eugene V. Debs, Wilson won a landslide victory in the electoral college despite receiving less than 42 percent of the popular vote.

For many the 1912 election signified a battle of contrasting progressivisms. Roosevelt's New Nationalism, championed by journalist Herbert Croly, called for countering the power of big business with that of big government, with labor viewed as something of a third wheel. Wilson's New Freedom, influenced by attorney Louis D. Brandeis, urged a restoration of competition through greater application of antitrust measures. During his inaugural address on March 4, 1913, Wilson acknowledged the rich abundance of American life but charged, "The evil has come with the good. . . . With riches has come inexcusable waste." Notwithstanding industrial advances, the American people failed to consider "the human cost, the cost of lives snuffed out, of energies overtaxed and broken, the fearful physical and spiritual cost . . . pitilessly" borne by adults and children alike. Too frequently, the American government had been employed selfishly, with the people "forgotten." Early in his first presidential term, Wilson, following New Freedom principles, supported the Federal Reserve Act, establishing a system of regional banks; the Underwood Tariff, reducing tariff rates and setting up a federal income tax system; the Federal Trade Commission, authorizing the investigation of "unfair methods of competition"; and the Clayton Anti-Trust Act. Less creditably, Wilson sang the praises of *The Birth of a Nation*, D. W. Griffith's epic film exalting the Ku Klux Klan, and he helped to cement segregation practices in the nation's capital. As the 1916 election approached, Wilson, who had recently married a Southern widow, Edith Bolling Galt, shortly after the death of his first wife, displayed a greater willingness to draw from New Nationalism tenets. Now he supported the Keating-Owen Act, prohibiting the interstate shipping of goods produced by children, and the Adamson Act, setting an eight-hour day for railroad workers. In another controversial move, Wilson also appointed Brandeis, a Jewish labor lawyer, to the U.S. Supreme Court. Those later moves helped Wilson narrowly defeat Republican presidential nominee Charles Evans Hughes in 1916.

Helpful too was Wilson's campaign pitch, "He Kept Us Out of War," although he warned repeatedly that "essential rights" must not be violated. As war broke out in Europe during the summer of 1914, Wilson urged his countrymen to adopt a policy of strict neutrality. He also sought to redirect U.S. foreign policy, viewing with dismay both Roosevelt's Big Stick approach and Taft's

Dollar Diplomacy, which relied on a potent military and expanded commercial interests, respectively. Wilson believed instead that the power of its ideas and the strength of its institutions would extend the global reach of the United States. Some eventually referred to this approach as Missionary Diplomacy, although Wilson simultaneously repeated the practices of his immediate predecessors. He maintained American troops in Nicaragua and Haiti, and twice authorized armed intervention during the Mexican civil war, as revolutionaries led by Pancho Villa spilled over the border. Nevertheless, it was the Great War, as the conflict that had erupted in Europe was called, that threatened to embroil the United States in a far deadlier conflagration. Furor arose in May 1915 following a German submarine's sinking of the *Lusitania*, a British liner, which led to the death of 1,200, including more than 120 Americans. Shortly thereafter Wilson moved to dampen calls for retaliation, declaring that a man could be "too proud to fight" and a nation could be "so right" that it hardly needed to demonstrate that to others. Wilson's unheeded efforts to serve as a mediator, his reluctance to expand the size of the American military as much as some desired, and his condemnation of German actions resulted in criticisms at home. Teddy Roosevelt considered Wilson's foreign policy weak, while Secretary of State William Jennings Bryan resigned because of fears that Wilson was steering the country into war. *The New Republic*, a new liberal publication, urged that the United States adopt a greater role in international affairs.

Writing to Senator William J. Stone of Missouri on February 24, 1916, Wilson agreed to do everything possible to prevent his country from going to war. However, he could not abide any encroachment on "the rights of American citizens," for otherwise the nation's "honor and self-respect" would be diminished. Two days later Wilson affirmed that America ought to avoid war but could not suffer the violation of its "sense of humanity and justice." He reminded Congress that the American people remained "the responsible spokesmen of the rights of humanity," shortly following the German attack on the British passenger ship *Sussex*. Increasingly troubled by secret conferences and the peace terms discussed by the Allies, Wilson began envisioning something he had considered earlier, a League of Nations, possessing the power of collective security, to be established following the war. Speaking before a crowd of 2,000 in Washington, DC, on May 27, 1916, he called for a different, healthier brand of diplomacy, in which nations across the globe joined together to prevent "selfish aggression." He asserted that all people possessed the right of self-determination, small nations to respect and territorial integrity, and the world to peace free from aggression. He supported the expansion of both the U.S. Army and Navy, along with the creation of a Naval Reserve Force. He also declared in early October, a month before the presidential election, that the United States would only fight for "the rights of humanity," which involved the "essence of free institutions."

On October 26 he predicted that the United States would be unable to remain isolated from future wars, for "the business of neutrality is over."

Mere weeks after his reelection, Wilson bemoaned the fact that the war was making neutrality "intolerable." On December 18, 1916, he sent a message to the warring nations, referring to the need for a satisfactory, permanent resolution of the present conflict. Wilson feared that the continuation of hostilities would lead to "exhaustion, reaction, political upheaval," and lingering resentment. Wilson's message received mixed responses at home too, with hawkish figures like General Leonard Wood infuriated at his purported lack of leadership and The New Republic applauding the president's sounding of a "call which will restore the morale of liberalism." The British responded with outrage, the French with a sense that Wilson's approach was quixotic, and the Germans by both questioning the president's motives and hoping his proposal for a meeting of all belligerents might lead to peace.

On January 22, 1917, in a speech before the U.S. Senate, Wilson extolled the virtues of progressive internationalism and prophesied that "a peace without victory" could be maintained. Considering himself the spokesperson "for liberals and friends of humanity" across the globe, as well as for "the silent mass of mankind" unable to speak freely, he called for all peoples, powerful or not, to be able to chart their own course, "unhindered, unthreatened, unafraid."

Wilson continued to hope that he could "keep the country out of war." However, the revelation on February 25 of the Zimmerman telegram from the German foreign secretary, which British cryptographers had recently decoded, stunned the president. That telegram urged that Mexico be drawn into a military alliance with Germany, enticed by the promise of help in the recovery of territories earlier lost to the United States. Wilson appeared before Congress on February 26, seeking authorization to arm American ships. Wilson still contended that only "the willful acts and aggressions of others" would result in U.S. intervention. Opposition failed to abate in Congress, led by Republican senators Robert M. La Follette and Henry Cabot Lodge, and an ensuing filibuster in the Senate doomed Wilson's proposal. Meanwhile, on March 5, 1917, Wilson delivered his second inaugural address, insisting that the American people, despite terrible losses endured on the high seas, had "not wished to wrong or injure in return." As the war continued, he underscored the fact that the American people had become "citizens of the world" and proclaimed "that governments derive all their just powers from the consent of the governed." In a telling statement, Wilson demanded that each nation "sternly and effectually" suppress and prevent its own citizens from fomenting revolutions in other states. He invoked "God's Providence" in calling for unity from the American populace.

A filibuster in the Senate prevented passage of the measure Wilson sought, leading him to complain on March 4 about "a little group of willful men," representing only themselves, who had reduced the American government to impotence and contempt. Nevertheless, one week into his second term, on March 12, Wilson called for American merchant vessels to be armed. German submarines continued to attack American ships. On the evening of April 1, Wilson informed Frank I. Cobb of the *New York World* that war unfortunately "required illiberalism at home to reinforce the men at the front." The next evening Wilson delivered his address to Congress, asking for a declaration of war. Thunderous applause followed his speech, with even Senator Lodge congratulating Wilson on his oratory. Two days later, on April 6, the Senate voted 82–6 in favor of the resolution, as did the House, by a margin of 373 to 50.

Notwithstanding the overwhelming margins by which both houses of Congress supported the declaration of war, not all Americans supported Wilson's decision. Some members of certain ethnic groups, including those of German and Irish ancestry, viewed the action with dismay, as did many associated with the Socialist Party and the radical labor organization the Industrial Workers of the World (IWW), along with pacifists. On April 20, the Wilson administration presented the Espionage Act to Congress, which became law on June 15. It called for lengthy prison sentences and hefty fines for those who, during a period when the nation was at war, knowingly delivered "false reports or . . . statements" designed to impede the country's military operations or assist its enemies, willfully sought to induce dissension within the ranks of the U.S. military, or knowingly obstructed military recruitment.

On August 17 Wilson did ask Attorney General T. W. Gregory to examine the contention contained in a telegram from the American Union Against Militarism, whose civil liberties branch was headed by Roger Nash Baldwin, that constitutional rights were being violated. Wilson noted that the signatories were "people whom I personally esteem," although "I am not always sure that they know what they are talking about." Responding to a letter from Max Eastman bemoaning abridgments of freedom of speech, assembly, and the press, Wilson wrote on September 18 that war was "wholly exceptional" and required viewing "things which would in ordinary circumstances be innocent as very dangerous to the public welfare." While admittedly the line to be drawn was "manifestly exceedingly hard," it had to occur. His administration was seeking to do that "without fear or favor or prejudice."

At noon on January 8, 1918, shortly following a second revolution in Russia spearheaded by the Bolsheviks, hard-line Marxist-Leninists who immediately moved to monopolize power, Wilson presented his Fourteen Points address to Congress, laying out his vision for the postwar world. As Wilson recalled, the United States entered the war because "violations of right" had "touched us to the quick." He called for "open covenants of peace, openly arrived at," rather than secret dealings that had helped ensnare the world in war. He urged freedom to navigate the seas, an end to trade barriers, and a reduction of armaments. Wilson spoke of the need for "a general association of nations," coupled with "specific covenants" to guarantee political autonomy and territorial integrity for all nations. His countrymen, Wilson insisted, bore no ill will toward Germany, only desiring that it "accept a place of equality among the peoples of the world—the new world in which we now live—instead of a place of mastery."

In early March 1918, on the fifth anniversary of his initial inaugural address, Wilson encountered an editorial in the *New York Times* that referred to him as among the "four or five chief men in the world, a great figure in the greatest drama of all time, the foremost spokesman in the cause of international morals, freedom and justice." American soldiers, sent abroad by President Wilson, helped to prevent an Allied defeat or further stalemate. Wilson's progressive internationalism seemed for many to be the best means of ensuring both liberty and peace, historian Alan Dawley suggests. In the process Wilson became "the first American to be recognized as a true world figure" and "the first world leader of the twentieth century." Wilson's role in shaping postwar events appeared greater still as the Bolsheviks concluded the Treaty of Brest-Litovsk in March, which took Russia out of the war. His Fourteen Points strengthened Allied morale, notwithstanding a frosty response on the part of French prime minister Georges Clemenceau, and cheered even American radicals such as Crystal Eastman and Eugene V. Debs.

That same spring witnessed another German offensive, and members of the American Expeditionary Force, newly arrived in France, joined the mass slaughter inherent in total war. However, the U.S. industrial machine enabled Allied forces to continue fighting and, by the fall, to turn the table against the Germans. During this same period, the Wilson administration continued resorting to heavy-handed practices at home, with the president, in May 1918, signing the Sedition Act, which amended the Espionage Act. It declared that criminal prosecution could await an individual who "willfully" delivered "false reports or false statements" when the nation was at war, incited "insubordination, disloyalty, mutiny, or refusal of" military duty, or obstructed military recruitment or enlistment. Again a lengthy prison sentence and a large fine could await anyone who did willfully attack the U.S. government, the Constitution, or the armed forces. George Creel, who headed the U.S. Committee on Public Information, denounced antiwar figures as slackers or worse. Postmaster General Albert S. Burleson halted the mailing of various issues of radical publications, while the Justice Department initiated prosecutions of leaders of the IWW, the Socialist Party, and the cultural Left, whose adherents had sought greater personal emancipation before the war began. Max Eastman, Crystal Eastman, Eugene V. Debs, Bill Haywood, John Reed, and Roger Baldwin all faced indictments.

Such activities occurred as President Wilson maintained his campaign to "make the world safe for democracy." On November 11, 1918, Wilson informed the public that an armistice had been signed, bringing an end to the fighting, and he declared that the United States would now help to spread "just democracy." In the months ahead, Wilson led the American diplomatic delegation at the Paris Peace Conference, where he hoped that the other Allies—Great Britain, France, and Italy—would agree to the Fourteen Points. Uninvited were Bolshevik leader Vladimir Lenin and German representatives. Received as a conquering hero by many in Europe, Wilson nevertheless failed to convince British prime minister David Lloyd George, French prime minister Clemenceau, and Italian prime minister Vittorio Emanuele Orlando of the necessity of a nonpunitive peace. Germany suffered reduced national boundaries, the loss of its overseas empire, and a bill for war reparations amounting to $35 billion. Wilson received affirmation of his belief in national self-determination and the creation of a League of Nations. His efforts led to receipt of the 1919 Nobel Peace Prize, but also resulted in the president's driving himself to exhaustion during an extended speaking tour back in the United States intended to drum up support for the treaty's ratification. Led by Henry Cabot Lodge and Robert La Follette, opposition in the Senate built up and an uncompromising Wilson instructed his supporters to oppose the Versailles Treaty, culminating in the refusal of the United States to join the League. Experiencing a series of strokes during the fall of 1919, Wilson became largely incapacitated, with the White House possibly governed in effect by his wife Edith.

The 1920 presidential election, a landslide victory for the Republican ticket of Warren G. Harding and Calvin Coolidge, served as a startling repudiation of Wilson and progressivism. Following his presidency, Wilson resided with his wife in a red brick house in Embassy Row in the nation's capital. He died on February 3, 1924, reportedly after informing Edith, "I'm a broken machine, but I'm ready." Wilson's brand of domestic and internationalism progressivism seemed in disrepute, something that warmed the hearts of many conservatives and radicals alike.

～ RANDOLPH BOURNE ～

The article appeared in the June 1917 issue of *Seven Arts*, one of the publications most closely identified with the band of cultural radicals referred to as the Lyrical Left and said to be participating in a "Little Renaissance." Many of the members of that loosely formed group dwelled and worked in the cozy confines of Greenwich Village, already considered an enclave of bohemianism and political radicalism. The timing of the article was propitious, as the U.S. Congress,

*Though burdened with serious physical disabilities, public intel-
lectual Randolph Bourne contributed greatly to the progressive
cause with his incisive analysis of critical national issues, which
were published in periodicals such as* The New Republic. *Bourne
broke decisively with his mentor John Dewey and with president Woodrow Wilson over the issue of American intervention
in World War I, arguing that democracy could not be spread
through force of arms. One of Bourne's major concerns was the
seductive lure of state power, to which be believed many progressives succumbed during the war. He died in 1918, the victim
of an influenza epidemic that took twice as many lives as had the
war. (Courtesy of Columbia University Archives, Rare Book and
Manuscript Library)*

following President Wilson's lead, had recently issued a declaration of war. Many
American intellectuals had roundly condemned the idea of U.S. participation
in the conflict, but the declaration of war compelled many to support the war effort. Their readiness to do so did not sit well with some of their contemporaries,
including a five-foot-tall hunchbacked young man who suffered from dwarfism,
was educated at Columbia University, and viewed American involvement in
the war as disastrous. Thirty-one-year-old Randolph Bourne proved to be one of
the most incisive critics of the seeming willingness of other intellectuals, including his one-time mentor, Professor John Dewey, and President Wilson himself,
to suspend critical analysis in their readiness to back the war effort.

In "The War and the Intellectuals," introduced by a full-page advertisement
in *Seven Arts*, Bourne scathingly examined that very willingness. He began
by stating that such support had proven "a bitter experience" to those who
remained irreconcilably opposed to the war. Bourne pointed to the fact that
socialists, university faculty, and Progressives had determinedly abandoned neutrality and adopted "the war-mind" so common among the American people. He
claimed that intellectuals went so far as to "deliberately" induce the reluctant
masses to support the war. And yet intellectuals reasoned that their involvement
had prevented the "hysteria or militarist madness" characteristic of other societ-

ies, resulting in "a war free from any taint of self-seeking." They, like President Wilson, believed this would be a war to safeguard democracy and create a new world order. Their counterparts who refused to support the drive toward war, Bourne indicated, sought to comprehend how intellectuals could readily "flood us with the sewage of the war spirit." He recalled "the virtuous horror and stupefaction" displayed by members of the professoriate on hearing their German counterparts cheer the outbreak of war. However, preparedness advocates, led by former president Theodore Roosevelt, shaped "the war sentiment" that now enveloped the American intelligentsia. In the process, this nation's intellectuals found themselves lined up with "the least liberal and least democratic elements." Ironically for intellectuals "in a time of faith, skepticism" became "the most intolerable of all insults." Sadly, Bourne feared, "the war has taught them nothing and will teach them nothing." Furthermore, the bellicosity of socialist intellectuals demonstrated "how thin was the intellectual veneer of their socialism."

More damningly still, Bourne observed, the "herd-instinct" became "herd-intellect." He pointedly wrote, "We go to war to save the world from subjugation!" just as German intellectuals supported war to prevent barbarism from sweeping over their culture, the French to defend France, the English to safeguard "international honor," and the Russians to stave off a small nation's decimation. Rational intellectuals, Bourne insisted, would have fought for peace, not for war. American intellectuals supported the war effort believing, as President Wilson indicated, that the present conflict would "internationalize the world!" Regarding the vision of a "League to Enforce Peace," Bourne dismissed that as "only a palpable apocalyptic myth." Moreover, such a league offered no guarantees of economic growth or justice, promising instead "to petrify" the existing international order.

American intellectuals proved prone to such ideas, Bourne indicated, because they had been unwilling to expend "emotional capital" on the downtrodden, the oppressed, and the racially excluded at home. Consequently they were all the more ready to do so on behalf of "the oppressed nationalities and ravaged villages of Europe." American universities appeared contented at present with "simple, unquestioning action" replacing "the knots of thought." The "myth of the League of Peace" afforded "a dogma" to hold onto and the kind of "certitude" that intellectuals craved. Additionally, intellectuals proved prone to intolerance, excommunicating dissenters and viewing "irreconcilable radicals" as "the most despicable and impotent of men." In the process, forgotten was the reality that "War," not the kaiser's Germany, was "the real enemy." Bourne warned that efforts must be undertaken to prevent the present war from being mythologized "as a holy crusade." A great need existed for "some irreconcilables" demanding peace and a democratic resolution of the conflict, able to dismantle "old ideals" and forge new ones.

The author of this scathing indictment of his fellow American intellectuals was born in Bloomfield, New Jersey, just outside Newark, on May 30, 1886, the child of Sarah Barrett Bourne and Charles Rogers Bourne, a "handsome gay blade" who sold real estate. Bourne's family lineage included English immigrants who came to America in the early seventeenth century, a distinguished abolitionist minister, and an officer in the Union army. Randolph's face became disfigured because of "a terribly messy birth," caused by forceps during a difficult delivery, and he subsequently contracted spinal tuberculosis at the age of four, leaving him a "grotesque hunchback." His growth remained stunted and he reached the height of only five feet as an adult. His left ear sagged considerably, his jaw and teeth became more prominent when he spoke, and he often experienced difficulty breathing and speaking. Financial difficulties beset Bourne's family, resulting in the departure of his alcoholic father and a female-dominated household. Sarah and her four children, Bourne later indicated, had to endure "the awful glowering family eye of rich guarding relatives." He later wrote that childhood was "perhaps the hardest time of all." Vainly striving to overcome his physical ailments, by futilely attempting to skate, climb trees, and play ball, Bourne blamed his troubles on "moral weakness," guided by what he described as "rigid" Calvinism. He considered himself "a homeless, helpless waif" who would remain lonely. As he grew older, his physical condition prevented him from having desired intimate relationships with women.

Notwithstanding his social difficulties, Bourne performed easily in the classroom, although the family's financial circumstances prevented him from attending college after his graduation in 1903 from high school, where he had been class president and editor of the school newspaper. Hoped-for financial assistance to attend Princeton was not forthcoming from a wealthy uncle, although that relative soon provided such support to two of Randolph's sisters, who attended Wellesley. Instead Bourne underwent an extended and largely unsuccessful period of attempting to carve out a useful niche, while confronting the fact that little was expected of him, a "deformed man." He also began to discard the Calvinism of his youth, becoming more attracted to liberal free thinkers and Unitarians.

Finally, in 1909, Bourne, backed by a scholarship, entered Columbia University, which under President Nicholas Murray Butler was becoming a great academic institution. At the campus located at Morningside Heights in the upper western sector of Manhattan, Bourne encountered formidable intellectuals like Felix Adler, Charles Beard, Franz Boas, John Dewey, and James Harvey Robinson. Initially intending to major in English, Bourne, an honor student, switched to sociology, but read widely outside that discipline. He joined the Intercollegiate Socialist Society and attended speeches by Morris Hillquit, Big Bill Haywood, and Victor Berger. He joined the staff of the *Columbia Monthly*, a literary journal, eventually becoming editor in chief. His physical deformities continued to literally mark him, as indicated by the reaction of Ellery Sedgwick, editor of *The Atlantic Monthly*, who on meeting Bourne found him "without a redeeming feature," and later admitted, "I could not bring myself to ask him to stay for lunch." No matter, in May 1911, *The Atlantic Monthly*, viewed in certain circles in New England as "the Magazine," presented Bourne's article, "The Two Generations," and several additional pieces in that publication soon followed. Noting that his parents' generation proved unwilling to live "for their children," Bourne wondered "if any generation was ever thrown quite so completely on its own resources as ours."

Although still an undergraduate at Columbia, Bourne was already making his mark as an important new voice who displayed the youthful angst of his generation. In an essay appropriately titled "Youth" that appeared in the April 1912 issue of *The Atlantic Monthly*, Bourne discussed "that showery springtime of life" associated with both "the fiercest radicalisms" and "the most dogged conservatisms," while acknowledging that he was "full of the wildest radicalisms," determined to avoid draining responsibilities. It was young people, he insisted, who possessed "the really valuable experience," regularly confronting "new situations" and "new aspects of life" while "getting the whole beauty and terror and cruelty of the world in its fresh and undiluted purity." He concluded that "the secret of life" was to ensure "that this fine youthful spirit should never be lost." To Bourne's delight, he was part of a cadre of like-minded young people at Columbia, determined to explore all sorts of matters. While celebrating youth Bourne was also attracted to radical possibilities, coming to view himself as a socialist. In an article published in early 1912 in the *Masses*, one of the most important magazines connected to the Lyrical Left, Bourne warned that only socialism would diminish "the essential, never-closing gulf" between the classes. At the same time, he chose to back Teddy Roosevelt, who was running as a genuine Progressive, during the lively 1912 presidential campaign, eventually won by Woodrow Wilson.

His outspokenness, seeming support for the IWW, association with the Lyrical Left, and determination to become "a prophet, if only a minor one," coupled with his physical condition, ensured that Bourne continued to experience difficulty in obtaining employment. In a letter to a friend in 1913, he predicted, "My path in life will be on the outside of things, poking holes at the holy, criticizing the established, satirizing the self-respected and contented." Indeed he possessed "a real genius for making trouble." In the end he anticipated remaining "poor and unloved and obscure." Having completed his undergraduate studies, Bourne began working on a master's degree at Columbia, which he referred to as "a real intellectual democracy." At the same time he typically criticized the institution, including its exploitation of workers, which hardly helped his chances of obtaining a desired lectureship.

Youth and Life, Bourne's first book and a collection of his essays, appeared in 1913. In the essay "For Radicals," Bourne acknowledged that young people had early recognized the need for "a regenerated social order," yet also bemoaned the propensity of the radical young to view compromise dismissively. Bourne concluded that while "radical life has its perils, it also has its great rewards," as socialism "does brighten and sweeten" the world "enormously." Moreover the radical's very faith had "already transformed the world in which he lives," offering "seeds of regeneration."

The Richard W. Gilder Fellowship, received from Columbia University, enabled Bourne, who had graduated the previous year and entered a graduate program in political science, to travel to Europe in August 1913. For nearly a year, he spent time in England and on the continent, including three months in both London and Paris. Bourne bemoaned "the artificiality of my life and ideas," deemed himself "a feeble little artist," and pointed to the difficulty of pursuing his craft "without the contact of some definite movement, some definite demand, some definite groups." He frequented meetings of suffragettes, savored the radical and avante-garde sentiments expressed by European intellectuals, and witnessed the final stages of a strike in Naples involving anarchists, republicans, and socialists. London, with its array of "cruel and unlovely" old institutions, had "immensely strengthened my radicalism," he revealed. Writing aboard a ship bound for New York, Bourne admitted that he had never anticipated being so glad to return to the United States. However, time had stopped altogether in Europe, he noted, as "this civilization that I have been admiring so much seems so palpably about to be torn to shreds."

Returning to Greenwich Village shortly after the outbreak of World War I, Bourne began sporting a "long black student's cape" and spending a good deal of time at the New York Public Library, where he completed a required report for the trustees of Columbia University. Bourne believed that the "cataclysm" sweeping Europe might transform it entirely. The very issues he focused on during his trip—"democracy, social reform, and international understanding"—had "been snapped off like threads, perhaps never to be pieced together again," he suggested. Having witnessed considerable opposition to conscription and mandatory military service, he proved wholly unprepared for "the impending horror." As he finished the report, Bourne again confronted the dilemma of how to make a living. "The life of a hermit philosopher living on a mere pittance," he fretted, "does not appeal to me; indeed even the bare pittance is wanting." Also to his dismay, he found it impossible to recapture the time previously spent at Columbia when he easily participated in "a sort of salon," discussing contemporary issues with good friends and acquaintances. While overseas he had determined to find a forum that would enable him to convey "disagreeable truths to [his] countrymen."

Fortunately, Ellery Sedgwick encouraged Herbert Croly to place Bourne, at an annual salary of $1,000, on the staff of *The New Republic*, a new magazine Croly and Walter Lippmann founded to provide a vehicle for progressive issues, backed by money from Willard Straight of J. P. Morgan Guaranty and Trust. Editorial sessions brought together an array of luminaries, including Columbia University's John Dewey, Charles Beard, and James Harvey Robinson, along with Van Wyck Brooks, Harold Laski, and Felix Frankfurter. Thrilled at his close proximity to such stellar intellects, Bourne once exclaimed, "I feel as if I were attending some incomparable school of journalism." Far more radical than his editors, which undoubtedly resulted in the rejection of various submissions, he nevertheless contributed a wide array of articles to *The New Republic*, particularly focusing on American education at the outset, which necessitated a dissection of John Dewey. In March 1915 Bourne applauded his former professor's "democratic attitude toward life," terming him the nation's "most significant thinker," with his "intensely alive, futuristic philosophy." Dewey's philosophy of instrumentalism envisioned the school as "embryonic community life" and challenged "the whole machinery of our world of right and wrong, law and order, property and religion," Bourne reported.

In *The New Republic* and in a pair of books of essays, *The Gary Schools* and *Education and Living*, which appeared in 1916 and 1917, respectively, Bourne continued exploring the field of American education, often in highly critical fashion. He discussed the firing of Scott Nearing from the University of Pennsylvania because of his pacifist views, which led Bourne to query, "Who owns the Universities?" Bourne bemoaned the control by corporate-minded trustees, who failed to appreciate that institutions of higher learning were becoming "effective scientific and sociological laboratories." In *The Gary Schools*, Bourne examined school programs that sought, in the fashion of Dewey, to educate "the whole child." *Education and Living* again focused on the need to nurture youth in a holistic manner, in keeping with the progressive school of educational thought most identified with Dewey, including "learning through doing."

With the passage of time, Bourne's stance on the European war proved at variance with that of *The New Republic*, where his support of American neutrality led readers to consider him "an impious, ungrateful, pro-German, venomous viper" or so he contended. To Bourne's dismay, the editors of the magazine, influenced by President Wilson, began to veer from a noninterventionist position. In the July 1, 1916, issue of *The New Republic*, Bourne responded by urging "more stirring and more creative" action to ward off "that militaristic trend." He recalled William James's proposal, ten years earlier, for a "moral equivalent of war," a suggestion that now appeared increasingly prescient. It was true, Bourne wrote, that Americans exuded a strong desire "for unity of sentiment, for service, for some new national life and broadening." He worried about the consequences of "military service, flag-reverence, patriotic swagger," applauding instead James's notion "of a productive army of youth" determined to battle "against nature and not against men." Universal military service, Bourne warned, would require "the most pernicious and revolutionary changes," while demanding a lengthy period of militaristic propagandizing. Moreover, universal military service was "a sham universality," with half the population excluded. By contrast the nation would benefit from national service for education, which could lead to food and factory inspections, relief efforts, nursing care, and conservation programs.

Increasingly estranged from The New Republic's editorial position, Bourne began contributing to other publications, particularly The Dial, Seven Arts, and the Masses. Guided by editor Martyn Johnson and influenced by Scofield Thayer, The Dial, the nation's most distinguished literary publication, had adopted a more pronounced political stance, and soon named Bourne a contributing editor. Founded by James Oppenheim, Seven Arts included the writers Waldo Frank, Van Wyck Brooks, and Paul Rosenfeld on its editorial board, which sought to become more influential than its counterparts at The New Republic and The Nation. Oppenheim admitted to experiencing "repugnance when I saw that child's body, the humped back," but asked him to join his staff anyway. The embodiment of the Lyrical Left, the Masses championed feminism and radicalism. In the meantime, Bourne, who was increasingly concerned about the drift toward war, joined with Amos Pinchot, Max Eastman, and Winthrop D. Lane in signing a full-page ad in The New Republic on February 17, 1917, blasting the American Rights League, which called for the United States to enter the war against Germany. Bourne soon produced biting antiwar essays for both The Dial and Seven Arts, among the most brilliant ever delivered by an American writer.

Two months after the U.S. Congress issued a declaration of war in April 1917, Bourne delivered "The War and the Intellectuals" for Seven Arts, which bore heavily on several of his personal relationships. Frederick Keppel, a dean at Columbia University who became third assistant secretary of war, informed a friend that Bourne considered this "unpardonable." Bourne was likewise enraged when Columbia dismissed Henry W. L. Dana and J. McKean Cattell, supposedly because of their pacifistic views. Even as he confronted fellow intellectuals, Bourne produced a series of other biting essays, including "Below the Battle," which discussed the lot of draft-age young men who felt "only . . . apathy toward the war" along with "a smouldering resentment" of its architects and supporters. No other nation, Bourne warned, faced "this appalling skepticism of youth" even at the onset of hostilities. However, as the fighting continued, Americans would be sent into battle, resulting in "bitterness" that would "spread out like a stain over the younger American generation" and crush "the only genuinely precious thing in a nation, the hope and ardent idealism of its youth." In "The Collapse of American Strategy," Bourne asserted that Allied policy was hardly progressive enough to set the stage for President Wilson's envisioned League of Nations.

In September 1917, Bourne's classic "A War Diary" appeared in *Seven Arts*, pointing to the widespread apathy that had enveloped the nation, with no group likely to help young men reject the call to arms. Losses would be suffered, taxes raised, and restraints on corporations lifted, but none of this would lead to revolt. Both human and material resources would prove "malleable" enough for the war effort, encouraged by "coercion from above," not "patriotism from below." Individual support for government policies did not matter, as long as large corporate enterprises backed the Wilson administration in moving toward "a semi-military State-socialism." In a brilliant observation, Bourne wrote, "The government of a modern organized plutocracy does not have to ask whether the people want to fight or understand what they are fighting for, but only whether they will tolerate fighting." He blasted "liberals," including his old professor John Dewey, for supporting U.S. involvement in the war.

While many still appeared "to believe in a peculiar kind of democratic and antiseptic war," pacifists recognized this was absurd, for war would prove crippling at home. Bourne declared, "For once the babes and sucklings seem to have been wiser than the children of light." In addition, many "of the more creative minds of the younger generation" remained "irreconcilable" regarding the war effort. They desired an end to the "carnage," genuine European reconstruction, and "a democratic peace," while recognizing "that the longer a war lasts the harder it is to make peace." These youths appreciated that "the peace of exhaustion" would amount to "a dastardly peace." Like those young critics, Bourne argued that a choice must be made between supporting either the war, which would "leave the country spiritually impoverished, . . . or American promise."

"Twilight of Idols," a scathing indictment of those who supported the war effort, particularly John Dewey, appeared in the October 1917 issue of *Seven Arts*. Bourne referred to the "slackening" of the thinking of his one-time mentor and its "inadequacy . . . as a philosophy of life in this emergency." To Dewey's discredit, Bourne reasoned, he failed to appreciate "the sinister forces of war," proved far more vexed by the purported "excesses of the pacifists," and dismissed the notion that thought could be conscripted, believing that "the war technique" could exist without "mob-fanaticisms . . . injustices and hatred." Dewey simply did not understand "the luxuriant releases of explosive hatred" exhibited in actions against antiwar activists like Max Eastman. Dewey's pragmatism or instrumentalism, "a philosophy of hope," worked well during a time of peace and prosperity. Unfortunately, pragmatist intellectuals, with Dewey taking the lead, had adapted their philosophy to champion war. Bourne regretfully concluded, "In this difficult time the light that has been in liberals and radicals has become darkness," with many of the latter seeking to demonstrate their loyalty by attacking the "enemies within." The seemingly accepted "policy of 'win the war first'" was necessarily one of "intellectual suicide" for radicals. As for young liberals, who helped to shape "State-socialism at home and a league of benevolently-imperialistic nations abroad," they could at best produce a soulless government that did nothing to touch "the quality of life." Only "thorough malcontents," Bourne offered, could do so, as they demonstrated "deep dissatisfaction" with the way things were.

His more radical offerings made Bourne a subject of suspicion and abuse as the war continued. John Spargo, a socialist who supported the war effort, viewed Bourne and his fellow antiwar critics as "copperheads," likening them to antiwar Democrats in the North during the Civil War. The *New York Tribune* referred to both John Reed and Bourne as "enemies within." The publisher of *The Dial*, Martyn Johnson, pressured Scofield Thayer to drop Bourne from the magazine, noting that John Dewey refused to be associated with him. Thayer insisted Bourne be retained as a book reviewer and be paid the same salary as before. *Seven Arts* folded in late 1917 when the major source of funding was withdrawn. Bourne reacted by writing to his good friend, Esther Cornell: "I feel very much secluded from the world, very much out of touch with the times, except perhaps with the Bolsheviki. The magazines I write for die violent deaths, and all my thoughts seem unprintable." As his writing was considered "seditious," Bourne wondered, "What then is a literary man to do if he has to make his living by his pen?"

The shutting down of *Seven Arts* and his diminished status at *The Dial* led Bourne to abandon his attempts to influence contemporary events and to grapple instead with "the field of theory," attested by his never-completed essay "The State," his colleague Paul Rosenfeld reported. Bourne bitingly observed that to most Americans of the "significant" classes, "the war brought a sense of the sanctity of the State." War, he declared, "is essentially the health of the State" and helped to foster the sensibilities that "its power and influence should be universal" and uniformity demanded of those lacking "the larger herd sense." Bourne concluded ruefully that war "unified all the bourgeois elements and the common people, and outlaws the rest."

Bourne retreated to Greenwich Village, where a smaller number of radicals and bohemians "clung together" as a "storm" raged, as Ernst Mayer later remembered. "We clung also to a few great names—Russell . . . Rolland . . . Bourne." Dwelling in a poorly lit small room, Bourne still exhibited his "raucous disturbing laugh" when friends visited. On December 19, 1918, Bourne began moving his books and clothes into the apartment of Esther Cornell, the beautiful young woman he planned to marry. As he headed into 18 West

Eighth Street in Greenwich, Bourne was afflicted with a cough, resulting from bronchial pneumonia. Within three days he was gasping for breath and died at the age of thirty-two. The socialist Norman Thomas delivered the eulogy, "The Truth Shall Make You Free," at the Spring Street Presbyterian Church. Two weeks following Bourne's death, Floyd Dell sang his praises in *The New Republic*, bemoaning the untimely passing of "a literary career of startling brilliance and peculiar value," which represented the younger generation and courageously traversed "unfamiliar ways in search of truth." Bourne joined in the revolt "in literature, in art, in politics, in all departments of life," participated in by that generation. Six years after Bourne's death, Paul Rosenfeld acclaimed him as "the great bearer of moral authority while America was at war. He was our ban-nerman of values in the general collapse." Bourne, Rosenfeld claimed, possessed "perhaps the strongest mind of the entire younger generation in America" as well as "one of the rarest, freest, sweetest spirits that have ever come out of this land." In 1927 Bourne's one-time colleague Van Wyck Brooks deemed Bourne "a guerrilla fighter along the whole battlefront of the social revolution." In 1932 the second volume of John Dos Passos's *USA* trilogy included a moving vignette on Bourne. Employing "a pebble in his sling," Bourne "hit Goliath square in the forehead with it," Dos Passos wrote. After elegantly encapsulating Bourne's life, Dos Passos concluded with the following observation:

> A tiny twisted unscared ghost in a black cloak hopping along the grimy old brick and brownstone streets still left in downtown New York, crying out in a shrill soundless giggle: *War is the health of the state.*

Conclusion

The entrance of the United States into World War I only heightened a divide that had already begun to appear in liberal or Progressive ranks. Progressives themselves, of course, were splintered between their Rooseveltian and Wilso-nian wings, as well as the faction identifying with Robert La Follette. Wood-row Wilson's vision of a New Freedom challenged Theodore Roosevelt's call for a New Nationalism, suggesting that a more concerted effort to restore competition and challenge the power of big business would better serve the nation. As Wilson campaigned for reelection and worried about events over-seas, he began adopting more of the tactics Roosevelt called for, as he did following the United States' declaration of war in April 1917. For his part Randolph Bourne proved wholly discomfited by the decision of many liberals and even a number of socialists to back the American war effort. This dispute between liberal and more radical members of the Progressive camp presaged future clashes that occurred during the Great Depression, the early Cold War, the Vietnam conflict, and when later events propelled the United States into conflict in the Middle East.

Study Questions

1. Examine Woodrow Wilson's support for strong executive leadership in American government.
2. Analyze Woodrow Wilson's belief in progressive governance.
3. Explain how his personal story influenced Randolph Bourne's worldview.
4. Discuss Randolph Bourne's involvement with the prewar Lyrical Left.
5. Analyze how U.S. entrance into World War I divided Woodrow Wilson and Randolph Bourne.

Selected Bibliography

Abrahams, Edward. *The Lyrical Left: Randolph Bourne, Alfred Stieglitz, and the Origins of Cultural Radicalism in America*. Charlottesville: University of Virginia Press, 1986.

Blake, Casey Nelson. *Beloved Community: The Cultural Criticism of Randolph Bourne, Van Wyck Brooks, Waldo Franks, and Lewis Mumford*. Chapel Hill: University of North Carolina Press, 1990.

Blum, John Morton, and Oscar Handlin. *Woodrow Wilson and the Politics of Morality*. Boston: Little, Brown, 1956.

Bourne, Randolph. *The Radical Will: Selected Writings 1911–1918*. New York: Urizen, 1977.

———. *War and the Intellectuals: Collected Essays, 1915–1919*. New York: Harper and Row, 1964.

Brooks, Van Wyck. "Randolph Bourne." In *Emerson and Others*. New York: E.P. Dutton, 1927.

Clayton, Bruce. *Forgotten Prophet: The Life of Randolph Bourne*. Columbia: University of Missouri Press, 1998.

Clements, Kendrick A. *Woodrow Wilson: World Statesman*. Lawrence: University Press of Kansas, 1992.

Cooper, John Milton, Jr. *The Warrior and the Priest: Woodrow Wilson and Theodore Roosevelt*. Cambridge, MA: Belknap Press, 1993.

Dawley, Alan. *Changing the World: American Progressives in War and Revolution*. Princeton, NJ: Princeton University Press, 2005.

Dell, Floyd. "Randolph Bourne." *The New Republic*, January 4, 1919, p. 276.

DiNunzio, Mario R. *Woodrow Wilson: Essential Writings and Speeches of the Scholar-President*. New York: New York University Press, 2006.

Dos Passos, John. *1919*. New York: Houghton Mifflin, 2000.

Filler, Louis. *Randolph Bourne*. Washington, DC: American Council on Public Affairs, 1943.

Levin, N. Gordon. *Woodrow Wilson and World Politics: America's Response to War and Revolution*. New York: Oxford University Press, 1970.

"Mr. Wilson's Five Years." *New York Times*, March 4, 1918, p. 10.

Pestritto, Ronald J. *Woodrow Wilson and the Roots of Modern Liberalism*. New York: Rowman and Littlefield, 2005.

———. *Woodrow Wilson: The Essential Political Writings*. New York: Rowman and Littlefield, 2005.

Rosenfeld, Paul. "Randolph Bourne." *The Dial*, December 1923, pp. 545–60.

Thompson, J. A. *Woodrow Wilson: Profiles in Power*. New York: Longman, 2002.

Vaughan, Leslie J. *Randolph Bourne and the Politics of Cultural Radicalism*. Lawrence: University Press of Kansas, 1997.

Vitelli, James R. *Randolph Bourne*. New York: Twayne, 1981.

Wilson, Woodrow, and Arthus S. Link. *The Papers of Woodrow Wilson*. Princeton, NJ: Princeton University Press, 1966.

CHAPTER FIVE

~

Popular Culture in the New Era

Two young men—one white, one black—symbolized the passion and energy associated with the decade that has been tagged with the label of the Roaring Twenties. Both grew up in troubled circumstances, each proving too difficult for their families to handle. As boys, they were placed in residential institutions that housed other wayward youth. There they refined skills while still teenagers that enabled them to leave those reformatories and begin to establish their marks as popular cultural icons. Even before the decade of the 1920s, George Herman Ruth Jr., tall, lanky, and white, although boasting something of a permanent tan, and Louis Armstrong, a skinny, ebony-hued African American, had become significant forces in the popular arenas of baseball and jazz, respectively. However, it was during the so-called Jazz Age that fans and critics alike began viewing them as stars of a rare dimension, with Ruth transforming organized sports and Armstrong altering American popular music.

All of this proved possible because of the very ingredients that enabled American popular culture to thrive. The nation, following involvement in the horrors of World War I, entered a period of prosperity in which American consumer culture underwent something of its own great leap forward. That relative affluence, although uneven and only minimally shared by certain groups, enabled American industry and technology to experience wholesale transformation resulting in a 40 percent jump in the nation's gross domestic product. Sports and popular music were but two of the realms, albeit among the most significant, that benefited from the generally prosperous times and the technological innovations fostering mass communications. During the 1920s and early 1930s, radio broadcasts, along with the sports and entertainment pages of leading newspapers, helped to bring word of Ruth's bat and Armstrong's trumpet into the homes of countless numbers of their fellow citizens. The two acquired nicknames along their path to stardom, as numerous Americans eagerly tracked the exploits of Babe and Satchmo. As Ruth's fame rose, his home runs altered America's national pastime, with batting stars now striving to belt long balls out of the park, rather than smacking doubles and triples or stealing their way to home plate. Ruth helped to make the New York Yankees, particularly the 1927 version, the most feared team in all of professional sports, as he compiled slugging marks that appeared insurmountable. Armstrong's extended instrumentals and his raspy voice, whether as part of Joe "King" Oliver's Creole Jazz Band or Louie's own Hot Five and Hot Seven groups, helped to change the shape and substance of American popular music. One discordant note in the rise to prominence of Ruth and Armstrong was the role played by race in their particular venues. Baseball remained segregated, with blacks excluded from the organized game, leading to the formation, at the beginning of the decade, of the Negro National League. Popular music, notwithstanding the complex roots of various genres, was targeted for separate white and black audiences. Still, black fans of baseball followed Ruth's exploits, just as white followers of contemporary music attended Armstrong's public performances and purchased his earliest records, whose reach extended far beyond the "race" crowd.

⌁ BABE RUTH ⌁

It was the fifth inning of game 3 of the 1932 World Series between the American League pennant–winning New York Yankees, led by Lou Gehrig and an aging but still feared Babe Ruth, and the National League champion Chicago Cubs. At the plate was Ruth, who had belted over forty homers that season for the eleventh time in his illustrious career. His first time up had resulted in a three-run homer in the top of the first inning, but the Cubs tied the score 4–4. The 50,000 fans at Wrigley Field rained down boos on a grinning Ruth, as Cubs players on the bench, especially pitcher Guy Bush, razzed him as the count reached two balls and two strikes. What followed next became one of the most celebrated and disputed moments in baseball history. Cubs catcher Gabby Harnett thought Ruth blurted out, "It only takes one to hit it." Gehrig heard Ruth point to Bush and holler, "I'm gonna cut the next pitch right down your goddamned throat." Taking hold of Cubs pitcher Charlie Root's curve, Ruth swung viciously, parking the ball deep in the center field bleachers, his fifteenth homer in World Series competition. Gehrig followed with another homer, chasing Root, and New York won 7–5. The Yankees won the next day, their twelfth straight World Series game victory, and their fourth championship during Ruth's reign with the team.

President Warren G. Harding shakes hands with George Herman "Babe" Ruth at Yankee Stadium in June 1923. Both personified aspects of the New Era of the 1920s, which brought a resurgence of conservative politics and burgeoning public interest in sports, as Americans rejected activist government and sought to relax following two decades of progressive reform and foreign interventions. Harding died later that year, shortly before revelations of widespread corruption in his administration. (Library of Congress, LC-DIG-ggbain-35844)

Onlookers and later baseball historians wrestled with the question of whether the headline in the *New York World-Telegram* rang true: "Ruth Calls Shot as He Puts Homer No. 2 in Side Pocket." Gehrig was quoted as saying, "What do you think of the nerve of that big monkey. Imagine the guy calling his shot and getting away with it." Charlie Root later insisted, "Ruth did not point at the fence before he swung. If he had made a gesture like that, he would have ended up on his ass." However, Yankee third baseman Joe Sewell reported, "I was there. I saw it. I don't care what anybody says. He called it."

The nation's greatest sports hero, Babe Ruth, was born George Herman Ruth Jr. on February 6, 1895, in Baltimore, Maryland, the son of Kate Schamberger-Ruth and George Herman Ruth Sr., both German Americans. Kate and Big George strove to make a go of a family grocery and saloon, while their rambunctious son roamed the streets of Baltimore. Along with other untutored youth, Little George harassed truck drivers and storekeepers, while attempting to avoid "coppers." Unable to control their "incorrigible" son, his parents, on June 13, 1902, placed him under the care of the St. Mary's Industrial School for Boys, where the Xaverian brothers, members of a Catholic order, took charge of 800 orphans, troubled boys, and poor lads whose families were unable to care for them. Ruth spent eight years at St. Mary's, when he did not reside with his family. Big for his age, Ruth possessed a sizable, flat nose and generous mouth, leading to a nickname, "Nigger Lips." While at St. Mary's, Ruth adopted the Roman Catholic faith, far removed from the Lutheranism of his parents. Embracing a work ethic as he experienced the required five-and-a-half-day work weeks, Ruth learned to expertly stitch tailor-made shirts at St. Mary's. More important for sports history's sake, he was tutored in baseball by the six foot, six inch, 250-pound Brother Matthias, whom he called "the greatest man I've ever known." Often snaring fungoes from Matthias, Ruth played baseball two or three hours a day, positioning himself behind the plate, at third base, or on the pitching mound.

Ruth's prowess on the diamond began to garner notices in local newspapers and from professional scouts. In February 1914 Jack Dunn, owner-manager of the Baltimore Orioles, a top minor league ball club in the International League, signed the nineteen-year-old Ruth, who both pitched and batted left-handed, to a contract after watching him strike out twenty-two batters in one contest. Dunn informed Brother Gilbert of St. Mary's, "This fellow Ruth is the greatest young ballplayer who ever reported to a training camp." Away from the ballpark, Ruth appeared untutored, without any polish or social graces, and veteran players referred to him as "Babe," indicating that he was "Dunn's baby," biographer Robert W. Creamer writes. The six foot, two inch, long-limbed Ruth starred on the pitching mound for the Orioles, compiling a 14-6 win-loss record. In midseason Dunn sold Ruth, star pitcher Ernie Shore, and another player to the Boston Red Sox for around $25,000. *The Sporting News* stated that "Ruth is considered a real star."

After warming the Boston bench for six weeks, during which time he won once and lost once on the mound, Ruth returned to the minor leagues to join the Providence franchise of the International League. Ruth pitched well for Providence, ending his International League season with a 23-8 mark, and having belted his first professional home run, along with the astonishing total of ten triples in only 121 official trips to the plate. This was the dead ball era in professional baseball, when the size of the stadiums and the makeup of the balls in play, seemingly used until the cover literally came off, made for low-scoring games, built around pitching and timely hitting, along with base running. Called back to complete the season with the Red Sox, Ruth managed his first two big-league hits, one a double, and recorded his second major league victory. On October 17, he married Helen Woodford, a pretty sixteen-year-old, and the two spent the winter at Big George's apartment located above his saloon in Baltimore.

Ruth won eighteen games against only eight defeats, while helping lead Boston to the 1915 American League pennant. He also batted .315 and smacked his first four major league homers, including one at St. Louis's Sportsman's Park called "the longest home run ever witnessed here." To Ruth's chagrin, Red Sox manager Bill Carrigan failed to select him to face the Philadelphia Phillies during the World Series. Nevertheless *The Sporting Life* termed Ruth's stardom "meteoric." During midseason of the following year, *Baseball Magazine* deemed the Babe "one of the greatest natural pitchers" ever to appear in the majors, while noting that he was "a dreaded batter" who delivered "tremendous wallops." He became baseball's top left-handed pitcher, notching a 23-12 record, with a league-leading 1.75 earned run average (ERA), and nine shutouts, a record for American League southpaws, as Boston swept to its second straight pennant. In game 2 of the World Series against the Brooklyn Dodgers, Ruth gave up an inside-the-park homer in the first inning, then shut down his opponents the rest of the way in a game won in the fourteenth inning by the Red Sox, 2–1, who took their second World Series title in a row. In 1917 "the giant southpaw pitcher-slugger," as *The Sporting News* referred to him, was even better on the mound, chalking up a 24-13 record, with a 2.01 ERA and a league high of 35 complete games, and he hit .325 at the plate. The Red Sox came up short that year, falling nine games behind the Chicago White Sox.

Despite losing thirteen of its players to the military, Boston rebounded the following season, shortened because of the U.S. entry into World War I, winning its third pennant in four years. Exempt from the draft because of his marital status, Ruth now doubled up, playing several games in the outfield. He still completed 18 out of 19 starts, winning 13 of 20 decisions, and carving out a 2.22 ERA. More strikingly he tied for the league in homers with 11, albeit all during the first half of the season, while driving in 66 runs and batting .300 in only 317 official plate appearances. F. C. Lane proclaimed, "The sensation of the closing baseball season is George (Babe) Ruth. . . . the Boston slugger bulks large as the dominating baseball figure of 1918." In game 1 of the World Series against the Chicago Cubs, Ruth twirled a six-hit shutout, then pitched scoreless ball into the eighth inning in game 4, before the Cubs finally scored. The Red Sox won that game and then took their third World Series crown during Ruth's tenure. In his three starts in World Series competition, Ruth garnered a 3-0 mark, along with a 0.87 ERA. He also broke Christy Mathewson's scoreless inning streak in the Fall Classic, having pitched twenty-nine and two-thirds consecutive innings without yielding a run.

During the off season, Ruth battled with Boston management over his salary demands, while *The Sporting News*, on January 30, 1919, referred to him as "unquestionably . . . the greatest slugger of all time. He hits the ball harder than any other man that ever lived." Although the Red Sox bumbled through the 1919 baseball campaign, Ruth's hitting exploits garnered considerable attention. By season's end he had established a new major league record with twenty-nine homers, and also led the league in runs scored with 103, runs batted in (RBIs) with 114, an on-base percentage of .456, and a slugging average of .647, while batting .322. He even led the league's outfielders in fielding with a .996 mark, and produced a 9-5 pitching record, with a 2.97 ERA. The National League home run champion, Gavvy Cravath, hit only twelve out of the park, while the second-best slugger in the American League managed but ten. Ruth belted all but four of his team's homers. This was seemingly still the dead ball era, with the great Ty Cobb hitting only one homer, Joe Jackson seven, and Rogers Hornsby eight. At the close of the 1919 season, the *New York Times* termed Ruth "the mastodonic mauler of the Boston Red Sox . . . the greatest batsman the game has ever known" and "the hardest hitter in the history of the game." *Spalding's Official Base Ball Record* termed Ruth's performance during the past season "the greatest achievement of any individual ball player in a generation." Grantland Rice of the *New York Tribune* called Ruth both "the world's greatest slugger" and "the game's greatest showman," possessing the "ability to deliver his choicest wares before the largest crowds."

In fact Ruth's legend was merely beginning. During the 1920s, after joining the New York Yankees, he compiled the greatest individual statistics of any athlete in professional sports while helping carry his new team to unprecedented heights. The sale of "baseball's biggest attraction" to New York for an unprecedented $125,000 and a $300,000 loan, resulting in the Yankees holding the mortgage on Fenway Park, jolted the baseball world, initiating an extended slide for the Red Sox and enabling the Yankees to soon surpass the New York Giants as the preeminent major league squad. Ruth's transfer to the Yankees also coincided with a decision by major league baseball's Joint Rules Committee to ban "freak deliveries" such as the spitter, as well as the possible introduction of a livelier ball. During the 1920 season, American League players smacked a record 369 homers with batting averages also soaring, as five players in the senior circuit hit over .370. One of those was Babe Ruth, who batted .376 in 458 official at-bats. Shattering all existing records, Ruth scored 158 runs, batted in 137, walked 150 times, produced a .532 on-base percentage, compiled an .847 slugging percentage, and stroked 54 homers, 35 more than second-place finisher George Sisler and a total surpassed by only one major league team.

Early in the season, the *Tribune's* W. O. McGeehan discussed Ruth's appeal, which drew record numbers of fans. "Baseball no longer is the chief attraction at the ball parks. Babe Ruth is. . . . Ruth doth bestride the baseball diamonds like a colossus." Ruth, McGeehan noted, "suddenly became a national idol."

Referring to "the swaggering swat king," the *New York Times* deemed him "a modern Goliath of the bludgeon" who had "become a national curiosity." Spectators remained riveted to their seats until it became apparent that Ruth was not likely to appear at the plate. "[W]hen Babe is through, they are through," F. C. Lane declared. Lane deemed Ruth's athletic feats "wholly unparalleled almost super-human." *Baseball Magazine* proclaimed "the mighty Babe" as "the huge noise of 1920," the game's "biggest drawing card" thanks to "the matchless, magnetic power of the Home Run Drive!" The publication called Ruth "the Whole Works, the Main Squeeze, and the Big Attraction." Sports writer W. A. Phelon called Ruth "the Goliath, the Sampson, the Superman of the season," who "gave the final proof that the American public worships The Solid Biff."

His epic feats could not have come at a better time for major league baseball, then America's most popular sport. On August 16 a pitch thrown by Yankee submariner Carl Mays crashed into the head of Cleveland Indians second baseman Ray Chapman, who died despite a late-night operation. Baseball decision makers soon determined that dirty, scuffed baseballs should be tossed aside, to be replaced by shiny new ones. This call, together with players' attempts to duplicate Ruthian uppercut swings, produced more balls being jacked out of big-league parks. As if Chapman's death were not disturbing enough, baseball was rocked by charges in September that the previous year's World Series competition between Chicago and the Cincinnati Reds had been fixed. Eight players from the Chicago White Sox, contending with the Yankees and the Indians for the American League pennant, were suspended. They included star pitchers Eddie Cicotte and Lefty Williams, third sacker Buck Weaver, and peerless outfielder Shoeless Joe Jackson, whose fluid swing had supposedly been copied by a young Babe Ruth. At season's end, the White Sox came up two games behind the Indians with the Yankees a game further back. Eventually, baseball moguls hired federal judge Kenesaw Mountain Landis to help restore the sport's good name, which had been tarnished by earlier accusations of gambling and crooked ballplayers. Landis permanently banished that version of the Chicago Eight from organized baseball.

Baseball historians still debate whether Landis or Ruth proved to be major league baseball's savior. Landis began a near-quarter-century tenure as baseball commissioner, one marked by arbitrary, dictatorial rule, as Ruth's stature continued to soar in a period that has been referred to as the golden age of American sports. Journalists Grantland Rice, Damon Runyon, Ring Lardner, Paul Gallico, and Heywood Broun helped to depict sports stars as mythical figures deserving of great respect, even adoration. Jack Dempsey, the Manassa Mauler, long ruled over the heavyweight division of the boxing world, before falling in a pair of epic battles with Gene Tunney. Bill Tilden strode atop the tennis circuit, winning seven U.S. Open and three Wimbledon titles, while leading the

United States to seven straight Davis Cup victories. Swimmer Johnny Weismuller captured fifty-two national championships, established sixty-seven world records, and took five Olympic gold medals. Golfer Bobby Jones won thirteen major titles, including the so-called Grand Slam of golf in 1930, when he swept the U.S. Open, the British Open, the U.S. Amateur, and the British Amateur championships, while retaining his amateur status. Man o' War, the Big Red thoroughbred, dominated horse racing, losing only once in twenty-one trips to the track. College football featured Notre Dame coach Knute Rockne and his stellar 1924 backfield, famously tagged with the label "the Four Horsemen" by sportswriter Rice, while Red Grange, first at the University of Illinois and later with the Chicago Bears, was a bigger individual star.

And yet Babe Ruth was the biggest star of them all, striding like a colossus above the pantheon of the American sporting world. As stellar as his first year with the Yankees had been, his 1921 campaign proved even more remarkable as he helped lead New York to its first American League title. Additionally, his batting prowess, *Baseball Magazine* offered, triggered a "home-run epidemic" with both leagues easily establishing new records. Ruth set the pace, smacking 59 homers, scoring 177 runs, driving in 171, and amassing 457 total bases, shattering his own records. He also batted .378, walked 145 times, and delivered an on-base percentage of .512 and a slugging average of .846. Many baseball chroniclers later referred to Ruth's 1921 campaign as the greatest in the game's history.

Following the Yankees' defeat at the hands of the cross-town Giants, Ruth and two teammates undertook a barnstorming series notwithstanding a decade-old rule that prohibited World Series participants from doing so. Perhaps determined to underscore who was organized baseball's biggest figure, Commissioner Landis suspended the three Yankees and demanded return of their World Series shares. As a consequence, Ruth's 1922 campaign did not begin until May 20, enabling him to play in only 110 of 154 regular season games. Still baseball's most feared slugger, Ruth's performance paled by comparison with the previous two years, as he scored only 94 runs, drove in but 99, and finished with 35 homers, the league's third best total, and a .315 batting average. The Yankees managed only a tie in five World Series contests against the Giants, with Ruth bumbling to a .118 performance in seventeen official plate appearances.

With more than 60,000 spectators present, Ruth began the 1923 season by cracking the first home run hit at newly constructed Yankee Stadium, referred to as the House That Ruth Built. Helping guide the Yankees to their third straight pennant, Ruth batted a career best .393, and led the American League with 151 runs scored, 131 RBIs, 41 homers, and a .764 slugging average, along with 170 base on balls and an on-base percentage of .545, both major league records. Roaring to the World Series title, the Yankees bested the Giants in six games, as Ruth batted .368 and delivered three homers. New York finished two games back of the Washington Senators in 1924, when Ruth captured his lone batting title with a .378 average. He also led the league with 143 runs scored, 46 homers, 142 walks, a .513 on-base percentage, and a .739 slugging average.

Out of shape, suffering from various physical ailments, saddled with a gambling debt of several thousand dollars, and juggling an increasingly unhappy wife, a paternity suit, and his mistress, Claire Merritt Hodgson, Ruth fell to earth with a resounding thud in 1925. Since his departure from St. Mary's eleven years earlier, Ruth had behaved like a man-child, gorging on food, drinking heavily, and philandering at will. Neither marriage nor stardom inhibited him in any fashion. However, a finger fractured during preseason, chills, and a fever underscored the very mortality of this baseball immortal, who soon experienced what reporters referred to as "influenza and indigestion," or simply "the bellyache heard round the world." Waxing eloquent, Damon Runyon wrote, "The Big Bam yesterday just about beat a long throw from Death, the outfielder in Life's game." Rumors floated that Ruth had been beset by syphilis or gonorrhea, although possibly he had suffered a hernia that helped to drive his weight down to 180 pounds, closer to what it had been when he first entered the majors.

In and out of the lineup, Ruth struggled at the plate while repeatedly violating team curfews. Eventually manager Millard Huggins informed the outraged Babe that he was being suspended and fined $5,000. Newspaper headlines of Ruth's troubles only continued as word got out that Helen Ruth was suing her husband for $100,000 and separate maintenance. Altogether he played in only ninety-eight games as the Yankees tumbled to seventh place in the American League, twenty-eight and a half games behind the champion Washington Senators. A late-season surge boosted Ruth's season totals to 61 runs scored, 66 RBIs, and 25 homers, still the league's second-best mark, along with 59 walks and a .290 batting mark, far below his career averages. His on-base percentage slid over 100 points, his slugging average twice that. The *New York Herald Tribune* indicated, "With the fall from glory of Babe Ruth, a million young Americans are bereft." And yet the *New York World* admitted, "There is something about him, even when he is under the dark cloud of disgrace, which makes us find excuses and love him still. That is probably because we realize he has never grown up. He started life as a bad boy, and he is still a bad boy."

The October 31, 1925, issue of *Collier's* magazine featured an article by Joe Winksworth titled "I Have Been a Babe and a Boob," referring to Ruth's declaration that in his experience with "pests . . . the good-time guys . . . and a few crooks I have thrown away over a quarter million dollars." On entering Artie McGovern's gymnasium in New York City later in the year, Babe was called "a physical wreck." McGovern put the badly overweight, out-of-shape ballplayer on a rigorous exercise program. Ruth returned to form in 1926, batting .372, with a league best 139 runs scored, 146 RBIs, 47 homers, 144 base on balls, .516 on-base percentage, and .737 slugging average. The Yankees regained the American League crown but were stunned in the decisive seventh game of the World Series by the St. Louis Cardinals, with the final out recorded when Ruth was caught attempting to steal second base. In the fourth game, Ruth belted three home runs, a feat never before accomplished in World Series competition.

Ruth and the Yankees' glory years continued, with many chroniclers considering the 1927 team baseball's finest. New York won 110 games, besting the second-place Philadelphia Athletics by 19 games, then swept the Pittsburgh Pirates in the World Series. Featuring their latest version of Murderer's Row, the Yankees included in their lineup the hard-hitting Earle Combs, Ruth, Lou Gehrig, Bob Meusel, and Tony Lazzeri. This was the season when Ruth, after a lengthy home run chase with Gehrig, surpassed his own home run mark, belting a record 60, along with the American League's top totals of 158 runs scored, 137 walks, a .486 on-base percentage, and a .772 slugging average, in addition to batting .356. The Yankees repeated their American League crown in 1928, as Ruth batted .323 and led the circuit with 54 homers, 163 runs scored, 142 RBIs, 137 walks, and a .705 slugging percentage. The Yankees blanked the Cardinals in the World Series, as Ruth hit a record .625 and Gehrig batted .545. Ruth again hit three homers in a single contest, the final game of that year's Fall Classic.

Still baseball's greatest slugger, Ruth watched his Yankees finish in second, third place, and second once more over the course of the next three seasons. He held onto his home run crown with totals of 46, 49, and 46, respectively, with the 1931 mark tying teammate Gehrig's, and he batted .345, .359, and .373. In 1930 Ruth's salary reached $80,000, an amount greater than President Herbert Hoover received, but the ballplayer asked, "Why not? I had a better year than he did." The Yankees captured another World Series title in 1932, when Ruth hit 41 homers and batted .341, in addition to delivering the homer against the National League champion Chicago Cubs that may have been a called shot. Age now seemed to catch up with both Ruth and the Yankees, as his home run totals fell to 34 and 22, along with batting averages of .301 and .288, as New York came in runner-up the next two seasons. With the Yankees unwilling to hand him the managerial title he desperately wanted, Ruth accepted a trade to the Boston Braves, but after a few weeks he retired from the game he so loved. Ruth completed his remarkable career having compiled a .342 batting average with 2,873 hits and 2,174 runs scored, along with record totals of 2,213 RBIs, 2,056 walks, a .474 on-base percentage, a .690 slugging average, and, above all else, the magical total of 714 homers.

In 1936, the Baseball Hall of Fame ushered in its five charter members: Ty Cobb, Honus Wagner, Christy Mathewson, Walter Johnson, and Babe Ruth. With no big-league team willing to name him its skipper, Ruth held court at his Fifth Avenue apartment, only occasionally attending ball games, and spending considerable time golfing, bowling, drinking, traveling, and hunting. During World War II, he helped to sell war bonds and also offered fifteen-minute radio shows, while maintaining an active social life with his second wife, Claire. Following the war, cancer raced through his body, although he appeared at Yankee Stadium in April 1947, when Commissioner Happy Chandler proclaimed a "Babe Ruth Day." The now gray-haired Ruth thanked the 58,000 fans in attendance, declaring, "The only real game, I think, in the world is baseball." The premiere of the Hollywood film *The Babe Ruth Story* took place on July 26, 1948. On August 15, 1948, baseball's greatest star died. Four days later tens of thousands of fans passed by Yankee Stadium or walked to St. Patrick's Cathedral, where Cardinal Francis Spellman presided over the funeral service.

⌒   LOUIS ARMSTRONG   ⌒

On June 28, 1928, Louis Armstrong and His Hot Five recorded "Don't Jive Me," "Sugar Foot Strut," and "West End Blues" in Chicago, Illinois. Formed three years earlier, the band no longer included Armstrong's estranged wife, Lillian Hardin Armstrong, but the well-rehearsed "West End Blues" featured trombonist Fred Robinson, clarinetist Jimmy Strong, pianist Earl Hines, banjo player Mancy Carr, drummer Zutty Singleton, and trumpeter-vocalist Armstrong. Their recording of "West End Blues," written by Armstrong's old mentor Joe Oliver and Clarence Williams, became one of the most celebrated American jazz records and possibly Armstrong's greatest single work. His opening, free-flowing trumpet salvo underscored how Armstrong's creative genius was altering improvisational jazz and recasting American music. The great blues singer Billie Holiday revealed how she had been "gassed" by Armstrong's scatting on "West End Blues": "It was the first time I ever heard anybody sing without using any words. . . . Ba-ba-ba-ba-ba-ba-ba-ba and the rest of it had plenty of meaning for me. . . . But the meaning used to change, depending on how I felt. Sometimes the record would make me so sad I'd cry up a storm. Other times the same damn record would make me so happy." Jazz critic Gunther Schuller termed the final blues chorus "the perfect climax, structurally and emotionally. It can only be described as ecstatic." In Schuller's estimation, Armstrong's 1928 rendition of "West End Blues" transformed American jazz "for several decades to come." Armstrong biographer James Lincoln Collier deemed the song "one of the masterworks of twentieth-century music."

Jazz trumpeter and singer Louis Armstrong, at right, with his band in 1937. His artistry was central in defining and popularizing jazz as a uniquely American musical form as early as the 1920s. Armstrong's influence and celebrity spanned five decades and his popularity endured even after his death in 1971. (Library of Congress, LC-USZ62-118977)

Born six years after Babe Ruth, on August 4, 1901, in New Orleans, Louis Daniel Armstrong was the son of fifteen-year-old Mayann Albert and her teenage, common-law husband William Armstrong, who quickly abandoned his family. Baptismal records counter Armstong's frequently delivered mythologizing, "I was a Southern Doodle dandy, born on the Fourth of July, 1900." Armstrong grew up in poverty in uptown New Orleans, shuffling back and forth between various relatives, including his grandmother, Josephine, as Mayann worked as a domestic but also engaged in prostitution in the segregated city. New Orleans was something of an untamed city, with numerous brothels, liquor and drugs aplenty, and white politicians and businessmen who commonly sported biracial or quadroon mistresses. At the same time, the city fathers increasingly turned to Jim Crow segregation laws, which also covered the red-light district. The Armstrongs lived in black Storyville, close to the famed white red-light district. Dilapidated housing with dirt- or mud-filled backyards, broken-down buildings, honky-tonks, and dance halls abounded, along with crime, alcoholism, drug addiction, and disease spawned by poor sanitation, crowded neighborhoods, and insufficient medical care.

Like the young George Herman Ruth Jr., Armstrong hung out in the city streets, and he frequented dance halls and brothels, drawn to the musicians who played ragtime there. He attended Fisk School for Boys, served as a paperboy, and, starting at the age of six, worked for a Russian Jewish family, the Karnofskys, hauling and selling junk. The Karnofskys insisted, as Armstrong later recalled, "that I had talent, perfect intonation when I would sing." On one occasion, the older Karnofsky son, Morris, advanced Armstrong two dollars to purchase an old, dirty cornet. His friendship with the Karnofskys left Armstrong with warm memories, and he later indicated, "I'm a Baptist and a good friend of the Pole, and I always wear a Jewish star for luck." Remaining enamored with music, he formed a vocal quartet. He also shot dice, sometimes returning home with his "pockets loaded with pennies, nickels, dimes and even quarters," thereby enabling his family "to go shopping."

Dropping out of the Fisk School after the fifth grade, Armstrong began carrying coal to Storyville. Finding a .38 pistol in Mayann's trunk, Armstrong fired it in the air on New Year's Eve in 1912 or 1913, leading to his arrest. Placed in the Colored Waif's Home, a rigidly run reformatory, by the juvenile court, Armstrong rejoiced on becoming bugler of the institution's band, which, attired in colorful uniforms, played in city parades, at private picnics, and at summer resorts. The band offered renditions of songs like "Swanee River" and "Maryland, My Maryland." Handed a cornet and taught "Home, Sweet Home," the proud Armstrong was, as he recalled, "in seventh heaven."

Released from the Colored Waif's Home in mid-June 1914, only one month after a tall, nineteen-year-old lad left the St. Mary's Industrial School for Boys to set the baseball world afire, Armstrong went to stay with his father, William's wife Gertrude, and their two young sons. After a short while, during which time he helped to take care of the two younger boys, Armstrong returned to live with Mayann. For a brief spell, he delivered milk for the Cloverdale Dairy, sold newspapers, worked as a stevedore, and drove a wooden coal cart for the C.A. Andrews Coal Company. Armstrong also became largely responsible for a mentally challenged little boy, Clarence, the son of his cousin Flora, who had died soon after her baby was born. While spending little time honing his own musical abilities, Armstrong managed to keep abreast of the bands that played in New Orleans, particularly following the cornet player Joe "King" Oliver, who, along with trombonist Kid Ory, spearheaded the top group in the city. In 1917 Armstrong headed a band, along with drummer Joe Lindsey, and sometimes received instruction from Oliver, whom he viewed as "the greatest of them all . . . a creator with unlimited ideas." New Orleans musicians began heading up north after the U.S. Navy shut down Storyville in 1917. By 1918 or 1919 Oliver departed for Chicago, opening a spot in Kid Ory's unit for the seventeen-year-old trumpet player.

On March 19, 1918, the five feet, eight inch, broad-shouldered Armstrong married Daisy Parker, a twenty-one-year-old prostitute from Gretna, Louisiana, and the two adopted the now three-year-old Clarence. Armstrong and Daisy fought constantly, sometimes ending up in jail as a consequence, and the marriage lasted only about four years. All the while he continued refining his musical skills, working with Kid Ory and also playing on riverboat excursions. In July 1922, Armstrong, now playing parades and funerals with the Tuxedo Band, received a telegram from King Oliver, tendering an invitation to join the Creole Jazz Band in Chicago. America's Second City, as Chicago was known, had undergone sweeping changes in the past several decades, experiencing a tremendous population boom, which included the migration of hundreds of thousands of African Americans from the Deep South. Race relations proved difficult at best, as exemplified by the terrifying, almost cyclonic disturbances that swept through the city during the summer of 1919, resulting in scores of fatalities and leaving hundreds homeless. Chicago was also known for its freewheeling ways, which included organized crime connected to brothels, gambling joints, drugs, and bootlegging. The Black Belt on the city's South Side, where the African American community largely resided, boasted its own crime boss, Dan Jackson, an ally of Mayor William "Big Bill" Thompson. As was true in New Orleans's black Storyville, the Black Belt contained dilapidated housing, prostitution, drugs, and illegal alcohol, but also an audience thirsting for the kind of music King Oliver's band offered.

On arriving in Chicago, Armstrong felt somewhat overwhelmed by the artistry of Oliver, Johnny and Warren Dodds, Honore Dutrey, Bill Johnson, and Lil Hardin, the petite woman who became Louis's second wife. His unusual appearance caught her attention, as Hardin later recalled. "Everything he had on was too small for him. His atrocious tie was dangling down over his protruding stomach and to top it off, he had a hairdo that called for bangs. . . . All the musicians called him Little Louis, and he weighed 226 pounds." Under her tutelage, Armstrong dropped fifty pounds and began dressing more stylishly. King Oliver's Creole Jazz Band was Chicago's hottest, in the very period when jazz was exploding into the national consciousness, with Armstrong garnering notice. The *Chicago Defender*, one of the nation's top black newspapers, indicated, "This newcomer brought us an entirely different style of playing than King Oliver had given us. He was younger, had more power of delivery, and could send out his stuff with a knack." Other musicians began to hear Armstrong play, including Bix Beiderbecke and Hoagy Carmichael, who recalled asking, "Why isn't everybody in the world here to hear that?" Carmichael thought that "something as unutterably stirring as that deserved to be heard by the world."

Black-based music thrived in cities like New Orleans and Kansas City before the end of the nineteenth century, drawing on complex African music—including call-and-response choruses, improvisation, polyrhythms, and syncopation—and the music that slaves and the freedmen made in the fields. Another source of inspiration was the music performed by individual troubadours and traveling bands after the Civil War. Black musicians, led by the brilliant Scott Joplin with his "Maple Leaf Rag," began playing ragtime music. Others, including W. C. Handy, who wrote the classic "St. Louis Blues" long played by Armstrong, helped to popularize the blues. One of the early hot spots for ragtime and blues players was New Orleans, particularly prewar Storyville, where brass or marching bands proved enormously popular. In the 1910s musicians were "playing hot," premiering an early version of jazz. Up north, James Reese Europe's orchestra, long the house band at the Clef Club in Harlem with its own brand of "hot" music, offered the first records produced by a black group in 1913. In 1920 Mamie Smith recorded "Crazy Blues" for the OKeh record label, one of the small but rapidly growing companies that targeted an African American clientele. Smith's recording sold 100,000 copies, convincing other companies, including Paramount, Vocalion, Columbia, and Black Swann, to join OKeh in marketing what the Chicago Defender referred to as "race records." In 1922 Kid Ory's Original Creole Jazz Band, which had played throughout California, was the first black jazz group to make a record. On April 5, 1923, in Richmond, Indiana, Armstrong participated in his first recording on the Gennett label, as the second cornetist with King Oliver's Creole Jazz Band. The next day his first recorded solo was made for "Chimes Blues."

The reception afforded jazz music demonstrated that its appeal reached far beyond the African American community. Consequently jazz and blues recordings sold well, sometimes performed by black artists but often as covers by white musicians. The increasingly popular medium of radio served jazz well, with Kid Ory broadcasting from New Orleans and Fletcher Henderson doing the same from New York City. In whichever guise, black-based music proved quite popular and seemed to provide a musical backdrop for the era that took its name, the Jazz Age, from the newest genre. At the same time, jazz and the blues were only the cutting edge of a broader cultural and social transformation affecting African Americans. In places like Harlem, where Armstrong headed in 1924 to join the Fletcher Henderson Orchestra, writers, artists, dancers, theatrical performers, and politicians all garnered attention. Harlem had its renaissance with the poets Langston Hughes and Claude McKay, the sculptor Aaron Douglas, the dancers Florence Mills and Josephine Baker, actors Charles Gilpin and Paul Robeson, and political figures W. E. B. DuBois, A. Phillip Randolph, and Marcus Garvey. But the New Negro movement cast a wider geographical sweep, influencing other leading urban centers on the order of Chicago, Philadelphia, and Detroit. Music was at the forefront of the black Renaissance, thanks to the artistry of Bessie Smith, King Oliver, and younger performers such as Armstrong and Duke Ellington.

In September 1924, Armstrong, evidently encouraged by Lil, began playing with Fletcher Henderson's orchestra, arguably the nation's top black dance band and one that was featured at leading clubs in New York City including the Apollo, the Roxy, and the famed Roseland Ballroom. The kind of hot music associated with Henderson was thriving in the nation's greatest city with young New Yorkers and out-of-towners alike flocking to speakeasies and cabarets where jazz and blues music wafted through the air. The most popular spots were located around Times Square, based at Broadway and Seventh Avenue and heading from West Forty-second to West Forty-seventh, and at Harlem's Lenox and Seventh Avenue on 135th Street. The Times Square locales excluded black patrons, but African American musicians played there, while in Harlem, clubs catered to segregated crowds or blacks alone, which whites could still frequent. In early January 1925 Armstrong played cornet on "Cake Walkin' Babies (From Home)," recorded by Clarence Williams's Blue Five, which included Sidney Bechet on soprano saxophone. The next month Armstrong and pianist Fred Longshaw recorded with Bessie Smith at Columbia Studios, producing the great blues singer's brilliant version of the W. C. Handy classic, "St. Louis Blues." Armstrong and Smith worked together again three months later, producing, among other recordings, "Careless Love Blues." During this period Armstrong also served as a studio sideman for Trixie Smith, Ma Rainey, and Clara Smith. On May 29, 1925, the Fletcher Henderson Orchestra, with Coleman Hawkins on clarinet and tenor saxophone and Armstrong on cornet and trumpet, recorded "Sugar Foot Stomp," a King Oliver standard. Although still receiving little public acclaim, Armstrong began attracting attention from other young musicians, just as he had in Chicago. Trumpeter Rex Stewart recalled what happened after Armstrong came to New York. "I went mad with the rest of the town! I tried to walk like him, talk like him, eat like him, sleep like him."

Shortly following a tour of New England, Armstrong returned to Chicago to play first trumpet in Lil's Dreamland Syncopators, his wife's band. Chicago stood as the headquarters of jazz, which was more popular than ever. By mid-November 1925 the *Chicago Defender* was advertising "The World's Greatest Jazz Cornetist, Louis Armstrong." Organized gangs were even more in control of Chicago than before and controlled entertainment venues of all kinds. Unquestionably some of Armstrong's managers had mob ties. Notwithstanding such connections, black musicians thrived in Chicago clubs, theaters, and hotels.

During the fall of 1925, OKeh signed Armstrong to an exclusive contract, quickly advertising him as "the hottest trumpet player in America" who conducted "the hottest, and most rhythmic dance record on sale." Made up of trombonist Kid Ory, clarinetist Johnny Dodds, banjo player Johnny St. Cyr, Lil on the piano, and Louis, Armstrong's Hot Five, and later his Hot Seven, soon began recording for OKeh Records in Chicago. Reshaping American music, the band produced renditions of "Heebie Jeebies," "Potato Head Blues," "Savoy Blues" (with guitarist Lonnie Johnson), and "West End Blues," among other Armstrong favorites. With "Heebie Jeebies" Armstrong began refining his wordless "scat" singing, establishing a new standard for musical vocalists. That record sold 40,000 copies within weeks of its release, during a period when 10,000 sales made for a hit.

The great African American writer Ralph Ellison later suggested, "If Louis Armstrong's meditations on the 'Potato Head Blues' aren't marked by elegance, then the term is too inelegant to name the fastidious refinement, the mastery of nuance, the tasteful domination of melody, rhythm, sounding brass and tinkling cymbal which marked his style." The recordings spread Armstrong's fame far beyond Chicago while stretching jazz's boundaries. Trumpeter Bill Coleman acknowledged, "Armstrong was my first inspiration and I listened to all of his records I could get hold of. . . . I used to copy Louis' records . . . in fact if he played a bad note, I'd put that in as well."

By early 1926 Armstrong had left Dreamland for Carroll Dickerson's orchestra, which played at the Sunset Café, while also working at the Vendome Theatre with Erskine Tate. The next year saw Louis lead his own band, Louis Armstrong and the Stompers, which included the pianist Earl Hines and trombonist Honore Dutrey. After establishing a small band that again featured Hines, Armstrong rejoined Carroll Dickerson's orchestra, now playing at the Savoy dance hall. Both black and white musicians, including Benny Goodman, Tommy and Jimmy Dorsey, and Bix Beiderbecke, now flocked to hear him play and sometimes jammed alongside Armstrong.

His personal life proved rockier, as the ever-ambitious Lil constantly pushed Louis, something their fellow musicians kidded him about, leading to fights between the Armstrongs. The presence of Armstrong's ward Clarence hardly helped matters, nor did Louis's growing fondness for Alpha Smith, his mistress who later became his third wife. Their relationship also was tumultuous, as Armstrong conceded. "Alpha was all right, but her mind was on furs, diamonds and other flashy luxuries, and not enough on me and my happiness. . . . [S]he went through my money and then walked out. We had some real spats."

Recognizing that Chicago cabarets were starting to founder, Armstrong moved back to New York in 1929, at the top of his game. Fellow musicians considered him the finest trumpet player anywhere while African Americans appeared to view Armstrong as a hero. He was about to become far more famous, thanks to the release of a series of hits. In 1929 he cut "I Can't Give You Anything but Love," "Ain't Misbehavin'," "Black and Blue," and "St. Louis Blues," among other records. "Black and Blue" underscored the harsh reality of racism with the plaintive cry, "My only sin is in my skin. / What did I do to be so black and blue?" His songs could be heard throughout Harlem and soon other communities across the country shared in the Armstrong hysteria. Significant too was the fact that Armstrong led the wave of black performers such as Duke Ellington and Clarence Henderson who began to mesmerize white jazz audiences as well as black ones. Armstrong played at Connie's Inn in Harlem, the main competitor to the Cotton Club and a club with gangster ties. He joined the cast of *Hot Chocolates*, a Broadway hit, for which he sang "Ain't Misbehavin'" and "A Thousand Pounds of Rhythm." He also played with the Carroll Dickerson band at the Lafayette Theatre, receiving a rave review from the *New York Age*, an African American newspaper that called him the "most remarkable of all cornetists," capable of producing "from his golden trumpet music such as has never been heard before."

Armstrong helped to spread the gospel of his brand of jazz on a musical journey across the country to California in the summer of 1930. At the New Cotton Club, located in Culver City outside of Los Angeles, movie stars, including Bing Crosby, showed up to listen to Armstrong and the house band, led by first trumpeter Vernon Elkins and then Les Hite. His latest recordings, including "I Surrender" and "Georgia," became big sellers, and other musicians eagerly awaited them. As the trumpet player Cat Anderson noted, "We played all Louis Armstrong's things note for note." Armstrong was arrested for marijuana possession while in California, spending nine days in the Los Angeles City Jail in November 1931. Receiving a six-month suspended sentence, Armstrong immediately returned to work. The following June, Armstrong was back to being celebrated as "maestro of jazz" by *Time* magazine.

Touring overseas in the summer of 1932, Armstrong appeared at the London Palladium on July 18. Among those present was Jack Johnson, the black former heavyweight boxing champion. Dan S. Ingman of the *Melody Maker* asserted, "[Armstrong's] technique, tone and mastery over his instrument (which he calls 'Satchmo,' a contraction, I am told, of 'Satchel Mouth') is uncanny. Top F's bubble about all over the place, and never once does he miss one." As for Louis's singing, Ingman continued, "Well, words just fail me. It's like it is on the records, only a thousand times more so! . . . His style is peculiarly his own, mostly long, high notes—there is no one else playing anything like it—they couldn't!" Still "the most amazing thing is his personality. He positively sparkles with showmanship and good humour the whole time." Ingman concluded, "He is, in short, an unique phenomenon, an electric personality—easily the greatest America has sent us so far. . . . Hail Louis, King of the Trumpet!" On a far less happy note, a columnist for the *Daily Herald* cried out, "Armstrong is the ugliest man I have seen on the music-hall stage. He looks, and behaves, like an untrained gorilla. He might have come straight from some African jungle and then, after being taken to a slop tailor's for a ready-made dress-suit, been put straight on the stage and told to sing."

Many jazz historians have criticized Armstrong's greater determination to seek a mass audience from the early 1930s onward, but his popularity continued to mount in both the United States and Europe. Lip troubles compelled him to concentrate more on melody rather than duplicating earlier, extended improvisational offerings. He began to record with big band orchestras but also performed with smaller jazz units that backed singers like Bing Crosby and Ella Fitzgerald. His music could increasingly be heard on Hollywood films such as *Pennies from Heaven*, released in 1936. In the introduction to *Swing That Music*, Armstrong's 1936 autobiography, entertainer Rudy Vallee acknowledged, "that Armstrong's delightful, delicious sense of distortion of lyrics and melody has made its influence felt upon popular singers of our own day cannot be denied. Mr. Bing Crosby, the late Ross Columbo, Mildred Bailey, and many others, have adopted, probably unconsciously, the style of Louis Armstrong." His "swinging," Vallee insisted, "antedated them all." In 1937 Armstrong broke through racial barriers by hosting his own radio program on NBC. The next year Armstrong joined in Paul Whiteman's Eighth Experiment in Modern Music, presented at Carnegie Hall on Christmas night, offering a pair of songs. In 1938 Armstrong divorced Lil Hardin and married Alpha Smith, although that relationship soon withered too. Four years later he married his fourth wife, the dancer Lucille Wilson.

Meanwhile, Armstrong's reputation suffered for a time during the heyday of both big band swing and bebop jazz, the latter particularly making his music seem stale by comparison. Also young blacks seemed to take offense at what they considered to be the humiliating Tomming exhibited by Armstrong, Cab Calloway, Step'n Fetchit, and several other leading African American entertainers. For his part Armstrong considered "these young cats now . . . [are] full of malice," wanting only "to show you up." At the same time trumpeters Miles Davis and Dizzy Gillespie both recognized Armstrong's genius, with Davis acknowledging, "You can't play anything on the horn that Louis hasn't played—even modern." Armstrong's popularity began to rebound with word of his participation in the upcoming movie, *New Orleans*, filmed in the summer of 1946. He appeared alongside a small group at a Los Angeles club, Billy Berg's, in mid-August 1947, with Johnny Mercer, Benny Goodman, and Woody Herman among those in attendance. *Time* reported, "Louis Armstrong had forsaken the ways of Mammon and come back to jazz." His fans listened to "the old, pure, easy phrasing and big, clear, ranging tone that had made Louis King of Jazz." The sextet Louis Armstrong and His All-Stars began touring in 1947 and Satchmo was soon being referred to as the most famous entertainer in the world. *Time* placed Armstrong's face, with a crown, on its February 21, 1949, cover and ran a lengthy article, "Louis the First." The story indicated that many jazz aficionados considered Armstrong "the greatest musical genius the U.S. has ever produced."

Recording for Decca and Verve, he produced hits like "Blueberry Hill," "La Vie en Rose," and "Kiss of Fire." In the December 31, 1952, issue of *Down Beat*, readers proclaimed Armstrong "the most important musical figure of all time." Louis Armstrong and His All-Stars, in 1954, presented the brilliant jazz album, *Louis Armstrong Plays W.C. Handy*. In 1956 he appeared in the box office hit *High Society*, which starred Frank Sinatra, Bing Crosby, and Grace Kelly, and released *Ambassador Satch*, one of his most popular albums. Acting as a "goodwill ambassador," Armstrong toured the world on behalf of the U.S. State Department. In 1957 CBS broadcaster Edward R. Murrow presented a documentary, *Satchmo the Great*, which tracked the musician on a tour of Europe and Africa, followed by a performance in New York City with Leonard Bernstein. That same year Armstrong exclaimed, "The way they are treating my people in the South, the Government can go to hell," in the midst of the attempt by Arkansas Governor Orval Faubus to prevent the public high school in Little Rock from being integrated. Armstrong proceeded to cancel a scheduled State Department–sponsored tour of the Soviet Union. On a happier note, Decca put out the four-album set *Satchmo: A Musical Autobiography*, a collection of forty-two of his songs reworked by Armstrong and the All-Stars. On May 9, 1964, Armstrong's recording of "Hello, Dolly," knocked the Beatles from the top of the *Billboard* chart. Heart and lung ailments afflicted him, but his 1967 release, "What a Wonderful World," became a number one hit in Great Britain. Increasingly, Armstrong could be seen on television talk shows, including *The Tonight Show*, hosted by Johnny Carson.

Following Armstrong's death on July 6, 1971, 25,000 gathered in New York City to pay homage. Honorary pallbearers at his funeral in the Queens borough of New York City included Governor Nelson Rockefeller, Mayor John Lindsay, Bing Crosby, Count Basie, Ella Fitzgerald, Duke Ellington, Dizzy Gillespie, and Frank Sinatra. The Russian poet Yevgeny Yevtushenko wrote, "Give to Armstrong a trumpet / Angel Gabriel." Jazz great Dizzy Gillespie remarked, "Never before in the history of black music had one individual so completely dominated an art form as the Master, Daniel Louis Armstrong. His style was equally copied by saxophonists, trumpet players, pianists and all the instrumentalists who make up the jazz picture." *The Life Millennium: The 100 Most Important Events and People of the Past 1000 Years*, published in 1998, asserted, "Armstrong's improvisational verve and technical virtuosity defined Jazz . . . and his engaging personality and ever-present grin made him a natural as the international ambassador of Jazz, America's greatest gift to the world." In its December 27, 1999, issue, U.S. *News and World Report* declared, "If jazz was the American Century's soundtrack, then Armstrong was its ambassador, the living embodiment of the nation's living art form."

Conclusion

During the 1920s a baseball player and a musician reshaped American popular culture. Taking a mighty uppercut swing with his thirty-six-inch, forty-six-ounce bat, Babe Ruth altered the way the national pastime was played for the rest of the century. Through his free-flowing cornet and trumpet and scat singing, Louis Armstrong transformed jazz, America's most original contribution to music. The two became giants in their respective fields, towering over those who followed in their footsteps. Boasting larger-than-life personas, the two seemingly enjoyed life to the fullest, as they conquered their respective arenas and freely partook of the women, alcohol, or drugs that came their way. At the same time they established never quite duplicated standards of excellence, performing at the highest level for extended periods and displaying their particular gifts at storied events that became part of American lore.

Study Questions

1. Explain the unique skills Babe Ruth brought to the baseball diamond.
2. Indicate how Louis Armstrong helped to reshape American popular music.
3. Discuss controversies that swirled around Babe Ruth and Louis Armstrong.
4. Analyze how Babe Ruth and Louis Armstrong serve as representative models of the 1920s.
5. Explain the ways in which both Babe Ruth and Louis Armstrong became iconic figures over the course of their lifetimes.

Selected Bibliography

Armstrong, Louis. *Louis Armstrong in His Own Words: Selected Writings*, ed. Thomas Brothers. New York: Oxford University Press, 1999.

Armstrong, Robert, ed. *The Life Millennium: The 100 Most Important Events and People of the Past 1000 Years*. New York: Life Books, 1998.

Berrett, Joshua. *Louis Armstrong and Paul Whiteman: Two Kings of Jazz*. New Haven, CT: Yale University Press, 2004.

———, ed. *The Louis Armstrong Companion: Eight Decades of Commentary*. New York: Schirmer Books, 1999.

Collier, James Lincoln. *Louis Armstrong: An American Genius*. New York: Oxford University Press, 1983.

Cottrell, Robert C. *Blackball, the Black Sox and the Babe: Baseball's Crucial 1920 Season*. Jefferson, NC: McFarland, 2002.

Creamer, Robert W. *Babe: The Legend Comes to Life*. New York: Fireside, 1992.

Jasen, David A., and Gene Jones. *Black Bottom Stomp: Eight Masters of Ragtime and Early Jazz*. New York: Routledge, 2002.

Jones, Max, and John Chilton. *Louis: The Louis Armstrong Story*. Boston: Little, Brown, 1971.

Montville, Leigh. *The Big Bam: The Life and Times of Babe Ruth*. New York: Doubleday, 2006.

Panassie, Hugues. *Louis Armstrong*. New York: Charles Scribner's Sons, 1971.

Schuller, Gunther. *Early Jazz: Its Roots and Musical Development*. New York: Oxford University Press, 1986.

Wagenheim, Kal. *Babe Ruth: His Life and Legend*. New York: Henry Holt, 1992.

CHAPTER SIX

~

Defending Democracy in Hard Times

Fierce ideological battles characterized the interwar period. On the international front, communism and fascism appeared increasingly ascendant as old imperial orders tottered or collapsed and democratic states foundered. Even the world's greatest democracy appeared shakier than it had since the Civil War as the Great Depression engendered great misery and a loss of hope. Beginning in the 1930s Americans lined up in ideological camps with some gravitating to the far Left or the far Right. Ultimately the presidency of Franklin Delano Roosevelt once again legitimized the American experience and seemingly democracy itself. Roosevelt's New Deal programs revitalized America's economy and the spirit of its peoples despite displeasing some on both sides of the ideological spectrum. The success of the New Deal—more in instilling hope than in putting all of the country's unemployed back to work—prevented a possible turn in a more radical direction. Things may well have turned out differently. The nation could have slid down a path more akin to that adopted by right-wing states leading to considerable restrictions on personal freedoms and economic opportunities. Or it might have tilted in the direction of a Soviet America as preferred by homegrown comrades who envisioned a communist utopia. Instead the United States proceeded to experience sometimes halting, sometimes more successful moves toward rectifying economic ailments while sustaining democratic practices and principles.

Many individuals were instrumental in ensuring that this was so. No one, of course, was more important in that regard than the president himself. Franklin Delano Roosevelt was a genuine American aristocrat residing in a land that supposedly lacked aristocracy of any sort. He was educated in the best private

114

schools before becoming a young state legislator in New York, thanks in part to his family name, which tied him to the most popular political figure in the country, former president Teddy Roosevelt. The young Roosevelt took on the same government role that his distant cousin had: assistant secretary of the navy during wartime. He then ran as the Democratic Party vice presidential nominee on a ticket that got trounced in 1920, before suffering the crippling effects of polio that threatened to abruptly terminate his promising political career. Encouraged by his wife Eleanor, another distant cousin, Roosevelt made a political comeback and soon successfully ran for the governorship of New York. His reputation as a progressive governor during the early years of the Depression catapulted Roosevelt to the top of the list of potential Democratic Party presidential candidates in 1932. Herbert Hoover's disastrous handling of the American economy led to a sweeping victory by Roosevelt and liberal Democrats in the fall elections.

The Great Depression altered the American political arena even before the advent of FDR's presidency. Roosevelt himself was hardly the only progressive governor elected to office during the early stages of the economic calamity that befell the nation. The progressive Republican Philip La Follette was the son of the late great United States Senator Robert La Follette and the brother of Robert La Follette Jr., who replaced his namesake in Congress. Philip was initially elected governor of Wisconsin in 1930, two years after FDR won his first statewide office. That same campaign season witnessed the election of young Floyd Olson as governor of Minnesota on the Farmer-Labor Party ticket. Olson triumphed in subsequent reelection bids as he shifted further to the Left, supporting legislation to assist farmers and workers. At the same time Olson proved a strong champion of the New Deal and intended to run for the U.S. Senate in 1936. That bid ended as cancer took the life of the forty-four-year-old Olson in August 1936.

While Olson's career was tragically shortened, First Lady Eleanor Roosevelt proved to be a progressive stalwart throughout her husband's tenure and for nearly two decades thereafter. Not only had she convinced Franklin to return to the political arena after he was afflicted with polio but Eleanor proved to be one of his most important advisers during his twelve years as president of the United States. Hers was also one of the more liberal voices that he heard, although Eleanor's concerns for the disadvantaged and people of color sometimes appeared even greater than his own. Following his death, Eleanor remained determined to sustain the Roosevelt legacy by championing internationalism, economic justice, and human rights. In the process she became the grand dame of the Democratic Party, both greatly respected and somewhat feared by those hoping to pick up the mantle once held aloft by FDR.

～ FLOYD OLSON ～

During the summer of 1934, truck drivers tied to the International Brotherhood of Teamsters undertook a strike in Minneapolis. The Twin Cities, Minneapolis and St. Paul, continued to experience depressed economic circumstances with unemployment at a high level and wages reduced. Truck drivers in Minneapolis hoped to rely on Section 7a of the National Industrial Recovery Act, which authorized labor to engage in collective bargaining. On May 16, truck drivers began a strike, which employers sought to break through public ridicule and the employment of force. Serving as the mouthpiece of business operators, the Employers' Committee condemned those who "have seized the city and dictated how, where, and when we are to obtain the bare necessities of life." As the strike proved effective, violence broke out with policemen and armed guards

Elected governor of Minnesota in 1930, Floyd Olson was the first member of the Farmer-Labor Party to hold that office. Faced with a multitude of economic and social problems spawned by the Great Depression, Olson enacted reforms that prefigured parts of Franklin Delano Roosevelt's New Deal, including social security for the elderly, a minimum wage, equal pay for women, conservation programs, and collective bargaining for labor. His hopes to place utilities and many Minnesota industries under state control was blocked by conservative legislators, who denounced his plans as "socialism." (Courtesy of the Minnesota Historical Society and the St. Paul Daily News)

beating male and female picketers. Soon backed by hundreds of deputized members tied to the pro-employers' Citizens Alliance, the police again battled with strikers, many of whom now sported clubs. Governor Olson mobilized the state guard but declined to deploy them while striving to mediate the conflict. An initial agreement that allowed for union recognition, improved wages, and reduced hours began falling apart, leading to another call for a strike on July 16. Violence ensued once more, and on July 26, Olson proclaimed martial law and ordered the state guard into action. Olson's declaration removed from Minneapolis's streets all trucks other than those carrying milk, bread, fuel, and basic necessities. Conservative publications assailed Olson, claiming he was abetting lawlessness, while the Teamsters denounced the resort to martial law. As *Time* noted, the governor, "who loves to proclaim his radicalism, found that martial law was gaining him no kudos with Labor." He allowed the state guard to arrest strike leaders, who included Trotskyists, proponents of communism who followed the lead of former Red Army commander Leon Trotsky, not Russian dictator Joseph Stalin, and to conduct a raid on the headquarters of the Citizens Alliance. Then on August 21, the National Labor Relations Board helped bring about an agreement that called for the rehiring of strikers, improved wages, arbitration in cases of labor dispute, and an election that would usher in union recognition. Olson acquired greater stature due to his handling of the labor strife, while he helped to plant the seeds for national labor legislation supporting collective bargaining.

Floyd Bjørnstjerne Olson was born in Minneapolis, Minnesota, on November 13, 1891, the son of Paul and Ida Maria Nelson Olson, both Scandinavian immigrants. Neither his Norwegian father nor his Swedish mother was well educated, and the unambitious Paul proved content to work for the Northern Pacific railroad. Highly critical of her husband's seeming laziness and fondness for alcohol, Maria had greater hopes for her son and only child, who nevertheless sided with his father during familial disputes. Floyd compensated for the coldness of his own home by frequenting those of his Jewish neighbors, who welcomed his participation during Sabbath celebrations. As a young lad Floyd performed odd jobs, including selling candy at the downtown Metropolitan Opera House, religious volumes for the Vir Publishing Company in the southern portion of the state, and farm equipment in Canada. Following high school, Olson, to his mother's displeasure, toiled for the Northern Pacific before enrolling at the University of Minnesota in 1910. His lone year there proved troublesome, resulting in clashes with campus officials about his unwillingness to go along with military drills required of male students and his battles with upperclassmen over his determination to sport a large derby, an act that violated university traditions. Leaving school behind, he worked in both Alberta and Alaska before ending up in Seattle, where he operated as a longshoreman.

Witnessing the seamier side of life, the nineteen-year-old Olson became a member of the radical Industrial Workers of the World (IWW), which championed anarcho-syndicalism in envisioning One Big Union that would contest corporate capitalism.

Returning to Minneapolis in 1913, Olson began clerking in a law office and enrolled at Northwestern Law College, which offered classes in the evening. Graduating in 1915, Olson joined the law firm of Larrabee and Davies, quickly acquiring experience as a trial attorney. In New Prague, Minnesota, he married Ada Krejci, who expressed little interest in politics, which he proved determined to enter. Becoming a member of the National Guard, Olson suffered a hernia that precluded his active duty in the military when the United States entered World War I in April 1917. In between unsuccessful bids for the Democratic Party nomination for a congressional seat, Olson joined the Committee of 48 that sought in 1919, albeit unsuccessfully, to convince Senator Robert M. La Follette of Wisconsin to undertake a third-party bid for the presidency. That same year Olson received an appointment from Republican county commissioners as assistant county attorney in Hennepin. Overcoming the reputation for corruption that afflicted Minneapolis and despite charges that he was too lax in prosecuting lawbreakers, Olson twice won reelection as Hennepin County attorney. Helping his reputation was his readiness to go after the Ku Klux Klan and various shady business operators. In 1923 Olson also prosecuted the heads of the Minnesota Citizens Alliance, a right-to-work organization that apparently employed a mobster to murder a local union leader. The left-of-center Minnesota Farmer-Labor Party, which championed the cause of farmers and workers, nominated Olson for the governorship in 1924, but he lost to the Republican candidate, who garnered 48 percent of the vote to Olson's 43 percent, with the Democratic nominee receiving a mere 6 percent. Governor-elect Theodore Christianson accused Olson of favoring public ownership as a road to socialism. The renamed Farmer-Labor Association desired to renominate Olson four years later, but he declined the honor. That year saw Olson prosecute Minnesotan graft-taking aldermen and leading businessmen.

Having acquired a statewide reputation for honesty, integrity, and a Robin Hood–like determination to pursue justice against the well heeled, Olson undertook another gubernatorial campaign in 1930, during the early days of the Great Depression. Downplaying the Farmer-Labor Party's early radicalism, Olson deliberately avoided visionary nostrums, to the dismay of forces on the Left and ridicule from those on the Right. The tactic worked nevertheless, enabling Olson to capture 59 percent of the vote in a four-man race in which he took all but five of the eighty-seven counties across Minnesota. A cartoon appearing in the December 17, 1930, edition of the *Farmer Labor Leader* underscored Olson's dilemma: how to appeal to diverse constituencies, including farmers, laborers, educators, clergy, and his fellow lawyers, who were concerned about everything from special privileges doled out to corporations to mismanagement of higher education. Little helping matters were the continued Republican dominance of the state legislature and concerns that proposals for strong action would lead to accusations of dictatorial designs on Olson's part. Attempting to be conciliatory, Olson delivered his inaugural address, calling for greater state involvement regarding conservation, securities, an old age pension plan, a uniform primary ballot, prohibition of the use of injunctions to resolve labor conflicts, and mandated minimum working standards on state-financed projects. At the same time, he feared that premature support for more radical nostrums would both damage him politically and cripple the reform movement in the state. As it was, few of his initial proposals sailed through the state legislature while the economic situation sharply deteriorated. By the close of 1931 unemployment stood at 21.4 percent and farm prices plummeted. Olson became more attentive to the plight of farmers but the Farm Holiday program envisioned a strike in several states, including Minnesota. In late August 1932 Olson threw his support behind the Farm Holiday Association, which supported cooperative action, but he also condemned the violence that broke out between angry farmers and truck drivers in Iowa. At the end of September farmers in western Minnesota compelled truckers to halt their operations. The calling out of special deputies by a county sheriff and moves by the State Highway Patrol helped to break a farmer-orchestrated blockade and picketing. Urban radicalism also heightened during this period, with demands heard for government to accept greater responsibility for the plight of the dispossessed and unfortunate.

Speaking to the League of Minnesota Municipalities in Red Wing earlier that summer, Olson foreshadowed the growing sensibility that government had a larger role to play in economic and social affairs. He asserted, "The old pioneer idea of government confined to police power has passed off the stage. We have now reached the socialized state." This was a simple fact and a matter "of practice and expediency" rather than theory, Olson continued. "The present economic system has shown its inability to provide employment and even food or shelter for millions of Americans." In fact, he insisted, "only government can cope with the situation." That fall Olson condemned capitalism as "steeped in the most dismal stupidity." Once again Olson swept to victory, winning a majority of votes in a three-person race with both nominees from the two major political parties. Still he again confronted a state legislature hardly amenable to the general platform of the Farmer-Labor party, let alone its more radical proposals. Nevertheless Olson's enhanced popularity and greater confidence resulted in his adoption of a role as "tribune of the people," his biographer, George H. Mayer, indicates.

During his second inaugural address, delivered in early January 1933, Olson demonstrated his readiness to tack Left. Referring to the dire distress experienced by many, he prophesied "rampant lawlessness and possible revolution" could ensue unless the state responded forcefully. He again proposed measures to alleviate the plight of farmers, called for unemployment insurance funded by employers, insisted the government should provide necessary relief, and urged that labor injunctions be prohibited. He also declared the need to increase taxes on corporations and to expand public ownership, including in the area of power resources. Looming over public officials in Minnesota was the recognition that the Farm Holiday Association had adopted more extralegal tactics, including showing up at public disclosures with shotguns in hand to coerce the return of property to indebted farmers. A. C. Townley, who had earlier helped to found the Nonpartisan League in North Dakota, called for a march of farmers to the state capitol to insist on debt repudiation. The Farm Holiday Association's John Bosch also appeared sympathetic to insurrectionary action. Responding to the brewing crisis, Olson on February 23 ordered a halt to mortgage sales, effective through April, in order to prevent "riots and insurrection." Determined to maintain "law and order in the state," he pledged to turn to the militia if necessary. The governor also indicated that he was tendering a final appeal to the state legislature. "If the Senate does not make provision for the sufferers in the State and the Federal Government refuses to aid, I shall invoke the powers I hold and shall declare martial law." He further warned, "A lot of people who are now fighting [relief] measures because they happen to possess considerable wealth will be brought in by provost guard and be obliged to give up more than they would now." He continued, "There is not going to be misery in this State if I can humanly prevent it." Olson asserted, "Unless the Federal and State governments act to insure against recurrence of the present situation, I hope the present system of government goes right down to hell."

Olson soon signed into law legislation designed to strengthen the tottering banking system in Minnesota. To his dismay, however, state legislators refused to support unemployment insurance, leading the governor to express his hope that the present system of local government would go "right down to hell" if aid for the unemployed were not forthcoming. Only partially more successful was Olson's attempt to shepherd legislation expanding municipal ownership of power plants. The legislature did back various labor laws, including those restricting the hours women could work in industrial jobs and precluding resort to injunctions to terminate labor conflicts. Equally pleasing was the decision to establish a series of state forests. Despite the mixed statutory accomplishments, one newspaper proclaimed Olson "the idol of the hour. He can do no wrong."

His strenuous endeavors to enact a progressive program for Minnesota proved taxing for Olson, who suffered from stomach ulcers, an inflamed appendix, and other physical ailments. No matter, by 1933 he had become something of a national figure. His general support for Franklin Delano Roosevelt's New Deal program hardly hurt Olson in that regard. At the same time he wished New Dealers would go further, stating on August 4, 1933, "I do not believe there can be any economic security for the common man and woman in this country until and unless the key industries of the United States are taken over by the government." Olson joined with a band of governors from the Midwest to petition Roosevelt to support the same kind of price fixing to stabilize agricultural prices that the new administration had for industry. A gradual rise in the prices for farm products served to diminish another call by the Farm Holiday Association for a strike by farmers. In late December 1933 Olson referred to "a dying social, economic order which brought about this catastrophe in American life, which we call a depression." That same season witnessed the state legislature pass, at long last, the relief program Olson had called for, which certainly heightened his appeal among Minnesota residents.

Olson's political standing became more precarious by the spring of 1934, however. On March 27, 1934, he proclaimed in a public address that the Farmer-Labor Party sought "a cooperative commonwealth wherein the government will stifle as much as possible the greed and avarice of the private profit system and will bring more equitable distribution of the wealth produced by the hands and minds of the people." Speaking extemporaneously, Olson now acknowledged, "I am frank to say what I want to be. I am a radical," which resulted in thunderous applause. The Farmer-Labor Party's platform for 1934 seemed to echo Olson, affirming, "only a complete reorganization of the social structure into a cooperative commonwealth will bring economic security and prevent a prolonged period of further suffering." Additionally it called for public ownership of mines, public utilities, transportation, banks, and factories. As a firestorm of criticism built, Olson stated, "I interpret the public ownership plank as approving federal and state ownership of public utilities and key industries" only. Later the governor insisted that his party desired "a cooperative commonwealth in which enterprises will be carried out cooperatively by organizations of producers and consumers." This amounted to support for "private business," he insisted, but "business carried on for mutual aid and not avaricious profit." The Farmer-Labor Party subsequently amended its platform, affirming its opposition to state control of small businesses.

With the Teamster strike of the summer of 1934 resolved, Olson headed into that year's gubernatorial campaign. Backing off from the spring platform of the Farmer-Labor Party, he insisted,

The Communists believe in the abolition of private property. We believe in its creation. The Communists would confiscate whatever little private wealth the ordinary man has. We would give him an opportunity to earn more. The Communists believe the individual is created for the service and benefit of the state. We believe that the state is created for the service and benefit of the individual. The Communists would abolish Christian morality. We would give Christian morality the first real test in commercial relations it ever had. The Communists would reduce all people to a dead level. We would uplift all people to a happier life.

He also likened the Farmer-Labor Party to the New Deal administration of Franklin Delano Roosevelt in its support of public ownership of utilities and government operation of dormant factories. Presenting himself as the candidate of the common man, Olson insisted, "There is a real issue in this campaign, a very vital issue, and it is not communism . . . nor the Third Internationale . . . nor Russia." Rather it was the following: "Shall our social and economic order be changed and so modified as to bring a more equitable distribution of wealth and a decent standard of living?" Although winning by a far smaller plurality than he had in the previous two campaigns, Olson captured a third term as governor of Minnesota because urban areas had shifted leftward and due, in his biographer's estimation, to "his tremendous personal prestige." Olson's own political orientation remained vague and he denied having even read Karl Marx's work. He expressed no interest "in names," declaring, "Results count."

As his third term began, Governor Olson confronted a hostile state legislature and continuing severe economic conditions that produced protests by farmers and condemnations of capitalism by those professing to speak for the unemployed. During the summer of 1935, Minnesota again confronted industrial conflict, with picketers fighting with so-called scabs and hard-line employers unwilling to readily accept labor unions. While that strife would abate, Olson was criticized by a federal district court that claimed "the menace to the liberty and property" of a plant operator arose "from the uncertainty that those who owe the duty of giving . . . protection will perform that duty." Meanwhile, talk surfaced about a possible presidential run by Olson on a third-party ticket. The *Minnesota Leader* offered that Olson's frequent criticisms of Roosevelt's administration should be placed into context. "Constructive criticism," the paper noted, was welcomed by the president. Additionally, the New Deal, through its Social Security program, determined to make the American tax system more progressive, and antipathy "to corporate greed" was more akin to the Farmer-Labor Party than were "Minnesota reactionaries." In November Olson predicted Roosevelt's reelection and the *Minneapolis Journal* suggested that the governor was looking ahead to the 1940 national election. Olson, the *Journal* declared, "would not sacrifice himself as leader of an abortive 1936 national drive against the devils of capitalism." Instead "the governor is evidently waiting for President Roosevelt to play out the role of Kerensky before he takes the part of Lenin in the new American revolution," referring to the leaders who held power after the first and second Russian revolutions in 1917 that culminated in the Bolsheviks' takeover.

In the meantime Olson continued with his current political plans: to run for the U.S. Senate in 1936. The likelihood of another political triumph for Olson seemingly improved when the little-liked blind incumbent and embittered foe of Roosevelt's New Deal, Minnesota Senator Tom Schall, suffered fatal injuries when hit by a car on December 22, 1935, as he attempted to cross a street in the nation's capital. Schall had helped trigger a vicious journalistic assault from Walter Liggett of the Rochester *Midwest American* that attempted to link the Olson administration and organized crime. Liggett drew up a list of a dozen reasons why Olson should be impeached, including a claim that the governor was, he insisted, controlled by banking interests and in league with mobsters who headed Minnesota's mob and liquor operations during Prohibition. Then on December 9, 1935, Liggett was gunned down, apparently by gangsters, in the presence of his wife and young daughter. Mrs. Edith Liggett charged, "Governor Olson's gang got Walter," and she said, "The murder would not have been committed without Governor Olson's permission." Few gave credence to such sensationalistic charges. Now Olson felt compelled to appoint his fellow Farmer-Labor politician and state commissioner of banks, Elmer A. Benson, to complete Schall's term.

Interest in the appointment quickly waned, however, when an announcement was made on December 31 that Olson, who had lost nearly forty pounds between August and November, was at the famed Mayo Clinic in Rochester, Minnesota, where he had undergone an "exploratory" operation. Rumors floated that Olson had stomach cancer and a reporter for *Fortune* indicated that the governor would "never run for anything again." It would later be revealed that Olson did indeed have pancreatic cancer and was projected to have no more than eight months left. His physicians evidently chose not to inform Olson of the severity of his illness, and he consequently determined to enter the race for the U.S. Senate in early February. He also remained adverse to the idea of running against Roosevelt on a third-party ticket, which, he worried, might result in Roosevelt's losing to "a fascist Republican." One group of disgruntled mavericks opted to form the Union Party, which placed William Lemke, a progressive Republican congressman from North Dakota, on the ballot alongside Roosevelt, Republican governor Alfred Landon of Kansas, and other minor candidates. Father Charles Coughlin, the famed "radio priest," was selected as Lemke's running mate.

Refusing to complain and continuing to lose weight, dropping to 135 pounds by mid-April, Olson remained hopeful enough to file as a candidate for the U.S. Senate. By the end of May cancer had spread to his esophagus, making it difficult to swallow. He was back at the Mayo Clinic for another operation on July 9, then returned to the clinic the following month, where he drafted a series of telegrams. The first went to Wisconsin Senator Robert M. La Follette Jr., stating, "In this campaign we must choose between President Roosevelt or Governor Landon. . . . For the liberals to split their votes is merely to play into the hands of the Wall Street gang." Olson expressed his "utmost respect" for Lemke and Coughlin, but insisted that the defeat of the Republican candidate was "of the utmost importance to the great masses of America." The next telegram went to President Roosevelt, who hoped to visit Olson at the end of the month. At 8:29 on the evening of August 22, Olson, only forty-four years old, died. Thousands paid their respects at the state capitol or the Minneapolis civic auditorium, where Wisconsin Governor Philip La Follette delivered the funeral oration. President Roosevelt paid tribute too: "The nation has lost a personality of singular force and courage. . . . Year by year since he assumed the Governorship of a great commonwealth he had become a more massive figure in our national life."

⌣ ELEANOR ROOSEVELT ⌣

By the spring of 1939 Eleanor Roosevelt, the wife of President Franklin Delano Roosevelt, was considered worthy of a cover story for *Time* magazine titled "Oracle." Having returned from a lecture tour across America, she was quoted as stating, "There are still people who think that we can cut ourselves off from the rest of the world, but more people are less secure in this belief." *Time* referred to the first lady as "Eleanor Everywhere," "the world's foremost female political force," who was "a woman of unequaled influence in the world." In contrast to Cleopatra, Queen Elizabeth, or Catherine the Great of Russia, Eleanor's "power is not that of a ruler." Rather "she is the wife of a ruler but her power comes from her influence not on him but on public opinion." Over the course of six years, Eleanor's image had transformed from a target of derision into "the prodigious niece of prodigious, ubiquitous, omnivorous Roosevelt I." *Time* continued, "Everything she says, everything she does, is genuinely and transparently motivated." Her writings reached a respectful and expanded audience, with her "My Day" column then appearing in almost seventy newspapers with a circulation of nearly five million. "My Day" increasingly dealt with controversial subjects such as her call for the release of labor leader Tom Mooney, jailed for the past twenty-three years after having been convicted of a bombing in San Francisco that resulted in the deaths of ten people; African American singer Marian Anderson's battle with the Daughters of the American Revolution (DAR); Adolf Hitler; Joseph Goebbels; and Francisco Franco. Her column

Eleanor Roosevelt with Marian Anderson, classical vocalist. In 1939, when Anderson was denied use of the hall owned by the Daughters of the American Revolution, the first lady arranged for a concert on the steps of the Lincoln Memorial. A champion of minority rights, Roosevelt boldly embraced civil rights in a way that the president, who needed the support of segregationist Southern Democrats, could not. (Library of Congress, LC-USZ62-116730. The authors wish to thank the National Association for the Advancement of Colored People for authorizing the use of the image of Mrs. Franklin D. Roosevelt presenting the Spingarn medal to Marian Anderson.)

warned that the "moral rearmament" favored by the antiwar Oxford Movement would not suffice against aggressor states. She indicated instead "that, much as we may dislike to do it, it may be necessary to use the forces of this world in the hope of keeping civilization going until spiritual forces gain sufficient strength everywhere to make an acceptance of disarmament possible." She opposed Indiana representative Ludlow's demand for a war referendum, asking, "I wonder whether we have decided to hide behind neutrality? It is safe, perhaps, but I am not sure that it is always right to be safe." Responding to a query, she answered, "The greatest danger to democracy seems to me to be apathy, a lack of personal responsibility and ability to look courageously at the world." Kathleen McLaughlin of the *New York Times* suggested that "after her hundreds of thousands of miles of industrious travel and sightseeing and myriads of questions and explanations, the probability exists that she is, except for the President, the best informed individual on the American scene."

Anna Eleanor Roosevelt was born on October 11, 1884, in New York City, to the beautiful Anna Hall and Elliott Roosevelt, brother of recently defeated mayoral candidate Theodore Roosevelt. Following their mother's death from diphtheria in 1892 and Elliott's incarceration in a mental asylum, Eleanor and her two younger brothers, Elliott Jr. and Hall, went to reside with their Grandmother Hall in Tivoli, New York, and in a brownstone in New York City. Two years later, Elliott, who had another child, Elliott Roosevelt Mann, the product of an affair with a young servant of Anna's, also died, his health wracked by alcoholism. Brought up in a family that was part of the New York social elite, the tall, elegantly attired Eleanor, who clearly lacked her mother's beauty, was afflicted with self-doubts. At the age of fifteen, she enrolled in the exclusive Allenswood Academy, a finishing school in England, whose headmistress, Marie Souvestre, was a well-known feminist educator. Eleanor thrived there, acquiring the self-confidence she had previously lacked. She received word in 1901 that her uncle Theodore Roosevelt had become president of the United States following the assassination of William McKinley. Eleanor returned to the States the following year and was officially introduced to New York society at the famed Waldorf-Astoria Hotel in Manhattan. In the fashion of well-bred, educated women of her generation, she participated in the social work movement. In 1903, as a member of the Junior League of New York, she offered calisthenics and dancing classes to immigrants at the Rivington Street Settlement House. She also joined the New York Consumers' League, which conducted investigations of the conditions under which women and children worked.

That same year Eleanor became engaged to her distant cousin, the handsome and dapper Franklin Delano Roosevelt, who was then an undergraduate at Harvard, where he edited the *Harvard Crimson*, and the two were married on March 17, 1905, with President Roosevelt giving away the bride, followed by a summer of honeymooning in Europe. Within the span of five years, she had four children, one of whom soon died of influenza. She would later give birth to two more children. The Roosevelts resided in a house on East Sixty-fifth Street in New York City located next to one owned by Sara Delano Roosevelt, in another house on the sprawling family estate astride the Hudson River in Hyde Park, New York, and at a cottage on Campobello Island in New Brunswick, Canada. Eleanor performed charity work; was tutored in French, German, and Italian; read widely; and attended classes on subjects ranging from art to the Bible held in the homes of friends. At the same time she was hardly content with her domestic duties and often brooded, feeling somewhat depressed. Eleanor later acknowledged, "For ten years, I was always just getting over having a baby or about to have another one, so my occupations were considerably restricted."

After Franklin attended Columbia Law School, he briefly practiced law before being elected to the New York State Senate as a Democrat, eschewing the Republican Party of his cousin Teddy. As Franklin's political career began, Eleanor, no matter how supportive, realized, "I had to stand on my feet now and I wanted to be independent. I was beginning to realize that something within me craved to be an individual." President Woodrow Wilson named Franklin assistant secretary of the navy in 1913, a post previously held by Teddy. With Franklin forced to attend to his government responsibilities, Eleanor attained "considerable independence" managing the family's trips from the nation's capital to the Roosevelt family estate in Hyde Park and to Eleanor and Franklin's home in Campobello. When the United States entered World War I in the spring of 1917, Eleanor supported the war effort, joining the Red Cross canteen, helping organize the Navy Red Cross, and serving on the Navy League's Comforts Committee, which provided apparel for thousands of American soldiers. She also hosted a number of foreign dignitaries but turned down an opportunity to travel abroad with the Red Cross, believing she could not leave her children behind. Eleanor had supported Franklin's move into politics, while enduring a difficult relationship with Franklin's overbearing mother, Sara. Eleanor also experienced heartbreak on learning of Franklin's affair with her social secretary, Lucy Mercer, in 1918, which almost led to the breakup of the Roosevelts' marriage. Franklin promised to end his relationship with Mercer but failed to do so.

Eleanor became involved with a number of reform activities back home, supporting campaigns to abolish child labor and provide protective legislation for workers. She spent a good deal of time at St. Elizabeth's Hospital in Washington, DC, visiting wounded soldiers. She also drew closer to a group of strong-willed women such as Marion Dickerman, Nancy Cook, and Frances Perkins, who were involved in reform efforts. Eleanor joined the League of Women Voters, which sought to educate women about their recently won right to vote and supported progressive legislation. Once more with his wife's support, Franklin served as Ohio governor James M. Cox's running mate during the 1920 presidential campaign, but the Democrats suffered a resounding defeat at the hands of their Republican foes, Warren G. Harding and Calvin Coolidge. Hardly thrilled by the experience, Eleanor was at best resigned, acknowledging that public service was Franklin's "great interest."

Then in 1921, Franklin, who had resumed the practice of law, suffered an apparently fatal blow to his political aspirations when he contracted polio, which left him partially paralyzed. Eleanor strove diligently to foster Franklin's recovery, amid the confusion their father's illness caused the Roosevelt children and with Sara hovering over the family. Encouraged by Franklin's adviser Louis Howe, Eleanor ensured that the Roosevelt name remained visible and that political contacts were made. In the process, she maintained her own political involvement, joining the Women's Trade Union League and supporting a reduced work week for women, improved relations between blacks and whites, and her country's joining the World Court. It was Eleanor who helped to convince her husband to return to the political fray, leading to his appearance at the 1924 Democratic National Convention, where he nominated New York governor Alfred E. Smith, whom he referred to as the "happy warrior," for the presidency. Now more of a political activist herself, Eleanor became a member of the Women's Division of the Democratic State Committee. She expressed her own political philosophy, writing, "The Democrats today trust in the people, the plain, ordinary, every-day citizen, neither superlatively rich nor distressingly poor, not one of the 'best minds' but the average mind." Along with her friends Marion Dickerman and Nancy Cook, she purchased the Todhunter School in New York City, a private school for wealthy girls that offered progressive education, where she taught American history, drama, English, and American literature. The three women also began running a small factory along a brook called Val-Kill, located on a 180-acre tract that had been part of the Roosevelt family estate, designed to produce faithful reproductions of old American furniture.

In 1928, Eleanor, who edited the *Women's Democratic News*, served as codirector of the Women's Division of national political operations for Smith, who had won the Democratic Party presidential nomination denied him four years earlier. She worked at the national party headquarters in New York City and delivered campaign speeches. Beseeched by party leaders, Franklin ran to replace Smith as governor of New York. He won resoundingly and the Roosevelts moved into the governor's mansion in Albany. Eleanor still taught classes two and a half days each week at Todhunter, admitting, "I teach because I love it. I cannot give it up." She maintained her position of prominence within the women's branch of the Democratic Party, albeit in a less overt fashion, and hosted a public celebration for the twenty-fifth anniversary of the Women's Trade Union League. With the Great Depression sweeping over the American landscape, Franklin initiated his bid for the Democratic Party presidential nomination in 1932. Eleanor appeared withdrawn at times, confiding, "From the personal standpoint, I did not want my husband to be president," but she never informed him of that fact. She recognized that "this meant the end of any personal life of my own." Notwithstanding her own reservations, Eleanor, during FDR's lengthy tenure in the Oval Office, helped to transform expectations regarding the first lady. She wrote in her autobiography, "I knew what traditionally should lie before me; I had watched Mrs. Theodore Roosevelt and had seen what it meant to be the wife of a president, and I cannot say that I was pleased with the prospect." One important early step Eleanor undertook was to hold press conferences that only female reporters could attend. She later admitted, "It was new and untried ground and I was feeling my way with some trepidation." She strove to maintain privacy at the same time, declining Secret Service accompaniment, telling her husband, "Nobody's going to . . . shoot me. I'm not that important." Eleanor also took train coaches, refusing private compartments, and walked to the White House from her hotel room, rather than ride in a limousine. She drove herself, protected by a revolver that Louis Howe insisted she carry, though she left it unloaded. At the White House, she had swings, slides, and a sandbox brought in for her grandchildren. Eleanor also ushered in more democratic practices at the executive mansion, running the elevator herself when she used it, replacing various white staff members with African American servants, and instituting an eight-hour workday.

All the while Eleanor served as her husband's emissary as she traveled widely around the country and outside the United States as well. She did so believing that his entire political career was focused on a determination "to help make life better for the average man, woman and child." She also appreciated his desire "to enlighten and lead the people," his confidence that problems could be solved, and his courage. Eleanor undertook numerous trips into economically distressed mining areas such as Logan County, West Virginia, where she encountered families residing in tents after employers evicted them from company houses following a strike. The tents were worn, illness abounded, and medical care proved nonexistent. Eleanor helped to set up a clinic for the children and Franklin promised to get the families out of the tents by early winter. Both Roosevelts backed the establishment of cooperative, subsistence homestead projects, designed to provide housing for the downtrodden, that were denounced by congressmen. Continuing her travels across the United States, Eleanor witnessed the results of public works projects, including reforestation and the building of recreation sites, bridges, schools, hospitals, and sanitation projects. She considered "such experiments" as the Tennessee Valley Authority to be "a mighty bulwark against attacks on our democracy." Five subsistence homestead communities appeared, including Eleanor's favorite, Arthurdale, located near Reedsville, West Virginia. Particularly concerned about the plight of women, she advocated the creation of camps for women like the ones the New Dealers set up under the Civilian Conservation Corps that targeted young men from eighteen to twenty-five years of age, even organizing a White House Conference on Camps for Unemployed Women. In 1933 she published her first book, It's Up to the Women, which underscored women's particular responsibilities during times of economic distress. While encouraging women to become involved in political affairs, she asserted, "Women are different from men, their physical functions are different, and the future of the race depends upon their ability to produce healthy children."

Eleanor asked young readers of her columns and editorials to write to her, expressing their interests and concerns. Considered accessible, she was on the receiving end of over 300,000 letters by year's close. In the spring of 1934 Eleanor visited dilapidated rural homes and urban slum areas in Puerto Rico and troubled areas in the Virgin Islands too. Like Jacqueline Kennedy and Lady Bird Johnson decades later, Eleanor encouraged government interest in different kinds of artistic expression. She insisted that slum areas in Washington, DC, housing African Americans be improved. Congress authorized the Alley Housing Bill in June 1934, with funding allocated to the Public Works Administration, headed by Secretary of the Interior Harold Ickes. The cabinet secretary named Eleanor an advisor on alley housing. In other ways too she supported a more progressive attitude regarding race than did her husband. In early 1934 she invited the head of the National Association for the Advancement of Colored People, Walter White, and other African American leaders to the White House. No administration since that of Theodore Roosevelt had welcomed a black luminary in such fashion. She strove to ensure that blacks participated in federal programs and helped ensure the addition of Mary McLeod Bethune to the staff of the National Youth Administration. Eleanor backed the call for a federal antilynching act, which the president, fearing a Southern white backlash, refused to do. In a speech delivered to the National Urban League on the organization's twenty-fifth anniversary in January 1936, she acknowledged "many grave injustices" meted out to black American citizens. Marveling at the patience displayed by so many, she also declared, "The Negro race as a whole must improve its standards of living, and become both economically and intellectually of higher caliber." Later in the decade she invited the black American contralto Marian Anderson, denied permission by the DAR to perform at Constitution Hall in Washington, DC, to sing at the White House. In protest of the DAR's denial, Eleanor resigned from the organization. Nevertheless, in the fashion of FDR, Eleanor failed to overtly contest Jim Crow practices, other than in selected instances. She could also parrot her era's racial insensitivities in the manner of one of her columns that repeated stereotypical black dialect. Still she publicly questioned how free people were if they were unable to vote, uncertain of receiving the same justice as a neighbor did, toiled "on a lower level" for lesser wages, or were "barred from certain places and from certain opportunities." She also pointed to the worker who lost a company house and employment because he belonged to a union.

One venue that enabled Eleanor to support both her husband's programs and progressive developments generally was "My Day," a syndicated newspaper column she first delivered on December 30, 1935. For the next twenty-six years, she produced that 500-word column, which appeared six days a week, garnering considerable criticism and applause too. The subjects of her columns were diverse, with many containing insightful comments on serious domestic or international issues. She also delivered paid public lectures, offered weekly radio broadcasts—for which she received $500 a minute—and undertook frequent travels around the nation. "My Day" championed FDR's reelection bid in 1936 with tales like the one involving a waiter in Detroit who informed her, "I'm for Mr. R. He saved my home and my family." Her initial autobiographical book, *This Is My Story*, appeared in 1937, was serialized in *Ladies' Home Journal*, and helped her income reach $75,000, the bulk of which was donated to charity. All the while she reinforced the notion that the Roosevelt administration cared about the American people, particularly perhaps the downtrodden and dispossessed. Throughout FDR's first two presidential terms, Eleanor stood as the administration's most stalwart champion of social welfare programs. Speaking to reporters in early 1935, she envisioned greater economic security that would "include old age pensions, a permanent ban on child labor, better unemployment insurance, better health care for the country as a whole, better care for mothers and children generally." That same year witnessed passage of the Social Security Act, which incorporated many of her suggestions, although not universal medical coverage, to her disappointment. Eleanor proved instrumental in convincing FDR to support the establishment of the National Youth Administration, which was part of the Works Progress Administration, and sought to assist students to remain in school, provided part-time jobs for high school and college students, and offered job training and work programs for those who had dropped out of school. She also helped to bring about the establishment of the WPA's Federal Theatre Project, which supported experimental, ethnic, and children's theater. Following FDR's second inaugural in 1937, *Literary Digest* wrote, "Alive, curious, seeking, actively humanitarian, pitying, sincere— Eleanor Roosevelt perfectly supplements the character of the man who is her husband." Moreover, "it is possible to say sincerely that without her, he might never have been president."

Critics castigated both Eleanor and Franklin while accusing them of being "communists" or, in the president's case, "a traitor to his class." As she followed the student peace movement that emerged on American university campuses in the mid-1930s, Eleanor expressed appreciation that young people were desirous of eradicating war. At the same time, she considered them "very indefinite as to the way in which it shall be done." She wondered if young Americans, such as those in the Left-dominated American Youth Congress, understood "that every new form of government, fascism, communism or our own democracy" initially sought to produce "a world in which people could be happy and content." She considered democracy's greatest strength to be that it "allowed people to shape their own government," in contrast to the authoritarianism spawned by fascism and communism. She hoped young people would come to appreciate that "their future success [lay] in controlling democracy." Moreover, "only if democracy makes individuals better able to attain their ideals will it survive the test of today." Eleanor grew close to many of the youth leaders, including Joseph Lash, one of the American Youth Congress figures who flirted with communism for a spell.

More than many of her countrymen who remained determinedly isolationist, Eleanor appeared prepared for the outbreak of World War II. She had joined in women's peace activities back in the 1920s, including the Women's International League for Peace and Freedom and the National Conference on the Cause and Cure of War. She supported the League of Nations, which the United States declined to join, and the World Court. In a small book, *This Troubled World*, published in 1938, she pointed to the need for a strengthened American military. She also became a committed antifascist, opposing the neutral stance her husband adopted regarding the Spanish Civil War, in which General Francisco Franco's Nationalist forces fought against the Loyalists who supported the Spanish Republic. Perhaps influenced by the State Department, Eleanor failed to speak out on German anti-Semitism. Behind the scenes she did contest discriminatory policies that impacted American Jews. She also began championing the cause of refugees following Kristallnacht, or "Night of Broken Glass," on November 10, 1938, when Jews across Germany were attacked. Shortly after the beginning of World War II the following September, Eleanor referred to the "horrors" meted out to Jews, Catholics, and some liberal German Protestants by Hitler "and his storm troopers." Eleanor revealed that she had encountered a number of concentration camp internees who had entered the United States. Somewhat inexplicably, she acknowledged, "there may be a need for curtailing the ascendancy of the Jewish people," while hoping "it might be done in a more humane way by a ruler who had intelligence and decency." She also expressed a hope that America could remain at peace but insisted, "no country can exist free and unoppressed while a man like Hitler remains in power." When Soviet forces attacked Helsinki, she bemoaned the fact that "little countries" now appeared to "have no rights."

In her next book, *The Moral Basis of War*, which came out in 1940, Eleanor contended that Americans were already involved "in a war—an economic war and a war of philosophies." They opposed "a force, which, under the rule of one man, completely organize[d] all business and all individuals," spent whatever he desired to on armaments, and compelled his people to obtain "the wages *he* decrees," to "work the hours *he* decrees." A similar effort seemed to be taking place in Japan. The North American continent, Eleanor warned, must become aware of what would occur should such ideas prevail. "Our Democracies must realize that from the point of view of the individual and his liberty, there is no hope in the future if the totalitarian philosophy becomes dominant in the world."

The democracies, including the United States, needed to be strengthened, with "a minimum standard of security" provided to ensure that each child reached equality of opportunity. Racial relations at home, Eleanor continued to recognize, had to improve. She wrote that it was impossible to honestly claim that American blacks were free. "We have poverty which enslaves and racial prejudice which does the same." Social justice was demanded to ensure "winning the peace." When A. Philip Randolph threatened to lead a march on Washington protesting race relations, Franklin asked his wife to speak with the black civil rights activist, who asked for "an executive order banning discrimination in the defense industry." After the president issued such a directive, Executive Order 8802, Randolph thanked Eleanor for her support. She later acknowledged "what a lot we must do to make our war a real victory for democracy," admitting that discrimination in the American military "makes you weep & yet I imagine all of it is true."

Following the Japanese attack on Pearl Harbor on December 7, 1941, Eleanor's column "My Day" indicated that American lives had been lost because of "an enemy, who attacked in the usual ruthless way which Hitler has prepared us to suspect." Displaying the same confidence associated with FDR, she prophesied that no one in the United States "will doubt the ultimate outcome." On January 1, 1942, she offered, "The English-speaking peoples will, probably, when peace first comes to this earth, have to bear a heavy burden." Together with "liberated people" across the globe, they would devise a program that conveyed "the hopes now hidden in the hearts of people throughout the world." In the fall of 1942 Franklin asked the restless Eleanor, who had hoped to represent the Red Cross in Europe, to go to Great Britain to ascertain what role British women were performing in the war and to visit American soldiers stationed there. She visited with King George VI and his wife, the former Elizabeth Bowes-Lynn, began a genuine friendship with U.S. Ambassador Gil Winant, and spent time with Prime Minister Winston Churchill. During the summer of 1943 Eleanor undertook a goodwill trip extending 23,000 miles to the South Pacific, going to Australia, New Zealand, Fiji, Guadalcanal, and a host of other islands. Admiral William J. Halsey Jr., who commanded American operations in the Pacific, initially resented Eleanor's visit but came to praise her highly. "I marveled at her hardihood, both physical and mental," he later wrote. "She walked for miles, and she saw patients who were grievously and gruesomely wounded. But I marveled most at their expressions as she leaned over them." Halsey declared, "She alone accomplished more good than any other person, or any other group of civilians, who passed through my area." During the spring of 1944, she conducted another goodwill tour at the behest of her husband, this time of American bases in the Caribbean and Latin America. In a "My Day" column dated December 28, 1944, Eleanor asserted, "This is total war, and we fight in spirit with our men overseas."

Throughout FDR's third term, Eleanor remained a stalwart liberal voice within administration ranks. At the same time she both justified and criticized—largely behind the scenes—the internment of Japanese Americans and Japanese aliens, the most egregious violation of civil rights undertaken by her husband's administration. On a more progressive note she supported unionization of farm workers, national health insurance, and the setting up of a Peace Production Board to ease the economic transition to peacetime, and opposed dropping Vice President Henry Wallace from the presidential ticket in 1944. She received with dismay revelations about the Holocaust and compared wartime American race riots with Nazism. Eleanor wrote that the treatment afforded Polish Jews "makes one ashamed that a civilized race anywhere in the world could treat other human beings in such a manner." In the pages of *Negro Digest*, she admitted, "If I were a Negro today, I think I would have moments of great bitterness. It would be hard for me to sustain my faith in democracy and to build up a sense of goodwill toward men of other races." She also underscored the fact that "even women of the white race still suffer[ed] inequalities and injustices," while many white Americans were "slaves of economic conditions." After traveling across the United States during the 1944 presidential campaign, she urged the planning of new housing for the postwar period. She also supported the idea of a year of national service for young people, both boys and girls, to help engender "passionate patriotism." "My Day" backed a proposed fair employment practices bill, writing, "If we do not see that equal opportunity, equal justice and equal treatment are meted out to every citizen, the very basis on which this country can hope to survive with liberty and justice for all will be wiped away."

On April 12, 1945, President Roosevelt died from a massive cerebral hemorrhage. Eleanor reportedly remarked, "I am more sorry for the people of the country and the world than I am for myself." In her first column following her husband's death, she asserted that during his tenure in Albany and his first years in Washington, DC, "his chief interest was in seeing that the average human being was given a fairer chance for 'life, liberty and the pursuit of happiness.'" As war threatened he became more involved with international affairs, while hoping for an organization that "might be built to prevent future wars," which he referred to as the United Nations. Departing from the White House, she resided in her cottage at Val-Kill on a now nearly 1,000-acre plot of land, retained her apartment on Washington Square in Greenwich Village, and, in keeping with Franklin's request and after consulting with their children, turned the estate at Hyde Park over to the government. FDR's estate amounted to about $1,000,000, but Eleanor continued delivering public lectures, earmarking her earnings for a charity fund, made radio and television appearances, and wrote extensively, determined to sustain her husband's legacy and to "build a peaceful world with justice and opportunity for all."

Throughout the rest of her life Eleanor Roosevelt remained a public figure while being treated as the grande dame of the Democratic Party, with suggestions that she run for office, including the vice presidency under FDR's successor. Shortly following the dropping of an atomic bomb over the Japanese city of Hiroshima, she exclaimed that humankind could choose either "destruction and death—or construction and life!" She served on the U.S. delegation to the United Nations, the only woman among ten Americans selected by President Harry Truman. She chaired the temporary committee chosen to establish a UN commission to promote human rights. In 1948, the UN Commission on Human Rights, headed by Eleanor, presented its Universal Declaration of Human Rights to the General Assembly. She referred to the document as "the International Magna Carta of all mankind" that "has no legal value but should carry moral weight." She highlighted the import of three articles of the declaration, pertaining to the right to a nationality, individual freedom of thought and conscience, and the right to participate in the government of one's country. Eleanor now acquired an international reputation herself, with references to "the First Lady of the World," and crowds eagerly gathered to see or hear her.

Back home she favored an extension of the New Deal–spawned welfare state and helped to establish Americans for Democratic Action, a liberal, anticommunist organization that nevertheless urged diplomacy to "make peace with the Russians." She joined the board of directors of the NAACP, encouraging Truman to create a permanent Fair Employment Standards Commission. For a year and a half, beginning in 1950, Eleanor hosted a television program, *Mrs. Roosevelt Meets the Public*, on which she interviewed such luminaries as Albert Einstein. She viewed with concern the anticommunist hysteria that culminated in the postwar Red Scare, condemning demagogues and criticizing those who refused to do the same. She warned that Red baiters were fostering "an atmosphere akin to that of communist countries, for we are using the very weapon those countries use." She felt compelled to defend friends, colleagues, and former New Deal administrators from verbal assaults. She viewed the Red-baiting Senator Joseph McCarthy of Wisconsin as "the greatest menace to freedom we have in this country." At a tribute held at the Waldorf-Astoria Hotel in honor of her seventieth birthday, Eleanor again championed the UN. "There I was part of the second great experiment to bring countries together and to get them to work for a peaceful atmosphere in the world, and I still feel it important to strengthen this organization in every way." She continued traveling widely, including to Israel, Pakistan, India, and Japan. She visited Yugoslavia, a communist state that had departed from the Soviet sphere, and the Soviet Union. She strongly backed the presidential campaigns of Adlai Stevenson, continuing to support him even in 1960, when Senator John F. Kennedy of Massachusetts headed toward the nomination of the Democratic Party. Initially distrustful of Kennedy, she agreed to once again serve as a delegate to the UN and also chaired the president's Commission on the Status of Women. She supported "the social revolution" regarding race relations in the United States. On November 7, 1962, seventy-eight-year-old Eleanor Roosevelt died, bringing to a close a golden chapter in American politics. The *New York Times* remarked, "We shall not soon see her like again." At Eleanor's memorial service, Stevenson wondered, "What other single human being has touched and transformed the existence of so many?"

Conclusion

Floyd Olson and Eleanor Roosevelt underscored the resiliency of American democracy during the Great Depression, when many other nations turned in extreme directions. Both Olson and Eleanor Roosevelt supported greater government involvement in economic affairs in the very period when capitalism was imperiled and the structural foundation of the American welfare state was planted. Olson favored more government ownership than Eleanor's husband Franklin would usher in during his lengthy presidency, calling for a "cooperative commonwealth" and proclaiming himself a socialist. Neither Eleanor nor Franklin, no matter their considerable popularity, could have offered such pronouncements without considerable and probably fatal political consequences. Nevertheless, both the Minnesota governor and the two Roosevelts recognized the need for government action, challenging still influential laissez-faire and social Darwinistic concepts that hindered more decisive responses to the era's unprecedented economic calamities. During World War II and its aftermath, Eleanor continued to stand as a tribune for democracy, both in America and around the globe.

Study Questions

1. Discuss how Floyd Olson adopted a more radical perspective by the early 1930s.
2. Explain Floyd Olson's vision for Minnesota and the United States.
3. Indicate how Eleanor Roosevelt helped to resuscitate the career of her husband Franklin while carving out her own political niche.
4. Indicate what social causes Eleanor Roosevelt was drawn to from the 1930s onward.
5. Analyze why Floyd Olson and Eleanor Roosevelt are viewed as two of the most significant American progressive figures in the first several decades of the twentieth century.

Selected Bibliography

Black, Allida M. *Casting Her Own Shadow: Eleanor Roosevelt and the Shaping of Postwar Liberalism*. New York: Columbia University Press, 1997.

Brands, H. W. *Traitor to His Class: The Privileged Life and Radical Presidency of Franklin Delano Roosevelt*. New York: Random House, 2008.

"The Congress: Senator Pro Tem." *Time*, January 6, 1936.

Harris, Cynthia M. *Eleanor Roosevelt: A Biography*. New York: Greenwood, 2007.

Mayer, George H. *The Political Career of Floyd B. Olson*. St. Paul: Minnesota Historical Society Press, 1987.

"Minnesota's Management." *Time*, August 13, 1934.

"Misery in Minnesota." *Time*, April 24, 1933.

Roosevelt, Eleanor. *The Autobiography of Eleanor Roosevelt*. New York: Harper and Brothers, 1961.

———. *Courage in a Dangerous World: The Political Writings of Eleanor Roosevelt*. New York: Columbia University Press, 1999.

———. *It Seems to Me: Selected Letters of Eleanor Roosevelt*. Lexington: University of Kentucky Press, 2005.

———. *My Day: The Best of Eleanor Roosevelt's Acclaimed Columns*. New York: Da Capo, 2001.

———. *On My Own: The Years Since the White House*. New York: Harper and Brothers, 1958.

Scharf, Lois. *Eleanor Roosevelt: First Lady of American Liberalism*. New York: Twayne, 1987.

Youngs, J. William T. *Eleanor Roosevelt: A Personal and Public Life*. New York: Longman, 2005.

CHAPTER SEVEN

~

Questions of Loyalty
in War and Peace

Following the conclusion of World War I, many Americans longed to isolate their nation from the complexities of international affairs and return to a not-so-distant past in which the republic's chief concerns were domestic. The modern age, however, of which the war was a harbinger, precluded any long-term American retreat into insularity. Radical ideologies springing from that cataclysm heightened the likelihood of future international conflicts even as new technologies born of the century's scientific revolution made it possible for aggressors to threaten destruction across great distances. The decades following the "war to end all wars" brought not global accord but rather new dangers, and Americans often found themselves divided over issues of peace, war, and the increasingly destructive weapons that modern science made possible. In some instances, disagreements over policy evolved into questions of loyalty, tarnishing or even destroying public reputations that had once seemed beyond reproach.

Described by some historians as the first truly international celebrity, aviator Charles Lindbergh was feted in unprecedented fashion following his 1927 solo transatlantic flight. The tall, handsome, quiet-spoken Midwesterner, hailed as the "Lone Eagle" and "Lucky Lindy," was a constant focus of national adulation as the pioneer of a new frontier and an exemplar of the national character. Nonetheless, Charles and his wife, Anne Morrow, had already grown weary of the public's attentions when their infant son was kidnapped and killed in 1932. The subsequent media frenzy drove the Lindberghs to seek refuge in Europe for most of the decade, but public controversy continued to surround Charles because of his advocacy of dubious racial theories and his uncomfortably close ties with Germany's Nazi regime. Returning to the United States in 1939, Lindbergh was quickly drawn into the rancorous debate over possible American intervention in the European war. Soon the most famous spokesman for the isolationist America First Committee, Lindbergh voiced the sentiments of many who viewed U.S. intervention as contrary to national interests. His opinions, however, convinced others, including President Franklin Roosevelt, that the famous aviator was an anti-Semite and a Nazi sympathizer. Lindbergh's stubborn insistence on nonintervention and his unwillingness to unequivocally condemn the Nazi regime ultimately cost him the heroic status that he had gained in 1927.

Born only two years after Lindbergh in 1904, Julius Robert Oppenheimer was likewise destined for both fame and controversy. Born to German Jewish parents in New York, Oppenheimer demonstrated an early affinity for the physical sciences, earning a PhD at the age of twenty-two. Pursuing advanced studies in Europe, Oppenheimer was absent for much of the Roaring Twenties, returning only in 1927 and entering academia. The social and economic inequities of the 1930s drew the young physicist into Progressive politics and by the later years of the decade, Nazi Germany's anti-Semitic policies and militaristic posture convinced him of the necessity of a more muscular American foreign policy. In June 1942, Oppenheimer accepted appointment as director of the Manhattan Project, the ambitious wartime program to develop a nuclear weapon. Thoroughly committed to the struggle to defeat fascism, Oppenheimer led the team of prominent scientists who successfully developed the weapons that ended the war in the Pacific. Lauded for his contribution to Allied victory, Oppenheimer was named chairman of the General Advisory Committee to the Atomic Energy Commission (AEC) in 1947. Only a few years later, however, Oppenheimer was embroiled in controversy, denounced by politicians and even some in the scientific community for his opposition to the development of a thermonuclear weapon. His publicly expressed doubts about the wisdom of developing a weapon with unparalleled destructive capacity led to claims that he was a security risk and a communist sympathizer. In the context of the Cold War and the Red Scare of the 1950s, such allegations often proved fatal to the careers of even the most illustrious Americans. Deprived of his security clearance, Oppenheimer was relegated to the backwaters of academia.

The lives of Charles Lindbergh and J. Robert Oppenheimer spanned approximately six decades during which America's role in the world underwent drastic fluctuations, and those changes directly affected the lives of both men. During the late 1930s, Lindbergh attained considerable public prominence and influence as he rode the crest of the isolationist wave. With the sudden advent of war in late 1941, however, Lindbergh's opinions became as irrelevant as the nonintervention that he had counseled. Determined to serve his country, he found opportunities to apply his aviation expertise to defense needs. As the United States emerged from the war with newly gained superpower status and unprecedented international obligations, it was Lindbergh who retreated into relative isolation, remaining largely out of the public eye and committing himself to environmental issues. During the isolationist 1930s, Oppenheimer rejected the idea that insularity would preserve American civilization, voicing his concern about the rise of militaristic fascism. During World War II, his fame grew as he turned his formidable scientific knowledge to achieving victory against the Axis powers. During the postwar era, however, Oppenheimer feared that superpower antagonisms, coupled with weapons of mass destruction, threatened human existence. Unwilling to accept that the exigencies of the Cold War required the unquestioning service of American scientists, Oppenheimer chose what amounted to internal exile rather than contribute to the development of the hydrogen bomb.

⌒ CHARLES LINDBERGH ⌒

September 1941 had proven to be a month of portentous occurrences when an Iowa audience of 8,000 assembled on the eleventh for the America First rally at the Des Moines coliseum. Only a week before, a German submarine had fired two torpedoes at the destroyer USS *Greer*, which had been aiding a British patrol bomber in locating the Nazi U-boat in the cold North Atlantic waters southwest of Iceland. Though officially neutral since the outbreak of the European war two years earlier, the United States had sold war materials to Britain and France. After the fall of France in June 1940, President Franklin Roosevelt had pushed for incrementally greater degrees of direct military support for beleaguered Britain, culminating with the Lend-Lease Act earlier in the year. That summer, the president had quietly authorized U.S. naval commanders to give all possible assistance to merchant convoys running the submarine-infested Atlantic. The attack on the *Greer* was the inevitable result of this decidedly nonneutral policy, and confirmed many isolationist members of the America First Committee (AFC) in their belief that FDR was leading the nation into a disastrous war. As the Des Moines crowd awaited the arrival of the speaker, the public address system broadcast the president's radio address in response to the *Greer* incident. FDR informed listeners that the *Greer* had been wantonly attacked by the Nazi U-boat and announced that henceforth, the United States would follow a "shoot on sight" policy. FDR in effect announced an undeclared naval war against Germany. The crowd barely had time to digest this information before the featured speaker strode onto the stage and took the podium.

Anne Morrow and Charles Lindbergh at a ceremony with German Luftwaffe chief Hermann Goering in July 1936. Lindbergh's embrace of controversial racial theories and anti-Semitic remarks, together with his acceptance of honors from the Hitler regime, led many Americans, including Franklin Roosevelt, to conclude that the famous aviator was at the very least a Nazi sympathizer. His controversial speeches on behalf of the isolationist America First Committee further tarnished his image. (Library of Congress, LC-USZ61-1362)

Tall, slender, and handsome, thirty-nine-year-old Charles Lindbergh was arguably the nation's most famous celebrity more than a decade after his 1927 transatlantic flight. But his fame had turned to controversy since September 1939, when he began a series of public speeches warning of the dangers of intervention in Europe's war. American civilization, he had cautioned, could be best preserved through a focus on hemispheric defense. Following the creation of the AFC in September 1940, Lindbergh had emerged as its most prominent spokesman and, as the Allied position in the war worsened, the famous aviator had become more insistent that Britain faced inevitable defeat, even in the event of U.S. intervention. The interventionists, Lindbergh claimed, were determined not so much to save Britain as to defeat Germany; the destruction of Hitler's anticommunist regime, he feared, would lead to the Bolshevization of Europe and the collapse of Western civilization. Some wary Americans discerned pro-Nazi sentiments and anti-Semitism in Lindbergh's odd perspective. Now, as his expectant audience settled down, Lindbergh spoke to the question, "Who are the war agitators?" "The three most important groups who have been pressing this country toward war," Lindbergh proclaimed, "are the British, the Jewish and the Roosevelt administration." The coliseum erupted in thunderous applause—such suspicions were commonly voiced in general-store conversations throughout the isolationist heartland. Lindbergh continued, laying out the evidence of British pressure for U.S. belligerence, an assertion that was difficult to dispute. When he addressed the extent and effect of Jewish influence, however, Lindbergh's rhetoric revealed a contorted perspective and some troubling prejudices. Anyone could understand why "Jewish people desire the overthrow of Nazi Germany," he declared, but Jews should understand that war would mean the end of tolerance and, "they will be among the first to feel its consequences." "Their greatest danger to this country," he argued, "lies in their large ownership and influence in our motion pictures, our press, our radio and our government. The British and Jewish peoples alike," Lindbergh concluded, "for reasons which are not American, wish to involve us in the war."

Though Lindbergh departed the Des Moines coliseum to enthusiastic applause, his remarks badly damaged his already tarnished public reputation. The famous aviator's comments stunned Jewish Americans like Arnold Foster, chief attorney for the Anti-Defamation League: "When I heard him utter those words, I—along with every Jew in America—felt as if we had been kicked in the gut. Here was this so-called hero saying these things. . . . [I]t said the Jews want to get your son killed." Popular indignation was so widespread that it transcended party, religion, and region, threatening to bring about the immediate collapse of the AFC. The *San Francisco Chronicle* typified the press response with its assertion, "the voice is Lindbergh's, but the words are the words of Hitler." The Texas House of Representatives passed a resolution warning the aviator to stay out of the Lone Star State. Trans World Airways distanced itself from its former adviser and dropped the motto "The Lindbergh Line." Some months before, FDR confided to Treasury Secretary Henry Morgenthau that he was "absolutely convinced that Lindbergh is a Nazi." After September 11, more Americans were willing to agree with the president's assessment. Only months later, the Japanese attack on Pearl Harbor signaled the end of isolation, the collapse of the AFC, and the beginning of a very trying period for a discredited national hero who struggled to determine how he might still serve the nation that had rejected him.

Like many Americans born in the early years of the twentieth century, Charles Augustus Lindbergh was the child of an immigrant parent. His father, Charles Sr., born in Stockholm, Sweden, in 1859, had traveled with his parents the same year to Minnesota, where the family endured the privations of a pioneer existence on their homestead. C. A., as he came to be known, graduated from Michigan Law School in 1883. He married Mary LaFond in 1887 and the two produced two daughters, Lillian and Eva, before Mary's death in 1898.

Recovering from his grief by 1901, C. A. married Evangeline Lodge Land, a schoolteacher. Settling in Little Falls, Minnesota, C. A. won a congressional seat in 1909 and supported progressive Republican policies in the House. His political career foundered after losing a 1916 U.S. Senate race, during which he ardently opposed American intervention in the world war, and he returned to practicing law.

Charles Augustus Lindbergh was born in Detroit, Michigan, on February 4, 1902. He spent much of his childhood between the urban home and a farm near Little Falls, gaining a reputation as a loner, in part because his father moved the family frequently and there was little opportunity to forge lasting friendships. An aggressive learner, young Charles showed special interest in mechanics and aviation. In 1912, Charles traveled with his mother to Fort Myer, Virginia, to witness the Aeronautical Trials, which left a lasting impression on the young Midwesterner. He entered the engineering program at the University of Wisconsin in 1920, but found it boring compared to the excitement that aviation offered. In 1922, as a first step toward realizing his dream of becoming an aviator, Charles left Madison and enrolled in a pilot and mechanics training program offered by the Nebraska Aircraft Corporation in Lincoln.

Aviation was entering an era of rapid technological advance as Charles began his study of aircraft design, maintenance, and construction at the renamed Lincoln Standard Aircraft factory, which renovated "veteran" war-era aircraft. World War I had quickly revealed the diverse utility of aircraft, which performed both tactical and strategic roles. Barely more than motorized box kites at the war's onset, aircraft were rapidly transformed by wartime demands into much more sophisticated machines. By war's end, multiengine bombers were raining explosives into enemy cities. The 1920s brought equally fast-paced innovations. Stronger airframes, the monocoque fuselage (in which the outer skin is stress bearing), improved aerodynamic designs, and more powerful engines were all indicative of the as-yet-unrealized potential of civilian and military aviation. Such was the promise in April 1922 when Lindbergh took his first flight in an Army surplus Curtiss JN-4 Jenny. The twenty-year-old later recalled that as the craft lifted off, he lost "all consciousness with the past," living "only in the moment in this strange, unmortal space, crowded with beauty, pierced with danger." Within weeks, Lindbergh, demonstrating a natural ease in the cockpit, had learned how to pilot the craft himself. Desirous of more experience, he soon left Lincoln Aircraft and spent several years as a barnstormer, along with other stunt pilots who made their living awing rural audiences with aerial acrobatics. Lindbergh livened up the shows by wing walking and parachuting from the Jenny, earning the nickname Daredevil Lindbergh.

In early 1924, Lindbergh forsook barnstorming and enlisted in the Army Air Service with an eye to additional flight training and future employment opportunities. The following March, reserve Lieutenant Lindbergh graduated from flight school and accepted employment with Robertson Aircraft as an airmail pilot, undertaking the route from St. Louis to Chicago. The dangerous work did not sate his desire to test the boundaries of aviation, and in 1926, he prepared to seek the Orteig Prize, established in 1919 to award $25,000 for the first transatlantic flight. Lindbergh convinced nine St. Louis businessmen to back him, then oversaw the design and construction of a craft named the *Spirit of St. Louis*. A high-wing monoplane with aluminum skin, the shimmering *Spirit* boasted a powerful radial engine but offered no forward vision—the pilot would need to look out side windows. As Lindbergh prepared to begin his flight from Garden City, New Jersey's Roosevelt Field, he was aware that other fliers had died in the attempt, and the fuel-laden *Spirit*'s wobbly takeoff on May 20, 1927, was an inauspicious start to a problematic journey. Alone for the next thirty-three and a half hours, Lindbergh fought sleep, hunger, anxiety, and hallucinations before touching down at Paris's Le Bourget airfield.

Unprecedented international acclaim followed Lindbergh's flight. The ecstatic French showered him with adulation and the Legion of Honor. He returned home aboard a U.S. Navy cruiser specially dispatched by President Calvin Coolidge, who also awarded him the Distinguished Flying Cross. As awards and honors were lavished on the quiet-mannered "Lone Eagle," his visage became a lucrative merchandising tool worldwide, appearing on items from shaving mugs to commemorative plates. Capitalizing on his new fame as the avatar of the aviation age, Lindbergh toured the nation as a spokesman for the Guggenheim Fund for the Promotion of Aeronautics. In late 1927, while in Mexico on a goodwill tour, "Lucky Lindy" met Anne Spence Morrow, daughter of Ambassador Dwight Morrow. The couple was wed in May 1929 and eventually had six children. It was the tragedy surrounding their firstborn, Charles Augustus Jr., that drove the couple to flee the United States. The twenty-month-old child was killed, probably accidentally, after being kidnapped on March 1, 1932, and the lengthy trial of the alleged murderer, Bruno Hauptmann, occurred in a grotesque, sensationalistic atmosphere that drove the bereaved couple to Europe. Lindbergh's activities in subsequent years brought growing disrepute.

The Lindberghs lived in both England and France during the worst years of the worldwide depression. Lindbergh worked with Alexis Carrel, a French surgeon who had collaborated with the mechanically minded American flier earlier in the decade to develop a perfusion pump to aid in cardiac surgery. Controversy developed when Lindbergh embraced dubious scientific theories of racism and eugenics that Carrel advocated. Pseudoscientific theories about purifying the human race through euthanasia and selective breeding were prolific in Nazi Germany when Lindbergh traveled there in 1938, having been asked by the American military attaché in Berlin to evaluate the state of Germany's newly built air force. Lindbergh made extensive inquiries into the state of German aviation technology and military preparedness, and Nazi officials granted the American broad access to their latest aircraft, some of which Lindbergh flew. In a subsequent report to American ambassador Joseph Kennedy in London, Lindbergh concluded that Nazi Germany was invincible. "Germany, on account of her military strength," he asserted, "is now inseparable from the welfare of every civilization, for either to preserve or destroy is in her power." It was "wiser to permit Germany's eastward expansion," Lindbergh concluded, "than to throw England and France, unprepared, into a war at this time." His evaluation circulated in British policymaking circles, bolstering the case made by those who advocated appeasing the Nazi dictator. Weeks later, at the Munich Conference in September 1938, British and French diplomats acceded to Hitler's demand for the Sudetenland region of Czechoslovakia. In October, Lindbergh attended a dinner with Nazi Luftwaffe chief Hermann Goering, who presented the American with the Service Cross of the German Eagle. The ceremony took place only weeks before Nazi savagery was unleashed on German Jews during the Kristallnacht pogrom. In the United States, the press brimmed with condemnations of Lindbergh's apparent affinity for the Hitler regime. Expressing her disgust at Nazi violence, first lady Eleanor Roosevelt asked a friend, "How could Lindbergh take that Hitler decoration?" In his journal, Lindbergh confided his own confusion about the Germans. "They have undoubtedly had a difficult Jewish problem," he conceded, "but why is it necessary to handle it so unreasonably? My admiration [for Germany] is constantly being dashed against some rock such as this." It was well that the public remained unaware of such private musings.

Charles and Anne had returned to New Jersey when the Nazi *Blitzkrieg* roared into Poland in September 1939, marking the beginning of the conflict that Lindbergh feared would lead to the destruction of Western civilization under the boots of Asiatic Bolshevik hordes. Though President Roosevelt proclaimed America's neutrality, he pointedly conceded in his radio address that he could not expect that Americans would remain "neutral in thought" as well as deed. It marked the beginning of a two-year effort by the president to gradually push public opinion toward greater degrees of aid for the European democracies. During those same years, Lindbergh quickly emerged as the leading voice of isolationism, taking to the radio on September 15 to establish a rationale for nonintervention. Lindbergh warned of the cost in lives and money, insisted that America could remain out of the conflict only by adopting a cold detachment from European events, then cautioned listeners to consider the source of every bit of war news: "We must ask who owns and influences the newspapers, the news pictures, and the radio station." The implicit anti-Semitism of this claim was evident to any who examined it, but Lindbergh's plea for noninvolvement resonated with the public. In a second radio address on October 14, Lindbergh made the absurd suggestion that the United States could remain out of the war by embargoing the sale of "offensive weapons" to the Allies. Of more enduring controversy was his interjection of racial themes. "Our bond with Europe is a bond of race and not of political ideology," he claimed. "Racial strength is vital." The "white race" could not afford internecine conflict if it were to avoid destruction, Lindbergh asserted. These words provoked a new barrage of editorial criticism, with journalist Dorothy Thompson deriding Lindbergh as "a somber cretin" who wanted to become "an American Führer."

Lindbergh was not deterred. In an article in the November 1940 issue of *Reader's Digest*, he argued that an exclusive monopoly on airpower could ensure the survival of the white race "in a pressing sea of Yellow, Black and Brown" and again warned of "racial suicide by internal conflict." Lindbergh's claim in a May 1940 speech that the greatest danger to America came from a small minority of influential interventionists provoked a presidential response five days later. FDR warned that the peril to the nation came not from "military weapons alone," but from the "Trojan Horse" of "spies, saboteurs and traitors." Growing popular suspicions about the Lindberghs were affirmed when Anne published *The Wave of the Future: A Confession of Faith* in September. Many readers interpreted her assertion, "There is no fighting against the wave of the future" as an endorsement of fascism. That same month, Charles attended a meeting at Henry Ford's Dearborn, Michigan, office, where the organizers of the recently established America First Committee hoped to persuade him to accept a leadership role. Founded by Yale University students, the AFC was organized to marshal public opinion against intervention. It eventually claimed 650 chapters and 800,000 members, mostly in the isolationist heartland. It attracted a diverse following that included socialist Norman Thomas, isolationist Republican congressmen, Alice Roosevelt Longworth, and Walt Disney. The AFC leadership believed that Lindbergh's voice would be a potent weapon in the battle of persuasion that was taking shape in the midst of a presidential election campaign in which Republican nominee Wendell Willkie sought to convince voters that a third term for FDR meant inevitable war. Promising that "your boys are not going to be sent into any foreign wars," FDR won reelection as the war in Europe entered a critical phase.

Roosevelt, who described the intensifying foreign policy debate as a struggle for "the soul of the nation," infuriated isolationists in a fireside chat radio address in late December 1940 when he proposed that the United States become the "Arsenal of Democracy" and supply the weapons that Britain required to remain in the fight with Nazi Germany. The subsequent Lend-Lease Act, introduced in Congress early in 1941, provoked a new barrage of outrage from the AFC, and Republican Hamilton Fish asked Lindbergh to testify before the House on the bill's likely effect. For more than two hours, Lindbergh reiterated his well-known rationale for nonintervention and proclaimed his desire that "neither side should win." In the course of subsequent Senate hearings, when Florida Democrat Claude Pepper questioned Lindbergh's unwillingness to publicly denounce Nazi atrocities, Lindbergh unconvincingly asserted that "nothing is gained by publicly commenting" on personal opinions. Such evasions fed growing public doubts about the Lone Eagle's loyalty. Interior Secretary Harold Ickes warned FDR that Lindbergh was "a ruthless and conscious fascist" and publicly denounced him as "the first American to hold aloft the standard of pro-Nazism." In speeches in Chicago and New York in April, an undeterred Lindbergh insisted that Britain had lost the war and urged that Americans not be too quick to judge Nazi Germany. Newspaper accounts of the AFC rallies noted an alarming "sprinkling of Nazis, fascists, anti-Semites, [and] crackpots," some of whom offered Nazi salutes. In July, *Time* magazine described the AFC's membership as "Jew-haters, Roosevelt-haters, England-haters and Coughlinites." That same month, Secretary Ickes again questioned Lindbergh's unwillingness to denounce Nazi barbarity and suggested that he return his Nazi decoration. Lindbergh's assertion that a public condemnation of Nazi Germany would be contrary to his personal policy of absolute neutrality was increasingly unconvincing for most Americans, and public opinion slowly began to turn against Lucky Lindy that summer. The September speech identifying Jews as "war agitators" marked the beginning of the rapid decline of Lindbergh's reputation. "Lindbergh's halo," remarked popular commentator Walter Winchell, "has become his noose."

In subsequent weeks, Lindbergh proved willing to put his neck deeper into that noose, despite polls indicating that a majority of Americans rejected his claims of Jewish pro-intervention influence. In late September, Lindbergh warned an AFC rally in Fort Wayne, Indiana, that FDR intended to suspend the 1942 elections as a prelude to a presidential dictatorship. In October, after Roosevelt announced that he would ask Congress to revise the 1935 Neutrality Act to allow arming U.S. merchant ships, Lindbergh again assailed the president's course before a Madison Square Garden audience of 20,000. Nonetheless, the Lone Eagle's blindness to the growing Nazi threat in Europe, together with his alleged anti-Semitism, contributed to his growing isolation from majority opinion. Anne's sister Constance later recalled her realization that "in just fifteen years, he had gone from Jesus to Judas." Despite Lindbergh's declining stature, the AFC had stood by him throughout the fall as the organization charged Roosevelt with responsibility for the escalating crisis with Japan. On December 6, the *America First Bulletin* headline charged "Blame for Rift with Japan Rests on Administration." The following day, events in Oahu, Hawaii, ended the "great debate" over foreign policy, signaling the end of the AFC and new trials for Charles Lindbergh.

Lindbergh was slow to recognize the extent to which his reputation had suffered as a result of previous public comments that to many seemed defeatist if not pro-Nazi and callous if not anti-Semitic. After the AFC's leadership agreed to disband on December 11, Lindbergh recapitulated his bizarre perspective before the guests at a private dinner party in New York. He was appalled that the United States was "fighting on the side of the Russians and the Chinese," given that "the only danger in the world [is] the yellow danger." China and Japan, he argued, were in league "against the white race." Only Germany, he asserted, could have successfully blunted this threat, had that nation allied with Britain. "The British envied the German and wanted to rule the world," he asserted. "Britain is the real cause of all the trouble in the world." The famous flier also projected that the AFC could again play a role in public affairs when Nazi military invincibility became manifest. "There may be a time," he suggested, "when we can advocate a negotiated peace." It was well that such remarks remained private. Though Lindbergh publicly agreed that the United States now had no alternative other than to fight, his efforts to offer his services to the government were openly spurned. Having previously resigned his Air Corps commission during his AFC days, he was now unable to regain it in 1942, but he found employment as a consultant to Ford Motor Company, which was building bombers for the Army Air Force. Later, as a consultant for United Aircraft, Lindbergh was given permission to travel to forward areas in the Pacific to evaluate aircraft performance in combat. Though a civilian, Lindbergh participated in about fifty combat missions, once shooting down a Japanese observation plane. His wartime journals reveal a thoughtful, introspective individual who recognized and deplored the racial animosity inherent in the Pacific War, but who seemed more willing to condemn American atrocities than those of the Japanese enemy. "What the German has done to the Jew in Europe," he wrote in July 1944, "we are doing to the Jap in the Pacific." The bizarre analogy, no doubt offensive to many, seemed characteristic of Lindbergh's obtuse perspective.

Time and seclusion gradually eroded public distaste for Lindbergh. In the postwar era, the famous flier settled in Connecticut, serving as a consultant to the U.S. Air Force (USAF) chief of staff and to Pan American Airways. He reemerged into the public spotlight in 1953, when his book *The Spirit of St. Louis* won a Pulitzer Prize, though the subsequent film version bombed. The following year, President Dwight Eisenhower restored Lindbergh's commission, appointing him a USAF brigadier general. As of the 1960s, Lindbergh devoted his energies to conservation, stressing his belief that a balance should be sought between technological advancements and the preservation of the natural world. He died of lymphoma in Maui, Hawaii, on August 26, 1974. Lindbergh's legacy is a decidedly mixed one. An American public hero of immense stature during the 1920s, Lindbergh squandered a huge reservoir of

public goodwill when he embraced dubious racial theories and the appeasement of Hitler's Germany. While his determination to keep America out of
the European war mirrored that of many fellow Americans, his rationale for
abandoning the European democracies and seeking a modus vivendi with the
Axis powers struck many as the product of tortured logic or, even worse, anti-
Semitic and pro-Nazi sympathies. Contemporaries and historians alike have
speculated on the origins of Lindbergh's often bizarre beliefs, and some have
concluded that his experience with the disorder and indiscipline of American
society in the aftermath of his son's kidnapping may have soured him on the
long-term prospects of democracy. His approving remarks about the relative
order of totalitarian Germany and his expressed dismay at the comparative
weakness of British society suggest an implicit affinity for the former. Though
Lindbergh's later years were generally bereft of controversy, his status as the
heroic Lone Eagle of the 1920s would always be offset by the troubling positions he took as his nation stood on the brink of war.

～ J. ROBERT OPPENHEIMER ～

During the early months of 1954, a number of events combined to give the
Cold War confrontation between the United States and the Soviet Union a
new and frightening immediacy. On March 1, shortly after Secretary of State
John Foster Dulles announced that the Eisenhower administration's defense
strategy would rely on a policy of "massive retaliation" in response to any Soviet
attack, American scientists conducted a test of the newly developed hydrogen
bomb at isolated Bikini Atoll in the Pacific. The "Castle Bravo" test produced
a detonation three times as powerful as predicted, alarming many of the ob-
servers who witnessed the four-mile-wide fireball. Stanford physicist Marshall
Rosenbluth, watching from a ship thirty miles distant, recalled, "It was pretty
frightening. There was a huge fireball with these turbulent rolls going in and
out. The thing was glowing. It looked to me like a diseased brain up in the sky.
. . . It was a pretty sobering and shattering experience." Radioactive fallout
from the massive blast sickened the crew of a Japanese fishing boat some eighty
miles away and also affected nearby islanders. The Castle tests confirmed the
unprecedented destructive power of thermonuclear or fusion bombs, even as
controversy over the history of the new weapon's development erupted. In
April, Red-baiting Republican Senator Joseph McCarthy, on the eve of Senate
hearings inspired by his charges that the U.S. Army was sheltering subversives,
charged in a televised address that communist sympathizers in the government
were behind a "deliberate eighteen-month delay" in the development of the
hydrogen bomb. On April 13, Americans awoke to the news that J. Robert Oppenheimer, famed director of the wartime Manhattan Project, was the subject

Atomic physicist J. Robert Oppenheimer (right) accepting a Medal for Merit from Secretary of War Robert Patterson in March 1946. Hailed for his crucial contributions to the wartime Manhattan Project, Oppenheimer later faced scrutiny as a potential security risk because of his political beliefs and his opposition to the development of the hydrogen bomb, which he considered of dubious military value and morally indefensible. (Library of Congress, LC-USZ62-41884)

of an Atomic Energy Commission investigation. At issue were Oppenheimer's past political beliefs, his alleged connections to communists, and finally, his opposition to the hydrogen bomb program. Coming as it did in the aftermath of years of startling revelations about Soviet espionage, sometimes abetted by Americans like Julius and Ethel Rosenberg, who provided classified information to Soviet agents, this was troubling news to many Americans. Even before the hearing began, some were willing to credit right-wing commentator Walter Winchell's sensational claim that Oppenheimer had been "an active Communist Party member" and "leader of a Red cell including other noted atomic scientists." For Oppenheimer, long accustomed to the plaudits of a public that credited him with contributing the knowledge essential to the construction of the weapon that ended the Pacific war, the next several weeks of hearings were agony, as his past associations and policy recommendations were relentlessly examined for indications of subversive actions or disloyalty. At stake were both his government security clearance, which, in an age of suspicion, served as an official confirmation of loyalty, and his personal reputation. The hearings during that tumultuous spring of 1954 deprived Robert Oppenheimer of each.

Born in New York City on April 22, 1904, Julius Robert Oppenheimer was the son of Julius S. Oppenheimer, an immigrant German textile manufacturer, and Ella Friedman, a painter from Baltimore. Robert grew up in a secular Jewish household, where he was soon joined by younger brother Frank. Both boys were drawn to cerebral activities at an early age, though Robert was especially precocious and attended the Ethical Culture School, acknowledged as one of the city's best. Always somewhat introverted, Oppenheimer later remarked, "It is characteristic that I do not remember any of my classmates." His focus on academic achievement was rewarded in 1922, when he was accepted at Harvard University. There he was diverted from chemistry to physics, but also studied Latin and Greek prior to his summa cum laude graduation in 1925. He spent the next four years in Europe, studying at Cambridge before traveling to the University of Göttingen at the invitation of physicist Max Born, whose work in the new field of quantum mechanics intrigued the young American. Having earned a PhD in the remarkably abbreviated span of two years, Oppenheimer accepted a joint position at the University of California at Berkeley and the California Institute of Technology, where he remained for the next thirteen years, establishing the renowned School of Theoretical Physics.

Oppenheimer's graduate study and early professorial years corresponded to an era during which the field of physics underwent a revolution that equaled, or perhaps even surpassed, the Newtonian revolution of the seventeenth century. Albert Einstein, Ernest Rutherford, Max Planck, and Erwin Schrödinger laid the foundations for a radically new physics, and Oppenheimer's generation of younger scientists were quick to build on it throughout the 1930s. At Berkeley, Oppenheimer's incisive intellect and personal affability endeared him to his students, who often enjoyed a close relationship with the tall, slender, mild-mannered physicist. Not all of "Oppie's" time was dedicated to science; he studied Sanskrit and read widely in the classics and modern literature. Those around him noted, however, that because of his intense absorption with physics, he was often disengaged from external events. Oppie disdained newspapers, telephones, and radios and was said to have learned of the 1929 stock market crash only long after it occurred. His detachment ebbed in the late 1930s, however, as he reacted to news of the Nazi persecution of German Jews, some of whom were relatives. His growing concern about the spread of fascism led him to contribute to groups supporting the Loyalists against General Francisco Franco's Nationalists in the Spanish Civil War. The impact of the Great Depression awakened Oppenheimer to the social and economic inequities within the United States, and his political beliefs reflected a leftward tilt as the decade wore on. His brother Frank and his wife were members of the American Communist Party, and though Oppie shared some of their views, he never joined the party. According to colleague Hans Bethe, after the Nazi-Soviet Nonaggression Pact of August 1939, Oppenheimer made clear his disgust with the communists. Appalled at Germany's rapid defeat of France in 1940, he told friends that he saw fascism as a threat to Western civilization.

That same year, as the world descended deeper into war, Oppenheimer married Katherine "Kitty" Harrison, a Berkeley student who was both a widow and a divorcee, as well as a former member of the Communist Party. Having forsaken radical activities, Kitty devoted herself to advancing Robert's career and beginning a family, which eventually included a son and daughter. As the debate over U.S. intervention built in 1941, Oppenheimer, now a full professor, was elected to the U.S. National Academy of Sciences. With a new wife and a comfortable home in San Francisco, he seemed destined for a stellar academic career, but American entry into the world war put Oppenheimer on a path toward international renown as the director of the project to develop an atomic bomb.

The Manhattan Project grew out of a small research project begun in 1939 in response to warnings from European and American scientists about the possibility that German scientists might feasibly pursue the development of atomic weapons. A letter from Albert Einstein to President Roosevelt triggered a rapidly expanding program that drew American scientists, including many recent European émigrés, into the U.S. Army Corps of Engineers project that eventually employed more than 130,000 people working at over thirty different sites to develop a nuclear weapon. The project was overseen by General Leslie Groves, who appointed Oppenheimer director of scientific research in 1942. Robert Wilson, an Oppenheimer student, recalled Oppie's ardent commitment to the work, which the physicist saw as an ideological struggle between democracy and fascism. Oppenheimer's dedication to this "people's war" was so deep that he dismissed the moral qualms that some of the scientists voiced, telling Isidor Rabi, "I do not think that the Nazis allow us the option of [not] carrying out that development." One of the physicists that Oppie brought to the research center at Los Alamos, New Mexico, was Hungarian émigré Edward Teller, who sought to interest his colleagues in the concept of the "Super," a thermonuclear fusion bomb. Given the extremely problematic science behind the fusion bomb, Oppenheimer insisted that the focus remain on the development of a fission weapon, and a resentful Teller refused to participate in the effort. The rift between the two men would have momentous consequences a decade later, when Teller's envy of Oppie's fame intensified to the point of obsession. Oppie's team nevertheless saw their quest through to completion in July 1945, when the "Trinity" test detonation in the New Mexican desert near Alamogordo demonstrated the awesome power of the new weapon. In a

1965 interview, Oppenheimer recalled that the horrific blast reminded him of words attributed to the Hindu god Vishnu: "I am become Death, the destroyer of worlds." "We all knew," he recounted, "the world would not be the same." Nonetheless, as a member of the War Department's Interim Committee on Atomic Energy, Oppenheimer, together with the others on the scientific panel, affirmed in the summer of 1945 that there was no alternative to using the new weapon on Japan. In early August, two atomic bombs obliterated the Japanese cities of Hiroshima and Nagasaki, bringing World War II to a close.

Widely hailed as the genius behind the weapon that ended the war, Oppenheimer basked in the new status and prominence that wartime exigencies had conferred on scientists as well as military leaders. As chairman of the AEC's General Advisory Committee (GAC), Oppenheimer and other top scientists could directly shape national policy and supported the effort to increase the production of fissionable material for military applications. Oppie, named as director of Princeton's Institute for Advanced Study in 1947, successfully advocated the development of a program for the detection of foreign nuclear tests, which proved its value when the Soviets detonated their first atomic bomb in August 1949. He also participated in the Vista project study group, which recommended a developmental focus on tactical rather than strategic nuclear weapons, a decision that irritated some high-ranking Air Force officials, whose latent animosity toward Oppenheimer later had serious consequences. The greater controversy came in the aftermath of the Soviet atomic test, when Teller perceived an opportunity to push once again for the development of the Super, a project that, if successful, would allow Teller to supplant Oppenheimer as the nation's preeminent nuclear weapons expert. Though Teller was seconded by physicist Ernest Lawrence, the GAC rejected the idea, arguing that the technical problems involved in a thermonuclear bomb had not been resolved and that pursuing such a weapon would escalate the arms race with the Soviet Union. The debate was abruptly ended in January 1950 when President Harry Truman announced his decision to proceed with the hydrogen bomb program, given that Soviet behavior remained antagonistic and unpredictable. Most congressmen, believing that a "bigger" bomb was inevitably better, endorsed the idea. Air Force officials argued that the H-bomb's vastly increased radius of destruction, ten times greater than a fission weapon, would "compensate for bombing error." Subsequent events ensured that the public was receptive to the idea of upping the nuclear ante even as many atomic scientists expressed serious misgivings about the endeavor. On February 1, Manhattan Project scientist Klaus Fuchs confessed to passing atomic secrets to the Soviets, which seemed to explain recent Soviet gains as well as casting suspicion on others in the scientific community. Even as the Fuchs revelations garnered headlines, two dozen scientists announced their opposition to the Super in the *Wall Street*

Journal, denouncing the H-bomb as "a betrayal of all standards of morality of Christian civilization itself." Einstein warned that the accelerating nuclear arms race meant "general annihilation." Hans Bethe, who publicly questioned the morality of "this weapon of total annihilation," confided to a friend, "I cannot in good conscience work on this weapon."

This broad expression of concern on the part of leading scientists occurred as Teller attempted to entice recruits to the Super program at Los Alamos, and he was quick to insist that scientists should not concern themselves with questions of morality, but rather with national security, and should go "back to the laboratories." Teller also undertook a systematic effort to cast suspicion on Oppenheimer's judgment and loyalty, telling senatorial assistant William Borden that the physicist had delayed the H-bomb program and had sought to close the Los Alamos laboratory after the war. Doubts about Teller's proposed design for a Super, together with his reputation as contentious and egotistical, ensured that he was not chosen to direct the development of the Super at Los Alamos. The aggrieved and resentful Teller accepted a position at the new Livermore laboratory in California, having successfully convinced government officials that the Los Alamos scientists were too slow in their work. The first thermonuclear device, produced by the Los Alamos team, was detonated at Eniwetok Atoll in November 1952, producing a blast ten times as powerful as the Hiroshima bomb, vaporizing the test island of Elugelab, and creating a characteristic mushroom cloud 100 miles across. Though Teller had no direct role in the "Ivy Mike" test and the bomb was not based on his original proposals for a Super, the media deemed him the "father of the hydrogen bomb." In less than two years, the opportunity would arise for Teller to contribute to the discrediting of Robert Oppenheimer, the man whom he held responsible for denying him the stature he deserved.

Though a driving force behind the atomic bomb, Oppenheimer had questioned the utility and morality of the Super since Teller first proposed it during World War II. Oppie was also among a number of scientists on the State Department's Disarmament Panel who had hoped to convince authorities to postpone the Mike test as a step toward heading off a burgeoning U.S.-Soviet nuclear arms race. His cautionary stance on the Super was the final straw for a number of individuals, government officials and scientists alike, who believed that the famous physicist was a "pinko" or even a "Red," intentionally seeking to sidetrack the American nuclear program. In 1952, AEC chairman Lewis Strauss and AEC commissioner Thomas Murray, together with scientists Kenneth Pitzer, Luis Alvarez, and Teller, were among those who began to privately voice concerns about Oppie's influence. In May 1953, *Fortune* magazine took the issue before the broader public in an unsigned article provocatively titled, "The Hidden Struggle for the H-Bomb: Dr. Oppenheimer's Persistent Campaign to Reverse U.S. Military Strategy." Rife with inaccuracies, the article asserted that Oppenheimer was among a number of arrogant scientists who sought to block the construction of the Super; both Teller and Strauss were depicted as heroically resisting this misguided effort. The article also posited the existence of a sinister conspiracy referred to as ZORC, an acronym ostensibly comprised of the initials of a shadowy cabal of scientists—Jerrold Zacharias, Oppenheimer, I. I. Rabi, and Charles Lauritsen—that was said to be dedicated to ending SAC's offensive capabilities in favor of a more "moral" defensive strategy. The tide of suspicion grew through 1953, when William Borden, executive director of the Joint Committee on Atomic Energy and a confidant of Strauss and Teller, submitted his own investigatory findings about Oppenheimer to the Federal Bureau of Investigation. Borden offered twenty-one reasons why he believed, "more probably than not, J. Robert Oppenheimer is an agent of the Soviet Union." Upon learning of the report, President Dwight Eisenhower told his national security advisers that it was necessary to build a "blank wall" between the physicist and the classified information that he had previously had access to.

As he would do with the troublesome Senator Joseph McCarthy that same year, Eisenhower delegated to others the onerous task of disposing of a controversy. The AEC's Personnel Security Board, headed by Gordon Gray, was assigned the task of weighing the charges and Oppenheimer's defense. Oppenheimer and his counsel, Lloyd Garrison, were at a considerable disadvantage as the hearing opened in April in a temporary government building in Washington, DC. There was no discovery process and no rules of evidence; the defense was prevented from seeing Oppenheimer's FBI files; and the confidential conversations between the physicist and his lawyer were known to AEC attorney Roger Robb through electronic surveillance. Robb quickly put the chain-smoking scientist on the defensive, quizzing him about a wartime conversation with his friend Haakon Chevalier, a Berkeley colleague and self-professed communist who told Oppenheimer that he was in contact with a third party who could pass classified information to Soviet agents. Oppie's response had been to warn that such an action would be treasonous, and he later notified Army counterintelligence, naming the contact that Haakon had mentioned. Robb's allegation was that Oppie subsequently concealed his friend Haakon's role in the event for more than a year. Compelled to acknowledge that he had lied to shield a friend, Oppie was now vulnerable to questions about his truthfulness about other issues. Robb mercilessly quizzed the scientist about an extramarital affair in the 1930s with Communist Party member Jean Tatlock, and Oppenheimer admitted to the affair and conceded that during that era, he had been a "fellow traveler," in support of the communist struggle against fascism, though not a party member. Kitty Oppenheimer was also brought before the board and questioned about her past Communist Party membership, which she explained as growing out of the unique circumstances of the 1930s, when capitalism seemed to have failed and the Soviet Union was seen as the only major power actively combating fascism. A parade of twenty-eight defense witnesses, all of whom testified to Oppenheimer's character and loyalty, could not undo the damage done. During the last full week of the hearing, Teller appeared as a prosecution witness and took his revenge. Asked if he believed that Oppenheimer was a security risk, Teller disingenuously suggested that while he would not challenge Oppenheimer's loyalty, he seriously questioned his judgment, claiming that Oppenheimer's resistance to the Super had delayed the program for four years. When Gray asked whether national security would be threatened if Oppenheimer retained his security clearance, Teller opined that Oppenheimer would not "knowingly and willingly" endanger the nation, "but if it is a question of wisdom and judgment, as demonstrated by actions since 1945, then I would say that it would be wiser not to grant clearance." Subsequently, the Security Hearing Board and the AEC agreed that Dr. Oppenheimer's security clearance, already suspended, would be revoked.

The verdict shocked the American public, and the scientific community generally rallied around their beleaguered colleague; 282 Los Alamos scientists signed a letter to Strauss defending Oppenheimer. Carson Mark, who worked on the Super, denounced the hearing as another "Salem witchcraft delusion." McCarthyism was still a dynamic force, however, and columnist Walter Winchell was among the right-wing voices lambasting Oppenheimer. The scientist, Winchell reminded readers, had admitted an adulterous affair with "a fanatical Redski" and "knew his Doll was an active member of the Commy apparatus." The ultraconservative *American Mercury* gloated over the humiliation of the "longtime glamour-boy of the atomic scientists" and condemned his defenders as those "who would coddle potential traitors." That fall, James Shepley and Clay Blair's *The Hydrogen Bomb: The Men, the Menace, the Mechanism* proclaimed that Oppenheimer had ensured the Los Alamos lab was "loaded with Communists and former Communists." In the rarefied atmosphere of Cold War America, Oppenheimer's progressive political views, past associations, and qualms about developing a weapon of mass destruction were interpreted by some as tantamount to treason.

Shorn of his security clearance and public stature, Oppenheimer was restricted to an academic career at Princeton and, as Hans Bethe noted, "was never the same man." Colleague Robert Serber, noting that the Gray Board hearing "broke his spirit," explained how Oppenheimer's universe had precipitously shrunk: "He had spent the years after the war being an adviser, being in high places, knowing what was going on. To be in on things gave him a sense of importance. That became his whole life." In one of the Cold War's greatest ironies, Oppenheimer, effectively exiled to Princeton because of little more than allegations about his loyalty and judgment, became a nonperson, as had uncountable "enemies of the state" in the Soviet Union. Edward Teller quickly superseded the lanky scientist as the acknowledged national expert on nuclear affairs and maintained that stature well into the 1980s, when he convinced President Ronald Reagan of the feasibility of the Strategic Defense Initiative. Oppenheimer, who now had to deal with Kitty's deepening alcoholism, rarely made public appearances, though he alluded to his dilemma in a 1954 address at Columbia University. "This is a world," he observed, "in which each of us, knowing his limitations, knowing the evils of superficiality, will have to cling to what is close to him, to what he knows, to what he can do, to his friends and his tradition and his love, lest he be dissolved in a universal confusion and know nothing and love nothing." The words offered a rare window into the complexity of the inner man. The famous physicist returned to the public eye in 1963 when President John F. Kennedy announced that he would be awarded the Enrico Fermi Prize and a medal for public service. This effort to undertake Oppenheimer's political rehabilitation in a more liberal era produced conservative outcries. Kennedy's assassination in November delayed the ceremony, but in early December, Oppenheimer appeared in the White House Cabinet Room to receive the award from Lyndon Johnson. Oppenheimer supporter David Lilienthal saw his friend's ordeal written in the appearance of the "figure of stone, gray, rigid, almost lifeless, tragic in his intensity." The presentation, Lilienthal felt, was an "expiation for the sins and hatred and ugliness" that the scientist had endured. Oppenheimer thanked the president for his political courage and, in an amazing act of graciousness, accepted the extended hand of his nemesis Edward Teller. Aware that the ceremony had not expunged the controversy his name provoked, Oppenheimer withdrew from public life during one of the most tumultuous decades in American history, never publicly commenting on the growing nuclear tensions, the Vietnam War, or unprecedented domestic dissent. He resigned his position at the institute in June 1966 even as his health deteriorated rapidly. Diagnosed with throat cancer, Oppenheimer died at home on February 18, 1967. His passing occasioned the expected tributes, perhaps the best of which David Lilienthal offered: "The world has lost a noble spirit—a genius who brought together poetry and science." Others who knew him acknowledged that the subjective quality of poetry defined his character perhaps more than the scientific objectivity that he sought. Isidor Rabi identified Oppenheimer's charisma as emanating from an indefinite "spiritual quality." "He never expressed himself completely," wrote Rabi. "He always left a feeling that there were depths of sensibility and insight not yet revealed."

Conclusion

There are some intriguing superficial commonalities in the lives of Charles Lindbergh and Robert Oppenheimer. Both were drawn to new areas of science and technology, though Lindbergh's focus was on application, whereas Oppenheimer's forte involved theory. Both men contributed significantly to advances in their respective fields and enjoyed subsequent celebrity. The domestic and international developments of the 1930s compelled their political engagement, though they diverged greatly over the question of the fascist threat. Both saw their public stature diminished when their political beliefs and actions, alleged or otherwise, were deemed questionable during an era of rapidly shifting international and domestic dynamics. Charles Lindbergh was never able to fully restore his reputation with the American public, and historians still debate the motivations that drove him to advocate controversial positions in often incautious speeches. Robert Oppenheimer, however, was widely regarded even in the 1950s as an unfortunate martyr to the burgeoning national security state and the Red Scare of the postwar years, and contemporary historians have endorsed that perspective. The lives of both men testify to the tenuous quality of fame and, more important, to the potential for conflict between individual beliefs and public opinion even in a democratic society committed to the free expression of ideas.

Study Questions

1. In what ways did rapid advances in science and technology shape the lives of Charles Lindbergh and Robert Oppenheimer?
2. Discuss the foreign policy perspectives that Charles Lindbergh formed in the later 1930s and explain why they were controversial.
3. Was the America First Committee's insistence on maintaining U.S. neutrality realistic? Why or why not?
4. Why did Robert Oppenheimer enthusiastically direct the atomic bomb program but oppose the development of the Super?
5. Do you agree with the AEC's decision to revoke Oppenheimer's security clearance in 1953? Explain why or why not.

Selected Bibliography

Berg, Scott. *Lindbergh*. New York: G.P. Putnam's Sons, 1998.

Bethe, Hans. *The Road from Los Alamos*. New York: Simon and Schuster, 1991.

Bird, Kai, and Martin Sherwin. *American Prometheus: The Triumph and Tragedy of J. Robert Oppenheimer*. New York: Alfred A. Knopf, 2005.

Cole, Wayne S. *Charles A. Lindbergh and the Battle against American Intervention in World War II*. New York: Harcourt Brace Jovanovich, 1974.

Dumenil, Lynn. *The Modern Temper: American Culture and Society in the 1920s*. New York: Hill and Wang, 1997.

Groves, Leslie. *Now It Can Be Told: The Story of the Manhattan Project*. New York: Harper, 1962.

Herken, Gregg. *Brotherhood of the Bomb: The Tangled Lives and Loyalties of Robert Oppenheimer, Ernest Lawrence and Edward Teller*. New York: Henry Holt, 2002.

Lindbergh, Anne Morrow. *War Within and Without: Diaries and Letters, 1939–1944*. New York: Harcourt Brace Jovanovich, 1980.

Lindbergh, Charles. *Autobiography of Values*. New York: Harcourt Brace Jovanovich, 1976.

———. *Wartime Journals*. New York: Harcourt Brace Jovanovich, 1970.

McMillan, Priscilla J. *The Ruin of J. Robert Oppenheimer and the Birth of the Modern Arms Race*. New York: Penguin, 2005.

Milton, Joyce. *Loss of Eden: A Biography of Charles and Anne Morrow Lindbergh*. New York: Harper Collins, 1993.

Parrish, Michael. *Anxious Decades: America in Prosperity and Depression, 1920–1941*. New York: Norton, 1994.

Rhodes, Richard. *Dark Sun: The Making of the Hydrogen Bomb*. New York: Simon and Schuster, 1995.

———. *The Making of the Atomic Bomb*. New York: Simon and Schuster, 1988.

Wallace, Max. *The American Axis: Henry Ford, Charles Lindbergh and the Rise of the Third Reich*. New York: St. Martin's Press, 2003.

CHAPTER EIGHT

~

The Cold War at Home

Following in the wake of World War II, the Cold War altered the shape of American politics for at least two generations. It helped to weaken the Democratic Party's hold on the political allegiance of the American people and diluted the appeal of liberalism associated with government action during the Great Depression. The bid for the presidency by New York Governor Al Smith in 1928 had garnered support from new immigrants, many of them Jewish or, like the Democratic Party standard bearer, Catholic. The advent of the Great Depression and Franklin Delano Roosevelt's ensuing presidency enabled the Democrats to supplant the Republicans as the dominant political force in the United States. While championing activist government in the fashion of the Progressives, Roosevelt similarly helped to make liberalism the nation's dominant political philosophy. Workers, farmers, intellectuals, urban political machines, supportive businessmen, Catholics, Jews, Southerners, blacks, and various ethnic minorities formed the New Deal coalition that allowed FDR to capture four consecutive presidential elections and to enable his successor, Harry S Truman, to grab the next one as well. In the process, belief in the need for greater government involvement in the nation's social and economic affairs resulted in larger control of both the industrial and agrarian sectors. That belief led to the structural foundation of the American welfare state and the apparent discrediting of the ideas of laissez-faire and social Darwinism.

Not everyone was pleased with this turn of events, as forces on both the left and the right proved critical of New Deal operations and Rooseveltian liberalism. Socialists and communists envisioned far greater structural transformation of the American economic order, with the former desiring more movement in the direction of economic democracy and the latter favoring a "Soviet America" in which communism would prevail, at least theoretically. Conservatives and those further to the right viewed with alarm the Roosevelt administration's purported socialistic tendencies, evident in programs ranging from the Tennessee Valley Authority to the Social Security Act. In the manner of former president Herbert Hoover, they warned that America was treading a line that could not be crossed without heading down a slippery slope toward another system altogether. American far rightists had their own vision of an authoritarian state headed by a strong man on the order of Benito Mussolini or Adolf Hitler. World War II and the horrors it unleashed, including the Holocaust and the bloody fighting across Europe and Asia, appeared to discredit the most extreme views on the right side of the American political spectrum.

The disintegration of the wartime Grand Alliance—the partnership of imperialist-parliamentary Great Britain, the capitalist-democratic United States, and the communist Soviet Union—led to heightened tensions following the end of humankind's most terrible conflagration. Little helping matters was the Soviet determination to set up first friendly, then overtly Stalinist communist regimes throughout Eastern Europe, and the United States' belief that it possessed the right to serve as something of a world hegemon. Embittered rhetoric flowed from both Soviet dictator Joseph Stalin and former British prime minister Winston Churchill suggesting that amicable relations between East and West were not possible. The deterioration of relations with the former World War II ally played into the hands of those determined to use anticommunism as a political club in the United States.

Anticommunism was hardly a new force in American life, having been wielded by employers, strikebreakers, and politicians during labor strife following the Civil War. It had resurfaced with a vengeance during World War I, especially after the Bolsheviks, led by Vladimir Lenin and Leon Trotsky, came to power in Russia, helping usher in the postwar Red Scare. During the interwar period, anticommunism waxed and waned but never fully dissipated. It heightened, even among liberals and anti-Stalinist radicals, during the Moscow purge trials of the 1930s and after the Nazi-Soviet Pact of August 1939 was announced. The German invasion of the Soviet Union enabled the communist state to land back on the side of the angels, at least rhetorically, and the Communist Party of the United States of America (CPUSA) acquired thousands of new members. As communists held sway in Poland and other Eastern European states, American anticommunism reemerged with considerable potency, allowing figures like World War II veterans Richard Nixon of Orange County, California, and Joseph McCarthy of Wisconsin, to sweep into political office.

As the Republicans regained control of Congress for the first time in a generation following the 1946 midterm elections, President Truman and many liberals in the Democratic ranks adopted more overtly anticommunist approaches of their own in an effort to deflect allegations that they were "soft on communism." Truman required federal employees to take a loyalty oath and allowed Attorney General Tom Clark to devise a list of purported subversive organizations. Hardly placated, Congress proceeded with a series of investigations, including some targeting the entertainment industry. In the process even well-known and previously highly regarded individuals got caught up in something of a dragnet, although nothing akin to the terrors that had been unleashed in totalitarian states like Nazi Germany and the Soviet Union under Stalin. Standing on opposite sides of the political and cultural divide that characterized the domestic Cold War were Democratic Senator Pat McCarran of Nevada and the acclaimed black actor-singer Paul Robeson. Both before and after Republican Senator Joseph McCarthy of Wisconsin launched his well-publicized campaign to ferret out domestic subversives, McCarran spearheaded Red-baiting efforts of his own. One of those victimized by the anticommunist fervor of the late 1940s and early 1950s was Robeson, long considered one of America's greatest and seemingly unassailable performers.

The anticommunist mania that enveloped both McCarran and Robeson recast American politics for decades to come. It strengthened American conservatism, caused liberals to adopt anticommunist approaches of their own, and crippled the Left, virtually eviscerating its Stalinist branch. Anticommunism influenced U.S. policymakers, many of whom considered it necessary for their nation to serve as an international police force, some guided by political calculation, others by conviction, and a number by fear of standing on the wrong side of the ideological spectrum in a time when hysteria, at least on occasion, prevailed. McCarran came to symbolize patriotic zeal for some and fanaticism for others. Robeson too was viewed in different lights, either as a puppetlike, anti-American shill for brutal authoritarianism, or as a well-intentioned man of conviction whose artistic career was blunted because of witch-hunting, little better than that which residents of Salem had endured long ago.

～ PAUL ROBESON ～

A large crowd congregated on September 4, 1949, to hear the famed singer and controversial political activist Paul Robeson, the Weavers, and other singers perform at a benefit concert put on by the left-wing People's Artists Inc. The proceeds were to be delivered to the Harlem chapter of the Civil Rights Congress in the largely blue-collar community of Peekskill, New York. This was the

Paul Robeson as Othello in the 1943–1944 Theater Guild production of the Shakespeare drama. Defying racial conventions as well as political orthodoxy, Robeson was a highly controversial figure throughout his career. His leftist political views and criticisms of American foreign policy during the early years of the Cold War brought intense scrutiny from the Federal Bureau of Investigation and public condemnation of the famous baritone. (Library of Congress, LC-USW33-054945)

second attempt for such a gathering, the previous week's effort having been canceled after a baseball-bat-wielding, jeering mob attacked would-be concertgoers. Many appeared angered at the statement the Associated Press falsely attributed to Robeson: "It is unthinkable that American Negroes would go to war on behalf of those who oppressed us for generations against a country [the Soviet Union] which in one generation has raised our people to the full dignity of mankind." The Peekskill *Evening Star* repeatedly referred to the ebony-colored, still-handsome Robeson as a "Communist," although he was not officially a member of the CPUSA, and a "subversive."

With only four deputy sheriffs on hand on August 27, angry veterans refused to allow most ticket holders to enter the concert grounds, and Robeson's car never arrived. A cry had gone out from the pack of men and boys: "Give us five minutes and we'll murder the white niggers." Other common epithets included

"Dirty Commie" and "Dirty kike." Brass knuckles, billy clubs, bottles, and rocks rained down on the would-be concertgoers. Holding a press conference in Harlem at the Hotel Theresa, Robeson demanded an investigation by the Justice Department, declaring that what happened in Peekskill amounted to "an attack on the whole Negro people." The *New York Daily Mirror* headlined, "Robeson: He Asked for It," although an FBI agent would report that the riot was "started by the vets." The *New York Times* offered an editorial, defending the concertgoers' rights and confirming the singer's right to perform, no matter the "twisted thinking" regarding the Soviet Union "that is ruining Robeson's great career." The editor of the *Washington Post* placed most of the blame for the violence on Robeson's shoulders while condemning "his disparagements of his native country and his fulsome glorification of Soviet Russia."

A large crowd congregated on September 4 to hear the famed entertainer sing at a picnic ground close to a sign reading "Peekskill Is a Friendly Town." Thousands of veterans and members of New York City unions established something of a defense perimeter. Robeson appeared in the late afternoon, offering renditions of "Let My People Go" and "Ol' Man River." All the while 1,000 or so veterans protested near the concert grounds but were initially held in check, this time by a large number of state troopers and policemen. In the late afternoon, however, departing concertgoers were attacked over a wide swath of territory. Eventually, "a nightmare of crashing rocks, flying glass, blood, and swerving cars," with many tipped over, resulted. The *Times* noted that the rioters included housewives, young people, and older men and women. Some frightened bus drivers abandoned their posts, leaving the concert attendees to the mercy of the mob. Police were heard to warn, "Go back to Jew town, if we catch you up here again we'll kill you." At a lengthy press conference the following day, Robeson denounced the out-of-control state troopers as "fascist storm troopers who will knock down and club anyone who disagrees with them." Governor Thomas Dewey dismissed the concertgoers as "followers of Red totalitarianism," who sparked "this incident." A grand jury later declared that communists, not anti-Semitic or antiblack sentiments, had triggered "racial and religious hatred" in Peekskill. The Peekskill affair underscored the transformed public image of Robeson, once considered iconic but now increasingly viewed as beyond the pale because of his political perspectives.

Paul Leroy Bustill Robeson was born on April 9, 1898, in the then informally segregated community of Princeton, New Jersey, the fifth surviving child of the former slave turned Presbyterian clergyman William Drew Robeson and schoolteacher Maria Louisa Robeson. A scholarship enabled Paul to attend Rutgers University in New Brunswick, where he lettered in four sports, was a two-time all-American, and became class valedictorian. The student magazine contended that he was "the leader of the colored race in America." Robeson went on to graduate from Columbia Law School, residing in Harlem, where he befriended leading figures in the Harlem Renaissance such as writers Countee Cullen and Langston Hughes, artist Aaron Douglas, and sociologist E. Franklin Frazier. Robeson financed his legal education largely by playing semipro basketball and professional football, then still in its infancy and at the time open to black players like Robeson and Fritz Pollard, another former collegiate all-American, despite the racism they confronted. Just before his second year in law school, Robeson secretly married the light-skinned and highly ambitious Eslanda Cardozo Goode on August 17, 1921. They later had one son, Paul Jr.

While still at Columbia, Robeson began to appear on Broadway, performing in *Taboo* in the spring of 1922, and in the acclaimed all-black musical revue *Shuffle Along* that featured Florence Mills. Robeson entered the London stage, where he repeatedly returned, to star in *Voodoo*, a retitled version of *Taboo*. Returning home, he completed his law degree in 1923 and briefly served as a law clerk with a Wall Street firm but quit, enraged by the racism he encountered from a stenographer there. He became involved with the Provincetown Players, starring in productions of Eugene O'Neill's *All God's Chillun Got Wings*, about an interracial marriage, and *The Emperor Jones*, in the lead role initially performed by Charles Gilpin on Broadway. The *Philadelphia Record* praised Robeson's performance in *All God's Chillun*, calling him "a strapping man with a voice that rolls out of him like a vibrant tide." The *New York Telegram* said of his performance in *The Emperor Jones* that Robeson was "as fine an actor as there is on the American stage." By contrast, a review in the *Chicago Defender* termed the plays "genius productions of subtleness of the most insidious and damaging kind."

Robeson remained one of the leading theatrical performers in both the United States and abroad over the next two decades, often starring in productions on Broadway or the London stage. He also made the first of several cinematic appearances, accepting a leading role in 1924 in the silent melodrama *Body and Soul*, taking on twin roles as a convict and his well-meaning brother. He frequently toured with his friend, accompanist-arranger Larry Brown, offering the kinds of spirituals that led a critic in the *New York Times* to applaud their ability to exude "universal humanism, that touches the heart." As Robeson's fame soared, women flocked to him, and his relationship with Essie took on an on-again, off-again pattern. They nevertheless sailed for London in September 1925, living in Chelsea as Paul starred in a British production of *The Emperor Jones*, with the *New Statesman and Nation* terming him "magnificent." Back home, he discovered that his recently released records had sold more than 50,000 copies within four months of their release. Over the next several years, he starred in theatrical productions of *Black Boy*, *Porgy*, *Show Boat*, *Othello*, and *The Hairy Ape*. King George V and Queen Mary attended *Show Boat*, while a reviewer proclaimed Robeson's performance in *Othello* "one of the great moments in the history of Shakespearean drama." He gave concerts at the Royal Albert Hall in London and Carnegie Hall in New York City. He also was seen on the silver screen in such films as *The Emperor Jones* (1933), which led the *New York American* to claim Robeson had delivered "the finest acting ever seen on stage or screen," *Showboat* (1936), and *King Solomon's Mines* (1937).

Responding to an invitation from famed film director Sergei Eisenstein, Robeson visited the Soviet Union for two weeks with Essie—their relationship remaining in flux—starting in late December 1934. When asked by an interviewer in London before his departure, Robeson insisted, "Oh no. There is absolutely no color prejudice" in the Soviet Union. Passing through Berlin, Robeson was taken aback by the militarism that had enveloped Germany since the Nazi takeover. Received like a welcomed celebrity in Moscow, Robeson met Foreign Minister Maxim Litvinov and spent a good deal of time with Eisenstein. In an interview with the communist *Daily Worker*, published in New York City, he declared, "I was not prepared for the happiness I see on every face in Moscow." Regarding the deadly show trials that Joseph Stalin had begun to initiate, Robeson exclaimed, "From what I have already seen of the workings of the Soviet Government, I can only say that anybody who lifts his hand against it ought to be shot! . . . It is the government's duty to put down any opposition to this really free society with a firm hand." He continued, "This is home to me. I feel more kinship to the Russian people under their new society than I ever felt anywhere else. It is obvious that there is no terror here, that all the masses of every race are contented and support their government." During the next few years, Robeson would make several trips to the Soviet Union, which he saluted as "the bulwark of civilization against both war and fascism." Broadcasting from Moscow in 1937, where he had enrolled Paul Jr. in a Soviet Model School attended by children of Stalin and Vyacheslav Molotov, a top Soviet official, Robeson praised "this wonderful country" and its "unforgettable, great Socialist Constitution," which he acclaimed for laying out "the glorious highway to Socialism . . . symbolic of the future path of mankind." He compared "the boundless hope and aspiration of the Soviet family of free peoples" with "the tragic lot of the people of Spain," caught up in a brutal civil war involving the democratically elected government and fascist forces led by General Francisco Franco.

After departing from the Soviet Union, Robeson continued to speak out on behalf of the Spanish Republic, asserting in the summer of 1937, "The freedom of all the Peoples of the world is at stake in this conflict in Spain." On December 19, 1937, Robeson spoke once more at a rally in Albert Hall, put on by the Labour Party, with 12,000 in attendance. Delivering a new rendition of "Ol' Man River," Robeson altered the closing refrain from "I gets weary and sick of tryin'; / I'm tired of livin' and scared of dyin'" to "I keeps laughin' instead of cryin'; / I must keep fightin' until I'm dyin'.'"

Robeson determined to go to Spain to demonstrate solidarity with those fighting Franco, who was backed by fascist Italy and Nazi Germany. The U.S. State Department now opened a file on him. Arriving in Spain on January 23, 1938, Paul and Essie Robeson met top CPUSA leaders there, including Robert Minor, Earl Browder, and William Rust. When asked during his visit why he was in Spain, Robeson answered, "It is dishonorable to put yourself on a plane above the masses, without marching at their side . . . and it is not only as an artist that I love the cause of democracy in Spain, but also as a Black. I belong to an oppressed race, discriminated against, one that could not live if fascism triumphed in the world." Republican troops everywhere recognized and warmly greeted Robeson, who later termed the trip "a major turning point in my life." Considering Spain "our Front Line," Robeson was appalled at the unwilling-ness of the Western democracies, in contrast to the Soviet Union, to assist the Loyalists. Little desirous of another major war or not well disposed to the radical aspects of the Spanish government, the United States, England, and France failed to provide assistance to the Spanish Republic; Germany and Italy, by contrast, funneled a great amount of support to the right-wing forces led by General Franco determined to crush the Republicans.

Back in London he enrolled Paul Jr. in a school attended by the children of Soviet diplomats. Young Paul confronted his father at one point about the Moscow purges, now in their deadliest phase. The great artist finally admitted to his son that "terrible" deeds had been committed, that innocent individuals were "sacrificed to punish the guilty," but that the Soviet Union was facing "the equivalent of war" and could not tolerate dissent. Following the collapse of the Spanish Republic in January 1939, Robeson again spoke on behalf of those flee-ing from Franco. He seemed untroubled by the announcement that the Soviet and German foreign ministers had signed a nonaggression pact on August 23, 1939, which stunned many Communist Party members. He arrived in New York City on October 12, having spent most of the previous decade residing in London. Speaking to the press, he denied being either a communist or a fellow traveler who failed to join the party but supported many of its positions. However, he readily admitted communists had befriended him. He proclaimed himself an antifascist, who felt "closer to my country than ever." Refusing to criticize the Soviet Union or the CPUSA openly, even following the Soviet invasion of Finland in November, Robeson instead spoke of the Soviet Union as waging a "defensive war."

Robeson garnered acclaim across the country, however, when he joined in a radio broadcast, "The Pursuit of Happiness," a celebration of democracy for which Paul sang an Earl Robinson-John LaTouche song, "The Ballad of Uncle Sam." Refrains included "Man in white skin can never be free / While his black brother is in slavery" and "Our Country's strong, our Country's young / And her greatest songs are still unsung." At the same time, Robeson's procommunist stance was beginning to evoke greater concern. An appearance on a national radio program was temporarily delayed due to growing concerns that he was a communist.

Robeson continued to be lauded for his theatrical and musical performances, including a revival of *Show Boat* in mid-1940. He also lent his name to the Committee to Defend America by Keeping Out of War. Following the German invasion of the Soviet Union in June 1941, Robeson, in line with the CPUSA, shifted course, discarding an anti-interventionist stance for one demanding aid to the beleaguered communist state. He also insisted on the release of CPUSA leader Earl Browder, who had been imprisoned for passport violations. With the formation of the Grand Alliance after the Japanese attack on Pearl Harbor, the issue of Russian war relief seemed noncontroversial, as evidenced by a rally on June 22, 1942, in Madison Square Garden, where the podium boasted New York mayor Fiorello La Guardia, labor chieftain William Green, presidential adviser Harry Hopkins, Supreme Court Justice Stanley Reed, Soviet Ambassador Maxim Litvinov, and Robeson.

All the while the FBI tracked the great entertainer, tapping phone conversations and bugging apartments he visited. An earlier report noted he was "reputedly" a member of the Communist Party and the Bureau now considered him "a Communist functionary," Robeson biographer Martin Duberman writes. Special agents tailed him, reporting on his movements. On January 12, 1943, FBI director J. Edgar Hoover recommended that Robeson "be considered for custodial detention in view of the existing emergency." The FBI eventually compiled a large file containing nearly 3,000 pages on Robeson, whom Hoover considered "a confidant of high officials of the Party" and "undoubtedly 100% Communist."

Robeson remained a luminous star throughout the war, a period when the CPUSA regained a measure of respectability as the Soviet Union, Great Britain, and the United States partnered to defeat the Axis powers. His singing of "Ballad for America" at the Southern Conference for Human Welfare, held in Nashville, Tennessee, led Eleanor Roosevelt to acclaim in her "My Day" column of April 22, 1942, that hearing him was "a thrilling experience. . . . [L]ast night there was something peculiarly significant about it." The present war, Robeson announced, was "a war for the liberation of all peoples, all races, all colors oppressed anywhere in the world," something FDR "very clearly" recognized. He told *PM*, the left-liberal newspaper, that he now believed "America gives her minority groups more of a chance than just about any country," and he had no intention of living anywhere else again. Robeson was on stage for the Broadway opening of *Othello* in October 1943, which the black press declared a racial milestone and led to the New York Newspaper Guild handing him a Page One Award for his "distinguished performance."

On April 16, 1944, 12,000 people—thousands more were turned away—joined in the celebration of Robeson's forty-sixth birthday and the anniversary of the Council on African Affairs, held at the Armory located at Thirty-fourth Street and Park Avenue in New York City. Congratulatory notes arrived from a host of luminaries ranging from Vice President Henry Wallace to Babe Ruth. Robeson participated in a USO tour in Germany, Czechoslovakia, and France in August 1945. He received the Spingarn Medal two months later, an award delivered annually by the NAACP for "the highest achievement" by a black American. Speaking at the Biltmore Hotel, with several hundred in attendance, Robeson roundly praised the Soviet Union, to the dismay of NAACP executive secretary Walter White. Robeson intoned, "The Soviet Union can't help it as a nation and a people if it is in the mainstream of change." He warned about fascism's resurgence and the restoration of monarchies. Robeson, now standing at "the apex" of his career, soon began to experience the loss of public esteem.

Investigative committees started calling on Robeson to testify. On October 7, he spoke before the legislature's Joint Fact-Finding Committee on Un-American Activities in California about race relations. Asked by Chairman Jack Tenney if he was a communist, Robeson denied that he was, calling himself "an anti-Fascist and independent." Questioned about the Soviet purges, Robeson refused to compare them with lynchings in the United States and then said that dissenters in the USSR "ought to get out of there or get shot."

Such provocative statements ensured that Robeson remained a target of Red hunters. Columnist Hedda Hopper reviled Robeson in March 1947 for delivering the "People's Battle song" associated with the Soviet Union, while the House Committee on Un-American Activities named Paul and almost 1,000 other individuals, such as former Vice President Wallace and Tennessee Valley Authority director David E. Lilienthal, as "invariably found supporting the Communist Party and its front organizations." In several instances Robeson was allowed to give concerts with the stipulation that he refrain from offering political commentary. *Newsweek* soon offered a "Paean from *Pravda*," charging that the Soviet Union felt "gratitude" to figures like Albert Einstein, former U.S. ambassador Joseph E. Davies, Harvard professor Ralph Barton Berry, and Robeson. *New York Times Herald* columnist George E. Sokolsky warned that "better men than Paul Robeson have been thrown to the lions." Robeson's support for Henry Wallace's controversial presidential bid under the banner of the Progressive Party, largely run by figures associated with the CPUSA, helped to bring that about, at least figuratively. The artist called Wallace a "progressive capitalist" and said the "whole talk about Communism is absurd. Either we get along with the Communists, jump in the ocean, or blow up the whole world." Testifying before the Senate Judiciary Committee in May 1948, Robeson referred to his "many dear friends who are Communists" and pledged to violate a proposed law, which he deemed "part of that hysteria," requiring the registration of all communists and communist-front organizations.

In November of that year, President Truman upset the highly favored New York Governor Thomas Dewey, the Republican nominee. Performing more poorly than another minor party candidate, South Carolina Governor Strom Thurmond of the States' Rights Democratic Party, Wallace captured little more than one million votes. The Progressive Party's abysmal showing appeared to provide further impetus for those determined to attack the American Left, particularly the CPUSA and those, like Robeson, who remained supportive of it. In early 1949 the U.S. government initiated its prosecution of communist leaders, indicted for having violated the 1940 Smith Act, which made it a criminal offense for anyone to "knowingly or willfully advocate, abet, advise or teach the duty, necessity, desirability or propriety of overthrowing" the federal government or any state government "by force or violence." Appearing in Manhattan at the courthouse in Foley Square where the trial occurred, Robeson declared, "I, too, am on trial," pointing to his leadership in the Progressive Party, the Civil Rights Congress, and the Council on African Affairs.

In April 1949 Robeson attended the World Congress of the Partisans of Peace held in Paris. Among those participating were W. E. B. DuBois, Pablo Picasso, and the poet Louis Aragon. Robeson spoke briefly, charging that American wealth was derived from "the backs" of white European laborers and "millions of blacks." He exclaimed, "And we are resolved to share it equally among our children." He then stated, "And we shall not put up with any hysterical raving that urges us to make war on anyone. . . . We shall not make war on anyone. We shall not make war on the Soviet Union." The Associated Press mistakenly quoted Robeson as comparing U.S. government policies to those of the Nazis. Denunciations came fast and furious, with American black leaders like Walter White, NAACP legal strategist Charles Houston, and Harlem congressman Adam Clayton Powell Jr. condemning Robeson's alleged statement. A *New York Times* editorial termed Robeson "mistaken and misled" and offered, "We want him to sing, and to go on being Paul Robeson." At a contentious press conference in Stockholm, a defiant Robeson now affirmed that American blacks would never fight against the Soviet Union.

Landing at La Guardia Airport on June 16, 1949, Robeson blasted the throng of reporters for having distorted his overseas remarks. He soon urged fellow American blacks not "to die in vain any more on foreign battlefields for Wall Street and the greedy supporters of domestic fascism. If we must die, let it be in Mississippi or Georgia." Headlines cried out, "Loves Soviets Best, Robeson Declares" and "An Undesirable Citizen."

The House Un-American Activities Committee held hearings with well-known African Americans regarding the controversy surrounding Robeson. Brooklyn Dodger Jackie Robinson, the first black player in the major leagues in the twentieth century, acknowledged on July 18 that African Americans possessed authentic grievances and called Robeson "a famous ex-athlete and a great singer and actor." But he declared that if Robeson had actually delivered the statement attributed to him, it "sounds very silly to me." The black community proved divided, with some calling Robeson "as loyal an American as any other." And yet while Robeson was himself being assailed, he followed the CPUSA line in supporting the government prosecution of American Trotskyists, adjudging them "allies of fascism" who falsely accused Stalin of leading a "police state."

The furor surrounding Robeson threatened to boil over, as evidenced by the Peekskill concert on September 4, 1949. Robeson refused to mute his voice, conducting a nationwide tour sponsored by the Civil Rights Congress. More and more large civic centers were closed to him, but Robeson appeared at smaller venues and churches to overflowing crowds and still occasionally drew huge crowds. He continued operating as if he wanted to become a pariah in his homeland. Speaking in early November at a dinner held at the Waldorf-Astoria honoring Soviet Foreign Minister Andrei Vyshinsky and the anniversary of the Bolshevik Revolution, Robeson insisted Eastern Europeans were "masters of their own lands"; denounced Joseph Tito, the Yugoslav leader who had broken with the Soviet Union; and referred to President Truman as an "imperialist wolf disguised as a benevolent watchdog."

The number of venues available to Robeson steadily diminished. This situation worsened after Wisconsin Senator Joseph McCarthy began hurling charges of widespread communist involvement in the Truman administration. More frequently Robeson was invited only to speak at peace rallies, many communist-directed. He attacked U.S. intervention in Korea, while asserting, "a new wind of freedom blows in the East," as long-oppressed peoples attempted to throw off the yoke associated with "robber barons and white-supremacists of Europe and America." During the summer of 1950, the U.S. State Department voided Robeson's passport. In "The Strange Case of Paul Robeson," which appeared in the February 1951 issue of *Ebony*, Walter White called his old friend "a bewildered man . . . more to be pitied than damned." The State Department tightened its grip around Robeson in January 1952, refusing to allow him to travel to Canada to offer a concert in Vancouver, British Columbia. Now facing something of an unofficial blacklist, Robeson extolled Stalin's "deep humanity" following the dictator's death in early 1953 and celebrated the "new magnificent society" in the Soviet Union. Even following Soviet premier

Nikita Khrushchev's revelation of Stalinist horrors at the Twentieth Communist Party Congress in February 1956, Robeson, recently allowed to give a concert in Toronto, refused to publicly criticize the Soviet state. By contrast, communist parties around the globe were thunderstruck, with many individuals deciding to leave the train of the revolution.

Now experiencing obvious signs of depression, Robeson was compelled to testify before HUAC in June 1956. When asked if he belonged to the CPUSA, Paul asked, "What is the Communist Party?" A heated exchange between Chairman Francis Walter and Robeson ensued when the legislator acknowledged being desirous of keeping "only your kind" of people out of the country. Robeson retorted, "Colored people like myself." Additional insults flew back and forth before Robeson shouted that the members of the committee were the authentic "un-Americans, and you ought to be ashamed of yourselves." The committee soon voted to cite him for contempt of Congress but the House of Representatives failed to follow suit. That fall, Robeson refused to support the Hungarian rebels who were striving to replace Stalinist communism with democratic socialism.

English friends formed the National Paul Robeson Committee in the spring of 1957 to pressure the U.S. State Department to reissue his passport. By early 1958, Robeson, in an apparent desire to be viewed once more as black spokesperson, lessened his public support for the Soviet Union. To the evident dismay of the FBI, he completed a series of concerts that played to enthusiastic crowds. Improving his public image too was the release of a slim volume, *Here I Stand*, an autobiographical treatment that effectively proclaimed his allegiance to black Americans and to this country. He insisted, "I am not and never have been involved in any international conspiracy or any other kind, and do not know anyone who is." Robeson also likened himself to Frederick Douglass, the great nineteenth-century black leader, who believed he was acting as "a true patriot; for he is a lover of his country who rebukes and does not excuse its sins." After seven years away from a commercial studio, Robeson began recording again. Around the globe, celebrations in honor of his sixtieth birthday occurred. For the first time in over a decade, he delivered a concert at Carnegie Hall. Then, in June 1958, the U.S. Supreme Court ruled that the Secretary of State was not entitled to deny a passport because of a citizen's political beliefs.

On July 11, 1958, Robeson arrived in London, where he was greeted by political heavyweights and a bevy of journalists, and soon flew on to Moscow. After nearly a month's stay in the Soviet Union, he returned to London to kick off a three-month concert tour. He was back in Moscow late in the year and was welcomed by Khrushchev to the Kremlin. In the spring Robeson starred in another presentation of *Othello* in London's West End, directed by Tony Richardson. He also sang in Trafalgar Square before a large disarmament rally in

April 1959. While the U.S. State Department proved troubled by his criticisms of American foreign policy, the British received him enthusiastically. Robeson returned to Moscow for a three-week visit in January 1960, spent a good deal of time on the continent performing, and toured in Australia beginning in October of that year, followed by a stint in New Zealand.

Though the Red Scare waned in the 1960s, Robeson remained both controversial and afflicted by bouts of depression that led to a pair of suicide attempts, electroshock treatments, and continued poor health. He made few public appearances, but on April 15, 1973, more than 3,000 people arrived at Carnegie Hall to celebrate his seventy-fifth birthday. Former U.S. Attorney General Ramsey Clark lauded Robeson's "grace and beauty" that his own country seemed "afraid of," and Coretta Scott King noted that Paul had "tapped the same wells of latent militancy" earlier than her slain husband. Less than a month after suffering a stroke, Robeson died on January 23, 1976. Thousands paid tribute four days later at the Mother A.M.E. Zion Church in Harlem.

～ PAT McCARRAN ～

In January 1939, Nevada senator Pat McCarran attended the Senate Judiciary Committee's hearing in which Harvard Law School professor and American Civil Liberties Union member Felix Frankfurter fielded questions regarding his nomination by President Franklin D. Roosevelt to serve on the U.S. Supreme Court. McCarran, who easily tossed around the epithet "kike," asked the Austrian-born Frankfurter, "Doctor, you were born abroad?" before hurling a series of additional queries about purported communist influence inside the ACLU. McCarran asked, "Doctor, do you believe in the Constitution of the United States?" Frankfurter responded, "Most assuredly." McCarran then asked if Frankfurter had ever "enrolled" in the Communist Party. Frankfurter replied, "I mean that I have never been enrolled and have never been qualified to be enrolled because that does not represent my view of life, nor my view of government." Thunderous applause filled the Caucus Room and the hearing ended. At a luncheon with Henry Ashurst, who chaired the Senate Judiciary Committee, Frankfurter asked about McCarran, who appeared "obsessed about Communism." When Frankfurter asked if there were any communists in Nevada, Ashurst answered, "No, no, he's never seen one." The subcommittee's vote on Frankfurter's nomination was unanimous, with the exception of McCarran, who returned an unmarked ballot.

Patrick Anthony McCarran was born in Reno, Nevada, on August 8, 1876, to Irish immigrants Patrick and Margaret McCarran. The elder Patrick arrived in the United States in 1848, as a terrible potato blight swept through Ireland, leading to the death of one million Irish and the emigration of a million

Nevada senator Pat McCarran in 1947. Though Wisconsin senator Joseph McCarthy was generally acknowledged as the nation's most prominent communist hunter during the Red Scare, McCarran began his crusade to oust subversives at an earlier date. (Library of Congress, LC-USZ62-83708)

more. Illiterate when he first landed in the new country, Patrick entered the U.S. Army in 1857 and briefly served with the California Volunteers during the Civil War. Deserting from the army, he acquired land in the Nevada territory. Margaret landed in the United States in 1872, working as a domestic servant. Three years later the twenty-three-year-old met Patrick McCarran, then nearly twice her age and noted for his ill temper and financially profligate manner, and the two married that October. When Patrick Jr., destined to be an only child, was still a toddler, the family settled on a ranch situated about fifteen miles outside of Reno. The ranch's isolation ensured that Patrick Jr.'s early years were marked by social isolation, hard work, and sporadic education. Patrick Jr. enrolled in school for the first time when he was ten years old, and graduated from high school, valedictorian in a class of sixteen students, when he was nearly twenty-one. In the fall of 1897, McCarran began attending the University of Nevada, still a fledgling institution, where he was most drawn to political science classes, played on the football team, starred in track and field, joined the debate squad, and served as sports editor of the school newspaper.

With his grades sliding and his father in ill health, McCarran dropped out of the university during his senior year, opting for sheep raising instead. However, in 1902, the nephew of powerful banker William Sharon asked McCarran to run for the state legislature.

Admitted to the Union as a state in 1864, at the encouragement of President Abraham Lincoln, Nevada remained safely in the Republican Party camp until hard economic times and the Free Silver movement converged in the last decade of the nineteenth century. That movement called for remonetization of silver to ensure that more money was in circulation, something that the hard-money Republicans opposed. In 1892 Populist Party candidate James Weaver captured the electoral votes of four states, including Nevada. In the next election, William Jennings Bryan, running as a fusion candidate backed by both Democrats and Populists, captured 81.2 percent of Nevada's votes. The following campaign cycle saw Bryan again easily take the state. Thus the offer to McCarran to run on the Democratic Party ticket in 1902 had to have been welcome news to the ambitious, politically concerned young man. Propounding a Progressive platform that supported an eight-hour work day, the right of workers to organize, and restraints on trusts, McCarran was elected to the state assembly. The following year he married Martha Harriet Weeks, a teacher at a one-room school in Clover Valley; the McCarrans eventually had five children. Meanwhile the *Reno Evening Gazette* lauded the young McCarran as being one of the state legislature's "most careful and painstaking members."

Narrowly defeated in a bid for the state senate in 1904, McCarran continued reading law, passing the bar examination and moving to the boom town of Tonopah. He was elected district attorney of Nye County in 1906, having been praised by the *Tonopah Bonanza* as "a fine orator, a shrewd lawyer, and a worthy gentleman." He criticized the use of federal troops during a labor struggle pitting members of the Western Federation of Miners, led by Big Bill Haywood, against mine owners, headed by George Wingfield, soon to become McCarran's nemesis. McCarran charged, "The Plan of Governor Sparks to equip a body of Texas Rangers and vest these horsemen with power to use their shooting irons at will in the settlement of labor controversies would be more than a state disgrace." McCarran then made an unsuccessful bid for a seat in the U.S. House of Representatives. At the time he remained a Bryan Democrat, calling the perennial Democratic Party presidential candidate "the greatest living exponent of Jeffersonian principles." Ironically, given his later positions, McCarran's candidacy and his opposition to strikebreaking tactics led some to view him as a radical. Others deemed McCarran unscrupulous, with Democratic Party leader Key Pittman referring to his unfettered ambition and "reputation as a double-crosser."

In 1909 Pat and Martha McCarran moved with their two young daughters to Reno, the largest city in the state, albeit one with a population of only 10,000.

There he practiced law and again envisioned a political future that would carry him to the nation's capital. He began in 1912 by winning a seat on the Nevada Supreme Court, easily defeating former congressman George Bartlett. Four years later, McCarran made a futile bid for the U.S. Senate seat now held by Key Pittman, despite a prohibition in the state constitution regarding sitting judges running for nonjudicial government posts. McCarran insisted he would better represent Nevada in Congress and proclaimed himself a champion of women's right to vote in federal elections. As the United States entered World War I McCarran's term on the state supreme court continued, proving by all accounts to be a distinguished one, although he later considered the period to have amounted to "six years of exile." His judicial record was characterized by strong concern for the rights of criminal defendants, including the need for adequate counsel, and by firm support for progressive legislation. With his political career having foundered, McCarran hoped for an appointment to the federal court, and at one point senators Pittman and Francis G. Newlands backed him, hoping to be rid of a potential foe at the ballot box. Deciding to run for reelection to the state supreme court only five months before the election, McCarran was defeated, to the delight of powerful fellow Democrats in Nevada. He remained enamored with the idea of serving in Washington, DC, but an extended period in the political wilderness soon began.

McCarran's notoriety continued, hardly hurt by his handling of a divorce case involving the actress Mary Pickford. After biding his time, McCarran initiated another run for the U.S. Senate in 1926. Speaking on July 4, McCarran demanded that his country "avoid participating involvement with any court, compact or league which may endanger our being drawn into foreign wars." Six years later, the fifty-six-year-old McCarran finally garnered the Democratic Party nomination for the Senate seat held by Republican Tasker Oddie, who was running for a third term. Campaigning vigorously, McCarran now paid little attention to foreign policy other than expressing support for diplomatic recognition of the Soviet Union, along with other nations where American products might be sold. As the Great Depression deepened, McCarran called for a reduction in tariff rates, a six-hour day for American workers, stronger immigration measures, and an end to Prohibition. He proclaimed himself a supporter of Democratic Party presidential candidate Franklin D. Roosevelt and blasted the Hoover administration's decision to violently expel the Bonus Army, a group of protesting World War I veterans that had gathered in Washington. With Roosevelt winning Nevada by a better than two-to-one margin and Oddie soundly outspent, McCarran won a narrow triumph of his own, promising to dedicate himself to the welfare of his nation and state, and to recall "the forgotten man." He informed his daughter Margaret that he would enter

the Senate "independently," owing his success to "the people . . . especially
. . . the laboring element."

Named to the Appropriations and Judiciary committees, McCarran quickly
displayed a readiness to both support and oppose the Roosevelt administration,
while offering support for workers and veterans. George Creel deemed him "a
large and prickly cocklebur in the cushion of the presidential chair," who "always fought for the masses." *Time* magazine indicated in its March 5, 1934, issue
that McCarran was "already one of the best liked members of the Senate . . .
considered intellectually honest, frank, and logical . . . potentially a bigger up-
setter of administration plans than almost any other member of the Senate." He
demanded that federal employees receive their full pay and that the government
public works projects meet prevailing wage standards, to the chagrin of the president, who remained concerned about budgetary imbalances. McCarran joined
with Idaho Republican William Borah and other Senate Progressives in blocking Roosevelt's proposal that the United States become a member of the World
Court. The junior senator from Nevada promised, "I will never vote to send the
boys of America across the water again." Some likened McCarran to Louisiana
Senator Huey Long, as a demagogue determined to wreak havoc. Following
Roosevelt's sweeping reelection triumph in 1936, McCarran insisted, "Those
who would tear down the New Deal are the ones who encourage anarchism,
Communism and other Red programs bent upon the destruction of Democratic
government." Within a few months he was attacking the administration more
strongly than ever, blasting the president's effort to pack the Supreme Court
through a series of liberal appointments. McCarran's stand on the court-packing
plan only strengthened his support in Nevada, enabling him to sweep to an easy
reelection victory, trouncing Tasker Oddie, despite FDR's opposition.

As world war returned in September 1939, McCarran joined the camp of
the diehard isolationists led by the famed former aviator Charles Lindbergh.
At an early rally of the Keep America Out of War Congress, the Nevada legislator exclaimed, "I think one American boy, the son of an American mother,
is worth more than all Central Europe." He opposed Roosevelt's bid for an
unprecedented third term, backing instead the former Postmaster General
James Farley, chairman of the Democratic National Committee. McCarran
followed Lindbergh to the podium at a mass rally in Chicago's Soldier Field
in August 1940, urging, "Watch out for propaganda which may lead us into
the new world war" and warning, "Mass murder is on again." McCarran voted
for Republican Party nominee Wendell Willkie in the general election, but
Roosevelt easily won again. McCarran opposed Roosevelt's plan, announced
in early January 1941, to lend or lease weaponry and ships to Great Britain,
enabling the United States to stand as "the arsenal of democracy." Orating in

the Senate, McCarran charged, "This is a program that begins in peace and ends in hell—in worse than hell!" In December, following the Japanese attack on Pearl Harbor, he delayed his return to Washington until a declaration of war had already been issued.

McCarran won the Democratic Party nomination for the U.S. Senate in a bitterly contested primary campaign in 1944, and then more easily captured a third term of his own. The powerful Congress of Industrial Organizations (CIO), the left-tilted labor confederation established in the mid-1930s, backed his opponent, Lieutenant Governor Vail Pittman, something McCarran never forgot. *Labor*, put out by the rival American Federation of Labor, slammed the CIO's purportedly "Communist-controlled" Political Committee for opposing McCarran. Already fixated on the issue of communism, McCarran had charged in a radio address in October that "Communism is not just knocking at the door of our democracy—it is using a battering ram on the portal of our democratic home." The communists had particularly targeted him, McCarran complained.

Both McCarran and Franklin Delano Roosevelt began new terms in January 1945, with McCarran becoming chair of the Senate Judiciary Committee, but the president's death in early April carried Harry S Truman into the Oval Office. McCarran and Truman little liked one another, but the senator voted for his country's entrance into the United Nations, something the new president favored.

Early in the postwar period, McCarran returned with a vengeance to the issue of communist influence in various walks of American life, including the federal government. He demanded and got a rider included in an appropriations measure in June 1946 enabling the secretary of state to summarily dismiss any employee from the State Department. The *Washington Post* suggested that the rider was designed to be another means to attack "members of CIO's United Public Workers who actively supported the Communist line." McCarran was in fact targeting figures like Alger Hiss, the former top State Department official suspected of communist ties and a willingness to funnel information to the Soviet Union. McCarran solicited information about Hiss from FBI director J. Edgar Hoover, and he began blasting the State Department's supposedly lax attitude regarding security matters. Speaking before the San Francisco Bar Association in September, McCarran cried out, "It is our duty to make sure that those forces seeking to destroy the American form of government—and I am sorry to say they exist in high places—shall not succeed."

The unpopularity of the Truman administration, beset by soaring inflation and labor unrest, helped lead to a resounding Republican triumph in the 1946 congressional elections. Among those slated to go to Washington were former naval officers Richard M. Nixon of Orange County, California, and Wisconsin's Joseph McCarthy, elected to the U.S. House of Representatives and Senate, respectively. Shortly after the elections, health problems, including a heart attack and prostate difficulties, temporarily sidelined McCarran.

However, when the Democrats recaptured control of Congress following the 1948 elections, McCarran actively resumed his chairmanship of the Senate Judiciary Committee. In late February 1949, McCarran proposed the China Aid Act to provide over a billion dollars in assistance to the faltering Nationalist regime of Chiang Kai-shek, which was engaged in a civil war with Mao Zedong. McCarran aggressively attacked newly appointed secretary of state Dean Acheson, charging, "the State Department Division of Far Eastern Affairs is definitely soft to Communist Russia" and Mao Zedong. That summer McCarran demanded the State Department provide financial support to Spain, still ruled by the anticommunist dictator Francisco Franco. Even more insistently, McCarran employed his stature as Senate Judiciary Committee chair to highlight the threat of subversion in the United States. In the midst of hearings in May 1949, McCarran demanded a revision of the nation's immigration statutes to ensure that subversives, including those serving as diplomats, were not allowed to enter the country. As McCarran assailed UN employees, claiming they were communists, and ordered subpoenas served on Attorney General Tom Clark and Assistant Secretary of State John Peurifoy, the *Washington Post* proclaimed him "a one-man Un-American Activities Committee in the Senate."

McCarran eventually convinced Congress to provide economic assistance to Spain and to recognize the Franco regime, which soon welcomed American military bases. Back in Washington, DC, McCarran spoke at a naturalization ceremony where he warned, "If any of you come with the ulterior motive of tearing down our government it were better a thousand times if a millstone had been tied around your neck." Thanks to McCarran, the percentage of refugees admitted into the United States who were Jewish shrank considerably.

The domestic Cold War heightened thanks to dramatic events in both 1949 and 1950. On August 29, 1949, the Soviet Union successfully completed its first test of a nuclear bomb, and five weeks later, Mao Zedong and his communist forces took control of China. Senator Joseph McCarthy initially charged in late February 1950 that fifty-seven individuals belonging to or loyal to the CPUSA worked for the U.S. State Department. North Korean troops tore across the thirty-eighth parallel on June 25 in an effort to oust the South Korean government of Syngman Rhee. American soldiers soon entered the Korean conflict. That September, McCarran steered to passage the Internal Security Act, which tightened immigration procedures, demanded that communist organizations register with the U.S. attorney general, and set up the Subversive Activities Control Board to investigate individuals believed to be involved with subversive activities. The measure precluded those who belonged to the CPUSA or its front organizations from using passports. It also allowed for the detention of suspect individuals during times of "internal security emergency." Congress quickly overrode President Truman's veto, which came complete with his warning that the measure posed "the greatest danger to freedom of speech, press, and assembly since the Alien and Sedition Laws of 1798." McCarran easily won reelection to a fourth term in the Senate, where his power appeared unmatched.

The following December, McCarran, determined to discover how effectively the Internal Security Act was being administered, urged Mississippi's James Eastland to introduce a resolution that led to establishment of the Senate Internal Security Subcommittee. The subcommittee, headed by McCarran, was further authorized to explore "the extent, nature and effects of subversive activities." President Truman responded by forming his own Commission on Internal Security and Individual Rights, chaired by Admiral Chester Nimitz but soon headed by former president Herbert Hoover, thereby hoping to ward off the mania associated with both McCarthy and McCarran. FBI director J. Edgar Hoover continued feeding information to McCarran, whom he considered more reliable than Joseph McCarthy. McCarran could toss out sensationalistic charges as easily as his Senate colleague from Wisconsin. On March 4, 1951, McCarran charged that President Truman's firing of General Douglas MacArthur for insubordination was communist directed.

In mid-May, McCarran triggered a congressional battle regarding the nation's immigration and naturalization practices. Congress passed the Immigration and Nationality Act of 1952, also called the McCarran-Walter Act, which continued the three-decade-long practice of favoring immigration from Western Europe. The measure discarded racial restrictions but allowed immigration officials to deny entrance to accused subversives. It also enabled the federal government to order the deportation of immigrants or naturalized citizens who were participating in subversive activities. McCarran charged that Truman's refusal to sign the measure was "one of the most un-American acts I have witnessed in my public career." Congress again overrode the president's veto.

On October 17, 1952, former vice president Henry Wallace testified before McCarran's subcommittee, having received a subpoena to do so. The Nevada legislator had long hoped for the opportunity to humiliate Wallace, whose Farm Bureau he had viewed back in the 1930s as "a Soviet organization" that most imperiled American democracy. McCarran went after former State Department China experts John Carter Vincent, Edmund Clubb, and John Paton Davies Jr., along with Johns Hopkins University professor Owen Lattimore and renowned columnist Joseph Alsop, a fervent anticommunist who condemned mindless Redbaiting. In the midst of Vincent's testimony, McCarran insisted that membership in the CPUSA was hardly the only peril the nation faced. "It is sympathy with the Communist movement that raises one of the gravest threats that we have." The *Washington Post*, which had recently referred to McCarran as the "most important member" of the U.S. Senate, assailed his subcommittee, declaring it "an attempt to perpetuate another fraud and hoax on the American people."

In a letter to his wife, Birdie, McCarran worried that both leading candidates in the 1952 presidential race, Republican Dwight D. Eisenhower and Democrat Adlai Stevenson, were being misled by "the Jews." In another note to his wife, he vented, "Truman will go down in history as the dirtiest as well as the most ignorant of all presidents. This pissant in human form is a disgrace to his country." He told Birdie, "It's a stormy time for me but . . . [t]hese Commie rats can't cower me with their threats. . . . So we fight on."

Early in the Eisenhower administration, McCarran opposed appointments to key foreign policy slots, when the secretary of state picked Scott McLeod as the department's security head and Chip Bohlen as ambassador to the Soviet Union. Having been informed by J. Edgar Hoover that the FBI had compiled a report on Bohlen, McCarran insisted that the "clique" of subversives had "just won one of its greatest victories." Republican Senator Joseph McCarthy joined McCarran in assailing Bohlen. The *Washington Star* warned that the confirmation hearing provided "the acid test of whether a corporal's guard of reckless senators is going to be able to butcher the reputation of a respected public servant—and get away with it."

During the Army-McCarthy hearings, which ran from March through June 1954, McCarran defended the senator from Wisconsin. Talking in New Hampshire to the Catholic War Veterans, McCarran asserted to thunderous applause, "Joe McCarthy has done one thing and that is he has routed a lot of Communists in this country." McCarran nevertheless worried that McCarthy's notoriety could cripple the anticommunist crusade. In the early fall of 1954, following an announcement that a Senate committee was unanimously recommending that McCarthy be censured for conduct contrary to senatorial practices, McCarran continued to worry that the United States had never "been in such jeopardy as it is today." McCarran insisted during a public oration in Hawthorne, Nevada, on September 28, 1954, "It is beset with enemies from within and from abroad in greater numbers than ever before." Leaving the stage, McCarran suffered a fatal heart attack.

Leading Nevada newspapers offered mixed analyses of McCarran's public record, underscoring his devotion to his home state but also noting his insistence on "complete subservience" from those receiving his favors. The *Washington Post* reported that McCarran's passing "removes from the Senate one of its most formidable influences—a controversial man of passionate convictions made effective by extraordinary force of personality and an adroit wielding of political power." Radio host Fulton Lewis acknowledged, "For twenty-two years I have loved and respected this man. He told me once . . . that it was more important to be hated by the right people, than it was to be admired by others."

Conclusion

The early Cold War period witnessed heated ideological confrontations between the Left and the Right, with liberals sometimes standing on one side of an issue, sometimes on the other. Even storied reputations came under question, including that of the legendary black singer-actor Paul Robeson, whose sympathetic stance toward the Soviet Union and blanket condemnation of racism offended many. Robeson's career suffered too as he confronted something of a blacklist along with vilification by those who considered him un-American, in the common parlance of the time. One of those tossing around charges of that sort at liberals and radicals alike was Nevada senator Pat McCarran, whose political affiliation did not preclude him from attacking political leaders, even presidents, of the Democratic Party. As Robeson's star dimmed, that of McCarran seemed to soar, with his name attached to some of the most important congressional legislation of the era. While many associate the heightened Red Scare of the early 1950s with McCarran's Republican colleague Joseph McCarthy, the Nevada legislator was at least equally instrumental in fostering the anticommunist mania that dominated American political life for some time to come.

Study Questions

1. Indicate how Paul Robeson exemplified the New Negro of the 1920s.
2. Explain why Paul Robeson began to shift leftward in the 1930s and thereafter.
3. Discuss Pat McCarran's support for and opposition to the New Deal.
4. Analyze Pat McCarran's growing attraction to anticommunism.
5. Explain the contrasting ways in which the domestic Cold War influenced the lives and careers of Paul Robeson and Pat McCarran.

Selected Bibliography

Boyle, Sheila Tully, and Andrew Bunie. *Paul Robeson: The Years of Promise and Achievement.* Boston: University of Massachusetts Press, 2001.

Brown, Lloyd L. *The Young Paul Robeson: "On My Journey Home."* New York: Basic Books, 1998.

Dorinson, Joseph, ed. *Paul Robeson: Essays on His Life and Legacy.* New York: McFarland, 2002.

Duberman, Martin. *Paul Robeson.* New York: Alfred A. Knopf, 1989.

Edwards, Jerome E. *Pat McCarran: Political Boss of Nevada.* Reno: University of Nevada Press, 1982.

Pittman, Von V., Jr. *Senator Patrick A. McCarran and the Politics of Containment.* PhD dissertation, University of Georgia, 1979.

Robeson, Paul. *Here I Stand*. New York: Houghton Mifflin, 1971.

———. *Paul Robeson Speaks: Writings-Speeches-Interviews 1918–1974*. New York: Carol Publishing Group, 1978.

Robeson, Paul, Jr. *The Undiscovered Paul Robeson: An Artist's Journey, 1898–1939*. New York: Wiley, 2001.

Whited, Fred E., Jr. *The Rhetoric of Senator Patrick Anthony McCarran*. PhD dissertation, University of Oregon, 1973.

Ybarra, Michael J. *Washington Gone Crazy: Senator Pat McCarran and the Great American Communist Hunt*. Hanover, NH: Steerforth Press, 2004.

CHAPTER NINE

⁓

New Frontiers in Activism

A palpable sense of expectancy pervaded American society in the early 1960s, an era when the future seemed to offer great, if as yet undefined, prospects. Most Americans enjoyed material circumstances far beyond any that might have been imagined at the end of World War II. The dynamic prosperity of postwar America, joined with the benefits of science and technology, gave promise of a society in which meeting basic human needs was no longer a burdensome concern; attention might now be directed to ensuring a better quality of life. During his 1960 presidential campaign, John F. Kennedy had articulated the compelling belief that America, great nation that it was, could be much more. As president, Kennedy made this theme of the nation's unfulfilled potential a chief component of the "New Frontier," his vision of a direction for the United States. Though vague on specifics, Kennedy enjoined the American people not only to defend their ideals, but to fully realize them. Many Americans accepted the challenge. Some sought to live their ideals by helping others, as did those who joined Kennedy's Peace Corps, while others struggled on the frontiers of civil rights.

While the drama of the civil rights movement often placed that struggle at the center of national attention, other significant movements were also beginning to coalesce. The new environmentalism, a popularly based conservation movement, developed out of several concerns. One was a growing awareness that science and technology, when not wisely used, could significantly degrade the national quality of life. Pesticides, herbicides, and other industrial chemicals, the new environmentalists warned, threatened to introduce toxins and mutagens into the food chain, ultimately endangering human health. The impact of pollutants on air and water quality was another major area of concern, as was the need to preserve wilderness areas from development. A new environmental ethic, activists believed, was crucial to the preservation of the natural quality of life in America. Science would afford one component, providing the rational basis for understanding the interconnection of life and the necessity of ensuring the health of the whole planet. Aesthetics would provide another, offering a compelling justification for the preservation of wilderness areas, not only as national legacies but as critical to human spiritual needs. Though many individuals contributed to the creation of a new environmental consciousness and movement, one was especially influential. Rachel Carson, a marine biologist, introduced the American public to the crucial theme of interconnectedness in nature through several best-selling books. Her writings acquainted the reading public with the science of oceanography, which explored the mechanisms that regulate the oceans and the life in them, both critical to the future of the human race and the planet's health. By the late 1950s, Carson was increasingly concerned about the impact of environmental toxins such as pesticides and herbicides. Carson's *Silent Spring*, a clarion call to address the poisoning of the environment, appeared in 1962. Later acknowledged as one of the most influential books in American history, *Silent Spring* played a crucial role in engendering a new concern about the environment. Though Carson died in 1964, her work was central to the rapid emergence of the new environmentalism as a mainstream movement with growing political clout.

The year after *Silent Spring* appeared, another book of both immediate and enduring impact was published. In 1963, the publication of Betty Friedan's *The Feminine Mystique* did much to give focus and direction to the women's rights or feminist movement. The struggle for women's rights was not new; in one form or another, it had existed since the founding of the republic. The movement's goals, which shifted with each incremental success, had included suffrage, divorce and property rights, women's work conditions, birth control, and, as of the 1920s, a broader definition of gender equality elaborated in the Equal Rights Amendment. During the 1930s, the teenaged Friedan had first become aware of the limits that society placed on women. During the war years, which brought new employment opportunities and financial independence to American women, Friedan became aware of workplace gender discrimination and compensation inequities. The genesis of *The Feminine Mystique*, however, was in Friedan's experience in the 1950s. A married mother of three, Friedan initially sought fulfillment as a suburban housewife, but found little satisfaction or personal growth in a life that was lived primarily for others. Seeking to identify and define what she called "the problem with no name," Friedan began her research with a survey of her graduating class at Smith College. Somewhat to her surprise, she discovered that she was not alone in wondering, "Is this all there is?" The product of five years of research and writing while Friedan also met all the obligations of a housewife and mother, *The Feminine Mystique* was a call to action that catalyzed the modern women's movement.

Following the publication of Friedan's book, the modern women's movement seemed to take shape almost overnight. With the goal of bringing women into the mainstream of American society, the National Organization for Women came into being in 1966, with Friedan among the founders. In their struggle for equal rights, feminists adopted many of the strategies and tactics that had served the civil rights movement so well. Protests, boycotts, mass demonstrations, and efforts to gain political voice were all put to the service of the cause. Though they were generally spared the violence inflicted on civil rights activists, women's rights activists were met with derision, condescension, and denunciation from those who felt threatened by female equality. Condemned as man haters, home wreckers, political radicals, and lesbians, feminists worked through their own organizations and the political system toward a major transformation of American society. The battles that feminists fought were not always against the "system" or "male chauvinism." As has been the case with every major social protest movement, a significant portion of the struggle took place within the women's movement as activists debated over principles, tactics, and objectives. In these heady years, the intellectual dynamism that the movement generated contributed significantly to new analyses of major social issues, even as feminists made discernible progress in gaining entrée into theretofore restricted areas of American life. At the forefront of these changes through the formative decades of the movement and into the twenty-first century, Betty Friedan established a legacy as a major, if controversial, icon of the American women's movement.

∽ RACHEL CARSON ∽

To those assembled at the Women's National Press Club meeting in Washington, DC, on December 5, 1962, it seemed improbable that the speaker that day could have generated the intense controversy that had followed her in recent months. Modest in appearance and demeanor, scientist Rachel Carson seemed anything but a "hysterical" fanatic manipulated by "sinister influences," as critics had recently charged. An examination of her résumé would have shown that, since the early 1930s, she had quietly pursued a career in marine biology, working for the Fish and Wildlife Service (FWS) until her resignation in 1952. In addition to the writing required by her official duties, Carson was the author of numerous articles and books about nature, perhaps most notably *The Sea Around Us*, a 1951 best seller that explored the natural history and

Rachel Carson's 1962 bestseller Silent Spring, *which warned of the dangers of chemical toxins to animals and humans alike, played a crucial role in awakening environmental consciousness during that decade. A marine biologist in an era when few women pursued scientific careers, Carson stressed the concept of interconnectedness in her popular books about the world's oceans such as* The Sea Around Us. *(Library of Congress, LC-USZ62-107991)*

environmental role of the world's oceans. She was, as a biographer described her, an "improbable revolutionary." The growing furor surrounding the petite, fifty-five-year-old brunette in late 1962 stemmed from the recent publication of her findings concerning the damaging consequences of the widespread use of chemical herbicides and pesticides, most notably the common insecticide dichlorodiphenyltrichlorethane (DDT). *Silent Spring* was the product of four years of intense research, addressing the impact of environmental toxins on water supplies, soil, plants, and animals. Carson's study pursued the theme of interconnectedness to demonstrate the inescapable impact of chemical toxins on humankind. Chemically induced changes in human cells, she concluded, not only caused degeneration of the human liver and nervous system, but were undeniably linked to cancer.

Praised for her courage, Carson had also been challenged by critics who questioned her methods and motivations. Now, in early December, she took to the podium to respond to them. The quiet-spoken biologist first addressed the criticism aimed at *Silent Spring*, noting that it had drawn denunciations from government agricultural agencies, agribusiness, and, most notably, from the chemical industry. Not surprisingly, Carson observed, chemical trade associations had launched a counteroffensive aimed at discrediting both her and her findings. One line of attack was to depict Carson as a sentimental and naive woman whose romanticization of nature had overcome her scientific objectivity. A secondary strategy of her critics in the chemical industry, she observed, was "the soft sell, the soothing reassurances to the public." Carson countered with a litany of recent news items that confirmed the very dangers she had warned of, citing incidents in which chemical toxins had affected humans, animals, and commercial crops. She also noted the close connection between the chemical industry and research funding, warning that "research supported by pesticide manufacturers is not likely to be directed at discovering facts indicating unfavorable effects of pesticides." The available evidence, Carson asserted, could only lead to the conclusion that industry research was shaped "to accommodate to the short-term gain, to serve the gods of profit and production."

Rachel Carson had thrown down the gauntlet before one of the nation's most powerful and influential industries. Though hopeful that her new book might spur discussion over the effects of pesticides, Carson could not have anticipated the central role *Silent Spring* would play in shaping the new environmentalism that was coalescing in the early 1960s. In 1970, Robert B. Downs, writing in *Books That Changed America*, described *Silent Spring* as "comparable in its impact on public consciousness, and demand for instant action, to Tom Paine's *Common Sense*, Harriet Beecher Stowe's *Uncle Tom's Cabin* and Upton Sinclair's *The Jungle*." *Silent Spring* arrived in bookstores as many Americans were beginning to give serious consideration to the costs of progress. In the popular media of postwar America, science was hailed as the invariably benign instrument of progress, eliminating the inconveniences and uncertainties of an earlier age. Even as the "peaceful atom" was promoted as providing an inexpensive and inexhaustible energy source, newly developed chemical compounds were extolled as the solution to problems as diverse as agricultural production, bacteria-free homes, brighter laundry, and weed-free lawns. A new consciousness about environmental toxins had become manifest in the years preceding the publication of *Silent Spring*, and now Carson's book galvanized interest in the issue. Tragically, Rachel Carson would not be present to witness the tremendous effect that *Silent Spring* had on American environmental awareness. Even as she spoke on that December day in 1962, Carson was fighting a losing battle with breast cancer and heart disease. She had less than two years to live, but she dedicated her remaining time to the cause.

The rural landscape of Springdale, Pennsylvania, may well have been instrumental in establishing Rachel Carson's affinity with the natural environment. Born on May 27, 1907, Rachel Louise Carson was the third child of Robert Warden Carson and Maria McLean. Extensive unspoiled woods and meadows near the family home served as Rachel's playground, and her blossoming interest in birds, animals, and fish was often reflected in her childhood drawings and stories. Graduating from high school in 1925, Carson traveled to Pittsburgh to enroll at the Pennsylvania College for Women, where she soon discovered that the study of biology could provide a topical focus for her writing, which she hoped to seriously pursue. Graduating with a bachelor of arts degree in science in 1929, Carson was awarded a summer fellowship at the Woods Hole Marine Biological Laboratory. There she undertook research projects, explored the nearby coastline, and participated in a deep-sea collecting voyage. That fall, she registered as a graduate marine science major at Johns Hopkins University and completed a master's degree in marine zoology in 1932. For the next several years, her future seemed indeterminate, as she taught part-time at Johns Hopkins and the University of Maryland. As Carson was partially supporting five family members at home, she turned once again to writing, though her submissions were uniformly rejected.

In October 1935, Carson accepted part-time work at the U.S. Bureau of Fisheries in Washington, DC, writing scripts for a series of brief educational radio programs on marine life. Subsequently assigned to write a general introduction to marine life for a government brochure, Carson composed an essay titled "The World of the Waters," a revised version of which was published in the September 1937 issue of *The Atlantic* as "Undersea." The article proved to be a milestone in her literary career, establishing both a lyrical style and themes that characterized much of her mature work, such as the paucity of knowledge about the undersea world and the interrelatedness of ocean life. In the meantime, Carson, already responsible for her aging mother, faced new burdens. In the spring of 1937, her sister Marian died of pneumonia, leaving two young daughters orphaned. Carson purchased a house in Silver Spring, Maryland, where she and her mother could provide a home for the girls. Over the next several years, Carson struggled to balance family needs with her work and writing, but she did extrapolate a book from the "Undersea" article—*Under the Sea Wind* was published in late November 1941. The following month, however, Japan's attack on Pearl Harbor pulled the United States into World War II and public interest in natural history abated. Her career as a nature writer suspended for the duration, Carson focused primarily on her duties at her agency, which was now part of the FWS. In July 1945, she sought unsuccessfully to interest *Reader's Digest* in an article about some early government reports on the effects of the new synthetic pesticide DDT, which Carson warned "may upset the whole delicate balance of nature if unwisely used." The article was rejected, though some early warnings about DDT use were published in both *Nature Magazine* and *Time* that year.

By late 1948, Carson had risen as close to the top of her chosen profession as gender then commonly allowed. Classified as a ranking biologist, she was appointed as editor in chief of the FWS's Information Division. Carson's work at FWS provided priceless opportunities to expand her understanding of the ocean world, the subject that still commanded her greatest interest. In July 1950, Carson traveled to south Florida to gather information for planned FWS publications. There she explored the Everglades, Florida Bay, and the Florida Keys, where she finally experienced the undersea world of which she had written. Donning a cumbersome diving suit and helmet for a look at the complex life of a coral reef, Carson was entranced. The experience, she wrote to oceanographer William Beebe, "formed one of those milestones of life." Such experiences greatly broadened Carson's scientific horizons, and inspired the completion of her next writing project, *The Sea Around Us*, which largely established Carson's reputation as an acknowledged nature writer when published in July 1951. In nontechnical terms, she described the interrelated geological, hydrological, and climatic mechanisms that, together with almost inconceivably complex biological relationships, determined the natural history of the world's oceans. She also made clear her concern about the impact of human agency. In writing about the natural history of islands, Carson observed, "Man, unhappily, has written one of his blackest records as a destroyer on oceanic islands. He has seldom set foot on an island that he has not brought about disastrous changes." She also warned of the consequences of misguided efforts to alter the natural environment for human convenience, potentially compromising the oceans' integrity. "For the globe as a whole," Carson warned, "the ocean is the great regulator, the great stabilizer of temperatures." *The Sea Around Us* proved immensely popular, winning both the John Burroughs Medal for natural history and a National Book Award. This success presented an opportunity for the rerelease of the previously neglected *Under the Sea Wind*, which soon gave Carson two titles on the national best-seller list.

Resigning from government service in 1952, Carson was free to pursue nature writing, and she quickly purchased land for a summer cottage in Southport, Maine. In subsequent years, her explorations of the tide pools along the rocky coast afforded endless hours of fascination and material for her writing. Carson's resignation from the FWS also accorded her the latitude to openly criticize questionable federal environmental policies. The 1952 elections had brought a new Republican administration, and Carson was appalled at the policies of the new secretary of the interior, Oregon businessman Douglas McKay, derided by critics as "Giveaway McKay." In a letter to the *Washington Post*, Carson expressed her fear that McKay's policies constituted "a raid upon our natural resources that is without parallel in the present century," including "the proposed giveaway of our offshore oil reserves and the threatened invasion of national parks, forests and other public lands." The event that galvanized Carson and other environmentalists to action in 1954 was the government's proposal to build the Echo Park Dam on the Colorado River, which would flood Dinosaur National Monument and inundate pristine canyonlands. "It is part of the general problem that is close to my heart," she wrote to friend Dorothy Freeman, "the saving of unspoiled, natural areas from senseless destruction." Carson's expanded environmental concerns reflected the first stirrings of the new environmentalism. Coalescing in the early 1950s and drawing support from a broad segment of society, the movement began to define itself and organize. Like Carson, the new environmentalists questioned the cost of the "progress" that seemed to bring greater environmental degradation and a lessened quality of life.

In 1953, even as RKO studios was releasing an award-winning documentary film based on *The Sea Around Us*, Carson was working on a new book that focused on the natural history of the seashore. *The Edge of the Sea* attained best-seller status in 1955 and Carson found the demands on her time increasing as she was sought as a consultant, lecturer, and author. After 1958, however, Carson's attention was increasingly drawn to the issue that she had raised briefly in 1945. She had continued to follow research on the environmental effects of pesticides and had remained in contact with colleagues with a shared interest in the subject. For the next several years, Carson reviewed research, conferred with colleagues, and conducted her own meticulous research at the National Institute of Health and the National Cancer Institute. Her deteriorating health slowed her progress considerably. Minor infections, a duodenal ulcer, temporary blindness, and ultimately breast cancer posed increasingly difficult challenges. Overcoming immense obstacles, Carson completed *Silent Spring* in the summer of 1962. Within days of its publication, it became apparent that powerful interests were determined to discredit both the author and her conclusions.

Carson dedicated *Silent Spring* to Albert Schweitzer and prefaced the book with a grim warning from the renowned humanitarian-scientist: "Man has lost the capacity to foresee and forestall. He will end by destroying the earth." The body of the book focuses on the environmental impact of chemical toxins, and especially chlorinated hydrocarbons like DDT, as Carson traces them from water to earth and then to air, offering specific and documented examples of the damage done. Carson concluded that pesticides held the potential to affect human life at the cellular level, causing cancer, sterility, and birth defects. Ultimately, *Silent Spring* argued that man's arrogant efforts to control and modify nature could bring unforeseen disaster. The book provoked a storm of controversy. In one of the first responses to the *New Yorker* serialization, a reader complained that Carson's criticism of the chemical industry showed "her Communist sympathies" and observed that while "we can live without birds and animals . . . we cannot live without business." In a postscript, the writer warned, "She's probably a peace-nut too." Personal attacks on Carson were one aspect of a massive industry-funded campaign to discredit the scientist. Questions about her marital status were raised. Former Secretary of Agriculture Ezra Taft Benson was quoted as wondering "why a spinster with no children was so concerned about genetics" and suggested that Carson was "probably a Communist." A food industry scientist dismissed Carson and her supporters as "organic gardeners, the antifluoride leaguers, the worshippers of 'natural foods' and those who cling to the philosophy of a vital principle, and other pseudo-scientists and faddists." In the months after *Silent Spring's* publication, industry forces marshaled funds and their own scientific spokesmen to challenge the book's conclusions. Ironically, the controversy generated the public discussion that Carson desired. Many prominent scientists confirmed the validity of her research and much of the public agreed that the issues she raised were legitimate. By late 1962, more than forty bills to regulate pesticides had been introduced in state legislatures. Recently elected President John F. Kennedy had already made known his interest in the issue and that spring, the President's Science Advisory Committee issued its report on pesticide use, confirming the concerns that Carson had raised. The following day, a Senate subcommittee made preparations to begin an investigation of government and industry regulations concerning pesticides.

The year was, in many other regards, one of personal triumph. Carson was the recipient of numerous honors and awards, and was elected to the American Academy of Arts and Letters. Sadly, these achievements were increasingly overshadowed by her failing health. Weakened by a succession of illnesses and fighting the ravages of breast cancer, Carson was determined to continue to publicly speak on the issue of environmental pollution as long as was physically possible, but her public activities were increasingly limited by the advance of her disease. As she confronted the imminence of her death in early 1964, she made preparations to settle her estate, much of which was bequeathed to the Sierra Club and the Nature Conservancy. On April 14, 1964, Rachel Carson, her body worn out by months of struggle, died at home of heart failure. That summer, a close friend scattered her ashes along the rocky shores of the Maine coast, fulfilling Carson's wish that, in death, she be reunited with the sea that figured so prominently in her life.

In the years that followed, Carson's vision of a new environmentalism gained growing popular and governmental support. The membership rolls of groups such as the Sierra Club, the Wilderness Society, the Nature Conservancy, and the Natural Resources Defense Council grew exponentially as increasing numbers of Americans acknowledged the necessity of environmental protection and wilderness preservation. By the mid-1960s, Congress, at the urging of President Lyndon Johnson, had passed a broad array of environmental protection legislation, prefiguring continuing interest in the issue in subsequent decades. In 1970, several parcels of land on the Maine coast were set aside as the Rachel Carson National Wildlife Refuge. Carson's final crusade achieved a major victory in June 1972, when the newly established Environmental Protection Agency issued an order that banned almost all use of DDT. In 1980, she was posthumously awarded the Presidential Medal of Freedom, the nation's highest civilian honor. In 1999, *Time* magazine recognized Rachel Carson, the "unlikely revolutionary," as one of the century's 100 most influential individuals.

⌒ BETTY FRIEDAN ⌒

Only a half-dozen years earlier, few Americans could have imagined the scene that unfolded on Manhattan's Fifth Avenue on that late summer day in 1970. It was August 26, the fiftieth anniversary of the ratification of the Nineteenth

Betty Friedan, telling reporters during the April 1967 session of the New York State Assembly of her intention to "put sex into section I of the New York constitution." Friedan's The Feminine Mystique *(1962) was a major catalyst of the women's rights movement, which took organizational form in 1966 when Friedan helped found the National Organization for Women. (Library of Congress, LC-USZ62-122632)*

Amendment to the U.S. Constitution, which had granted women the right to vote. In recognition of that advance, Betty Friedan, outgoing president of the National Organization for Women (NOW), had announced a Women's Strike for Equality the previous February. Chief among the issues that the demonstrators would march for in a number of major cities were abortion rights, free day care, and equal employment and educational opportunity. All were essential issues of "second-wave feminism," a reconfiguration of the women's rights movement that was manifest by the mid-1960s. The new feminists sought to identify and remedy the social and legal roots of gender inequity, and an expanding base of popular support gave new political force to this movement. As the latest incarnation of this phenomenon, the Women's Strike drew considerable media attention. The media focus was inevitably on the protest in New York City and, to a large degree, on Friedan, who had already established a reputation as the nation's most prominent advocate for women's rights. Friedan lived up to her reputation that day, leading a crowd of between 35,000 and 50,000 marchers up both sides of Fifth Avenue toward Bryant Park, where the crowd listened to speakers Gloria Steinem, Bella Abzug, Kate Millett, and Eleanor Holmes Norton. The most enthusiastic applause was reserved for the forty-nine-year-old Friedan, who put her aggressive, fist-pumping rhetorical style to the service of lauding the need for sisterhood and an end to all gender, racial, and class divisions. She reminded her listeners of a traditional morning prayer recited by Jewish men, giving thanks that they had not been born female. In this new era, she proclaimed, women could thank God that they had been born as they were.

By all measures, the Women's Strike for Equality was a huge success. The organizers brought together a wide array of groups that mirrored the dynamism and diversity of second-wave feminism. Within the coalition were organizations that ranged from the relatively conservative to the self-professedly radical. Prominent officeholders, including congresswomen Bella Abzug and Shirley Chisholm, had endorsed the event. New York Governor Nelson Rockefeller had proclaimed August 26 a holiday, and President Richard Nixon, who often catered to a socially conservative constituency, issued a proclamation recognizing the anniversary of the Nineteenth Amendment.

Not all the response to the Women's Strike was benign, however. West Virginia Senator Jennings Randolph denounced the marchers as "braless bubbleheads" and Vice President Spiro Agnew joked that "three things have been difficult to tame: the oceans, fools, and women." As the first feminist event to gain extensive media coverage, the Women's Strike provoked numerous print and broadcast comments that revealed a deep-seated unwillingness to take the movement seriously. A New York Times article on Friedan headlined the fact that she had visited a beauty salon prior to the march. Another Times article derided Kate Millett, "the principal theoretician of the women's liberation movement," as an elite college professor who cursed "like a gunnery sergeant" and who stood "to make $100,000 from a book on how tough it is to be a woman." Television coverage likewise emphasized the radicalism of feminist leaders and the opposition of "average" women to the movement's objectives. CBS anchorman Walter Cronkite described the marchers as "a militant minority of women's liberationists." Several networks featured interviews with women who disparaged the event as "stupid" and "ridiculous," while an ABC interviewee proclaimed that she opposed women's liberation because, "I like being a girl. It's fun." Media coverage of the Women's Strike, often dismissive and condescending, revealed the distance that had yet to be traveled before a majority of Americans embraced the objectives of the women's movement.

These were not the only challenges that Betty Friedan faced as a movement leader. The unity demonstrated on August 26 was fragile and would experience growing strains in the future. Friedan, who focused on achieving legal and social equality for women, was often at odds with radical feminists who saw the roots of gender discrimination entwined in the most fundamental social relationships and institutions. For radical feminists, true liberation was not simply a question of equitable salaries for women in the workplace, but rather in a wholesale transformation of human relationships. Fearful that the excesses of radical feminism might fatally wound the movement, Friedan distanced herself from the advocates of "sexual liberation," warning fellow activists against the "bra-burning, anti-man, politics-of-orgasm school." Another issue with tremendously divisive potential was sexual orientation The question of lesbian rights had arisen several years earlier, and Friedan provoked considerable controversy when she expressed concerns about the damage that the "lavender menace" might do to the movement. Then there was the issue of Friedan's personality. While revered by many as the "mother of modern feminism," Friedan had a nearly universal reputation for contentiousness. Another difficulty for Friedan was the media's predisposition toward focusing on the glamorous. Long cognizant that she did not meet many traditional standards of physical beauty, Friedan was annoyed when media attention shifted to more photogenic activists such as Ms. magazine editor Gloria Steinem, with whom Friedan often clashed. As of 1970, Friedan, aware of both the achievements to date and the challenges that awaited, began to stake out her own ground in a movement that was gaining momentum even as it diversified. In subsequent decades, Friedan sought to understand and realize her full potential as an individual, a quest that had driven her since childhood.

Betty Naomi was born in Peoria, Illinois, on February 4, 1921, first child of Harry and Miriam Goldstein. The young girl suffered from a multitude of physical problems, including bowlegs requiring braces, asthma, poor eyesight, and crooked teeth. As an adolescent, Friedan wrote, "All in all, I have not been well endowed physically, neither with health nor with beauty." A stable home life partly compensated for these disadvantages. Harry Goldstein, an immigrant Russian Jew, was a successful jeweler who lavished attention on his intellectually precocious but ill-tempered daughter. Betty's distemper stemmed partly from conflicts with her mother, a controlling woman who often chided Betty for her inattention to personal grooming. Beyond the Goldstein household, anti-Semitism was yet another trial. Peoria's gentile society excluded the Goldsteins and Betty ascribed her exclusion from a high school sorority to anti-Semitism. She endured painful social isolation during these years, graduating in June 1938. Her political awakening began that same year at Smith College in Northampton, Massachusetts. She immersed herself in undergraduate life, majoring in psychology, writing poetry, and editing *The Smith College Associated News*. Under her direction, the paper took up some significant contemporary issues, and Friedan soon developed a reputation as the campus radical. Her growing interest in Marxist ideology and labor activism was not unusual for college students in the Depression years and, during her junior summer in 1941, Betty spent several weeks at Tennessee's Highland Folk School, famous as a training center for labor activists. In 1942, she graduated from Smith with numerous honors, but her academic achievements masked a growing personal crisis. Plagued with psychosomatic illnesses and feelings of panic, she began to fear that she was mentally ill. Only many years later would she recognize her discomfort as the product of a severe identity crisis. As she later wrote in *The Feminine Mystique*, "I thought I was going to be a psychologist. But if I wasn't sure, what did I want to be? I felt the future closing in—and I could not see myself in it at all."

There was a future, but it brought no immediate resolution of Betty's personal crisis. In 1942, she enrolled at the University of California's Berkeley campus to pursue a doctorate in psychology. She was still torn by doubts as to her future and, to reassure herself of her personal worth, she initiated a series of short-lived romantic relationships. One of her lovers, graduate student David Bohm, came under investigation by the FBI because of his membership in the Communist Party of the United States, which made Betty a subject of an FBI inquiry. She soon left Berkeley, later claiming that her boyfriend, threatened by her intellect, pressured her to abandon her doctoral studies.

Goldstein found no refuge when she returned to Peoria in the spring of 1943. Her family had dispersed since her father's death earlier that year, and she soon moved to New York City. There she found employment as assistant news editor for the *Federated Press*, a labor-oriented publication. After July 1946, she further honed her skills as a labor reporter while working for the *UE News*, the publication of the United Electrical, Radio and Machine Workers of America, one of the nation's most left-leaning unions. That same year she met Carl Friedan, a veteran who was pursuing a career in theatrical management, and they married in 1947. It was fated to be a stormy union, due to Betty's temperament and Carl's insecurities and indiscretions. In October 1948, Betty Friedan gave birth to Daniel, the first of her three children. Much to her chagrin, she lost her UE job when she became pregnant a second time in 1952.

Friedan often portrayed the next period of her life as exile in a materially comfortable but sterile suburban Siberia. The family moved to Parkway Village in the Jamaica area of Queens in 1951, where Betty sought to come to grips with her disillusionment with leftist politics and labor activities. She wrote freelance articles for women's magazines, but even here she encountered frustration. Women's magazine editors were almost always men who rejected any article that conflicted with their preconceived notions of what interested women. Topics beyond the bounds of family, children, cooking, and homemaking were inevitably dismissed. Friedan later lamented that her articles undoubtedly reinforced the prevailing stereotype of the 1950s American housewife: "frivolous, almost childlike; fluffy and feminine; passive; gaily content in a world of bedroom and kitchen, sex, babies and home." Meanwhile, with two children having joined the Friedan family by 1956, Betty felt increasingly torn between her familial duties and the persistent desire to accomplish something more.

In 1957, Friedan took the first big step toward defining the "problem with no name" when she attended the fifteenth reunion of her Smith College graduating class. One of Friedan's objectives was to discover whether her classmates, almost all ambitious and intelligent women, felt the same persistent sense of dissatisfaction that she did. To test her thesis that suburban domesticity smothered many intellectually vibrant women, she passed out a survey questionnaire to her former schoolmates. Many of the responses confirmed Friedan's own feelings. Some of her classmates noted the frustrations of being identified primarily as someone's wife; others complained that the roles of mother and housewife did not allow for the full realization of intellectual potential. Friedan discovered that 60 percent of those questioned did not find fulfillment in the role of homemaker. She was convinced that the subject demanded a book-length examination and, having sold W.W. Norton Publishers on the idea, she went to work in the New York Public Library, pursuing the background research that provided a solid conceptual framework for her findings.

Friedan began work on *The Feminine Mystique* in 1957 in the midst of an extraordinary profusion of critical social, economic, and political analysis that signaled the end of an era of relative complacency. The writings of C. Wright Mills, William Whyte Jr., Daniel Bell, David Riesman, Vance Packard, John Kenneth Galbraith, Rachel Carson, and Michael Harrington challenged virtually every aspect of American civilization. *The Feminine Mystique* was destined for publication in the midst of a rich intellectual exchange that was redefining Americans' conceptions of themselves and their society. These were also difficult years for Friedan personally. Her marriage to Carl had grown increasingly stormy as loud arguments gave way to more frequent physical altercations between the couple, often leaving Betty bruised. However, after years of research, interviews, and revisions, *The Feminine Mystique* was published in February 1963, with excerpts appearing earlier in *McCall's* and *Ladies' Home Journal*. Friedan proclaimed the book's central theme on the first page, where she described "the problem with no name" that suburban housewives confronted: "As she made the beds, shopped for groceries, matched slipcover material, ate peanut butter sandwiches with her children, chauffeured Cub Scouts and Brownies, lay beside her husband at night—she was afraid to ask even herself the silent question—'Is this all?'" Friedan's wide-ranging analyses drew heavily on the theories of psychologist Abraham Maslow, who stressed the human need for self-actualization, as well as Theodore Veblen's *Theory of the Leisure Class* (1899). Though her analytical framework also drew from the writings of Karl Marx and Friedrich Engels, Friedan avoided any reference to the founders of Marxist socialism. The second Red Scare was a very recent memory in 1963, and Friedan feared that her past political activism might be used to discredit her work. Even so, *The Feminine Mystique* generated considerable controversy. Friedan questioned virtually every dimension of the prevailing "feminine mystique," examining in detail the social, psychological, and economic forces that reinforced a restricted life for women. Reviews were mixed, but the subsequent controversy helped to ensure that the book would be a best seller. Friedan's analysis and presentation of the feminine dilemma may well have been, as some later critics proclaimed, flawed, but she had succeeded in compelling the American public to confront it. The next challenge was to organize the revolution.

During the next few years, Friedan grappled with her newfound fame and the slow unraveling of her marriage. She and Carl had moved to an upscale apartment in Manhattan, and her social circle soon included an impressive array of intellectuals and celebrities. Carl's resentment at becoming "Mr. Betty Friedan" was evident in his frequent public sarcasms; he often greeted strangers with the remark, "I'm the bitch's husband." Struggling to chart her own course, Friedan began to focus on how women might most effectively organize to demand equal rights. The legal foundation for such a movement was evident in the 1964 Civil Rights Act, which prohibited discrimination on the basis of race or sex. What was needed, though, as African American lawyer Pauli Murray suggested in a speech to the National Council of Women, was "an NAACP for women." Existing women's organizations were either too moribund or too cautious. The origins of the National Organization for Women can be traced to a series of meetings between Friedan, civil service professional Catherine East, and Justice Department lawyer Mary Eastwood in late June 1966 at the Third National Conference of the Commission on the Status of Women in

Washington, DC. Over lunch, Friedan, Eastwood, Murray, and others sketched out a plan for NOW. Friedan played a central role in events through the formal organizing meeting in late October, where members of the infant NOW elected her president. The group's statement of purpose, coauthored by Friedan and Murray, was a stirring declaration of ideals and intentions, proclaiming that "the time has come for a new movement toward true equality for all women in America, and toward a fully equal partnership of the sexes, part of the world-wide revolution of human rights." Friedan's influence was evident in the statement, "NOW is dedicated to the proposition that women are first and foremost human beings, who, like all other people in our society, must have the chance to develop their full human potential." The manifesto also proclaimed the intent to "protest and endeavor to change the false image of women now prevalent in the mass media, and in the texts, ceremonies, laws and practices of our major social institutions."

NOW was established just as a broadening current of social transformation swept across the nation. The civil rights movement, from which many feminists took inspiration and guidance, had already achieved striking legal victories. A new consciousness within other minority groups, such as Hispanic Americans and Native Americans, further widened the scope of social protest. Simultaneously, the expansion of the American war in Vietnam gave birth to a dynamic antiwar movement that challenged the legitimacy of American policy abroad. It was a heady era for reformers and radicals alike, and the relatively conservative leadership of NOW was determined that neither sectarian quarrels nor radicalism should taint the organization. Friedan felt that NOW could best achieve its objectives if its members demonstrated that they were "not battleaxes or man haters." NOW's priority was to lobby for the remediation of sex discrimination, challenging it everywhere it could be discovered. One target was newspapers that segregated help-wanted ads according to gender; another initiative supported airline stewardesses whose employment had often been dependent on appearance, single status, and avoiding pregnancy. Other issues proved immediately divisive. NOW endorsed the right to abortion, despite Friedan's concern that the position would harm the organization's reputation, and some members left to form the Women's Equity Action League, which focused on employment and education issues.

A potentially more dangerous threat, as Friedan saw it, was the division between those feminists like herself, who sought to remedy inequality through the political and legal system, and the radical feminists, whose theoretical musings often challenged fundamental social relationships and institutions. Identifying women as an oppressed class, the radicals advanced theories that many Americans found disturbing. "Sexism" was the nemesis of the radicals, and they found it in virtually every aspect of American society. Should this perspective ever become associated with NOW, Friedan feared, it would alienate those who might otherwise support the group's relatively moderate goals. As of 1967, the NOW president struggled to preserve the organization from any taint of unwholesome radicalism. Given the growing diversity of feminist perspectives, it was not an easy task. Ti-Grace Atkinson, the elegant, aristocratic president of the New York NOW chapter, became an issue in 1968 due to her provocative views. Atkinson had also plunged into the controversy surrounding the attempted murder of pop artist Andy Warhol in the summer of 1968. Warhol was seriously wounded when Valerie Solanas, a young writer-actress, shot him at his famous New York studio, the Factory. Solanas, the founder and sole member of SCUM (Society for Cutting Up Men), had authored the SCUM manifesto promising to "bring about a complete female takeover, eliminate the male sex and begin to create a swinging, groovy, out-of-sight female world." With little regard for the consequences, Atkinson publicly rose to Solanas's defense, describing her as a "feminist heroine." The New York NOW president also denounced marriage as legalized prostitution and slavery. That fall, Friedan and the moderates successfully pressured Atkinson to resign the presidency of New York NOW.

The battle with the radicals was only beginning, however, as the dramatic tactics of the younger activists often overshadowed the more restrained actions organized by NOW. The radical-led assault on the Miss America pageant in Atlantic City in the fall of 1968 demonstrated their advantage in drawing media coverage. Robin Morgan, founder of the Women's International Terrorist Conspiracy from Hell (WITCH), organized the event protesting the commodification and exploitation of women. Morgan's in-your-face radicalism, often aimed at white, male, corporate America, was most famously established in an underground newspaper article in which she proclaimed that the male establishment would "have to make up their own minds as to whether they will be divested of just cock privilege or—what the hell, why not say it!—divested of cocks." It was not the sort of social analysis that Friedan endorsed, and she was aware of the potential damage that such unrestrained rhetoric could bring. WITCH actions at Atlantic City included crowning a sheep as Miss America and, more famously, the Freedom Trash Can, into which activists tossed the burdensome accoutrements of artificial femininity—bras, girdles, false eyelashes, and wigs. Contrary to popular myth, there was no bra burning, though critics would erroneously apply that descriptive to feminists in future years. The rapid radicalization of some parts of the women's movement mirrored the intensifying militancy of many dissidents that year. Greater civil unrest occurred in 1968 than at any time since the Civil War, as black militants, radical college students, and antiwar demonstrators raised the level of rhetoric and action. Friedan was struggling against the current of history as she sought to keep NOW in the political mainstream. Nevertheless, she did not shrink from embracing controversial issues when she saw them as fundamental to female equality. In 1969, Friedan attended the organizing meeting of the National Association for the Repeal of Abortion Laws, where she encouraged the participants to endorse a charter that proclaimed "the right of a woman to control her own body, her inalienable human, civil right, not to be denied or abridged by the state, or any man." It was among the few issues about which Friedan and feminist radicals agreed. Unfortunately, another issue soon arose, bringing with it the potential to severely disrupt the movement and damage Friedan's leadership status.

The "lavender menace," as Friedan termed it, had concerned the NOW president for some time. The role of lesbians in the movement was a controversial issue, given that many critics derided all feminists as "mannish" or anti-male. Yet, as Friedan knew, lesbian women had no other movement to turn to. Friedan's own homophobic sentiments were evident in passages in *The Feminist Mystique* in which she had condemned "the shallow unreality, immaturity, promiscuity, lack of lasting human satisfaction that characterize" homosexual life. Should lesbians ever gain prominence in the movement, she feared, the public would equate lesbianism with feminism. In 1969, she warned that the younger radicals needed to understand that the central issues were employment and education, "not sexual fantasy." Her concerns heightened the following year when bisexual Kate Millett became the new focus of media attention with the publication of *Sexual Politics*. *Time* magazine described Millett as the "Mao Tse-tung of Women's Liberation" and proclaimed her as the "ideologue" of the new "assault on patriarchy." The *Time* article gave new life to the controversy over lesbians in the women's movement, and several NOW leaders decided that they would proclaim their support for lesbians in an upcoming December demonstration. Friedan, knowing nothing of the plan, arrived at the New York City event to find the NOW leadership wearing lavender armbands. She angrily hurled to the ground the armband offered to her. Later that day, she was horrified and angered to learn that other leaders were planning a news conference to affirm "We are all lesbians." Friedan insisted that her name not be used in association with any such event. Comfortable with her own heterosexuality, Friedan saw the lesbian issue as an unnecessary and potentially dangerous diversion.

No longer a NOW officer as of 1970, Friedan could look back on the years since the group's founding with some satisfaction, cognizant that second-wave feminism already had significant victories to celebrate. In 1967, Lyndon Johnson had signed Executive Order 11375, which required federal agencies and contractors to adopt affirmative action policies toward women. The following year, the Equal Employment Opportunity Office ruled that gender-specific help-wanted newspaper ads were illegal. In 1969, when Friedan's marriage to Carl finally ended, California adopted a no-fault divorce law that allowed divorce by mutual consent, and elsewhere laws regarding the equal division of common property were passed. More dramatic events often swept these reforms from newspaper headlines, but they marked major advances toward gender equity. Friedan now focused on political reform and passage of the Equal Rights Amendment (ERA), while taking up teaching and writing. Her titular leadership of the movement diminished as the media focused on Gloria Steinem, whose visage soon graced the covers of *Time* and *McCall's*, the latter naming the more glamorous Steinem as 1971's Woman of the Year. Deeply resentful, Friedan strove to focus on empowering women politically, having in 1970 cofounded with New York congresswoman Bella Abzug the National Women's Political Caucus (NWPC), dedicated to electing women to public office. Much to Friedan's chagrin, the NWPC council selected Steinem as the group's spokesperson at the 1972 Democratic Convention. Undeterred, Friedan threw herself into black congresswoman Shirley Chisholm's long-shot presidential campaign. Chisholm's candidacy was purely symbolic, but in the November elections, five women gained congressional seats and dozens were elected to state legislatures. These achievements did not mask continuing divisions within the movement, however, as the younger, more radical feminists staked out positions in contrast to which Friedan appeared overly cautious and even conservative. Steinem criticized *The Feminine Mystique's* failure to take into account the tribulations of lower-class women and women of color. Shortly afterward, Friedan lost her leadership position in NWPC in the course of a contentious election. The movement that she catalyzed seemed to be moving on without her.

The 1970s brought frustrations for Friedan and some setbacks for the women's movement. Friedan took some satisfaction in a series of academic appointments and in efforts to organize an international women's movement. In June 1975, she traveled to Mexico City to attend the first International Women's Year conference, which attracted women from eighty countries. Friedan's chief focus at middecade was, however, the ratification of the ERA, the progress of which had slowed after thirty states ratified the amendment in 1972. Only three states did so in 1974, signaling the mounting strength of the new conservatism that emerged in response to the perceived liberal excesses of the turbulent 1960s. Alarmed at the 1973 *Roe v. Wade* decision that affirmed the right to abortion, social conservatives began marshaling their forces for a counterattack on moral permissiveness. For many adherents of the New Right, feminism was an insidious cloak for a radical transformation of American society, and the ERA was its Trojan horse. Despite Friedan's intense work for ERA, the amendment stalled short of ratification, in large part due to the effective opposition of groups like Phyllis Schlafly's Eagle Forum. Schlafly, a right-wing lawyer, was an extremely effective ERA opponent, arguing that it would deprive women of existing legal protections, make them eligible for the military draft, require unisex public restrooms, and hasten the collapse of Western civilization. In the midst of this crucial debate in 1977, Friedan traveled to the National Women's Conference in Houston, where she discovered that an antifeminist delegation from ultra-conservative Mississippi was participating, with some delegates carrying signs reading "Kikes for Dykes" and "Abzug, Friedan and Steinem are Anti-Christian Jews." The presence of the antifeminists within this inner sanctum so shocked Friedan that she impulsively decided to publicly support the "lesbian plank," which advocated equal rights for homosexuals. Friedan's speech in support of "our lesbian sisters" provoked an emotional outpouring of cheers and tears from the delegates, and brought some unity to a fractured movement. Such sentiments could not, however, halt the conservative floodtide that was sweeping the American heartland and setting the stage for decades of conservative political dominance. Time ran out on the ERA in 1982 when, still three states short of ratification, it died.

In many ways, the women's movement that emerged in the mid-1960s died with the ERA. The era of mass protest movements had clearly ended, and though the struggle for women's rights continued, it did not advance under a single banner or leader, but rather along many different avenues. As of the onset of the conservative 1980s, however, there were many accomplishments to be celebrated. During the previous decade, U.S. Supreme Court decisions granted feminists some of their goals. *Eisenstadt v. Baird* (1972) established that the right to privacy permitted unmarried individuals to purchase contraceptives. Many feminists hailed the 1973 *Roe* decision legalizing abortion as another major advance in reproductive rights. During these same years, women's athletic programs were given equal status through Title IX of the Education Amendments. The Equal Credit Opportunity Act of 1974 prohibited gender discrimination in consumer credit practices, while the Pregnancy Discrimination Act (1978) banned discriminatory treatment of pregnant women. Perhaps the more accurate register of the movement's success, however, was the increasing visibility of women in virtually all areas of American life, including law enforcement, law, public service, the corporate world, and the armed services. The stifling, male-dominated world that Friedan described in *The Feminine Mystique* was clearly giving way to a more equitable society.

Friedan continued to seek to define her past and present roles as a feminist, and to prod what remained of the movement in a direction she approved of. Her second book, however, did her reputation little credit. *It Changed My Life* (1976) reaffirmed Friedan's commitment to the cause, but contained allegations against former compatriots that generated heated rebuttals. She garnered far more attention with *The Second Stage* (1981), in which she argued that feminism's first stage, characterized by an overemphasis on the priority of women's needs, was selfish. The next stage, she contended, required renewed attention to the "new frontier" of the family and drawing men into the effort to establish an equitable society. Friedan's apparent embrace of home and hearth was partly a response to the New Right's monopolization of family values, but it was also intended as criticism of those radical women who forsook family for careers. Friedan propounded the necessity of balance between the two and the need to reconsider such concepts as abortion on demand, which she condemned as reflecting irreverence for life and sexual indiscipline. The book generated a storm of controversy, with some offering praise for Friedan's thoughtful midstream reappraisal of the movement, though many feminists denounced the book as a betrayal.

Friedan devoted most of the 1980s to activities outside the movement, such as supporting Democratic vice presidential candidate Geraldine Ferraro's ill-fated 1984 campaign and working for the American Jewish Congress. Having moved from New York to California, she returned to public attention in 1993 with the publication of *The Fountain of Age*, which addressed issues of aging. The book was a modest success, and Friedan followed up in 1997 with *Beyond Gender*. Her concerns now mirrored those of many Americans in the 1990s: growing corporate power, the vast disparities in wealth, a struggling middle class, and the continuing decline of labor unions, an issue that brought her full circle with her interests as a young woman. Remaining intellectually engaged but largely absent from public view during the last decade of her life, Friedan died on February 4, 2006, her eighty-fifth birthday. In a eulogy published shortly afterward, Germaine Greer, who had in the past made clear her differences with Friedan, offered the most succinct summation of Friedan's life: "She changed the course of human history almost single-handedly."

Conclusion

Though Rachel Carson and Betty Friedan were of different generations and came from significantly different family backgrounds, they both found the heady years of the early 1960s conducive to the realization of their long-term endeavors. Having achieved some modest prominence by the time she published *Silent Spring* in 1962, Carson found a public responsive to her warnings about the fate of the earth if human heedlessness were not corrected. A quiet and unassuming woman who dedicated her life to science and family, Carson was an unlikely crusader for environmental protection. Through painstaking research, however, she provided the empirical evidence that gave both support and impetus to a broadening environmental movement that, in coming decades, literally changed the way that Americans looked at and interacted with the natural world. She died before she could know the extent of her success, but the new environmentalism that blossomed in subsequent years stands as adequate testament to her achievement.

Betty Friedan, on the other hand, typifies the passionate activist who has been central to the definition and realization of American ideals since the founding of the republic. Bright and assertive, keenly aware of fundamental injustices, Friedan wrote her most famous work from a position of middle-class privilege that for many years cloaked her earlier association with the radical left politics of the Depression era. The lingering specter of McCarthyism in the early 1960s may well have led Friedan to downplay, if not to conceal outright, her radical past. Notably absent from *The Feminine Mystique* was any significant class-based analysis that might have hinted at a Marxist perspective or any consideration of race. Later criticized by more radical feminists for its shallow, middle-class perspective, *The Feminine Mystique* nonetheless lit the fire that stoked second-wave feminism and its diversity of viewpoints. Friedan's abrasive personality and persistent fear that radicalism would undermine popular support for feminism hindered her efforts to establish her leadership of the movement. Like others who initiated great movements for change, Friedan seemed unwilling to acknowledge that, once set in play, the dynamics of social transformation often defy restraint and follow new paths that could not have been foreseen. From the perspective of the twenty-first century, however, it is clear that Friedan played a signal role in bringing about a revolution in the way that American women live their lives.

Study Questions

1. Describe the events that led to Rachel Carson's interest in environmental issues.
2. Why were Americans more responsive to environmental concerns by the 1960s?
3. Discuss the central thesis of and public response to *Silent Spring*.
4. Explain Betty Friedan's importance to the emergence of the modern women's movement.
5. What were the chief successes of the women's rights movement between the publication of *The Feminine Mystique* and the end of the century?

Selected Bibliography

Boucher, Joanne. "Betty Friedan and the Radical Past of Liberal Feminism." *New Politics* 9, no. 3 (2003).

Carson, Rachel. *The Edge of the Sea*. Boston: Houghton Mifflin, 1955.

———. *The Sea Around Us*. New York: Oxford University Press, 1951.

———. *Silent Spring*. Boston: Houghton Mifflin, 1962.

Cohen, Marcia. *The Sisterhood: The True Story of the Women Who Changed the World*. New York: Fawcett, 1989.

Davis, Flora. *Moving the Mountain: The Women's Movement in America since 1960*. New York: Simon and Schuster, 1991.

Echols, Alice. *Daring to Be Bad: Radical Feminism in America, 1967–1975*. Minneapolis: University of Minnesota Press, 1989.

Friedan, Betty. *The Feminine Mystique*. New York: Dell, 1964.

———. *It Changed My Life*. New York: Random House, 1976.

———. *The Second Stage*. New York: Summit, 1981.

Gartner, Carol B. *Rachel Carson*. New York: Frederick Ungar, 1983.

Gitlin, Todd. *The Sixties: Years of Hope, Days of Rage*. New York: Bantam, 1987.

Hays, Samuel P. *Beauty, Health and Permanence: Environmental Politics in the United States, 1955–1985*. New York: Cambridge University Press, 1987.

Hennessee, Judith. *Betty Friedan: Her Life*. New York: Random House, 1999.

Hole, Judith, and Ellen Levine. *Rebirth of Feminism*. New York: Quadrangle, 1971.

Horowitz, Daniel. *Betty Friedan and the Making of the Feminine Mystique*. Amherst, MA: University of Massachusetts Press, 1998.

Lear, Linda. *Rachel Carson: Witness for Nature*. New York: Henry Holt, 1997.

Lytle, Mark H. *The Gentle Subversive: Rachel Carson, the Silent Spring and the Rise of the Environmental Movement*. New York: Oxford University Press, 2007.

MacKenzie, G. Calvin, and Robert Weisbrot. *The Liberal Hour: Washington and the Politics of Change in the 1960s*. New York: Penguin, 2008.

McCay, Mary A. *Rachel Carson*. New York: Twayne, 1993.

Millett, Kate. *Sexual Politics*. Garden City, NY: Doubleday, 1970.

Morgan, Robin, ed. *Sisterhood Is Powerful: An Anthology of Writings from the Women's Liberation Movement*. New York: Vintage, 1970.

Murphy, Priscilla Coit. *What a Book Can Do: The Publication and Reception of Silent Spring*. Amherst, MA: University of Massachusetts Press, 2007.

O'Neill, William. *Feminism in America: A History*. New York: Quadrangle, 1994.

Rome, Adam. "'Give Earth a Chance': The Environmental Movement and the Sixties." *Journal of American History* 90, no. 2 (2003): 525–54.

Rosen, Ruth. *A World Split Open: How the Modern Women's Movement Changed America*. New York: Penguin, 2001.

Rossiter, Margaret. *Women Scientists in America*. Baltimore, MD: Johns Hopkins University Press, 1982.

Rothman, Hal K. *The Greening of a Nation? Environmentalism in the United States since 1945*. New York: Harcourt Brace, 1998.

———. *Saving the Planet: The American Response to the Environment in the Twentieth Century*. Chicago: Ivan R. Dee, 2000.

CHAPTER TEN

~

Racial Justice

Thought and Action

During the 1950s, the first portents of what would later be acknowledged as a civil rights revolution appeared, as civil rights organizations, both new and long-standing, mobilized a mass movement demanding "Freedom Now." Though the American civil rights movement had deep roots, extending back well before the Civil War, World War II afforded new impetus to the dynamic movement of the postwar era. Demanding that their nation live up to the ideals that it was professedly fighting for, civil rights activists wrested a wartime executive order prohibiting racial discrimination in defense industry employment. While racial segregation in the armed services continued for the duration, African Americans demanded and gained access to combat assignments, acquiring new self-confidence as they mastered the military skills and experiences denied them in the past. Many black servicemen returned from the conflict determined to no longer quietly suffer the racist insults and violence that had been a common part of their lives. The foundations for an energized, popularly based civil rights movement were forged in the crucible of World War II.

Several developments in the 1950s further catalyzed rising expectations. Long-established civil rights organizations such as the National Association for the Advancement of Colored People (NAACP) focused on legal challenges to de jure racial segregation, winning a major victory in 1954 when the U.S. Supreme Court ruled on *Brown v. Topeka Board of Education*. The court's conclusion that "separate facilities are inherently unequal" provided a legal basis for further challenges to segregation in every area of public life, inspiring such direct actions as the Montgomery bus boycott of 1955, which brought both the Southern Christian Leadership Conference (SCLC) and Martin Luther King Jr.

to national prominence. That same year, the savage murder of fourteen-year-old black Chicagoan Emmett Till in Money, Mississippi, provoked widespread outrage among African Americans. The farcical trial that led to the acquittal of the white murderers revealed to a horrified nation the degree to which grotesque violence, shielded by injustice, preserved an entrenched system of racial inequality throughout the South. A clear consensus existed among African Americans that there would be no more propitious time to press for fundamental change, although leaders debated about strategies to tackle America's racial problems. These questions demanded the attention of both intellectuals and activists among African Americans; thought and action would have to be coordinated to further the monumental campaign for racial justice.

The African American intellectual tradition took shape well before the Civil War, producing such leaders as Frederick Douglass, and the twentieth century produced numerous worthy successors. W. E. B. DuBois, James Weldon Johnson, Langston Hughes, and Richard Wright were among those black Americans who devoted their lives to defining African American identity and examining the nation's racial challenges. In the years after World War II, James Baldwin emerged as arguably the nation's most influential African American intellectual. Distraught over the pervasive racism he experienced as a young man, Baldwin fled his New York City home in 1948 for France, where distance accorded him a trenchant perspective on his country's racial dilemmas. A novelist and playwright, Baldwin became best known for his incisive essays, in which he addressed a multitude of issues related to black identity and American racism. By the 1960s, as the crusade for racial justice accelerated, Baldwin became more directly engaged in the movement, insisting that the federal government enforce constitutional guarantees of every American's civil rights and embracing an increasingly militant stance throughout the 1960s.

The struggle for racial justice had always required the personal courage of activists as well as thinkers, and there too can be found a lengthy tradition that includes such diverse individuals as David Walker, Marcus Garvey, A. Philip Randolph, and Martin Luther King Jr. As the civil rights revolution advanced in the early 1960s, younger activists, often college students, assumed greater leadership roles through organizations such as the Student Non-Violent Coordinating Committee (SNCC). One such activist was Stokely Carmichael, a native of Trinidad whose family moved to New York in the early 1950s. A bright and articulate student, Carmichael participated in most of the major actions undertaken by SNCC in the early 1960s and, like many of his peers, adopted an increasingly militant perspective. Most famous for popularizing the slogan "black power" in 1966, Carmichael was one of many activists who abandoned King's nonviolent philosophy for one of armed self-defense. Carmichael's radicalism drew him to the Black Panther Party, third-world revolutionary ideology, and eventually pan-Africanism, as he grew increasingly pessimistic about racial conciliation in the United States. His personal journey, which ended in Africa, was testament to the sometimes irreconcilable dilemmas that ran through the issue of racial justice in America.

⌒ JAMES BALDWIN ⌒

The year 1963 was hardly a propitious time to have an impassioned discussion about race in America, as Attorney General Robert F. Kennedy soon discovered. Named to head the Justice Department by his brother John when the latter won the 1960 presidential election, the attorney general was deeply aware of the disquieting dilemma that their administration faced. An increasingly active civil rights movement demanded that the Justice Department combat segregation and protect demonstrators. Both Kennedys recognized that doing so would put them squarely at odds with powerful Southern Democratic elected officials and risk alienating Southern whites prior to the 1964 election. They were also aware that some civil rights activists considered the Kennedy administration far too cautious in its initiatives and too meek in responding to racist violence against activists, but Attorney General Kennedy was taken aback by the tone of the telegram he received from James Baldwin on May 12. Baldwin, an African American writer, had spent much of his early adulthood in self-imposed exile in France, where he struggled with his racial and sexual identities, though the burgeoning civil rights movement periodically drew him home. In his telegram, the thirty-nine-year-old New Yorker excoriated Kennedy for permitting the police brutalities that occurred during recent demonstrations in Birmingham, Alabama. Stunned at the allegation, Kennedy asked that Baldwin join him at his New York City apartment, where the two planned a subsequent gathering that would include prominent black entertainers and activists.

Any expectations Kennedy had that the subsequent meeting would produce polite and civil discourse were immediately dashed when a group of about a dozen influential African Americans assembled in his apartment on May 24. Kennedy, accompanied by assistant Burke Marshall, began by recounting his administration's civil rights achievements. When some suggested that much more could have been done, the attorney general expressed his dismay at the apparent ingratitude of black Americans and his fear that the growing influence of extremist groups, such as the Nation of Islam, would inevitably mean trouble. The tone of the meeting deteriorated as Jerome Smith, a Congress of Racial Equality (CORE) activist, announced, "It makes me nauseous to have to be here," and then declared, "You don't have any idea what trouble is, because

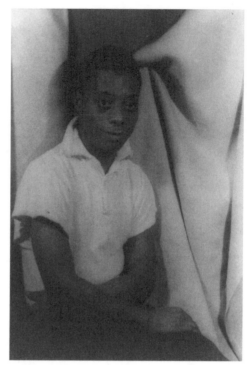

Novelist and essayist James Baldwin in a photographic portrait by Carl Van Vechten in September 1955. An articulate and forceful commentator on American race relations, Baldwin wrote extensively on the issue of racial identity during an era when the modern civil rights movement was compelling the American government and public to address these controversial issues. (Library of Congress, LC-USZ62-42481)

I'm close to the moment when I'm ready to take up a gun." The problem was not Black Muslims, Smith proclaimed, but white liberals who failed to comprehend the depth of black rage. "I've had enough shit," an angry Smith told the shocked attorney general. "I'm gonna kiss it off and pull the damn trigger!" Such sentiments were no surprise to Baldwin, whose numerous essays addressed the rage and frustration that African Americans commonly experienced. Kennedy was genuinely stunned at the extent of Smith's alienation, but suggested that his own Irish forebears had also faced discrimination and had nonetheless gained acceptance and influence. It was conceivable, he presciently suggested, that a black man might be president in about forty years. Baldwin interrupted to condemn Kennedy's analogy as "absurd." Irish immigrants arrived long after black slaves, he observed, and their descendants had already gained the White House. The black man, Baldwin reminded him, was "still required to supplicate and beg you for justice."

The distance between Kennedy and his black guests became evident as he cited statistics demonstrating African American advancement. When attorney Clarence Jones suggested that President Kennedy might prove his commitment to the cause of civil rights by personally escorting black students into segregated schools, Kennedy derisively laughed aloud. Those present, including celebrities Lena Horne and Harry Belafonte as well as prominent civil rights activists, realized that they were unable to convey to Kennedy the depth of black anger and resentment. The four-hour meeting broke up when disgusted black participants departed. Baldwin recounted later that "Bobby Kennedy was a little surprised at the depth of Negro feeling. We were all a bit shocked at the extent of his naïveté." Kennedy later confided that he believed Baldwin had "played" the meeting for publicity and that it "put him in the center of things and gave him a position of leadership." Baldwin's motives, however, were otherwise. He was sincerely committed to racial justice and feared that white incomprehension of the black perspective would inevitably lead to violence. That same year brought the publication of Baldwin's *The Fire Next Time*, the latest in a series of essay collections that explored black identity and racial issues. This work took its title from the lyrics of a black spiritual: "God gave Noah the rainbow sign; no more water, the fire next time." It was a warning that Baldwin had hoped to convey to Kennedy. There would be no more second chances—America had to resolve its race question justly and immediately, or face apocalyptic consequences. It was a message born of the despair and alienation that Baldwin had felt since childhood, sentiments that were widespread among black Americans, and which he sought to give voice to throughout his lengthy literary career.

James Baldwin's troubled passage through life began on August 2, 1924, in New York City, where he was born to a single mother, Emma Berdis Jones, who married David Baldwin when James was three years old. It was not a happy household, as the stepfather, a laborer and Baptist preacher from New Orleans, tyrannized his wife and the nine children that he eventually fathered. He was especially cruel to James, regularly telling him how ugly he was and addressing him as "frog eyes." In 1974, Baldwin summarized these hellish years in an interview with a French journalist. "I never had a childhood," he noted. "I was born dead." Despite his detestation of his religious stepfather, Baldwin was drawn to Pentecostalism and became a "Holy Roller" preacher at fourteen. The impact of this early period, when James became intimately familiar with the gospels, spirituals, and the role of religion in African American life, was apparent in his later writing. Baldwin demonstrated an early affinity for literature and in the 1941 DeWitt Clinton High School yearbook he listed his ambition as "novelist-playwright," an aspiration enhanced following his first meeting with African American artist Beauford Delaney in 1940. In later years, Beauford's neighborhood in Greenwich Village became a frequent refuge for Baldwin. His literary ambitions would not be easy to realize—though Richard Wright had won acclaim as a significant writer by this time, the opportunities for African Americans to gain recognition as anything other than "Negro writers" were limited. Even more daunting, his labor was needed to help support his large family, which compelled him to delay plans to attend City College and to devote his energies to a succession of manual labor jobs.

Regular racial insults compounded his personal hardships, building to a seminal event in New Jersey in 1943. Depressed and angry, Baldwin had sought a meal at a diner, where he was told, "We don't serve Negroes here." He subsequently recounted his reaction in *Notes of a Native Son*, noting that he purposefully strode into another restaurant where he knew that "not even the intercession of the Virgin would cause me to be served." He accosted a clearly alarmed white waitress and decided "that if she found a black man so frightening, [he] would make her fright worthwhile." Met with the expected explanation that blacks were not served there, Baldwin picked up a water jug and flung it at the woman. He fled the restaurant pursued by an angry mob, but aware of an important lesson: "My life, my real life, was in danger, and not from anything other people might do but from the hatred I carried in my own heart." Baldwin's inner turmoil grew that summer when he was fired from a defense plant job and learned that his insane and dying eighty-eight-year-old stepfather had again impregnated Emma as "a mocking farewell present." Reluctantly visiting David at his deathbed, Baldwin experienced an epiphany—he could not hate his stepfather anymore. "I imagine that one of the reasons people cling to their hates so stubbornly," he later wrote, "is because they sense, once hate is gone, they will be forced to deal with pain."

Baldwin's journey of self-discovery began as he left home for Greenwich Village, where he broadened his intellectual horizons through interactions with numerous artists and writers, including not only his friend Delaney, but seminal figures in the Beat movement such as the poet Allen Ginsberg and the writer Jack Kerouac. Baldwin was also in search of his sexual identity. Though he pursued at least one heterosexual relationship, he had already confided his homosexuality to close friends and believed that any other orientation was "many light-years too late." Baldwin toyed as well with radical politics, briefly joining the Young People's Socialist League and later proclaiming himself a Trotskyist, but he ultimately dismissed the value of ideologies. More important, he began to write, working on a father/son-themed novel he planned to call *Crying Holy*, but which would eventually be published as *Go Tell It on the Mountain*. Baldwin met Richard Wright in the winter of 1945, and the famous author of *Native Son* offered encouragement to the younger man. With Wright's recommendation, Baldwin received a Saxton Foundation Scholarship, and he established connections that ensured his entrée into publishing, writing articles for *Commentary* and *The New Leader*. He remained troubled, however, unable to shape the novel he wanted so much to write, and still "fighting with my shame," as he described his struggle for sexual identity. A former girlfriend advised him, "Get out—you'll die if you stay here." In November 1948, Baldwin boarded a passenger ship for Paris. "Once I found myself on the other side of the ocean," he told a *New York Times* interviewer years later, "I could see where I came from very clearly, and I could see that I carried myself, which is my home, with me. You can never escape that. I am the grandson of a slave, and I am a writer. I must deal with both."

Postwar Paris was a mecca for an international aggregation of intellectuals and writers, who luxuriated in the heady, historical ambience of the City of Light and peopled its multitude of cafés, discussing philosophy, literature, art, and music with luminaries such as Jean-Paul Sartre, Simone de Beauvoir, and Albert Camus. For black Americans like Baldwin, Paris promised social acceptability in a relatively racially tolerant climate, together with intellectual stimulation. Though Baldwin would discover that France and Europe were not immune from racial tensions, Paris offered the psychological space that he required, and he made the city his chief place of residence for the next nine years, with only brief journeys elsewhere. Living in a succession of cheap hotels, often on the brink of total impoverishment, the aspiring writer often depended on the goodwill of friends and acquaintances, gaining a reputation as a not always gracious or thoughtful guest, given as he was to moody behavior and frequent pleas for funds. In 1949, his writing turned to the topics of homosexuality and race, the former being addressed in his essay "The Preservation of Innocence," which was published in the literary magazine *Zero*. Baldwin attributed American violence against homosexuals to prejudices that could be "traced to the Rover Boys and their golden ideal of chastity." *Zero* also published his essay "Everybody's Protest Novel," a stinging criticism of Harriet Beecher Stowe's *Uncle Tom's Cabin* (1852), which Baldwin rejected as "a very bad novel" because its characters were not fully realized human beings, but rather only superficial categorizations. Despite this achievement, Baldwin's precarious equanimity was disturbed when he was arrested for receiving stolen goods after accepting a purloined hotel bed sheet from a friend. His week in jail terrified him, and he felt humiliated at his subsequent trial, where those in the courtroom seemed to dismiss him as a buffoon, reminding him of "what being a black man meant." Race prejudice, he was learning, could be vulgar and violent, as it was in the United States, or subtle and nuanced, as it appeared to be in France. Baldwin undertook a feeble attempt at suicide following his release, but the botched hanging had the effect of bringing a temporary end to the emotional tension that had shackled him since his arrival in Paris.

His life gained some nominal stability when he began a long-term relationship with Lucien Happersberger, a Swiss teenager who pursued numerous heterosexual affairs while he was Baldwin's lover, even fathering two children. Lucien's anarchic love life rarely disturbed Baldwin, who devoted more time to completing the novel that had obsessed him since his adolescence, *Go Tell It on the Mountain*. A semiautobiographical work, the novel draws from Baldwin's Harlem youth, telling the story of several generations of African Americans through a Harlem storefront church. The novel, he conceded, was also a delayed confession of forgiveness for David Baldwin. Editors at Alfred A. Knopf expressed interest, and with a loan from his friend Marlon Brando, the renowned Hollywood actor, Baldwin took the transatlantic voyage home in 1952. In addition to a reunion with his family, Baldwin negotiated with Knopf's editors over changes to *Mountain*, brushing off the unhelpful suggestion that the book might be better "without all the Jesus stuff." Advance monies went to his family and a return ticket, and in August he left a nation stewing in McCarthyite hysteria and racial tensions. *Go Tell It on the Mountain* was published in May 1953, to glowing reviews. A *New York Times* reviewer ranked the young novelist alongside Ralph Ellison, whose brilliant and troubling exploration of racial identity, *Invisible Man*, had just won the National Book Award.

Baldwin led a wayward existence for the next several years, often unsettled in Paris but refusing to return to New York. The tensions stemmed in part from unresolved issues confronted during his work on the novel that would become *Giovanni's Room*, which explored a white man's homosexual love affair. He had completed work on a play, *The Amen Corner*, another work drawing on the black Pentecostal experience. Baldwin stepped onto the dock in New York harbor in June 1954, but again racial prejudice intruded into his life. While staying with friends in the city, he was arrested in a police sweep of a Harlem street one evening and briefly jailed. A friend detained with him recalled that Baldwin was furious, complaining, "I'm a nigger, they arrested me because I'm black." Receiving a suspended sentence for disorderly conduct, Baldwin headed for a writer's colony in New Hampshire, where he worked productively on the novel, several articles, and the essay "Notes of a Native Son," which became the title of his first collection of essays in 1955. That work, which established Baldwin's reputation as an astute observer of the psychology of race, dealt with the identity of the "Negro," black life in America, and the perspective of the European expatriate. Later hailed as Baldwin's most incisive social criticism, *Notes of a Native Son* did not sell well initially, though it garnered positive critical response. Baldwin was pleased to have *The Amen Corner* produced at Howard University that year, but the play, like *Notes of a Native Son*, went largely ignored until the publication of *Giovanni's Room* in 1955 brought the author wider renown. That novel's subject guaranteed the caution of American publishers, but Baldwin found a London house willing to publish it. *Giovanni's Room* offered no graphic sexual activity, but was rather a nuanced examination of an individual who is conflicted over his sexuality. Still, it was a daring venture given the social conventions of an era in which homosexuality was generally dismissed as perversion or a form of mental illness.

Events in 1956 compelled Baldwin to reengage with the race issue. After continuing reflection, the expatriate writer was convinced that the questions about race that he wished to address could only be framed in the United States, where such events as the murder of Emmett Till and the *Brown v. Topeka Board of Education* decision had fueled a popularly based civil rights movement. Paris increasingly seemed less hospitable, as the Algerian crisis exposed French racist sentiments. In September 1956, Baldwin attended the Conference of Negro-African Writers at the Sorbonne. It was a disillusioning experience. Most of the attendees were proponents of *negritude*, an ill-defined outlook that saw Africa's future in the adoption of some peculiarly African form of socialism. Baldwin found little new or noteworthy at the conference and realized that it was time to return again to his native land.

Baldwin traveled to New York in July 1957 and though he periodically returned to Europe and Africa, his focus for more than a decade was race and American society. The nation was in the midst of the "second Reconstruction," as Congress passed a new civil rights act that summer and racial antagonism erupted at Little Rock, Arkansas's Central High School that fall. One of Baldwin's first contacts was African American intellectual Kenneth Clark, who described the writer as "resembling an Old Testament prophet" in his determination to seek and reveal truth. Clark was convinced that Baldwin could be a major contributor to the civil rights campaign. The young author had received funding for a trip through the South from *Harper's* and *Partisan Review* and began his journey of discovery from Washington, DC, in September, traveling to Charlotte, North Carolina, and then to Atlanta, interviewing both the foot soldiers of the movement and the leaders, such as Martin Luther King Jr. Once a preacher himself, Baldwin saw greatness in King's speeches and his work. Completing his journey with stops in Nashville and Little Rock, Baldwin was moved by the dedication of those in the movement, and shocked at the racial volatility in the region. More important, he had found new purpose in his life. "I realized that great things were happening," he told journalist Harold Isaacs, "and that I did have a role to play. I can't be happy here, but I can work here." Meanwhile, Baldwin took a small apartment in Greenwich Village, where he produced two essays, "The Discovery of What It Means to Be an American," and "Nobody Knows My Name," which did much to establish his reputation as an astute observer of racial issues. He also received a Ford Foundation grant to work on his novel *Another Country*.

By 1961, Baldwin was financially secure, due in part to the success of the essay collection *Nobody Knows My Name*, which largely dealt with his reflections on the American South as well as black identity. The book was rife with prophetic warnings about the consequences of ignoring American racial injustices, leading an *Ebony* writer to style Baldwin "The Angriest Young Man." "I love America," Baldwin was quoted as declaring, "but I'm angry about America calling itself the leader of the free world when there are twenty million captive people living within its borders." In such pronouncements Baldwin was finding his public voice, while quickly rising to celebrity status through numerous television appearances. He was also beginning to question King's strategy of nonviolence and in August 1961 met with the leader of the Nation of Islam, Elijah Muhammad, which inspired the essay "Down at the Cross." Baldwin found some admirable qualities in Elijah, but within a year wrote that he found the Black Muslims "frightening" and "irresponsible," feeding "on the despair of black men." Several projects drew Baldwin's attention in these years, including a proposed play about the Emmett Till murder and a trip to Africa. He was conflicted about the latter, fearing that seeing the African continent would provide no answers and "only more questions." Meanwhile, his novel *Another Country* (1962), which included interracial sex as well as bisexuality, drew more attention from the FBI than from readers because of allegations of obscenity. The controversy was not significant enough to preclude an invitation to the Kennedy White House, however, where American Nobel laureates were feted. Baldwin's trip to Africa that same year brought no epiphanies concerning his identity. He could not comprehend those African Americans who were proclaiming a newfound affinity for their ancestral homeland. "I think of the poor Negroes of the US who identify themselves with Africa," he remarked, wondering, "on what basis?" The relevant questions and answers, he concluded, were to be found in America.

In early 1963, as the civil rights movement approached floodtide, many of those issues were explored in *The Fire Next Time*, where Baldwin's essays assumed the tone of the jeremiad, warning of the consequences of ignoring the nation's racial sins. Though he criticized the Black Muslim movement and racial separatism, he expressed admiration for the articulate former spokesman for the Nation, Malcolm X. Baldwin could not contain his outrage at President Kennedy's timid handling of the "Ole Miss" crisis the previous year, in which the state's governor blocked the registration of black applicant James Meredith at the University of Mississippi, and he grew less tolerant of the administration's unwillingness to acknowledge the depth of black rage. These were chief among the concerns that he had made clear to Robert Kennedy at the explosive May meeting. Angered at the course of events, the attorney general had requested that the FBI provide him with files on the black author. The bureau report tied

Baldwin to "pro-Castro organizations" and alleged that he had declared that "only in revolutions could the problems of the United States be solved." The file also noted that Baldwin opposed capital punishment and had "criticized the Director," the latter considered a dire offense within the bureau. Director J. Edgar Hoover, always alert to information that could be used to defame prominent African Americans, penned an internal memo the following year asking, "Isn't Baldwin a well-known pervert?" The reply concluded dryly, "While it is not possible to state that he is a pervert, he has expressed a sympathetic viewpoint about homosexuality on several occasions." The bureau file also erroneously identified Baldwin, who shunned ideology, as a communist.

The months after the ill-fated meeting with Kennedy in 1963 brought soul-shaking news. First came the murder of Mississippi NAACP head Medgar Evers, gunned down in his driveway, then, close on the heels of King's dramatic August speech on the Washington mall, the bombing of a Birmingham church that killed four black girls. These events pushed Baldwin away from nonviolence, and he observed in a televised debate with theologian Reinhold Niebuhr that "the only time that non-violence has been admired is when Negroes practice it." By 1964, Baldwin, now an acknowledged prominent public intellectual whose views on racial topics were commonly sought, had completed his play based on the Till murder. *The Blues for Mr. Charlie*, premiering that April, captured the volatile racial atmosphere of the mid-decade, provoking acclaim from blacks and expressions of dismay from whites. To Baldwin's disappointment, the play closed down after a brief run and Baldwin, distraught over the racial impasse in the United States, briefly fled abroad.

In February 1965, Baldwin, then in England, debated conservative pundit William F. Buckley Jr. at the Cambridge Union, comparing himself to the prophet Jeremiah and decisively winning over the student audience. News of the assassination of Malcolm X soon diminished this triumph, however, and reporters quickly sought Baldwin's reaction. Baldwin recalled that Malcolm had once told him, "I'm the warrior of this revolution and you're the poet," and the murder deeply affected the writer. Baldwin's increasingly militant perspective comported with a change of attitude among many civil rights activists, and he more frequently abandoned writing to participate in history-making events such as the Selma-to-Montgomery march in March 1965. His new collection of short stories, *Going to Meet the Man*, was published late that year, stressing Baldwin's view that the "Negro problem" had always been in actuality a "white problem." The year had brought both hope, with the passage of the Voting Rights Act, and ominous portents of building black rage, which erupted in a deadly riot in the Watts section of Los Angeles in August. By 1966, Baldwin, radicalized by Malcolm's death, endorsed a more radical future direction for organizations such as CORE and SNCC. He was especially drawn to SNCC director Stokely

Carmichael's concept of black power, which promised black liberation through black agency. The writer was also supportive of the new Black Panther Party, which organized in paramilitary fashion to protect black communities from white police violence. Like both Carmichael and the Panthers, Baldwin saw in the expanding war in Vietnam a manifestation of America's historical pattern of self-righteous injustice, denouncing the conflict as "a desperate and despicable folly." He was quick to defend Carmichael and Panther founder Huey Newton when both became targets of government persecution, and their tribulations, together with a horrifying series of deadly urban riots in 1967, drove Baldwin toward a bleaker outlook on American race relations. In February 1968, the same month when Baldwin hosted a combined birthday party and fund-raiser for Black Panther Huey Newton, the Kerner Commission released its report on the roots of the nation's racial violence, concluding that racism was the chief catalyst and that America was "moving toward two societies, one black, one white—separate and unequal." It was a devastating finding, given even greater force when King was assassinated in Memphis that April. Near complete despair, Baldwin could only lament that there was little left to do but "pray to those gods who are not Western . . . not Christian."

The year 1968 was a disheartening one for the American people, and it proved equally difficult for Baldwin. His hope of producing a film version of the life of Malcolm X foundered, and his new novel *Tell Me How Long the Train's Been Gone* was a critical disaster. Derided as overly long, self-indulgent, and burdened with prose that lacked Baldwin's characteristic clarity, the novel convinced many critics that the writer had surrendered his critical acuity to mundane political rhetoric. Baldwin's affiliation with the ideas and leaders of the new black militancy, some suggested, came at the cost of his independence of mind and powers of objective observation. Baldwin's literary reputation rested on his ability to articulate the complex sentiments of black Americans, and, as of the late 1960s, he seemed to have forsaken that to become a spokesman for what proved to be an ephemeral movement. Black power, the Black Panthers, and black radicalism in general, though the products of genuine rage, soon came up against the limitations that reality imposed upon rhetoric. There would be no black revolution in America. Black radicalism, as well as that evolving from the New Left, sputtered out fitfully as the decade drew to a close, with neither utopian dreams nor apocalyptic nightmares realized.

Though the era of dramatic mass actions and radical dreams was clearly over by the early 1970s, America still faced considerable racial challenges. With public racial discrimination barred and voting rights protected through federal legislation, the stage for conflict was less often the streets and more often the nation's courtrooms. Though he retained a residence in New York City, Baldwin, despairing of any resolution of America's racial ills, increasingly sought refuge abroad, most often in France and Turkey. Though devoting more time to a long-delayed ambition, literary criticism, Baldwin continued to produce essays in the style that proved so potent in earlier decades. A 1972 collection, *No Name in the Streets*, included autobiographical essays together with the author's continuing reflections on racial issues. His bitterness was unconcealed, evident in his characterization of white Americans as "probably the sickest and certainly the most dangerous people of any color, to be found in the world today." His 1974 novel *If Beale Street Could Talk* dealt with the familiar topics of race and sex, drawing mixed reviews. Two years later, he returned to the essay in *The Devil Finds Work*, in which he examined the history of blacks in film. A 1979 novel, *Just Above My Head*, returned to the theme of homosexuality, leading Baldwin to comment that he "had come full circle" and was "set free to go someplace else." His last essay collection, *The Evidence of Things Not Seen* (1985), reflects his lifelong interest in racial issues, as Baldwin examines the controversial Atlanta serial murders of African American children in 1980–1981. A marked tone of pessimism about racial reconciliation marks these last essays.

From the late 1970s, Baldwin held teaching positions at several American universities, though he confided to friends that his penultimate hope was to establish enduring renown as a novelist. The literary landscape of African American writing was rapidly changing, however, transformed by Ishmael Reed, Toni Morrison, and Alice Walker, and though Baldwin pursued several writing projects during the 1980s, none gained for him the literary fame that he had aspired to since childhood. Though he had quieted some of his personal demons, the path to racial brotherhood that he had sought to uncover still seemed cruelly elusive. He died of stomach cancer in Saint-Paul-de-Venice, France, on December 1, 1987.

～ STOKELY CARMICHAEL ～

Though the civil rights activists of the 1960s often faced threats throughout the South, many considered Mississippi to be the most dangerous ground upon which their struggle was waged. It was there that Emmett Till had been brutally murdered in 1955, after which an all-white jury acquitted the smirking killers. It was the Magnolia State's segregationist governor Ross Barnett who in 1962 helped set the stage for the bloody Ole Miss riots, which erupted in response to the enrollment of black student James Meredith at the state university. It was there, in the summer of 1964, that white racists murdered three SNCC workers, then buried their bodies in an earthen dam. The intensity of racial hatred in the state was so infamous that black comedian and activist Dick Gregory had commented, "A white moderate in Mississippi is a cat who wants to lynch you from a *low* tree." It was there in March 1965, in the small

Civil rights activist and black power advocate Stokely Carmichael addresses an audience in 1966. A participant in many of the decade's most notable civil rights protests, Carmichael became in the minds of many Americans the public face of the black power movement, which saw black economic, political, and social empowerment as the path to racial justice. Unsparing in his condemnations of American racial injustice, Carmichael eventually left the country to live in Guinea. (Library of Congress, LC-USZ62-119500)

Delta town of Greenwood, that SNCC organizer Stokely Carmichael decided to try out a provocative slogan indicating a new direction in the movement, a phrase that would mobilize young black activists as well as outrage and frighten white Americans well beyond the borders of Mississippi.

The twenty-four-year-old Carmichael had been drawn into the civil rights movement while a student at Howard University, joining the SNCC after completing a philosophy degree in 1964. He was not unfamiliar with what might be expected in Mississippi, having worked there during the Freedom Summer program shortly after he left Howard. He and other SNCC activists were back in the state because of what had befallen James Meredith, who, on June 5, 1966, had undertaken a solo "March against Fear," vowing to walk from Memphis, Tennessee, to Jackson, Mississippi, to challenge that "pervasive fear" that black Southerners lived in. On the second day of the event, a shotgun-wielding white man repeatedly blasted Meredith from a concealed position before surrendering to police. Badly wounded, Meredith was furious that lax police protection had enabled the assailant to shoot him "like a goddamn rabbit." The hospitalized activist also expressed regret that he had not been armed; as casualties among civil rights workers had multiplied, more were coming to reject passive nonviolence and ponder the necessity of a new strategy of self-defense. In solidarity with Meredith, a cadre of prominent activists, including Martin Luther King

Jr. and Carmichael, pledged to undertake the "Meredith March," and complete the 194 miles of Meredith's planned trek. As the march proceeded, it quickly became apparent that nerves on both sides were frayed. State troopers assigned to the event were clearly hostile, roughly handling some marchers and knocking both King and Carmichael to the ground. The famous Atlanta minister had to struggle to restrain a visibly angered Carmichael, who was increasingly less willing to endure physical abuse and convinced that circumstances demanded a more militant movement strategy.

Following completion of the march, it was decided that separate groups of activists would move deeper into the Delta region to organize local blacks to vote, an activity that the Voting Rights Act had recently facilitated. Though the voter registration teams were welcomed by black residents, whites frequently harassed and threatened them. On June 16, Governor Paul Johnson Jr. announced the withdrawal of heavy police protection, refusing to "wet nurse a bunch of showmen." It was a virtual invitation to vigilante violence. In Greenwood, town officials did their best to disrupt SNCC activities and Carmichael was briefly jailed after a confrontation with local authorities. Angry and frustrated, Carmichael was released that evening and went to the SNCC campsite at Broad Street Park, where he stepped onto the bed of a tractor-trailer and addressed the assembled activists and locals, first recounting his previous work in Greenwood. Then, his pent-up rage spilling forth, Carmichael declared, "This is the twenty-seventh time I've been arrested. I ain't going to jail no more. The only way we gonna stop them white men from whuppin' us is to take over! We been sayin' 'Freedom' for six years and we ain't got nothing! What we're gonna start sayin' now is 'Black Power!'" Encouraged by the crowd's enthusiastic response, an agitated Carmichael continued, "The white folks in the state of Mississippi ain't nothin' but a bunch of racists!" He began a call and response that the crowd instantly joined. "What do we want?" he shouted, to which the crowd yelled back, "Black power!" The exchange continued for some moments as Carmichael played to the assembly's growing frenzy. "Every courthouse in Mississippi," he finally declared, "ought to be burned to the ground to get rid of the dirt!" Carmichael's inflammatory rhetoric accurately mirrored a major shift in attitude within the civil rights movement at mid-decade. Henceforth, the traditional objective of "Freedom Now" would have to compete with the seductive appeal of a new battle cry, "black power," the meaning of which remained for many, black and white alike, disturbingly ambiguous. Over the next three decades, Stokely Carmichael sought to both define and realize the controversial concept.

Stokely Carmichael was eleven years old when his father Adolphus moved his family to the United States from Trinidad, where Stokely had been born in Port of Spain on June 29, 1941. Adolphus had been active in his island's independence campaign, but family needs trumped politics, and the move to the Harlem section of New York City brought improved economic opportunities. Adolphus worked as a cab driver while Stokely's mother, Mabel, found employment as a maid. Stokely, though a black West Indian in a predominantly white ethnic neighborhood, established a niche, even joining an otherwise all-white street gang. Race, he later remembered, did not seem much of an encumbrance at this point, and he even dated white girls. When the Carmichaels moved to the Bronx, Stokely, recognized as a superior student, attended the borough's prestigious High School of Science. He relinquished his gang affiliation as his interest in politics, especially socialism, blossomed. During this period, inspired by news film of black protestors at a variety store lunch counter being assaulted by white hoodlums, he joined in the CORE-sponsored boycott of the F.W. Woolworth chain, which was infamous for its discriminatory treatment of blacks. Carmichael also traveled to Virginia and South Carolina to participate in sit-ins, a favored tactic to challenge segregation in the early 1960s, and endured physical assaults by racists.

By the time he was admitted to Howard University in 1960, where he was awarded an SCLC scholarship, his race consciousness had clearly emerged, and it was further piqued through interaction with African American scholars Sterling Brown, Nathan Hare, and Toni Morrison, destined to become one of the century's outstanding black authors. Carmichael was quickly drawn into the civil rights movement, joining the Nonviolent Action Group and participating in protests against segregation in the Washington, DC, area. The young student's baptism of fire occurred in 1961 when he hurried to finish exams so that he might join a group of Freedom Riders who were riding buses into the Deep South to challenge segregated bus station facilities. It was an eye-opening experience for Carmichael, who together with other demonstrators was menaced and attacked by racist mobs in several towns. He was among dozens arrested and jailed, spending forty-nine days in Mississippi's notorious Parchman State Penitentiary. Despite the abuse and privations he endured, Carmichael's commitment was strengthened, in large part by the resolve and courage that he witnessed on the part of his fellow activists. He demonstrated his total commitment to the cause after his 1964 graduation, when he joined the Mississippi Freedom Summer program, a daring operation organized by the Council of Federated Organizations (COFO), which brought together CORE, the NAACP, SCLC, and SNCC, a youth-oriented offshoot of SCLC, for an ambitious program of voter registration among the state's black citizens. Freedom Summer also included Freedom Schools, where activists like Carmichael tutored black children in the cultural heritage and history of African Americans as well as basic subjects. SNCC, which schooled activists in the tactics and strategy of nonviolent civil disobedience, attracted the best and brightest among college-age African Americans, but even among that group, Carmichael's personal presence and charm caused him to stand out, leading acquaintances to refer to him as "Stokely Starmichael." Carmichael's primary devotion was to the cause, however, and he demonstrated consistent personal courage that summer in the face of violent retaliation from white Mississippians. Over the course of the ten-week project, four rights workers were murdered, four severely injured, some eighty activists assaulted, over 1,000 jailed, and thirty-seven black churches and thirty homes bombed. Carmichael accepted the need for out-of-state activists to participate in such actions in the South but believed that significant local participation was crucial to lasting success. That same summer, black Mississippians like Fannie Lou Hamer were at the forefront of organizing the Mississippi Freedom Democratic Party (MFDP), which demanded the inclusion of blacks in the state's delegation at the Democratic Convention in Atlantic City. The controversy proved a political minefield for President Lyndon Johnson, whose support for civil rights legislation endeared him to many black Americans, but also infuriated white Southerners, whose support Johnson hoped to retain in his reelection bid. Eventually a compromise was worked out granting the MFDP two at-large delegates. Carmichael was among those disappointed with the outcome but determined to forge ahead.

Events in early 1965 caused both despair and hope among black Americans. On February 21, Malcolm X, a compelling and articulate advocate of a more aggressive strategy to advance racial justice, was assassinated by Nation of Islam gunmen. Only days later, a Selma-to-Montgomery march led by King was disrupted when Alabama police viciously attacked the demonstrators at the Edmund Pettus Bridge. Televised images of the unprovoked assault shocked the nation. It was the violence attending the Selma-to-Montgomery march that decisively turned Carmichael away from nonviolence. Having watched helplessly as police battered demonstrators in downtown Montgomery, Carmichael recalled, "I knew I could never be hit again without hitting back."

It was against this backdrop that Carmichael and an SNCC contingent undertook the task of organizing black voters in "Bloody Lowndes," Alabama's most notoriously violent county, where only two black voters had dared to register in 1965. Excluded from the state's all-white Democratic Party, the seal of which boasted "White Supremacy," the SNCC workers organized the Lowndes County Freedom Organization (LCFO) with a black panther as its symbol. Carmichael was forthright about the objective of the Black Panther party, as the media dubbed it. "It's very simple," he declared. "We intend to take over Lowndes County." SNCC worker John Hulett informed a Justice Department observer that they did not intend to start trouble, but, "We are within our rights. We will come armed. You tell the crackers not to start any trouble, because if they start something, we are going to finish it." SNCC rallies in Lowndes were protected by groups like Louisiana's Deacons for Defense, whose members had on past occasions fired on white attackers. LCFO succeeded in registering many of the county's black residents and challenging the Democratic Party's monopoly on political power by organizing their own party. That May, Carmichael replaced veteran activist John Lewis as SNCC chairman, signaling a more militant direction for the organization. Carmichael had concluded that the path to racial justice was not through integration, but rather by way of the empowerment of black Americans, politically and otherwise. This was the message that he introduced the following summer in Greenwood.

Carmichael's black power address in Greenwood drew immediate national media attention, even as the Meredith March concluded in late June 1966. Appearing on *Face the Nation*, Carmichael fended off the suggestion that black power was synonymous with violence, a common allegation in subsequent months. Black power, he asserted, meant that where black people were the majority, they should "organize themselves politically and . . . take over those counties from the white racists who now run it." He appeared together with King at a concluding rally at the state capitol on June 21, telling the crowd that the goal was to build a political base so formidable blacks could "bring them [whites] to their knees every time they mess with us." The national media soon mirrored the response of most of white America. *Time* denounced black power as "a racist philosophy," while *Newsweek* termed it "a distorted cry" and, like the *Saturday Evening Post*, warned of an inevitable "white backlash." Within the civil rights movement, the concept caused significant division, driving John Lewis out of SNCC and leading King to decry black power as "a nihilistic philosophy born out of the conviction that the Negro cannot win." "It is at bottom," King warned, "the view that American society is so hopelessly corrupt and enmeshed in evil that there is no possibility of salvation from within." Ironically, King had accurately described the perspective of many of the radical activists. Though the NAACP's Roy Wilkins and Vice President Hubert Humphrey denounced black power at the organization's 1966 convention, CORE announced its embrace of the concept that July. Carmichael gained recognition as the chief spokesman for the new direction, described by *Ebony* as the "architect" and personification of black power, who "walks like Sidney Poitier, talks like Harry Belafonte and thinks like the post-Muslim Malcolm X."

In subsequent months, Carmichael demonstrated that he could be every bit as provocative as the martyred former Black Muslim. Speaking in Cleveland, Carmichael declared, "When you talk of black power, you talk of bringing this country to its knees." His assertions that black power would bring about the end of Western civilization and his demands that blacks refuse service in Vietnam seemed calculated to alarm white Americans and provoke authorities. His prediction in a Chicago speech that blacks would control "all major cities" within a decade and that black power would "smash any political machine that's oppressing us" likewise drew cheers from black militants and disapproval from mainstream media. Carmichael's conception of how racial justice might be achieved did not, however, comport with that of Black Muslim leader Elijah Muhammad. The two met in August 1966 but found no room for common cause, given Elijah's insistence on being acknowledged as the unchallenged prophet. Later that month, Carmichael appeared on *Meet the Press*, where he was introduced as one of "six of the nation's top Negro leaders." Carmichael's criticism of the Vietnam War, together with his frequent calls for blacks to resist the draft, led the FBI to consider whether he might be charged with sedition. That September, in a *New York Review of Books* article, "What We Want," Carmichael made clear that the era of cooperation with white liberals was over, that blacks should cease trying to reassure whites with ingratiating rhetoric, and stated, "SNCC reaffirms the right of black men everywhere to defend themselves when threatened or attacked." As a journalist noted at the time, "If scaring whites is an art, Carmichael seems to be well on his way to becoming a master." Stymied in efforts to pass additional civil rights legislation, Lyndon Johnson blamed Carmichael and black power. Following Carmichael's inflammatory address at a Black Power Conference at the University of California's Berkeley campus in October, FBI director Hoover warned the White House of the growing threat, noting that the meeting had "received a great deal of support" from communists.

In May 1967, journalist-photographer Gordon Parks acknowledged Carmichael's rapid rise to prominence in an article in *Life* magazine. The SNCC activist, Parks wrote, was "damned, lionized, and simply discussed more than any other Negro leader." Parks offered a succinct summary of Carmichael's recent activities, confirming that he was a whirlwind of energy and a magnet for controversy:

> He speaks in Nashville, the Negroes riot there, and the Tennessee House of Representatives calls for his deportation. He parades in Harlem on the second anniversary of the death of Malcolm X. He's in Bimini for a *tete-a-tete* with my congressman-in-exile Adam Clayton Powell. He's in Puerto Rico making common cause with nationalists. . . . He stands in the United Nations Plaza, pouring invective on Johnson, McNamara, Rusk and the Vietnam war—"Hell no! We won't go!"

Indeed, 1967 marked a new phase in Carmichael's evolution as an activist. That same month, he turned over the chairmanship of SNCC to Hubert "H. Rap" Brown, who, according to one historian, soon exceeded Carmichael as "the nation's prime symbol of uncontrolled black anger." Brown's transformation into "America's Negro ogre of choice" was in part the result of the inevitable competition among black radical groups to grab media attention through increasingly fiery rhetoric. Brown, who characteristically titled his 1969 autobiography *Die, Nigger, Die!*, gained permanent notoriety with his contention that "violence is as American as cherry pie" and his promise, "If America doesn't come around, we are going to burn it down!" Brown inevitably drew scrutiny from law enforcement authorities when he advocated armed resistance to white oppression, urging black military veterans to utilize their skills in ghetto uprisings. Despite Brown's provocative activities, Carmichael retained the national media spotlight as chief spokesman for black power militancy, as well as the FBI's continuing surveillance. His proclamation in a Chicago speech that he intended to "take over" the nation's capital "lock, stock and barrel" led Hoover to inform a House committee that Carmichael was in communication with the Revolutionary Action Movement, which the director ominously described as "a highly secret all-Negro, Marxist-Leninist, Chinese-Communist group." That July, when deadly riots broke out in Newark, New Jersey, and then Detroit, Michigan, the FBI was quick to draw a connection between the inner-city rebellions and Carmichael's radical rhetoric. Having identified Carmichael, along with King and Elijah Muhammad, as among the nation's potential "black messiahs," the bureau gained approval for the expansion of COINTELPRO, the Counter Intelligence Program, to investigate "black nationalist, hate-type organizations."

That same summer, Carmichael undertook an extensive foreign tour, denouncing American racism abroad and at the Organization of Latin American Solidarity meeting in Havana, Cuba, condemning U.S. foreign policy and praising Cuban socialism as "the system we like best." He defined black power as part of a worldwide anticolonial struggle that was taking place with the United States and, laying out the position that would define his perspective in subsequent years, proclaimed to the conference, "We must internationalize our struggle, and if we are going to turn into reality the words of Che [Guevara] to create two, three or more Vietnams, we must recognize that Detroit and New York are also Vietnam." From Havana Carmichael traveled to communist North Vietnam, where he conferred with President Ho Chi Minh, before heading to Algeria to meet with Arab nationalists there, and finally flew to Guinea, where he met President Ahmed Sékou Touré. His meeting with one of the most renowned proponents of pan-Africanism had profound long-term consequences for Carmichael, who would later embrace that ideology. The American also met with deposed Ghanaian leader Kwame Nkrumah, another famous pan-Africanist. The two African leaders indicated their belief that Carmichael would be the next torchbearer for their dream. "The concept of black power will be fulfilled," Nkrumah asserted, "only when Africa is free and united." It was a conclusion that Carmichael eventually endorsed. More immediately, his life was transformed when he met South African singer Miriam Makeba, whom

he married within a year. The couple later separated and Carmichael married
Guinean physician Marylatou Barry, and the two had one son, Bokar.

That fall Carmichael and coauthor Charles Hamilton published *Black Power:
The Politics of Liberation in America*, which argued that black people were responsible for formulating the goals, strategies, and tactics for black liberation,
though the authors offered no single strategy. Before returning to the United
States in December, Carmichael had met with white American radicals in
Denmark, proposing that New Left organizations like Students for a Democratic
Society could advance domestic revolution by organizing in white communities. Back in New York, Carmichael was immediately drawn into a mounting
controversy concerning the Black Panther Party (BPP), which had been formed
in Oakland, California, in 1966. Panther "minister of defense" Huey Newton,
whose memo had drafted Carmichael into the party as a "field marshal" the previous June, had been arrested for manslaughter following a shootout with police,
and Carmichael believed that the growing "free Huey" movement offered an
opportunity to influence Panther ideology. Though he was named "honorary
prime minister of the Afro-American nation," Carmichael was soon at odds
with the Panther leadership over the utility of alliances with white radicals.
Forging ties with groups like the leftist Peace and Freedom Party, Carmichael
feared, would turn the Panthers into "the black shock troops of the white New
Left and the 'counterculture.'" Carmichael's rejection of socialism and communism also did not bode well for his continued association with the BPP, which
moved in a Marxist direction later in the decade. Instead, he continued to assert
that the liberation of Africa was crucial to the success of black power around the
globe. A whirlwind of nightmarish events in 1968 only confirmed him in this
belief. In a press conference subsequent to Martin Luther King Jr.'s assassination
in April, Carmichael proclaimed that "when white America killed Dr. King," it
declared war on black people. As black Americans expressed their rage in riots
in over 100 cities, the FBI saw more evidence of the dangers posed by provo-
cateurs like Carmichael and armed revolutionaries like the Black Panthers. As
racial polarization intensified, discord divided black radicals; a failed alliance
between SNCC and the BPP led to Carmichael's expulsion from the former.
Though Carmichael continued to speak at Panther rallies, his disenchantment grew as SNCC moved inexorably in a Marxist direction. In speeches at
California colleges in the fall of 1968, Carmichael, still dedicated to black liberation, denounced the hypocrisy of white liberals and the "cowardice" of dope-
smoking hippies, who had opted out of the revolution. "We are for revolutionary violence," he told a student audience at San Jose State. "We are for spitting
to killing, whatever is necessary to liberate us." He had concluded, however,
that the revolution could not be organized in the United States, where police
repression was increasing. In December 1968, boarding a freighter with his wife,

he headed for West Africa and a new home in Guinea. "The revolution," he explained, "is not about dying. It's about living."

Following Carmichael's departure, black radicalism in the United States stumbled into the same dead end of revolutionary fantasy that seduced the radical remnants of the New Left. The BPP, which responded to growing police harassment with greater rhetorical violence and ideological extremism, was decimated by the concerted efforts of law enforcement agencies to arrest or eliminate its leadership. In 1969, Panthers Fred Hampton and Mark Clark were killed in Chicago in what some journalists termed a "police murder." By 1970, thirty-four Panthers had died in confrontations with the police, and some survivors, such as Eldridge Cleaver, sought refuge abroad. Though Carmichael and Cleaver met in Algeria in July 1969 at the Pan-African Cultural Festival, the ideological chasm between the two was unbridgeable, and Carmichael shortly published a repudiation of the BPP's strategy. With the eclipse of organized black radicalism in the United States, Carmichael was compelled to chart a new course of black liberation from Africa.

Living in Conakry, Guinea, Carmichael divested himself of his American roots, adopting the name Kwame Ture in honor of the Guinean prime minister and the deposed Ghanaian leader, both of whom represented the pan-African perspective he had adopted. In 1971, he published *Stokely Speaks: Black Power Back to Pan-Africanism*, an explication of his personal philosophical journey. Rejecting the theatrical militancy that made him famous, he told an audience at the University of Texas, "The period of entertainment is over" and demanded a new ideological clarity that he never succeeded in defining.

Harnessing international black liberation to the progress of black Africa created a multitude of dilemmas, as the political, economic, and social progress of postcolonial African nations proved highly problematic, even under black governance. A quarter-century after 1960, Africa's Year of Liberation, much of the continent still suffered under the weight of stagnant economies and political oppression. Carmichael, who never challenged commonplace human rights violations of the Touré regime, was himself arrested by Guinean authorities after Touré's death in 1984 and charged with conspiring to overthrow the government. His enthusiasm for international revolution never flagged, however, and for the remainder of his life he routinely answered phone calls with the declaration, "Ready for revolution!" During the last decade of his life, Carmichael-Ture was increasingly given to speculations of government plots against him and, when he was diagnosed with prostate cancer in 1996, claimed that he had been infected with the disease by "forces of American imperialism and others who conspired with them." Ture was dismissive of evidence of the growing political power of African Americans, arguing that the election of black public officials remained meaningless because of the extent of "institutional racism," a phrase that he had popularized in the 1960s. When he died on November 15, 1998, the era of black radicalism that he had personified seemed only a distant memory, most of its leaders either jailed (H. Rap Brown, in prison for life for murder), dead (Huey Newton, shot to death in 1989 by a drug dealer), or converted to other causes (Eldridge Cleaver, who returned from exile as a conservative and born-again Christian). One survivor of that era, Jesse Jackson, offered this eulogy for his countryman who was buried in Guinea: "He was one of our generation who was determined to give his life to transforming America and Africa. He was committed to ending racial apartheid in our country. He helped bring those walls down."

Conclusion

The postwar era brought circumstances that allowed for the development of what was arguably the most important social protest movement in modern American history. The civil rights revolution was waged in many arenas: the nation's courts, legislative halls, the schools and streets, and the court of public opinion. Those who advanced this struggle did so as individuals and as members of organizations. Some, like James Baldwin, wielded their fierce intellect on behalf of the battle, striving to define the nature of racial identity and race relations in American society. Others, like Stokely Carmichael, advocated the importance of action through deeds that were the products of careful deliberation. Both men underwent personal transformations that paralleled the changes shaping the civil rights movement over the course of several decades, altering their perspectives as circumstances dictated. Despite the fundamental advances in American race relations that took place through these years, both men perceived deep flaws in American institutions and the persistence of prejudice as major obstacles to the full realization of racial justice in America. Ultimately, neither reconciled himself to life in a nation that failed to live up to its promise.

Study Questions

1. What led James Baldwin to move to France and how did that decision shape his perspective on racial issues?
2. What commonalities do you find in Baldwin and Carmichael's backgrounds and early lives?
3. Both Baldwin and Carmichael moved toward increasingly militant perspectives in the 1960s. How would you account for this?
4. Compare and contrast Baldwin's and Carmichael's understanding of the root causes of racial injustice in the United States.

5. How might Baldwin and Carmichael have reacted to the 2008 election of Barack Obama as president of the United States? Would it have altered their perspectives on American racial prejudice?

Selected Bibliography

Baldwin, James. *Collected Essays*. New York: Library of America, 1998.

Campbell, James. *Exiled in Paris: Richard Wright, James Baldwin, Samuel Beckett and Others on the Left Bank*. Berkeley: University of California Press, 2003.

———. *Talking at the Gates: A Life of James Baldwin*. New York: Viking, 1991.

Carmichael, Stokely. *Stokely Speaks: Black Power Back to Pan-Africanism*. New York: Random House, 1971.

Carmichael, Stokely, and Charles Hamilton. *Black Power: The Politics of Liberation*. New York: Vintage, 1992.

Carmichael, Stokely, and Ekwueme Michael Thelwell. *Ready for Revolution: The Life and Struggles of Stokely Carmichael*. New York: Scribner's, 2003.

Forman, James. *The Making of Black Revolutionaries*. New York: Macmillan, 1972.

Joseph, Peniel E. *Waiting 'til the Midnight Hour: A Narrative History of Black Power in America*. New York: Henry Holt, 2006.

Leeming, David. *James Baldwin: A Biography*. New York: Alfred Knopf, 1994.

Ogbar, Jeffrey O. G. *Black Power: Radical Politics and African American Identity*. Baltimore, MD: Johns Hopkins University Press, 2004.

Payne, Charles M. *I've Got the Light of Freedom*. Berkeley: University of California Press, 1995.

Schlesinger, Arthur M., Jr. *Robert Kennedy and His Times*. New York: Houghton Mifflin, 1978.

Van Deburg, William L. *New Day in Babylon: The Black Power Movement and American Culture*. Chicago: University of Chicago Press, 1992.

Weisbrot, Robert. *Freedom Bound: A History of America's Civil Rights Movement*. New York: W.W. Norton, 1990.

CHAPTER ELEVEN

~

Waging the Vietnam War

Beginning in the early 1960s, defense secretary Robert McNamara and *New York Times* reporter David Halberstam became first misaligned allies and then virtual antagonists regarding U.S. military operations in Vietnam. Initially both were strong believers in their nation's mission of sustaining the Republic of South Vietnam in the area south of the seventeenth parallel, which confronted guerrilla forces backed by the communist regime of North Vietnam headed by Ho Chi Minh. Within a short while, Halberstam questioned the effectiveness of U.S. and South Vietnamese operations, putting him at odds with the Kennedy administration that McNamara seemingly so brilliantly represented. Remaining in his post following the assassination of John F. Kennedy, McNamara initially appeared to be President Lyndon B. Johnson's most faithful servant. Indeed, historian George C. Herring suggests that "perhaps more than any other single individual . . . McNamara personified the American commitment in Vietnam." With the passage of time as American troops appeared bogged down in the quagmire Halberstam predicted, the defense secretary too came to question American involvement in what many called McNamara's War. Unwilling to openly challenge or depart from the Johnson administration, McNamara became increasingly frustrated as U.S. troop deployments accelerated, even as the number of casualties—Americans, troops from the Army of the Republic of South Vietnam (ARVN), enemy combatants, and civilians—grew alarmingly. To make sense of America's role in Vietnam, which was going so badly, McNamara instructed civilian assistants to begin exploring the causes and history of that involvement. Halberstam was undertaking his own examination of the war and of the instrumental actions of McNamara and those he referred to as "the best and the brightest," the cohort of seemingly impeccably qualified individuals who helped bring about and then sustained American participation in the Vietnam War.

Before the Vietnam War brought them together and then divided McNamara and Halberstam, each appeared to be on the periphery of the small group of Americans who shaped and guided their nation's policymaking. During the early postwar era, a liberal consensus, uniting liberals and conservatives, Democrats and Republicans, shaped the thinking of policymakers who subscribed to an anticommunist foreign policy. Those who embraced the liberal consensus generally viewed both the growing number of social eruptions and calls for national liberation in the developing postcolonial world through the prism of the Cold War, often seeing international communism as the chief culprit behind such upheavals. Like many called to serve in the Kennedy administration, which remained committed to a foreign policy centered on concerns about the Soviet Union, China, and third world revolutions, both McNamara and Halberstam possessed impressive academic credentials. Each man had graduated from Harvard University, where McNamara received an MBA after taking his undergraduate degree at the University of California at Berkeley, and Halberstam served as managing editor of the *Harvard Crimson*. Vaulting up corporate ladders, McNamara, at the age of forty-four, became the first president of the Ford Motor Company who was not a member of the Ford family. His success as a young business executive brought McNamara to the attention of president-elect John F. Kennedy, who offered him first the position of secretary of the treasury and then that of Pentagon chief. During the second year of the Kennedy administration, whose policy of counterinsurgency required a growing number of U.S. advisers in Vietnam to train ARVN forces, the *New York Times* sent Halberstam to cover the war. Joining a band of other young journalists including Neil Sheehan, Malcolm Browne, and Peter Arnett, Halberstam soon began questioning Pentagon and State Department statements regarding the effectiveness of U.S. policy in Vietnam, to the chagrin of President Kennedy. As McNamara continued to orchestrate Pentagon programs, Halberstam, even after departing from Vietnam, continued to track events there, writing a brief history of the conflict, a novel relating to the war, a biography of Ho Chi Minh, and finally, in 1972, a magnum opus examining men like McNamara, titled *The Best and the Brightest*. McNamara had resigned as defense secretary four years earlier, but his shadow continued to loom over the war, and Halberstam's treatment of him proved devastating. Notwithstanding his growing concerns about American operations in Vietnam, McNamara refused to go public about those misgivings until the publication in 1995 of his controversial memoir, *In Retrospect: The Tragedy and Lessons of Vietnam*.

His position as secretary of defense and identification with the dramatic escalation of U.S. operations in Vietnam led some to lament McNamara's War. When he took his post in the new Kennedy administration in January 1961, some 800 military advisers from the United States were stationed in Vietnam. Six years later, around 400,000 American troops were serving in that distant Southeast Asian land, and the total continued to escalate until peaking at approximately 540,000 soldiers in 1968 and 1969. Having strongly and publicly supported the expansion of American involvement in Vietnam, to the extent that he was viewed as the personification of the U.S. war effort, McNamara by early 1966 nevertheless increasingly experienced misgivings about the conflict. The following June, without informing President Johnson or Secretary of State Dean Rusk, he told John McNaughton, assistant secretary of defense for international security affairs, to begin gathering documents pertaining to U.S. involvement in Vietnam. McNamara instructed McNaughton to examine papers from the Department of Defense, the Department of State, the CIA, and the White House. "Tell your researchers not to hold back," McNamara ordered. "Let the chips fall where they may." Morton H. Halperin and Leslie H. Gelb, both of whom worked under McNaughton until the latter's death in an airplane crash on July 19, 1967, headed the project, which eventually involved thirty-six researchers and analysts. Known as the Pentagon Papers when leaked to the press in 1971, the study served as a devastating indictment of the conduct of the Vietnam War during McNamara's tenure at the Defense Department.

The Pentagon Papers took two years, 7,000 pages, and forty-seven volumes to complete and proved to be an illuminating treatment of U.S. policy toward Vietnam from 1947 to 1967. The top-secret study underscored the centrality of the domino theory, the belief of American policymakers that when one nation fell to communism, the likelihood of the same fate befalling surrounding states greatly intensified. In early 1971, Daniel Ellsberg, who had worked on the Pentagon Papers, and Anthony Russo, his one-time colleague at the RAND corporation, a leading think tank in Washington, DC, photocopied the documents and passed them on to *New York Times* reporter Neil Sheehan. Ellsberg had attempted, albeit unsuccessfully, to convince antiwar senators such as Arkansas's William J. Fulbright, chairman of the Senate Foreign Relations Committee, and South Dakota's George McGovern to release the papers in Congress. On July 13, 1971, the *New York Times* published its first article related to the study commissioned four years earlier by McNamara, under a banner headline: "Vietnam Archives: Pentagon Study Traces 3 Decades of Growing U.S. Involvement." In subsequent days, the *Times*, again drawing on the Pentagon Papers, printed articles about the Tonkin Gulf incident in August 1964 that led to the passage of a congressional resolution effectively providing President Johnson with a blank check to wage the war, the decision in February 1965 to initiate the systematic bombing of North Vietnam, and the introduction of ground troops. The *New York Times* offered a headline on July 16: "Judge, at Request of U.S., Halts Times Vietnam Series Four Days Pending Injunction." The *Washington Post* soon published its own account drawn from the Pentagon Papers titled "Documents Reveal U.S. Effort in '54 to Delay Viet Election." With injunctions in place precluding both the *Times* and the *Post* from relying on the Pentagon Papers, the *Boston Globe* published "Secret Pentagon Documents Bare JFK Rule in Vietnam War" on June 22, discussing Kennedy's support for covert operations. A week later, Alaska Senator Mike Gravel, having called a session of the Public Buildings and Grounds Subcommittee, began reading from the Pentagon Papers. The U.S. Supreme Court, in a 6–3 ruling the next day, lifted the injunctions against the *New York Times* and the *Washington Post* as unconstitutional prior restraints.

～   ROBERT McNAMARA   ～

The man most associated with the Pentagon Papers, Robert Strange McNamara, was born on June 9, 1916, in San Francisco, California, to an emotionally withdrawn and little educated father, Robert James McNamara, who served

Secretary of Defense Robert McNamara holds a press conference about the American war in Vietnam in April 1965. Serving presidents Kennedy and Johnson, McNamara played a central role in the decision to "Americanize" the conflict in the summer of 1965. Within six months, he came to seriously doubt that the United States could achieve its stated goals of securing South Vietnam from the communists, though he did not publicly voice his concerns. (Library of Congress, LC-USZ62-134155)

as a sales manager for a wholesale shoe distributor, and a mother, Clara Nell Strange, who watched over young Bobby and his younger sister Margaret. The ambitious and driven McNamara entered the University of California at Berkeley in the fall of 1933, graduating four years later, Phi Beta Kappa, with a BA in mathematics and philosophy. While at Berkeley he met Margaret McKinstry Craig, a bright young woman from Alameda, California, whom he later married. McNamara enrolled at the Harvard Graduate School of Business Administration in 1937, receiving his MA two years later and returning to San Francisco to work as an accountant with Price Waterhouse. He was back in Cambridge within a year, having married Marg, with whom he eventually had three children, and prepared to teach at Harvard. During World War II, the War Department sent McNamara, commissioned as a captain, to England, India, China, the Pacific, and across the United States. Working for the Army Air Force's Office of Statistical Control, McNamara instructed officers in analytical methods used in business and participated in a detailed statistical study of the U.S. strategic bombing campaign in Europe. By the time he departed from military service in January 1946, having devised new methods for cataloging damage assessments pertaining to B-29s, McNamara had received a Legion of Merit and been promoted to lieutenant colonel.

Having overcome a bout with polio, which afflicted Marg more seriously and led to mounting medical bills, McNamara declined to return to Harvard, instead accepting an offer to help reorganize and modernize the Ford Motor Company. Quickly moving up the corporate ladder while acquiring a reputation for both braininess and an intimidating demeanor, McNamara became president of Ford Motors in the fall of 1960. His tenure was brief, for he was named secretary of defense for the incoming Kennedy administration in December. President Kennedy quickly ordered McNamara to reexamine the American defense strategy, including commitments, warning systems, conventional weapons, and nuclear arms, "in light of present and future dangers." Together the two men strove to move the nation away from relying so completely on the concept of massive retaliation involving nuclear weapons associated with the previous administration, favoring instead a policy of flexible response. While acknowledging the fallacy of the alleged Soviet numerical superiority in ballistic missiles, which was discussed in the 1957 Gaither Report and became a key Democratic Party issue during the presidential campaign, McNamara considered it essential that his own country develop more sophisticated strategic weapons systems. The new young president, for his part, was particularly fascinated with the concept of counterinsurgency, as this was an era when wars of national liberation, championed by the Soviet Union, proliferated in the postcolonial world. Danger spots loomed in both Southeast Asia and Cuba, where 1,400 exiles trained by the CIA attempted to oust Fidel Castro at the Bay of Pigs in April 1961. That enterprise, supported by McNamara, ended disastrously, with the exiles routed and Kennedy forced to take responsibility. Another Cold War crisis threatened that summer, when Soviet premier Nikita Khrushchev asserted that Berlin belonged to East Germany, leading to Kennedy's insistence on increased defense spending, a larger army, the call-up of 150,000 reservists, and the threat of nuclear conflict.

By this point, McNamara, with his seemingly unmatched command of figures and theories, had become one of JFK's most important foreign policy advisers. Attorney General Bobby Kennedy acknowledged, "Bob is the most persuasive man in the cabinet, and that frightens me a little." During the Cuban missile crisis in October 1962, after American U-2 reconnaissance planes revealed Soviet attempts to place offensive nuclear weapons in Cuba, McNamara initially supported an air strike, along with a possible invasion of the island. As transcripts reveal, McNamara dominated discussions among Kennedy advisers, tossing around various ideas, including the possibility of a naval blockade, which Bobby and John Kennedy came to support.

McNamara became most associated, however, with administration policy regarding Vietnam, where the U.S.-sponsored government in South Vietnam struggled to hold off the communist-led Vietcong, southern guerrilla fighters who were backed by Ho Chi Minh's regime in the north. The defense secretary was little involved in policymaking regarding Vietnam until the fall of 1961, when President Kennedy received a report from General Maxwell Taylor and Walt Rostow warning of the deteriorating situation and calling for an increase in U.S. involvement. McNamara generally supported their recommendations, which included sending 8,000 troops, while indicating that such a commitment would hardly prove decisive and would not convince communist leaders "that we mean business." Largely subscribing to the domino theory, he warned that the fall of South Vietnam would lead to communist expansion or accommodation throughout Southeast Asia, but suggested the United States would probably not have to send more than 205,000 soldiers to prevent that from occurring. Adopting a different tactic, President Kennedy agreed only to increase the number of American advisers and provide greater logistical support for the ARVN.

With Secretary of State Rusk adopting a largely deferential role, McNamara became a still more important figure in determining Vietnam policy. After meeting with top American military commanders and Frederick Nolting, U.S. ambassador to South Vietnam, McNamara expressed pleasure that the ARVN forces were "carrying the war to the Viet Cong" but warned not to expect miracles immediately. He went to Vietnam for a mad-dash, forty-eight-hour visit in May 1962, receiving word that the South Vietnamese government was firmly in control. Reporters, including the *New York Times*'s Homer Bigart, contested that notion, declaring that the guerrillas deliberately refrained from attacking Americans. Another problem resulted from the fact that higher military figures, such as General Paul Harkins, who headed the Military Advisory Command, Vietnam, were determined to convince McNamara that the war was going well, even if that involved altering statistics and maps to downplay the strength of the Vietcong. McNamara later revealed that he knew briefs were tainted, but could decipher the truth from fiction. As he readied to depart from Saigon, McNamara insisted progress was being made, promised there would be "no large increase in numbers from those [Americans] now in country," and asserted his country "was not in a war." Instead he chastised journalists "for blowing up other things," further disappointing reporters like Bigart and Neil Sheehan. When Sheehan asked McNamara how he could be so optimistic, the defense secretary snapped at him, "Every quantitative measurement we have shows that we're winning this war."

In fact conditions in Vietnam were about to become more troubling still. On January 2, 1963, just outside the hamlet of Ap Bac, situated forty miles southwest of Saigon, Vietcong guerrillas battled with South Vietnamese army forces, killing scores, along with three American military advisers, with another five Americans wounded and eight helicopters destroyed. David Halberstam of the *New York Times* referred to Ap Bac as a "major defeat" for ARVN and its American advisers. Notwithstanding the setback at Ap Bac and the critical reports by young journalists, McNamara continued to exude optimism about the war, frequently citing statistics, including those indicating a favorable kill ratio regarding body counts. While those records continued to be inflated, McNamara adhered to the notion that the United States could successfully wage a war of attrition. Affirming that he pressed American military commanders for evidence of progress in Vietnam, McNamara later acknowledged in his memoirs that many of the "quantitative measurements such as enemy casualties . . . weapons seized, prisoners taken, sorties flown" proved to be "misleading or erroneous."

While McNamara remained hopeful about Ngo Dinh Diem, the South Vietnamese leader's hold on power faltered in the summer of 1963. A trip to Vietnam by McNamara and General Maxwell Taylor, chairman of the Joint Chiefs of Staff, led to their report that the military campaign had "made great progress" despite "serious political tensions" in Saigon and the growing unpopularity of Diem and his right-hand man and brother, Ngo Dinh Nhu. Urging that the Ngo Dinhs be pressured to reform, McNamara and Taylor also called for Vietnamese troops to be better trained so that most American military personnel could be withdrawn within two years. At the same time they reiterated, "The security of South Vietnam remains vital to United States security." Diem and Nhu were murdered following a coup on November 1 conducted by rebellious generals, who had the backing of U.S. Ambassador Henry Cabot Lodge. Three weeks later, President Kennedy was assassinated while riding in a motorcade in downtown Dallas, Texas. At the time of Kennedy's death, over 16,000 American military personnel were deployed in Vietnam, a twenty-fold increase over the commitment made by JFK's predecessor, Dwight Eisenhower. In his 1995 memoir, *In Retrospect*, McNamara contended that Kennedy would likely have withdrawn from that troubled state "rather than move more deeply in," having concluded that the South Vietnamese were unable to defend themselves.

The level of U.S. engagement in Vietnam soared over the next several years, under the administration of President Lyndon B. Johnson. Exuding "extraordinary self-confidence," McNamara proved to be a particular favorite of Johnson, becoming, as one official put it, something like the "executive vice president of the United States." Behind the scenes, as the Pentagon Papers later revealed, McNamara and the Joint Chiefs supported "intensified covert warfare against North Vietnam" under Operation Plan 34A, and the devising of strategy for overt war. McNamara privately warned President Johnson that if current trends continued, neutralization of a communist-dominated South Vietnam would result. In testimony before the House Armed Services Committee in late January 1964, McNamara indicated that the administration had "no plans to introduce large numbers, say hundreds of thousands, of U.S. combat troops," failing to reveal his concerns about the deteriorating military situation in South Vietnam. In April, after a reporter revealed that Oregon senator Wayne Morse, an early critic, referred to it as "McNamara's war," the defense secretary retorted, "I don't mind its being called McNamara's war. In fact I'm proud to be associated with it." In their discussions with President Johnson, McNamara and General Taylor both failed to convey objections expressed by the Joint Chiefs to the defense secretary's support for graduated pressure against North Vietnam. In the June 15, 1964, issue of *Aviation Week*, the magazine's editor, Robert Hotz, referred to the Defense Department's "credibility gap," declaring that McNamara's "optimistic reports" from Vietnam were "regularly contradicted by events." In August McNamara supported the use of air strikes against North Vietnamese patrol boats that had supposedly fired on American destroyers. He also supported passage of the Tonkin Gulf Resolution, capping off a series of incidents that provided President Johnson with a tremendous political boost in the midst of his campaign against Republican presidential candidate Barry Goldwater. In October McNamara angrily dismissed a detailed memo from Under Secretary of State George Ball that discussed various options regarding Vietnam, refuted the domino theory, and proposed a political solution that would result in a neutral regime. Meanwhile the Johnson administration did its best to keep discussion of Vietnam under wraps until LBJ safely won the presidential race.

Johnson even refused to strike back in the face of a Vietcong assault on an American air base at Bien Hoa on November 1, 1964, but he did allow for Operation Barrel Roll, a secret air campaign against trails in Laos used by North Vietnamese army forces. McNamara and National Security Adviser McGeorge Bundy informed the president in late January "that our current policy can lead only to disastrous defeat," supporting as a consequence the employment of American military power "to force a change in Communist policy." Following another Vietcong attack on an American barracks in Pleiku, McNamara and the National Security Council urged a reprisal strike against North Vietnam. He informed the House Armed Services Committee that the choice involved "whether to continue our struggle to halt Communist expansion in Asia." On March 2, 1965, the United States initiated Operation Rolling Thunder, a bombing campaign against the area north of the seventeenth parallel in Vietnam. McNamara later acknowledged that based on his World War II experiences, he did not believe a graduated bombing campaign would produce a military triumph but would, he hoped, put political pressure on the communist regime. As Operation Rolling Thunder unfolded, McNamara, who worried about possible entry into the war by the Soviet Union or China, placed restrictions on the bombing, insisting on military targets, which infuriated military commanders. Many of those restrictions diminished with the passage of time, as did early determinations to employ Marines around Da Nang for defensive purposes only. Although desirous of restricting air operations, McNamara proved far more receptive to calls by William C. Westmoreland, head of Military Assistance Command Vietnam (MACV), for combat troops. He also supported Westmoreland's determination to fight a war of attrition, something the French had unsuccessfully attempted against the Viet Minh and a policy questioned by General Harold K. Johnson, chief of staff of the U.S. Army. McNamara approved as well of Westmoreland's request for the raining down of bombs from B-52s, on purported enemy fighters in South Vietnam. McGeorge Bundy warned that McNamara's plan was "rash to the point of folly" and threatened "a slippery slope toward total US responsibility." Clark Clifford, a top Washington attorney and influential figure in Democratic Party ranks, worried that McNamara was helping to steer Johnson onto a disastrous course in Southeast Asia.

Despite additional admonitions by Ball pertaining to the Americanizing of the war, President Johnson agreed to McNamara's proposal that 185,000 troops be committed to Vietnam by the end of 1965, a figure that would nearly double by the close of the next year. Among those supporting that decision were the so-called Wise Men, a group of elder statesmen who included former secretary of state Dean Acheson, five-star general Omar Bradley, former secretary of defense Robert Lovett, and the one-time American proconsul in occupied

Germany, John McCloy, among others. McNamara for his part publicly acknowledged that the conflict in Vietnam promised to be "a long war" but he believed American firepower would lead the communists to acknowledge "they can't win in the south," thereby allowing for a settlement. At the same time he hoped to convince the North Vietnamese to "behave rationally," offering the carrot of a bombing pause in late 1965 and at other points during his tenure as defense secretary.

During 1965, the year of the initial great escalation of U.S. involvement in the Vietnam War, opposition to that conflagration burgeoned, beginning with teach-ins at a number of colleges and universities in the spring and including mass rallies. Antiwar rallies sprouted across the country, including the largest such gathering in the nation's history at the time, which took place in Washington, DC, in April, along with other actions against the war, ranging from protest against shipping young men off to Vietnam to draft card burnings and self-immolations that November by Norman Morrison and Roger Allen LaPorte, in front of the Pentagon and United Nations headquarters, respectively. When asked about the opposition, McNamara informed *Washington Star* columnist Mary McGrory, "The nation has a tradition of protecting free speech and the right of dissent. Our policies become stronger as the result of debate."

Still hoping for possible negotiations, McNamara sent a memorandum to President Johnson, dated November 7, 1965, acknowledging, "The question whether we should be prepared ultimately to settle for a 'compromise solution' . . . may have to be faced soon." He also urged both a further expansion of the number of troops deployed in Vietnam and a bombing pause. Should the cessation of bombing prove unavailing, he favored an intensification of Rolling Thunder to underscore that the Vietcong could not prevail and that North Vietnam would be punished for supporting guerrilla operations in the South. Following a major battle in the Ia Drang Valley, situated near the Cambodian border, that left 1,300 North Vietnamese soldiers dead, along with 300 Americans, General Westmoreland called for another 200,000 troops, an unsettling request that led McNamara to return to Vietnam. There he encountered mounting political instability, stalled pacification drives, and many more ARVN desertions. McNamara told President Johnson that he favored Westmoreland's request but warned that such deployment hardly guaranteed success, even as American casualties soared. The defense secretary also admitted that Chinese entry into the war could loom, particularly if the United States greatly increased the number of troops it deployed in Vietnam, threatening "a military standoff at a much higher level, with pacification still stalled" by early 1967.

McNamara clearly anguished over the costs and effectiveness of the war, seeming terribly stressed, as biographer Henry L. Trewhitt suggests, while others openly expressed misgivings about the war. Seeking "some fresh thinking,"

McNamara attended a dinner along with Carl Kaysen, Richard Goodwin, and John Kenneth Galbraith at Arthur Schlesinger Jr.'s home in Georgetown in early 1966. McNamara admitted that a military solution did not appear possible, appeared "skeptical about the value of enlarging our ground forces," and affirmed that he sought "withdrawal with honor." Bobby Kennedy, now serving as the junior senator from New York, expressed support in February 1966 for the Vietcong to "share . . . power and responsibility" in South Vietnam. Meanwhile, McNamara continued grappling with various plans that might help to salvage the Vietnam War. He welcomed an idea floated by Massachusetts Institute of Technology economist Carl Kaysen that a technological barrier might help to prevent movement of North Vietnamese soldiers across the seventeenth parallel. He allowed the Pentagon to escalate its bombing campaign in the North, with the number of sorties doubled, but the fighting in the South only intensified, along with the costs of the conflict, in economic, political, and, most tragically, human terms. Conservatives condemned McNamara and the president for not unleashing the U.S. military and for engaging in "shocking mismanagement," while the antiwar movement garnered more and angrier adherents, with talk of the need for draft resistance. Even the McNamara household was torn by the war, with two of his children becoming critics in their own fashion. A visit to Harvard on November 6, 1966, also proved highly unsettling as protestors confronted McNamara, who got into a shouting match and taunted the students, "I was tougher than you and I am tougher today," hearkening back to his own undergraduate days.

Remaining close to friends and allies of Bobby Kennedy, who had become increasingly critical of the Johnson administration's Vietnam policy, McNamara nevertheless later insisted, "I was scrupulously careful not to betray the president's confidences." He instructed one of his top aides to conduct a statistical analysis of troop deployments that suggested increased troop deployments would not prove decisive as General Westmoreland prophesied. Speaking before the Senate Armed Services Committee in January 1967, McNamara admitted, "I don't believe the bombing that I could contemplate in the future would significantly reduce the actual flow of men and materiel to the south." Notwithstanding the defense secretary's reservations, President Johnson allowed U.S. pilots to bomb sectors of Hanoi and Haiphong as well as North Vietnamese airfields. The American casualty count reached nearly 8,600 by April, as hundreds of thousands marched in protest against the war in New York and San Francisco. McNamara delivered a lengthy memo to President Johnson the following month, arguing against a heightened bombing campaign or the sending of 200,000 additional troops as requested by the Joint Chiefs. He warned that the war was "becoming increasingly unpopular as it escalate[d]" and declared, "There may be a limit beyond which many Americans and much of the world will not permit the United States to go." McNamara called for restricting the bombing campaign to below the twentieth parallel and limiting additional deployments to 30,000.

A controversy erupted within the Johnson administration, as well as between McNamara and the Joint Chiefs, that eventually led to his departure from the Defense Department. McNamara and his assistant Cyrus Vance warned Johnson in June, "Nothing short of toppling the Hanoi regime will convince North Vietnam to settle so long as they believe they have a chance to win the 'war of attrition' in the South," but such actions would likely result in war with China and the Soviet Union. That same month, McNamara initiated the process that led to publication of the Pentagon Papers. He also began to consider more seriously the possibility of accepting a position as president of the World Bank, which would enable him to leave his post as defense secretary. He also sent feelers to the Ford Motor Company, trying to ascertain whether he might return there, and received a multimillion-dollar offer to join a Wall Street firm. During that same period, after the latest of his many visits to South Vietnam, McNamara publicly indicated in July that the United States could "win" and during a White House meeting, asserted, "This is not a military stalemate." Still, on October 21, 1967, McNamara watched in dismay from his office as thousands of antiwar protestors ringed the Pentagon. In a meeting with top establishment figures ten days later, recounted in a letter to President Johnson, McNamara offered that continuation of U.S. policy in Vietnam "would be dangerous, costly in lives, and unsatisfactory to the American people." Instead he called for capping U.S. deployment figures at 525,000, beginning the process of Vietnamizing the war, and terminating the bombing. Johnson came to believe that McNamara was becoming emotionally unstable. The *Financial Times* of London announced the following month that McNamara was being nominated to serve as president of the World Bank. Bobby Kennedy, who was contemplating a bid for the 1968 Democratic Party presidential nomination, hoped his friend McNamara would come out openly against the war. However, as McNamara rationalized, "I wasn't about to do anything that wasn't in my opinion in the national interest." As 1967 neared an end, the United States had dropped 1.6 million tons of bombs on Vietnam, while suffering the loss of nearly 16,000 of its soldiers, a figure that almost doubled by the close of the next year.

The Tet Offensive, kicked off in late January 1968, resulted in Vietcong and North Vietnamese assaults on cities and villages throughout South Vietnam, astonishing the American public and many policymakers as well. According to biographer Deborah Shapley, McNamara was less surprised and he had in fact recently warned that an enemy attack in the South loomed. In a television address in February, McNamara reported, "The actions this government had followed, the objectives it has had in Vietnam, are wise." On February 27 he again urged that the war not be escalated. In awarding him the Medal of Freedom, the nation's highest civilian decoration, President Johnson declared the following day, "Bob McNamara's career is just about the textbook example of the modern public servant." Columnist Joseph Kraft saw matters differently, writing that McNamara's departure "expresses a failure in the managerial faith, a crisis of the whole postwar generation."

After leaving the Defense Department, McNamara headed the World Bank for thirteen years, then joined other top former national security officials in opposing the use of nuclear weapons as part of a defense shield for Europe. During a libel suit that Westmoreland brought against CBS News for accusing him of having deliberately falsified troop deployment levels that were needed, McNamara provided a deposition attesting to the general's character. After condemning the Gulf War in 1991, McNamara talked to reporter Carl Bernstein about Vietnam and partially blamed the death of his wife from cancer on that conflict, stating, "She was with me on occasions when people said I had blood on my hands." In 1995 McNamara saw the publication of his enormously controversial memoir, *In Retrospect: The Tragedy and Lessons of Vietnam*. Many proved outraged by McNamara's admission, "I believe we could and should have withdrawn from South Vietnam either in late 1963 amid the turmoil following Diem's assassination or in late 1964 or early 1965 in the face of increasing political and military weaknesses in South Vietnam." As for McNamara's admission that "we were wrong, terribly wrong," a *New York Times* editorial exclaimed, "His regret cannot be huge enough to balance the books for our dead soldiers. The ghosts of those unlived lives circle close around Mr. McNamara." *Newsweek*'s Jonathan Alter wrote, "For a major public official to admit profound error is extraordinarily rare, perhaps unprecedented, in American history." Vietnam War veteran and critic Ron Kovic declared, "McNamara's book and his comment will promote healing" and urged Americans to "embrace" and "welcome him home." In 2003 McNamara criticized the U.S. invasion of Iraq, the same year that a documentary film, *The Fog of War: Eleven Lessons from the Life of Robert S. McNamara*, was released. The next year, McNamara, having long been widowed, married Diana Masieri Byfield. He passed away in July 2009.

~ DAVID HALBERSTAM ~

In his magnum opus, *The Best and the Brightest*, published in 1972, David Halberstam contended that "McNamara lied and deceived the Senate and the press and the public," but "his greatest crime . . . was the crime of silence." Employing something of the New Journalism associated with Tom Wolfe and Hunter Thompson, Halberstam skewered McNamara and the Kennedy-Johnson advisers who supported the massive escalation of the Vietnam War. The hubris that

Pulitzer Prize–winning New York Times *correspondent David Halberstam with a squad of U.S. soldiers somewhere in South Vietnam. In the early 1960s, Halberstam initially supported the Kennedy administration's policies to secure South Vietnam from communist control, but his time in-country produced growing doubts about the effectiveness of those policies. His increasingly critical reporting of the war's course drew the ire of policymakers such as Secretary of Defense Robert McNamara, even as it matched building public opposition to the war. (AP/Wide World Photos)*

he condemned was present from the very outset of the Kennedy administration, exuded by "brilliant men, men of force . . . who acted rather than waited." They were determined "to get America moving again," in fact into something of "an Olympian age" in which "brains and intellect" would serve to "define a common good." These "tough" new men were determined to leave behind the stasis of the Eisenhower years, viewing themselves as "hard-nosed realists" who had been tested in war and succeeded impressively during the early Cold War period. Exuding "an exciting sense of American elitism," they were fascinated, in the manner of John F. Kennedy, by the vogue of counterinsurgency and viewed Vietnam "as a testing ground." Nevertheless they experienced disappointment along the way as 1961 proved to be "a terrible year" for the new administration, with the failures involving the Bay of Pigs foreshadowing the later disaster in Vietnam. Both were rooted in plans "so obviously doomed to failure" and "based on so little understanding of the situation." This proved even more unfortunate because, like Undersecretary of State Chester Bowles, Kennedy himself, as a young member of first the House of Representatives and then the Senate, had expressed doubts about the ability of the French to hold back the Viet Minh or to sustain colonialism in Algeria. Determined to act, in effect, as his own secretary of state, Kennedy believed he could carve out a "pragmatic and assertive" anticommunism, in contrast to his predecessor's hard-line approach. At the same time JFK proved enamored with guerrilla warfare, with the Special Forces trained at Fort Bragg his particular favorites, as was Brigadier General Edward Lansdale, who had spearheaded the effort to build a nation-state in South Vietnam under Ngo Dinh Diem. McNamara was one of the first of Kennedy's top advisers to point to the need for U.S. combat troops to prevent the collapse of that regime, but the president's own doubts immediately led the ever loyal secretary of defense to alter his position to merely support "the planning for a combat commitment."

As the U.S. level of engagement in Vietnam dramatically heightened under Kennedy, McNamara proved to be "the dominant figure," Halberstam indicated. "It was he who dominated the action, the play, the terms by which success in Vietnam was determined," as Secretary of State Rusk clearly took a back seat. McNamara proved, Halberstam charged, "intelligent, forceful, courageous, decent, everything, in fact, but wise." Embodying the Kennedy administration, McNamara "symbolized the idea that it could manage and control events, in an intelligent, rational way." For many in Washington, inside and outside of government, McNamara proved reassuring, leading to the sentiment that if he were in charge, "it would be a good war." Assisting him at the Pentagon were the so-called whiz kids, a young group of smart civilians who initially assisted McNamara in honing his statistical and supposedly factual analyses of the war. Following the assassination of JFK, his "brilliant, activist can-do" team, heretofore somewhat reigned in by the president's questioning nature, now became "harnessed to the classic can-do President," Lyndon B. Johnson. The new president retained Kennedy's advisers, viewing them with awe, possibly no one more so than McNamara, "the ablest man he'd ever met in government, so bright, so forceful, so intelligent." Halberstam for his part termed McNamara "the can-do man in the can-do society, in the can-do era." McNamara "was American through and through, with the American drive, the American certitude and conviction."

Early in his administration, LBJ relied on McNamara's perspective on Vietnam, as the defense secretary "set the tone and direction" in ensuring a military emphasis, taking the war to the North. While McNamara continued to be well regarded in Washington, DC, his visits to Vietnam proved troubling to a growing number of reporters who worried about his glibness, fixation on statistics, and cocksureness. McNamara's relationship with the Joint Chiefs of Staff was also problematic as they considered him manipulative and untrustworthy. They little appreciated his heavy-handed ways, notwithstanding his championing of a bombing campaign that he retained doubts about throughout his tenure. Others had to contend with McNamara's apparent absolute confidence in whatever position he was backing and his "ruthless" readiness to attack contrary opinions. Moreover, Halberstam offered, McNamara considered it "all right to lie and dissemble for the right causes," including demonstrating loyalty to President Johnson. However, as the war stalemated, McNamara grew "frustrated and divided," as he came to realize "all his forecasts were wrong." Even when he supported negotiations, he did so in a "disingenuous" manner, supporting the introduction of more troops, eventually losing credibility with President Johnson. Civilian administrators like McNamara and his assistant John McNaughton "completely lost control" by late 1965, no longer determining policies, although they remained ignorant about that. McNamara became "increasingly appalled by the war itself," particularly its impact on civilians, Halberstam reported. His "despair and frustration" induced McNamara to order the study that produced the Pentagon Papers and to attempt to halt the bombing. Despairing about McNamara and saying, "He's gone dovish on me," Johnson eventually pushed him out of the Defense post.

David Halberstam was born on April 10, 1934, to Charles A. Halberstam, who, despite growing up in poverty, became a surgeon with the U.S. Army, and Blanche Levy Halberstam, a teacher, both Jews of Eastern European ancestry. The fiercely competitive Halberstam attended Harvard University, where he saw himself as something of an outsider while managing to serve as editor of the *Harvard Crimson*, graduating with a degree in journalism in 1955. Determining to follow the most important domestic story of the era, the civil rights struggle in the American South, the lanky, six-foot, three-inch Halberstam wrote for first the West Point *Daily Times Leader* in Mississippi and then the *Nashville Tennessean*. Halberstam also contributed to the *Reporter*, a liberal, anticommunist publication, resulting in an offer by James Reston of the *New York Times* of a job with the nation's leading newspaper. He joined the *Times* in 1960 and began writing a novel, *The Noblest Roman*, about Southern political skullduggery. He was in the Congo the following June, along with a portable typewriter, a trench coat, bush clothes, and pills for stomach ailments, eventually discovering that he "was good enough to be a war correspondent" and could control his fears. His work, which admittedly frequently required extensive rewrites, led to receipt of an Overseas Press Club Award and a nomination for the Pulitzer Prize for international reporting, an award that went instead to Walter Lippmann.

Having learned more about Vietnam, Halberstam pressed the *Times* to assign him there. In late 1962, the newspaper sent the twenty-eight-year-old Halberstam, who deliberately had his name emblazoned on his fatigues, to replace Homer Bigart, in Saigon where the small Associated Press office was located at 153 Rue Pasteur, in covering the Vietnam War. On arriving in Vietnam with an already well-established reputation, Halberstam encountered AP photographer Horst Faas, who indicated that he would enjoy Vietnam because of the war and the fact that it was "much more dangerous" than the Congo. Saigon became for the ever-ambitious Halberstam "a reporter's dream," possessing "everything: a war, a highly dramatic and emotional story, great food, a beautiful setting and lovely women." He quickly befriended a group of young reporters, including Malcolm Browne, Peter Arnett, Faas, and Neil Sheehan, who proved critical of American policies in Southeast Asia; all would eventually win the Pulitzer Prize. These men viewed the conflict, as Halberstam later indicated, "more through the prism of Vietnamese history than of American history." Halberstam tirelessly traveled through South Vietnam, spending considerable time in the Mekong Delta, particularly My Tho, a provincial capital located south of Saigon. There he encountered Colonel John Paul Vann, a fierce critic of how the United States was waging the war. Halberstam heard Vann say, "They're not the greatest fighters. But they're good people and they can win a war if someone will show them how." Vann particularly sought to transmit his criticisms of the war to government leaders in Washington, including President Kennedy, through Halberstam's stories in the *New York Times*. Sheehan later indicated that the president pored over Halberstam's reports as carefully as he did dispatches from top American officials in Saigon. Halberstam's initial, relatively sunny accounts of American operations in Vietnam quickly gave way to more pessimistic reports, warning about the elusive nature of the enemy.

Vann eventually instructed Halberstam and his fellow young journalists about guerrilla warfare, stating, "The Vietcong know exactly where we are, but we don't know where they are." Vann opposed heavy-handed tactics that relied on the indiscriminate use of firepower, seeking instead to cultivate better relationships with the people in the vaunted effort to "win hearts and minds." He warned, "This is a political war and it calls for the utmost discrimination in killing. The best weapon for killing is a knife, but I'm afraid we can't do it that way. The next best is a rifle. The worst is an airplane, and after that the worst is artillery. You have to know who you're killing." Colonel Vann also explained that the Vietcong guerrillas were far more potent than official Washington pronouncements indicated and that the ARVN, riddled with political intrigue, engaged in mere "pillow punching." While considering the ARVN soldiers brave, Halberstam viewed the Vietcong as "absolutely sincere" in their determination to conduct "a war of revolution." The Vietcong knew that the conflict "was entirely political," employing all grievances, historic and recent, to that end. By contrast, "the American mission never understood the war as the enemy did."

In addition the Vietcong were "tough, indoctrinated men, willing and ready to die," with "equally good" leadership.

Like his journalistic cohorts, the so-called Young Turks, who also were mentored by Vann, Halberstam grew all but disdainful of both the South Vietnamese regime under Ngo Dinh Diem and its American sponsors, led by General Paul Harkins. Impatient, judgmental, and impassioned, Halberstam began to question the domino theory, determining that Ho Chi Minh might have been turned into "an Asian Tito" rather than a foe the United States unsuccessfully battled against for two decades. Little helping matters was the "outward rigidity and orthodoxy" displayed by top military brass, including Admiral Harry Felt, who responded to a question by Browne in late 1962 with one of his own: "Why don't you get on the team?" The process of disillusionment actually took awhile for Halberstam and his compatriots, who came to Vietnam every bit as gung-ho as many of the American soldiers. Having heard "how brilliant the Kennedy people were," the reporters assumed "these terrific guys wanted the truth." Instead they found out "that General Harkins was part of a lying machine" that followed General Maxwell Taylor's directive, "which was to lie." Taylor in turn submitted reports back to Secretary of Defense McNamara.

The American government attempted to silence the Young Turks, with "really nasty" innuendoes amounting to "character assassination" being spread about them. The Department of Defense went out of its way to send over other reporters who were viewed as "more malleable" than someone like Peter Arnett, who stayed in Vietnam for over a decade. The MACV in Saigon orchestrated press briefings involving ARVN, which reporters derisively referred to as the "five o'clock follies." Despite lacking verification by American operatives, those reports pointed to American sources and painted a favorable picture of developments in the war. Some of the *Newsweek* and *Time* correspondents, Halberstam believed, were hardly better, parroting the government line with their "meat-grinder journalistic style." By contrast, Halberstam helped to carve out a new, less amicable relationship involving journalists and the American government.

Developments like the battle of Ap Bac in early January 1963 greatly troubled both the Young Turks and field advisers. The disturbing turn of events hardly surprised the latter, who had long worried, as Halberstam indicated, that "the progress of the war was not so good as the high brass was claiming, and who felt that conditions in the field made a defeat like this virtually inevitable." The field officers continued to wonder if the Vietnamese really wanted their advice. The journalists were also stunned to hear General Harkins describe the Ap Bac battle as "a victory." Field advisers little appreciated such papering over of actual circumstances in Vietnam. For his part, Halberstam greatly respected the American officers serving with Vann, considering them "extremely well informed, honorably motivated, and intrigued by the problems of this war." Moreover, they happily treated him as an equal after he also went through the rice paddies.

Something of a generational divide seemed to separate the Young Turks from some of the correspondents who had earlier covered World War II and the Korean War. The younger journalists were more inclined to question the actions of their government, particularly those that seemed antagonistic to American democratic ideals. Still, Halberstam was shaken on being attacked by Richard Tregaskis, a journalistic veteran of World War II. While in the Mekong Delta, Tregaskis stated, "If I were doing what you are doing, I would be ashamed of myself." Eventually, however, older, more established reporters like CBS's Bernard Kalb, the *Saturday Evening Post*'s Stanley Karnow, *Time*'s Charles Mohr, and the *New York Herald Tribune*'s Marguerite Higgins also became critical of America's Vietnam operations. Disturbed by the reports of Halberstam, Sheehan, and others, President Kennedy went so far as to ask the *New York Times* to yank Halberstam, but the paper refused the request. By contrast, Mike Mansfield took to the Senate floor to speak favorably of the reporters. At the same time, the CIA, as analyst George Allen later informed Halberstam, looked to his reports and those of Sheehan to "find out what was going on" in Vietnam as "everything else was sanitized and doctored."

Halberstam particularly came to dislike McNamara, whom he acknowledged as possibly "this country's most distinguished civil servant of the last decade" and as "brilliant and tireless" in maintaining civilian control over the Pentagon. Halberstam lambasted McNamara with all "his vainglory and . . . arrogance," his fixation on statistics, and his readiness to be satisfied with "weird explanations and lame answers" regarding developments in Vietnam. There, the defense secretary had none of his famed whiz kids able to provide him with "objective viewpoints and alternatives," requiring him to rely heavily on the military. Halberstam viewed McNamara as loyal to the president alone, not to his country, and willing to operate as a vicious "hit man" who shredded the arguments of individuals who questioned his analyses. Halberstam came to see McNamara as "a pathological liar" who believed, like the French, that he could wield "technology, on the cheap" to prevail in Vietnam. As for McNamara's initial boss, John F. Kennedy, Halberstam considered him "a cool piece of work . . . very pragmatic" and lacking any desire to expend his second term as president "in the rice paddies of Vietnam." In contrast to his successor, Kennedy "was much more modern, much more sophisticated . . . much better read," and cognizant of the fact "that nationalism was the issue, not pure communism." At the same time, Kennedy increased the level of U.S. engagement in Vietnam and "gave us the McNamara team."

Arnett recalled Halberstam saving him from being pummeled by Saigon security forces when Buddhist protests erupted in mid-1963. Sheehan recalled

Halberstam tossing aside the Vietnamese who were beating Arnett and threatening, "Get back, get back, you sons of bitches, or I'll beat the shit out of you." Halberstam's reporting from Vietnam, including his coverage of the self-immolation of Thich Quang Duc, a Buddhist monk, led to his receipt of the coveted George Polk Award for American journalism in 1963 and the Pulitzer Prize for International Reporting the following year. Madame Nhu, the wife of Ngo Dinh Nhu, Diem's brother and right-hand man, viewed Halberstam less favorably. Reacting to his journalistic accounts, she exclaimed, "Halberstam should be barbecued, and I would be glad to supply the fluid and the match." The Nhus threatened to go further still, evidently including Halberstam and Sheehan on a list of journalists and supposedly "disloyal" South Vietnamese officers and civilians targeted for assassination. After Diem declared martial law, the two young reporters stayed for several weeks with the U.S. Information Service chief, John Mecklin. Meanwhile, a disillusioned Vann retired from the Army and returned home. Before he left Saigon, Vann met with several journalists and military officers who admired him. The reporters handed him a cigarette case with the inscription "Good soldier, good friend." Halberstam informed Vann that he had always worried that news stories might hurt him. Barely smiling, Vann replied, "You never hurt me anymore than I wanted to be hurt."

With his celebrity growing, Halberstam's coverage of the war also troubled some of his editors at the *Times*, including Turner Catledge and Clifton Daniel, who worried that the young reporter was causing an unbridgeable rift with the Kennedy administration. On August 15, 1963, the *Times* presented a story of Halberstam's affirming that the military situation in the Mekong Delta had deteriorated over the previous twelve months, despite the increased level of U.S. involvement. President Kennedy, the Pentagon brass, and Secretary of State Rusk all proved infuriated by Halberstam's warning that "a sizable military offensive" by the Vietcong loomed likely. During one meeting at the White House, Kennedy exploded: "Goddammit, I don't want you reading those stories in the *Times*. We're not going to let our policy be run by some twenty-eight-year-old kid." Major General Richard Stilwell of MACV refuted Halberstam in a press briefing in Saigon, but an MACV staffer later acknowledged that the journalists, not the generals, had been right about conditions in the Mekong Delta. Marguerite Higgins of the *New York Herald Tribune* also contested Halberstam's analysis, while some of the Hearst publications, including the *New York Journal-American*, charged that Halberstam was setting the stage "for a Vietnamese Fidel Castro," Sheehan noted. As the *Times*' editors proved even more doubtful about his treatment of the conflict, an enraged Halberstam threatened to resign, and the pressure subsided, but questions regarding his stories continued. Little helpful too was Halberstam's dismissive, "openly contemptuous" attitude toward General Harkins. During a visit by Arthur Ochs Sulzberger, publisher of the *Times*, to the White House on October 22, President Kennedy asked, "What do you think of your young man in Saigon?" When Sulzberger responded that he thought Halberstam was doing fine, Kennedy probed further: "Don't you think he's too close to the story?" The president also broached the possibility of Halberstam's being transferred out of Vietnam, but Sulzberger responded that he had not considered that. Unaware of JFK's entreaties, Halberstam nevertheless believed that Diem was about to kick him out of the country, with his visa soon to expire. Writing to Vann on October 29, Halberstam stated, "We all still miss you and refer to you as the Bible. There's damn little joy in covering something which has such a sour meaning for your country." Halberstam then praised U.S. Ambassador Henry Cabot Lodge, who had been consulting with rebellious ARVN military officers about the possibility of a coup, which occurred on November 1 and concluded with the murder of both Diem and Nhu. Reflecting on the turn of events, Lodge asked Halberstam, "What would we have done with them if they had lived? Every Colonel Blimp in the world would have made use of them." Halberstam's account of the coup seemingly all but ensured his receipt of the Pulitzer Prize.

Halberstam returned to the United States in December 1963, and the following year he, along with Sheehan and Browne, received the Louis Lyons Award for Conscience and Integrity in Journalism, delivered by Harvard. The reporters were praised for presenting "the truth as they saw it . . . without yielding to unrelenting pressures . . . from numerous sources including the United States government." Halberstam and Browne also received the 1964 Pulitzer Prize for International Reporting. That November, in an article published in *Esquire*, "The Ugliest American at Vietnam," Halberstam expressed concerns that "this pretty little country will be lost." He presented the tale of Colonel Vann, noting his personal courage and his efforts "to shame" ARVN officers to follow his lead "into walking in the rice paddies." Possibly Vann's "one great failing," Halberstam suggested, was characteristic of the finest American operatives in Vietnam. They believed that their Vietnamese counterparts would strive to duplicate "their own enthusiasm, dedication and effort." As for Vann, the reporters respected him enormously simply because "he cared so desperately about Vietnam." While recognizing the deficiencies in America's program there, Vann and like-minded critics of U.S. operations remained convinced the war "could be successfully prosecuted."

Random House published Halberstam's book, *The Making of a Quagmire*, in 1965. Concluding that work, Halberstam declared that "the American mission in Vietnam" began "with the highest hopes and idealism" but "failed for a number of reasons," although not because of an absence of good intentions, arduous efforts, and patience. Rather, that occurred due to the fact that too many mistakes were made over a lengthy period of time, and the U.S. failed to confront the situation in Vietnam realistically, responding instead "with clichés." As of the date of his book's publication, Halberstam believed, "our country's first major effort at counterinsurgency has failed." He also warned that there was "something to the Vietcong besides the terror" just as there was "something more to winning a revolutionary war than helicopters."

Stationed in Warsaw, Halberstam married Elzbieta Czyzewska, a Polish actress, but the communist government expelled the couple afterward because of the journalist's criticisms of the regime. On assignment from *Harper's Magazine*, Halberstam went back to Vietnam for a three-month stint in 1967, once again relying on John Paul Vann, who had been unable to remain outside that Southeast Asian country, to open up doors. Conditions deeply depressed Halberstam, who thought the great French journalist-historian Bernard Fall had it right: "We were fighting in the same footsteps as the French, although dreaming different dreams." Believing the war was lost, notwithstanding the "self-deception" of American officials, he began putting together *The Best and the Brightest*, highlighting the American architects of the war, while also serving as a contributor to *Harper's*. In extended articles on McGeorge Bundy, Robert McNamara, and other "architects of Vietnam," Halberstam spoke of "the worst tragedy to befall this country since the Civil War." Working for *Harper's* editor Willie Morris proved to be an enriching experience for Halberstam, who was clearly offering some of the finest examples of the New Journalism unrestrained by space limitations and time constraints. Covering America in the late 1960s, Halberstam recognized that there "was an electricity to everything," with *Harper's* and its "intelligent, concerned readers" appearing to be "at the center of the events." In 1968 *Harper's* offered Halberstam's article "Voice of the Vietcong," pieces on the antiwar movement, and a eulogy on Martin Luther King Jr.

That same year, Halberstam published *One Very Hot Day*, a novel on Vietnam. In 1969 he put out *The Unfinished Odyssey of Robert Kennedy*, while in 1971 Halberstam published *Ho*, a brief biography on the recently deceased Vietnamese communist leader. Ho Chi Minh and Vo Nguyen Giap, Halberstam indicated, adopted a similar strategy against both the French and the Americans—"frustrate the enemy, wear them out, bog them down in the quagmire, make victory elusive," by producing growing casualty figures. Halberstam's masterpiece, *The Best and the Brightest*, appeared in 1972, remaining on the best-seller list for thirty-six weeks and landing a contract for paperback rights amounting to $700,000. In the period following, Halberstam frequently alternated between writing sports books and those with seemingly weightier messages. The former included *Summer of '49*, *October 1964*, and *Playing for Keeps: Michael Jordan and the World He Made*, while the latter featured *The Powers That Be*, about the American media; *The Reckoning*, focusing on the automotive industry; *The Fifties*; *War in a Time of Peace: Bush, Clinton, and the Generals*; *Firehouse*, dealing with New York firemen and September 11; and *The Coldest Winter: America and the Korean War*. Halberstam died after an automobile accident in Menlo Park, California, on April 24, 2007. George Esper, who also covered the Vietnam War, said of Halberstam, "He didn't accept the word of generals and admirals. He stayed the course and kept the faith in the people's right to know. He was more honest with the American public than the government." Peter Osnos, publisher of PublicAffairs, stated that "the heirs of Halberstam . . . made the events of 9/11 and the wars in the Middle East and South Asia comprehensible," including Lawrence Wright and Thomas B. Ricks, while writers like Taylor Branch and David Maraniss were "heirs to Halberstam's writing ambition."

Conclusion

The Vietnam War was both the embodiment of the liberal consensus and, along with the racial conflagrations in the United States, its death knell. Escalating the level of involvement that had taken place under Dwight D. Eisenhower, first the administration of John F. Kennedy and then the one that followed under Lyndon B. Johnson adopted tactics that proved increasingly unpopular with the Vietnamese people and eventually with Americans in Vietnam and back home. Secretary of Defense Robert McNamara long appeared the personification of U.S. engagement in Vietnam, offering his crisp, seemingly cocksure analyses of events overseas that were invariably sprinkled with statistical evidence that the war was going well or would eventually succeed. The young journalist David Halberstam was also initially gung-ho about American activities in Vietnam in keeping with the activist, can-do spirit of the Kennedy era, but became increasingly disillusioned by the manner in which the war was being waged. For Halberstam, that promised to ensure disaffection by a growing number of the Vietnamese people, disaffection that would only mount as the number of American soldiers and the pace of military operations escalated. McNamara, who best represented the "best and the brightest" that Halberstam believed had led the United States into a major war in Southeast Asia, also became less convinced of the effectiveness of U.S. enterprises in Vietnam but failed to acknowledge this until many years after he had left government service.

Study Questions

1. Indicate how Robert McNamara seemed to exemplify President Kennedy's determination to offer an administration featuring the best and the brightest.
2. Explain how Robert McNamara's views on the Vietnam War developed over the course of time.

3. Analyze David Halberstam's early support for U.S. involvement in Vietnam.
4. Dissect David Halberstam's disillusionment with American operations in Vietnam.
5. Analyze how the antiwar movement in the United States would likely have viewed both Robert McNamara and David Halberstam.

Selected Bibliography

Halberstam, David. *The Best and the Brightest*. New York: Penguin, 1983.

———. "David Halberstam." In *Legacy of Discord: Voices of the Vietnam War Era*, ed. Gil Dorland. Dulles, VA: Potomac Books, 2001.

———. "Foreword." In *Breaking News: How the Associated Press Has Covered War, Peace, and Everything Else*, Associated Press. New York: Princeton Architectural Press, 2007.

———. *Ho*. New York: McGraw-Hill, 1986.

———. *The Making of a Quagmire*. New York: McGraw-Hill, 1987.

———. *One Very Hot Day*. New York: Houghton Mifflin, 1967.

———. "The Role of Journalists in Vietnam: A Reporter's Perspective." In *Vietnam Reconsidered: Lessons from a War*, ed. Harrison E. Salisbury. New York: HarperCollins, 1984.

———. "The Ugliest American in Vietnam." *Esquire*, November 1964.

Hendrickson, Paul. *The Living and the Dead: Robert McNamara and Five Lives of a Lost War*. New York: Alfred A. Knopf, 1996.

Herring, George C. "The Strange 'Dissent' of Robert S. McNamara." In *The Vietnam War: Vietnamese and American Perspectives*, ed. Jayne S. Werner and Luu Doan Huynh. Armonk, NY: M.E. Sharpe, 1993.

McMaster, H. R. *Dereliction of Duty: Lyndon Johnson, Robert McNamara, and the Joint Chiefs of Staff and the Lies That Led to Vietnam*. New York: HarperCollins, 1997.

McNamara, Robert S. *In Retrospect: The Tragedy and Lessons of Vietnam*. New York: Crown, 1995.

McNamara, Robert S., James G. Blight, and Robert K. Brigham. *Argument without End: In Search of Answers to the Vietnam Tragedy*. New York: PublicAffairs, 1999.

Prochnau, William. *Once Upon a Distant War: Young War Correspondents and the Early Vietnam Battles*. New York: Crown, 1995.

Shapley, Deborah. *Promise and Power: The Life and Times of Robert McNamara*. Boston: Little, Brown, 1993.

Sheehan, Neil. *A Bright Shining Lie: John Paul Vann and America in Vietnam*. New York: Vintage, 1989.

Trewhitt, Henry L. *McNamara: His Ordeal in the Pentagon*. New York: Harper and Row, 1971.

Twing, Stephen W. *Myths, Models, and U.S. Foreign Policy: The Cultural Shaping of Three Cold Warriors*. Boulder, CO: Lynne Rienner, 1999.

~

CHAPTER TWELVE

The New Right

Root and Branch

By the end of the 1960s, American liberalism appeared to be foundering on the shoals of untimely deaths, civil unrest, and the Vietnam conflagration. The silencing of the Kennedy brothers, Martin Luther King Jr., and Malcolm X proved devastating for progressive forces, now bereft of several leading spokespersons, including a president of the United States, a U.S. senator-presidential aspirant, a Nobel laureate who was an apostle of nonviolence, and a fiery black nationalist ready at the end of his life to discard a belief in racial separation. In the very period those men were gunned down, race riots tore across the United States, weakening the cords that had sustained the Democratic Party, dividing American liberals and radicals from one another, and alienating more conservative forces altogether. The coming to fruition of the warning by James Baldwin, the great black writer, in *The Fire Next Time*, tore at the nation's social and political fabric and, seemingly, its very soul. Then there was the Vietnam War, which not only separated liberals and radicals but splintered liberal ranks, along with the political consensus that had enabled the welfare state to thrive since the Great Depression. The ferocity of the challenge posed by the National Liberation Front and North Vietnamese forces produced mounting body counts, domestic tumult, and international outcries as American soldiers relied on such tactics as search-and-destroy missions, free fire zones, employment of chemical agents, and expansion of air and ground operations. The United States experienced its worst divisions since the Civil War, with both radicals and conservatives assailing liberals for having spawned the latest conflict or for having failed to prosecute it adequately.

Conservatives, who had appeared moribund following the seemingly disastrous presidential bid by Republican nominee Barry Goldwater in 1964, mounted a comeback as these events unfolded, defeating scores of Democratic congressmen in 1966 and weakening President Johnson's ability to conduct his War on Poverty or create the Great Society. Providing sometimes caustic, sometimes witty analyses for the conservative onslaught was William Buckley, editor of the *National Review*, a publication founded a decade earlier when conservatism appeared to be at a nadir, at least intellectually speaking. In the mid-1950s, particularly following the political demise of Senator Joseph McCarthy, whom Buckley insistently defended from liberal critics, influential commentators pondered whether conservatism had much of a role to play in American life. Indeed, writers like Richard Hofstadter and Louis Hartz questioned if conservative ideology ever had grown deep roots in American soil. True, Russell Kirk adopted a different tack, in his 1953 book, *The Conservative Mind*, in which he deliberately sought to underscore how embedded conservative thought had been in the American psyche since colonial times. However, it was not until the appearance of Buckley's well-regarded although often controversial magazine that conservatism appeared to have anything approximating the intellectual stature of liberalism. Too little noted at the time was Buckley's sponsorship of a meeting of the Young Americans for Freedom (YAF), which occurred at his estate in Sharon, Connecticut, and produced the Sharon Statement, a proud, even defiant pronouncement of conservative ideals. Rather, Richard Nixon's defeat at the hands of John F. Kennedy in the 1960 presidential election and, even more strikingly, the debacle suffered by Goldwater in the ensuing presidential race appeared to cement conservatism's demise in the United States.

In fact, by the mid-1960s, the politics of conservative backlash surged forth, rooted in anger over perceived liberal excesses involving government expenditures, social programs, judicial decrees, and acceptance of radical dictates, along with liberal inadequacies in prosecuting the war in Southeast Asia. Politicians like Alabama governor George Wallace, Ronald Reagan, and Richard Nixon, among others, benefited from the outrage as they reached out to elements within the Democratic Party, including members of the working class, ethnics, and Catholics, to break apart the New Deal coalition that Franklin Delano Roosevelt had helped to cement. The Nixon administration received backing from intellectuals such as Kevin Phillips, who insisted that Nixon could put together "the Real Majority" of heretofore silent Americans, and Daniel Patrick Moynihan, a Harvard professor and Democrat, who tried to convince the president to become "an American Disraeli" by backing federally supported guaranteed income levels. While Nixon accepted certain extensions of the welfare state and new legislation pertaining to the environment and consumer protection, his inclinations were otherwise, as demonstrated by his determination to "pack the Court" with conservative jurists like William Burger and William Rehnquist.

As antiwar opposition continued to surge during his administration, Nixon resorted to rhetoric intended to divide, not bring together, the American people; employed an enemies list; and unleashed the White House "Plumbers" to conduct break-ins and dirty tricks against political foes. Such developments, coupled with Nixon's attempts to cover up felonious acts by White House operatives, resulted in impeachment proceedings that appeared certain to result in his ouster from the presidency. Nixon's eventual resignation and the seemingly inept performance of his hand-picked successor, Gerald R. Ford, again appeared to cripple the conservative movement and to provide American liberals with the opportunity to mount their own comeback. The 1974 congressional and gubernatorial elections seemed to fit that very pattern with new Democratic officeholders, including Senator Gary Hart from Colorado, who had run George McGovern's 1972 presidential campaign, and Governor Jerry Brown of California. As matters turned out, Hart and Brown were hardly representative of the postwar liberalism identified with the welfare state and the Cold War consensus. Rather, they came to be viewed as new types of progressives, neoliberals who proved even more supportive of social equality than older liberals but less willing to back expansions of the welfare state or military actions overseas. Well-educated and articulate, they also frequently seemed to lack the passion that other liberals had brought to political fights in Congress or at the stump. In addition voters proved disinclined to back many of the firebrand figures who had taken lead roles in the civil rights, student, and antiwar movements of the previous decade.

All the while, conservative politicians and supporters steadily conducted campaigns of their own, adopting the tactic that the New Left had once pointed to: a steady, concerted march through establishment institutions in order to ultimately acquire power. Conservatives ironically followed the lead of the Movement, that amorphous but left-directed unfolding of a welter of political and social movements of the 1950s and 1960s that included the civil rights crusade, antiwar forces, and the women's rights campaign. Conservative activists, often championed by Buckley and the *National Review*, began to create counterinstitutions that helped to carry right-of-center ideas into the political mainstream. Veterans of both YAF and the Goldwater presidential run were instrumental in these efforts, providing a nucleus of skilled, dedicated activists determined to condemn the welfare state, support U.S. military preeminence, and link American liberals with the very radicals who so often damned them. Coupled with the turn to computerized direct mail that resulted in easy access to large numbers of like-minded individuals, this combination proved effective with liberalism eventually coming to be viewed by many Americans as alien and subversive, as communism had been in the early post–World War II period.

Both religious and secular figures, who themselves willingly drew on religious references and support, stood at the forefront of this conservative movement during the 1970s and 1980s. Individuals like Jerry Falwell, one of the founders of the Moral Majority, represented the rise of the Christian Right, while Ronald Reagan, two-term governor of California and successful candidate for the presidency in 1980, provided conservatives with a role model as beloved by their ilk as Franklin D. Roosevelt had been by liberals. Reagan received strong backing from the Christian Right, which condemned secular humanism, homosexuality, the Equal Rights Amendment, abortion, liberalism, and communism, often drawing little distinction between the last two. The former Hollywood actor adopted many of the same stances at the stump, notwithstanding his own more moderate position on social issues while serving as head of the nation's most populous state. The Reagan administration pushed for tax reductions, particularly for America's wealthiest individuals and corporations, and a whittling away at the welfare state. The administration also sharply increased military spending; directed rhetorical fire at the Soviet Union and left-wing guerrillas, including some then holding power in Nicaragua; and provided economic and military support to forces engaged in life-and-death struggles against those very forces.

⌐ WILLIAM F. BUCKLEY JR. ⌐

In what may have been a calculated move to shield the conservative movement from being tagged with an extremist label, Buckley met in January 1962 with Russell Kirk; William Baroody, who headed the right-wing American Enterprise Institute, a think tank in Washington, DC; and Jay Hall, who handled public relations for General Motors in the nation's capital. Buckley's standing among his fellow American conservatives demanded his appearance at this gathering. Conservative pundit Patrick Buchanan later referred to him as "the spiritual father of the movement," and historian Arthur M. Schlesinger Jr. denounced Buckley as "the scourge of American liberalism." The men congregated at the Breakers Hotel in Palm Beach, Florida, discussing the state of the conservative movement and the possibility of a Goldwater presidential run. Goldwater arrived and Baroody called attention to the John Birch Society, about which the senator obviously sought advice. Kirk charged that John Birch Society founder Robert Welch lacked rationality, given that he had accused President Dwight Eisenhower of being part of a communist conspiracy. Looking at Buckley, Kirk demanded that important figures in the conservative movement denounce the Birchers. Goldwater responded, "Every other person in Phoenix is a member of the John Birch Society. Russell, I'm not talking about Commie-haunted apple pickers or cactus drunks, I'm talking about the highest caste of men of affairs."

William F. Buckley Jr. around 1967, by which time he was widely acknowledged as American conservatism's chief intellectual voice. Founder of the flagship conservative magazine National Review *and instrumental in the organization Young Americans for Freedom, a conservative youth group, Buckley was a key figure in establishing the intellectual legitimacy of conservatism, which had lain largely fallow since the late 1920s, and making it the dominant ideology by the 1980s. (Library of Congress, LC-USZC4-8992)*

He then referred to Frank Cullen Brophy, a leading Arizona banker who was a member of the right-wing group, and said, "You just can't do that kind of thing in Arizona."

At another meeting the following morning, a decision was made to distance Goldwater from controversial statements made by Welch without attacking the John Birch Society. Buckley agreed to take on the task of exposing Welch to ridicule. In the pages of the *National Review*, Buckley roundly condemned him, asking how the John Birch Society could operate effectively while led by a man whose perspective on so many contemporary issues was "so far removed from common sense." A letter by Goldwater himself soon appeared in the magazine, calling for Welch to resign from the organization he founded. The twin-pronged attack badly damaged Welch, while the John Birch Society remained something of a force on the political right and within the ranks of the Republican Party. Goldwater went on to capture the 1964 Republican Party presidential nomination, asserting that "extremism in the defense of liberty is no vice." Goldwater's rhetoric and a media blitz by the Democratic Party doomed his chances in the general election, although a new political star, Hollywood actor

Ronald Reagan, captured the hearts of many conservatives in a televised speech supporting Goldwater near the close of the campaign.

William F. Buckley Jr. was born into a family of wealth and privilege on November 24, 1925, in New York City. His mother, Aloise Steiner, was from the South and boasted Swiss and German ancestors, while his father, William Frank Buckley Sr., possessing Irish-Catholic roots, was an attorney, who, like his own father, had made a fortune in the oil business, heading the Catawba Corporation, a network of six large oil companies. The Buckleys owned a large estate in Sharon, Connecticut. One of ten children, Buckley learned Spanish and French, thanks to Spanish-speaking nursemaids and French governesses, before receiving much exposure to English, and entered a day school in London at the age of seven. His father was a stickler for grammar, conveying a great respect for language. Buckley was drawn to many of the interests that became lifelong fascinations, including music, sailing, horseback riding, and skiing. He initially attended high school at the elite Catholic Beaumont College, run by the Jesuits at Beaumont Lodge in Old Windsor, outside of London, then went to another elite institution, Millbrook School, in Millbrook, New York. He graduated from Millbrook in 1943, where he ran the school's yearbook, *The Tamarack*. He then attended the National Autonomous University of Mexico before enrolling in U.S. Army Officer Candidate School, eventually receiving his commission as a second lieutenant.

Following World War II, Buckley enrolled at Yale University, where he joined the secret and highly select student society Skull and Bones, served as captain of the debate team, took on the assignment of editor of the *Yale Daily News*, taught Spanish to freshmen students, and studied political science, history, and economics before graduating with honors in 1950. Buckley's editorship of the school newspaper enabled him to produce editorials blasting individuals on the left he condemned as "traitors" or "fellow travelers." He claimed that the Yale faculty housed "Reds" and praised Senator Robert A. Taft from Ohio as a "bulwark against the socialization of this country." Although admitted into both Yale's law school and graduate school, Buckley decided against further academic studies, because of the outbreak of the Korean War and his desire to remain "a little bit more mobile." He married Patricia Taylor of Vancouver, who had attended Vassar and was a former Miss Vancouver, and kept teaching Spanish in New Haven; the two had one son, Christopher.

He also worked on his first book, *God and Man at Yale: The Superstitions of "Academic Freedom,"* released when he was only twenty-five. Published by the conservative Henry Regnery Company, after several New York houses refused to accept it, *God and Man at Yale* condemned the liberal bias purportedly displayed at the Ivy League institution, but as conservative analyst Peter Viereck rightly noted in a *New York Times* review, Buckley's intended target was the

American political scene. Viereck applauded the young author's insistence "that man has a moral nature" imperiled by statism, and that freedom required a moral base. At the same time, Viereck thought that Buckley only offered "the most sterile Old Guard brand of Republicanism, far to the right of [conservative Senator Robert] Taft." Viereck also was troubled by Buckley's easy coupling of "Adam Smith and Ricardo, Jesus and Saint Paul," and his failure to condemn McCarthyism. Viereck viewed with dismay Buckley's dismissal of social democracy and most social reform as nearly akin to "crypto-communism," and his blasting of "the income tax and inheritance tax" more fiercely than communism. Viereck was also taken aback by the book's denouement, which insisted on the banishing of both communists and anyone challenging Adam Smith's ideas from classroom teaching. Yes, Viereck acknowledged, "more conservatism and traditional morality," as Buckley indicated, were needed. However, "a profound conservatism" required, Viereck insisted, more than campus-honed glibness. In a review appearing in the *Atlantic Monthly*, McGeorge Bundy, then a professor of government at Harvard, proved still more critical of *God and Man at Yale*, stating, "As a believer in God, a Republican, and Yale graduate, I find that the book is dishonest in its use of facts, false in its theory, and a discredit to its author."

In 1951, the six-feet-tall, blue-eyed, blond-haired Buckley, possessing some celebrity of his own, joined the Central Intelligence Agency (CIA), serving briefly "as a deep cover agent" in Mexico City under Howard Hunt, who was later involved with the U.S.-sponsored overthrow of the democratically elected regime of Jacobo Arbenz in Guatemala, the disastrous Bay of Pigs invasion, and the Watergate fiasco. After leaving the CIA, Buckley worked for the *American Mercury*, but departed in 1952, supposedly troubled by the journal's seeming anti-Semitic tilt. He then toured the country as president of the newly founded Intercollegiate Studies Institute, which Frank Chodorov established in 1953, hoping to promote individual liberty, limited government, and the market economy, and to contest campus collectivism. That same year, Russell Kirk released *The Conservative Mind*, a book that Buckley took to heart. Kirk sought to trace a conservative intellectual tradition that had influenced American history, hearkening back to thinkers like John Adams and John C. Calhoun, and extolled a strict constructionist reading of the U.S. Constitution, states' rights, "divine intent," order, the indivisibility of property and freedom, tradition, and distrust of reform.

Along with his brother-in-law, L. Brent Bozell Jr., Buckley wrote *McCarthy and His Enemies*, released by Regnery in 1954, which contained a prologue from Willi Schlamm, one of many former radicals in the conservative movement. The book both criticized and praised the now beleaguered senator, pointing out "outrageous" and "reprehensible" actions but also indicating that McCarthyism "is a movement around which men of good will and stern morality can close ranks." Indeed, "on McCarthyism hang the hopes of America for effective resistance to Communist infiltration," the author warned. Ralph de Toledano, a former socialist who veered rightward during the early years of the Cold War, later indicated that McCarthy "loved [Buckley] and loved to have him around: he gave a sort of intellectual patent to the McCarthy movement." Later, Buckley admitted "that McCarthy did more damage to his cause than benefit." During this period, Buckley encountered a number of key figures on the American right, including Whittaker Chambers and Roy Cohn. Chambers, the one-time communist espionage agent turned *Time* editor, had accused New Dealer Alger Hiss of having been a member of an underground communist cell in Washington, DC, and of having illegally passed on State Department documents in the 1930s. A young attorney in the early 1950s, Cohn served as counsel to the Senate Permanent Subcommittee on Investigations headed by McCarthy. Buckley also met Vice President Richard Nixon, who had been placed on the presidential ticket with Dwight Eisenhower in 1952, in part to appease the right wing of the Republican Party.

Determined to articulate his own vision of America, while championing conservative principles, Buckley sought his own forum, initially attempting to buy *Human Events*, a weekly conservative publication. Buckley reasoned that intellectuals "have midwived and implemented the revolution. We have got to have allies among the intellectuals, and we propose to renovate conservatism and see if we can't win some of them around." Unable to purchase *Human Events*, Buckley and Schlamm envisioned a new publication, to be called the *National Weekly*. In soliciting financial support from wealthy conservatives, Buckley affirmed that the *National Weekly* would strive to provide a counterweight to American journalism's striving for "genteel uniformity of opinion, and even of style." Drawing on $125,000 in family money and $300,000 from others, Buckley garnered enough capital to begin his journalistic endeavor. Castigating "that decadent, lukewarm mood of indifference" characteristic of the liberal press, Buckley promised a magazine devoted to personal journalism, which he explained as "the manly presentation of deeply felt conviction," and "to revitalize the conservative position."

Buckley drafted a statement of intentions in which he foresaw his magazine directly contesting mainstream political thought. Moreover, its purpose, he stated, was "to *change* the nation's intellectual and political climate." Contending that liberal intellectuals had distanced themselves from the American public, Buckley also dismissed "Middle-of-the-Road" as "politically, intellectually, and morally repugnant." He affirmed that government should safeguard "citizens' lives, liberty, and property," while its growth should "be fought relentlessly." He saw the contemporary era's most significant crisis as involving the fight pitting social engineers, desirous of "scientific utopias," against "disciples of Truth" who championed "the organic moral order." The twentieth century's most horrific example "of satanic utopianism," Buckley continued, was communism, mandating the unacceptability of coexistence. Instead, the American people were "irrevocably at war with Communism" in a global battle that cried out for victory. Like Friedrich Hayek, who championed capitalism over collectivist solutions, Buckley insisted that free enterprise, "liberty and material progress," were necessarily linked.

On November 19, 1955, the first issue of Buckley's magazine, the *National Review*, appeared, just days before his thirtieth birthday. The corporate lawyer and former Office of Strategic Services officer William J. Casey, who later headed the CIA, incorporated the magazine. Happily, more than 120 investors, along with fifty individuals "of small means," had provided the capital for the *National Review*, Buckley reported. Its "Credenda and Statement of Principles" proclaimed that the *National Review* stood "athwart history, yelling Stop," when no one was doing so. The *National Review* was admittedly "out of place," Buckley acknowledged, because "literate America," as exemplified by columnist James Wechsler, historian Arthur Schlesinger Jr., poet and former Librarian of Congress Archibald MacLeish, and *Harper's Magazine*, had "rejected conservatism in favor of radical social experimentation." This was significant, he recognized, because "ideas rule the world." American conservatives, those who refused to accept the welfare state, were "non-licensed nonconformists," threatening "a Liberal world," he suggested.

Mere days after the initial issue of the *National Review* appeared, Buckley acknowledged that the American Right had a long way to go. "The few spasmodic victories conservatives are winning," he indicated, "are aimless, uncoordinated and inconclusive. This is so . . . because many years have gone since the philosophy of freedom has been expounded systematically, brilliantly, and resourcefully." Using the *National Review* as a forum, Buckley strove to attract conservatives and libertarians of different stripes. Traditional conservatives were represented by Russell Kirk, afforded his own column, "From the Academy"; libertarians included John Chamberlain and Frank Chodorov; and former radicals were prominent, including James Burnham, Whittaker Chambers, Max Eastman, Frank Meyer, and Schlamm. They were all, at the same time, staunch anticommunists. The eclectic nature of the contributors to the *National Review* was particularly fitting, in keeping with Buckley's determination to spearhead a movement that would bring together traditional conservatives and libertarians, a process called fusionism. Burnham's column, "The Third World War," and Buckley's own "The Ivory Tower" appeared regularly. While strongly, even stridently anticommunist, the *National Review* often targeted liberalism, insisting that a liberal "propaganda machine" relentlessly assailed the American public. By contrast, the magazine often praised Joseph McCarthy and McCarthyite-style tactics.

The *National Review* adopted other controversial stances, including some concerning segregation. In an editorial dated August 24, 1957, Buckley posed the question as to whether white Southerners could act to retain their stranglehold on the region's politics and culture. He answered, "Yes—the White community is so entitled because, for the time being, it is the advanced race," in spite of declarations to the contrary "by ever-so-busy egalitarians and anthropologists." Buckley asserted that it was "more important for any community . . . to affirm and live by civilized standards" than to adhere to democratic practices. The South did face "one grave moral challenge," he admitted, and that was to avoid exploiting "Negro backwardness" to keep blacks in a "servile" position.

Circulation figures hovered near 20,000 through 1958, at which point Buckley felt compelled to convert the *National Review* into a biweekly. Seeking financial aid, he claimed the magazine had "entered the mainstream of American thought, and it is now an institutional fact of American life." No more was it considered simply "a new experimental" publication or "a flash fire by the Neanderthal Right," but rather as "the voice of American conservatism." Buckley's celebrity became greater still with the publication in 1959 of *Up from Liberalism*, offering an introduction by conservative Senator Barry Goldwater of Arizona and a foreword by John Dos Passos, the great writer who had undergone his own pilgrimage from left to right. Buckley dissected what he referred to as "the failure of contemporary American liberalism," pointing to big government, violations of free market ideals, and the liberals' mistaken belief in humankind's perfectibility and social progress. In examining "the conservative alternative," Buckley criticized the modern Republicanism associated with President Dwight D. Eisenhower, which seemed to involve a basic acceptance of the welfare state and containment. Buckley insisted that "the distinctive challenge of our time" was "to resist the philosophical infiltration of the west by Communism"; in his estimation, "Coexistence . . . is death."

Buckley's influence on the American right lengthened following the establishment of the Young Americans for Freedom in 1960. On September 3 of that year, the *National Review Bulletin* called for college students "to establish a continuing youth organization dedicated to the achievement of political objectives." Six days later, about 100 students, drawn from forty-four colleges, gathered at the Buckley family estate in Sharon, Connecticut, to establish the group's goals and objectives. The Sharon Statement, produced between September 9 and September 11, undoubtedly delighted Buckley, who clearly was an inspiration. The YAF manifesto affirmed the belief that "liberty is indivisible, and that political freedom cannot long exist without economic freedom," declared that government should maintain order, provide national defense, and administer justice, proclaimed the diffusion of powers and reservation of "primacy to the several states" under the Constitution to be ideal, and extolled the market economy. The document asserted that "the forces of international Communism" posed the greatest threat to American liberties and demanded victory over such a "menace."

In the *National Review*, Buckley discussed the formation of the organization, praising its "young, intelligent, articulate and determined" members and declaring that YAF might well "influence the political future of this country." YAF's declaration of principles reflected "the great renewal of the last decade," Buckley wrote. Significantly, "here is mention of the moral aspect of freedom; of transcendent values; of the nature of man," along "with a tough-as-nails statement of political and economic convictions." Buckley, like Goldwater, a popular figure on college campuses, found most striking the students' "appetite for power." He also noted that Goldwater, not President Eisenhower or Vice President Richard Nixon, was the darling of young people gathered at the Republican Party convention in Chicago; Buckley himself participated in a "draft Goldwater" campaign. Those same youth spoke of "*affecting* history," Buckley wrote.

Like many others, the editors of the *National Review* viewed Goldwater as the leading political spokesperson for the conservative movement. L. Brent Bozell Jr. helped Goldwater write *The Conscience of a Conservative*, which laid out conservative ideals on its way to becoming a best seller. A sticking point for conservatives was the manner in which the movement could be tagged with the label of extremism. Some hearkened back to the stances of many leading conservatives prior to U.S. entrance into World War II, which had helped to diminish the luster of conservatism, fairly or not. President Herbert Hoover's refusal to provide federal assistance for individuals in the midst of the nation's greatest economic crisis hardly served the conservative movement well. But then neither did the embittered opposition of organizations like the American Liberty League to the New Deal, which sought to alleviate the suffering of millions of Americans and to strengthen the American economic system. Famed aviator Charles Lindbergh's apparent fondness for Nazi Germany and his isolationist stance caused many to view him with suspicion. The seemingly doctrinaire stance of conservatives regarding both domestic and foreign policy issues paled by comparison with the moves by Franklin D. Roosevelt to position himself first as "Dr. New Deal" and then as "Dr. Win the War." The Cold War induced many conservatives to discard isolationist positions in the arena of international affairs and Eisenhower's modern Republicanism suggested political gains to be achieved by moving away from laissez-faire and social Darwinist stances. Nevertheless, small groups on the far right garnered notice, as had the pro-fascist Silver Shirts and Black Legion in the 1930s. More recently,

Robert Welch's John Birch Society and the gun-toting Minutemen grabbed attention, thanks to Welch's easy tagging of Eisenhower with a communist label and the Minutemen's warning that communism was sweeping over America. Buckley's accusation in the *National Review* that Welch was "damaging the conservative movement" helped lessen the John Birch Society founder's appeal. That same editorial, "The Question of Robert Welch," asserted that the John Birch Society contained "some of the most morally energetic self-sacrificing and dedicated anti-Communists in America." As for Barry Goldwater, he went on to capture the 1964 Republican Party nomination. However, cast as an extremist, Goldwater went on to lose resoundingly to President Lyndon Johnson in the general election.

Buckley, whose column "On the Right" had been nationally syndicated in 1962, tossed his own hat into the political arena in 1965 after receiving the nomination of the recently formed Conservative Party for the mayoralty in New York City. He ran against the liberal Republican candidate John Lindsay, who also obtained the backing of the Liberal Party, and the Democratic Abe Beame. The Conservative Party anointed Buckley after an editorial of his in the *National Review* discussed the "crisis of the American city." In that piece, which appeared in both May and June of 1965, Buckley demanded harsh treatment of juvenile delinquents, urged that community groups patrol neighborhoods, supported a tax holiday for blacks and Puerto Ricans who set up businesses in depressed sectors, called for independent contractors to compete with labor unions, favored severe restrictions on welfare recipients, and supported the decriminalization of drug and gambling laws. Having promised he would "demand a recount" if he won the election, Buckley received 13.4 percent of the votes cast, over 340,000 of 2.6 million, despite being heavily outspent by his opponents. Writing in the *New York Journal-American*, Robert Donovan offered that Buckley, like Ronald Reagan, who had begun a gubernatorial campaign in California, was "trying to prove that right-wing conservatism still [was] on the march despite the Goldwater debacle of 1964."

In 1966 Buckley began hosting a public affairs television program, *Firing Line*, which originally appeared on WOR-TV in New York City and would have a thirty-three-year run. Buckley usually debated another intellectual about various issues of the day, while a group of panelists and later a third individual or "examiner," frequently far more liberal than the host, posed various questions to the host and his guests. A critic in the *New York Herald Tribune* had earlier underscored how important the new television host's style was: "The supercilious manner in which Buckley displayed his vast erudition, the flashes of wit and velvety insults that were sprinkled throughout his remarks, reminded me of Noel Coward acting in one of his own plays." The early period of *Firing Line* coincided, propitiously for Buckley's sake, with a weakening of liberalism's previously seemingly unassailable hold on the nation's allegiance. Liberalism seemed to crest in the midst of social unrest, topped off by racial riots, and the Vietnam quagmire that helped to divide the Democratic Party, pro-war hawkish liberals from so-called doves, and a good portion of the American populace from the liberal credo. Many of the very ideas that Buckley had long preached—restraint in government, albeit in certain areas; distrust of social engineering; and disdain for liberalism as an ideology, with its belief in the supposed goodness of humankind—resonated as the United States experienced its greatest divisions since the Civil War and became mired in a war that increasingly proved unwinnable.

Time magazine featured a cartoon sketch of Buckley on the cover of its November 3, 1967, issue and a companion article, "The Sniper." The piece pointed out that Buckley, in contrast to most American ideologues, hardly was "humorless" and was, in fact, "celebrated for his wit." Buckley operated on a daily basis "at some conservative Armageddon" although lacking "an army or even a division" of his own, *Time* declared. Buckley was in fact "too clever, too humorous, too well read, too . . . attractive," while serving as "a solitary sniper," blasting the Great Society, believers in coexistence, John F. Kennedy's acolytes, and John Lindsay–styled Republicans. Yale chaplain William Sloane Coffin Jr. acknowledged, "He is as brilliant an adversary as he is bankrupt an advocate." Buckley's column "On the Right" now appeared three times a week in over 200 newspapers; the *National Review*'s subscriptions had jumped to 94,000 (although the magazine still lost money annually); and *Firing Line* offered yet another national forum for his easy spewing of "polysyllabic vocabulary and an arsenal of intimidating grimaces." Liberals regularly appeared on his television program, including friends like economist John Kenneth Galbraith, columnist Murray Kempton, and writer Norman Mailer. With the radical right seeming to have dissipated and concerns about the radical left rife, Buckley was "in vogue as never before," solicited to produce "nonideological articles [for] nonconservative publications." He appeared to enjoy "the best of both worlds: a society that is especially vulnerable to criticism from the right and equally willing to take it."

Buckley got caught up in the cauldron of events swirling about in the late 1960s, including the Democratic Party national convention in Chicago during the summer of 1968. As police battled with demonstrators in the streets, Buckley and liberal author Gore Vidal appeared on national television alongside ABC anchor Howard K. Smith. After Vidal referred to Buckley as a "pro-crypto-Nazi," Buckley retorted, "Now, listen, you queer, stop calling me a crypto-Nazi or I'll sock you in your goddamn face and you'll stay plastered." During that same period, Buckley added Jeff Greenfield, a graduate of Yale Law School who had served as a staffer for Senator Robert F. Kennedy, to *Firing Line*. Greenfield contended that Buckley was no believer in small government when it came to civil liberties, having admitted, "I don't feel any obligation to protect the liberties of the Nazi or the Communist, or, for that matter, anybody who seeks class legislation or genocide." Buckley failed to act altogether even-handedly in dealing with his guests, Greenfield believed, adopting a hostile stance with antiwar figures like the noted linguist Noam Chomsky of the Massachusetts Institute of Technology, famed pediatrician Dr. Benjamin Spock, and radical attorney William Kunstler. *Firing Line* garnered an Emmy in 1969 and moved to public television two years later. In the mid-1970s, Buckley, who had watched his older brother James get elected to the U.S. Senate at the beginning of the decade, running on the Conservative Party ticket, began yet another career as a spy novelist.

Becoming something of an elder spokesperson for the American conservative movement, Buckley applauded the arrival of neoconservatives in the 1970s, many of whom had previously been stationed on the left side of the ideological spectrum. The neocons proved increasingly critical of the welfare state, supposed excesses associated with American liberalism, and the Soviet Union, which, like communism, continued to be viewed as something of a diabolical force, all stances that Buckley, the *National Review*, and *Firing Line* had long championed. Columnist George F. Will, who had once worked for the *National Review*, proclaimed in 1980, "All great biblical stories begin with Genesis. And before there was Ronald Reagan, there was Barry Goldwater, and before there was Barry Goldwater there was *National Review*, and before there was *National Review* there was Bill Buckley, with a spark in his mind, and the spark in 1980 has become a conflagration." Buckley happily backed President Reagan's drive to reduce taxes, particularly on the wealthy and corporations, moves to weaken the welfare state, and determination to battle the Soviet Union, whether rhetorically or through the use of surrogates in places like Central America and the Middle East. At a celebration of the *National Review*'s thirtieth anniversary in 1985, President Reagan saluted Buckley: "You didn't just part the Red Sea—you rolled it back, dried it up and left exposed, for all the world to see, the naked desert that is statism." In 1988, Nicholas Lemann, writing in *Washington Monthly*, noted that "the 5000 middle-level officials, journalists and policy intellectuals" who ran the Reagan administration were "deeply influenced by Buckley's example." Indeed, "some of these people had been personally groomed by Buckley, and most of the rest saw him as a role model."

Buckley relinquished his post as editor of the *National Review* in 1990 while retaining his title as editor in chief. He received the Presidential Medal of Freedom from President George Herbert Walker Bush the following year. In 1999 *Firing Line* offered its last in a series of over 1,500 episodes, with Buckley informing his audience, "You've got to end sometime and I'd just as soon not die onstage." William Kristol, editor of the decidedly conservative *Weekly Standard*, acknowledged, "For people of my generation, Bill Buckley was pretty much the first intelligent, witty, well-educated conservative one saw on television. He legitimized conservatism as an intellectual movement and therefore as a political movement." In 2004 Buckley carried out the divestiture of his controlling share of the *National Review*, which claimed a subscription figure of 155,000. At times, Buckley, through public addresses or his column with National Review Online, argued that conservatives had gone astray, proving particularly critical of the Iraq War that President George W. Bush initiated in 2003. On February 27, 2008, the eighty-two-year-old Buckley died at his home in Stamford, Connecticut, having recently lost his wife Patricia and having battled emphysema and diabetes. President Bush contended that Buckley "brought conservative thought into the political mainstream, and helped lay the intellectual foundation for America's victory in the Cold War." Right-wing radio talk show host Rush Limbaugh declared, "Bill Buckley is indescribable. He's irreplaceable. There will not be another one like him." Hendrik Hertzberg, writing in the *New Yorker*, criticized Buckley for championing Joe McCarthy and McCarthyism and for conflating liberalism and communism. But Hertzberg also praised Buckley for having done "his best to purge the right of anti-Semitism, overt racism, xenophobia and anti-intellectualism." Approximately 2,000 people attended the memorial service for Buckley held at St. Patrick's Cathedral in New York City. Liberal and conservative journalists, actors, and politicians paid their respects.

⌒ RONALD REAGAN ⌒

On Tuesday, January 20, 1981, sixty-nine-year-old Ronald Reagan, still movie-star handsome and sporting a mane of thick, dark hair, delivered his first inaugural address as president of the United States, speaking on the terrace of the western front of the Capitol. The favorite of American conservatives since his public speeches on behalf of Goldwater's presidential candidacy seventeen years earlier, Reagan now reiterated many of the themes and ideals associated with the conservative movement. He referred to the high inflationary rates that the country had recently endured, unacceptably high unemployment levels, and a tax system that "penalizes successful achievement and keeps us from maintaining full productivity." Crushing too, Reagan insisted, were the deficits that mortgaged "our future and our children's future for the temporary convenience of the present." Emphasizing that government "is not the solution to our problem" and needed to be reduced, he avowed that the American people had thrived "because here, in this land, we unleashed the energy and individual genius of man to a greater extent than has ever been done before." In America "freedom and the dignity of the individual have been more available and assured here than

President Ronald Reagan was renowned as the Great Communicator for his ability to effectively make the case for conservative principles and policies in an era in which liberal solutions were deemed to have failed. Since the 1950s, Reagan had been an articulate advocate for free market capitalism, fiscal conservatism, small government, and aggressive anticommunism. Though his presidency was not without controversy, he was instrumental in ushering in an era of conservativism. (Courtesy Ronald Reagan Library)

in any other place on Earth." Recent difficulties, Reagan charged, occurred due to "the intervention and intrusion in our lives that result from unnecessary and excessive growth of government." In characteristic fashion, he hopefully stated, "We are not, as some would have us believe, doomed to an inevitable decline." The American nation required "creative energy" to initiate "an era of national renewal," enabling the United States to "again be the exemplar of freedom and a beacon of hope for those who do not now have freedom." Reagan warned that "the enemies of freedom" would "be reminded that peace is the highest aspiration of the American people," but added, "we will not surrender for it—now or ever." Indeed, he said, "when action is required to preserve our national security, we will act." Moreover, the United States possessed the most "formidable" weapon: "the will and moral courage of free men and women."

On February 6, 1911, Ronald Wilson Reagan was born in Tampico, Illinois, approximately 100 miles west of Chicago, the second son of Nelle Reagan, a housewife, and her alcoholic husband John, who worked as a shoe salesman and resided with their family in a small apartment above a bank. The family surname was originally spelled "Regan" but was changed following the emigration of Reagan's great-grandfather from Ballyporeen, County Tipperary in Ireland, during the 1860s. Beset by economic troubles, the Reagans moved continuously during the 1910s before settling in Dixon in 1920. The next year, Reagan— referred to as "Dutch" by his father—received his baptism at Nelle's Disciples of Christ Church, while three years later, he enrolled at Northside High School, where he participated in football, basketball, and track; starred in class plays; and became class president. Thanks to a partial athletic scholarship, Reagan attended Eureka College, where he majored in economics and sociology, earned four varsity letters in football, again became student body president, and held the lead role in many school plays. Reagan received his degree in 1932, at the height of the Great Depression.

After unsuccessfully seeking a job as head of the sports department of a new Montgomery Ward store in Dixon, Reagan took to the road, hoping to find a position with a radio station. Eventually "Dutch" Reagan obtained a broadcasting job with WHO in Des Moines, recounting Chicago Cub baseball games by embellishing the information received from a ticker. Reagan entered the Army Reserve in 1937, soon receiving a promotion to second lieutenant in the Cavalary's Officers Reserve Corps. That same year the athletic-looking, six-feet-one-inch-tall young man took a screen test; had an agent declare about him, "I have another Robert Taylor sitting in my office"; signed a contract with Warner Brothers for $200 a week; and appeared in his first film. In 1940 he married the actress Jane Wyman and starred as the ill-fated George Gipp in *Knute Rockne, All American*. In the film, a dying Gipp told coach Rockne, "Someday when the team is in trouble . . . tell them to win one for the Gipper." Reagan later regularly employed that line during political addresses.

In 1941 the Reagans' daughter Maureen was born. Then, shortly following the United States' entrance into World War II, the Army Air Force ushered Reagan into active duty, placing him with the First Motion Picture Unit, which produced training and educational films. While repeatedly seeking overseas assignments, Reagan remained on the West Coast, due to his astigmatism, although he was eventually promoted to captain. Reagan's film career thrived during the war years, with an acclaimed performance in the 1942 film *Kings Row*, about a young man who suffered the amputation of his legs. He also appeared in such films as *For God and Country* and *This Is the Army*, and, in 1945, signed a seven-year, $1 million contract with Warner Brothers. The Reagans adopted a son, Michael, after the war, while their premature daughter died after only one day.

At this point, Reagan, who had been elected president of the Screen Actors Guild (SAG), remained a committed Democrat. The Reagans divorced in 1948, supposedly owing to Wyman's dismay over her husband's political ambitions and emotional reserve; she received custody of their two children. He served as head of SAG through 1952, at the height of the domestic Cold War. Reagan testified before the House Un-American Activities Committee as a friendly witness, and, evidently operating under the code name Agent T-10, informed the FBI about purportedly "disloyal" individuals but did not denounce them in public. Reagan supported blacklisting while insisting he would assist anyone who was unfairly targeted. He also believed that his principled anticommunism helped to doom his film career because of Hollywood's left-of-center propensities.

On March 4, 1952, as his film career continued to wane, Reagan married actress Nancy Davis, who came from a staunchly conservative Republican household. Their daughter Patti was born that October, while their son Ron arrived in 1958. By all accounts the Reagans' marriage was a happy one, with Ronald later indicating, "I want you to know that Nancy . . . is my everything. . . . [T]hank you partner for everything." Reagan worked briefly in Las Vegas as a master of ceremonies, before he began hosting *General Electric Theater* in 1954. Eventually he acquired an equitable stake in the television program and also delivered speeches around the country on the company's behalf, extolling the virtues of the free enterprise system. Increasingly drawn to a more conservative perspective, Reagan celebrated limited government, anticommunism, and individual responsibility. While again serving as SAG president, he backed Republican presidential nominee Richard Nixon during the 1960 campaign and spoke at Republican fund-raisers, even before officially switching parties (which he did in 1962). Referring dismissively to Democratic Party nominee John F. Kennedy, Reagan stated, "Under the tousled boyish haircut it is still old Karl Marx. . . . There is nothing new in the idea of a government being Big Brother to us all." The American Medical Association soon sponsored an album, *Ronald Reagan Speaks Out Against Socialized Medicine*. In an address in San Jose, California, in mid-October 1961, Reagan condemned the welfare state, contending that "our greatest defense against world revolution and communism is devotion to individual liberty, and the preservation of a free economy based on private ownership of property."

The British historian-journalist Godfrey Hodgson indicates that Reagan became "caught up in the excitement of the Radical Right in California," delivering versions of the same talk to Dr. Fred Schwarz's Christian Anti-Communist Crusade and during a fund-raiser for Republican congressman John Rousselot, a member of the John Birch Society. Reagan spoke of "the issue of our times—totalitarianism versus freedom." In January 1962, he avowed, "Today we are engaged in a great war to determine whether the world can exist half-slave and half-free. . . . Whether we admit it or not, we are at war." As Matthew Dallek notes, Reagan also showed up for political talks in which he joined diehard segregationist governors like Arkansas's Orval Faubus and Mississippi's Ross

Barnett. Reagan delivered articles for the right-wing journal *Human Events* and served on the national board of the Young Americans for Freedom.

Conservative Republicans now hoped to tape one of his speeches but technical difficulties arose, leading Reagan to suggest that he deliver a live address to a studio audience. Presented on NBC on October 27, 1964, "A Time for Choosing" condemned the Johnson administration's economic policies, pointing to the nation's heavy tax burden, the continued inability to balance the federal budget, the repeated raising of the debt ceiling, and the enormous national debt. In addition he recalled those who had lost loved ones in South Vietnam and questioned whether "this is a peace that should be maintained indefinitely." Reagan exclaimed, "We're at war with the most dangerous enemy that has ever faced mankind in his long climb from the swamp to the stars." The stakes were enormous, he suggested, for "if we lose freedom here, there's no place to escape to. This is the last stand on earth." The upcoming election, Reagan remarked, offered a choice between belief in self-government or abandonment of the ideals of the Founding Fathers and acknowledgment "that a little intellectual elite in a far-distant capitol can plan our lives for us better than we can." Rather than pitting left against right, Reagan continued, there was "only an up or down. Up to man's age-old dream—the maximum of individual freedom consistent with order—or down to the ant heap of totalitarianism." The largest risk, Reagan informed his audience, derived from "appeasement" or the "policy of accommodation," which he blamed "our well-meaning liberal friends" for accepting. By contrast, Barry Goldwater, Reagan asserted, favored "peace through strength." Reagan closed by informing the television audience, "You and I have a rendezvous with destiny," borrowing that phrase from liberal New Dealers. He went on to state, "We'll preserve for our children this, the last best hope of man on earth, or we'll sentence them to take the last step into a thousand years of darkness." Plaudits poured in following the Speech, as Reagan's address became known in conservative circles. Film director John Ford praised Reagan: "Great, Ronnie, Great." Phyllis Schlafly recalled that the address "just went through the country like electricity. As soon as it was shown on television, all of these unorganized grassrooters went around raising their last dollar to keep putting it on again." Moderate political columnist David Broder referred to Reagan's talk as "the most successful national political debut since William Jennings Bryan electrified the 1896 Democratic convention with the 'Cross of Gold' speech." At a minimum Reagan indicated that he, unlike Goldwater, could "present his views in a reasonable and eloquent manner."

Following Goldwater's devastating defeat, a group of California businessmen urged Reagan to run against Democratic governor Pat Brown. In 1965, remaining in the public limelight, Reagan published *Where's the Rest of Me,* an autobiography that underscored his "disillusionment with big government." Early the next year, he called for Republicans to unite, issuing what later became known as the Eleventh Commandment: "I have stated that I will not speak critically of any Republican and that I will wholeheartedly support whoever is the nominee of the Party." Hoping to quash Reagan's gubernatorial bid, the California Democratic Party put out a document, "Ronald Reagan, Extremist Collaborator—An Expose," insisting that the former actor was a "front man" who "collaborated directly with a score of the top leaders of the super-secret John Birch Society." Reagan nevertheless benefited from a backlash against liberal governance and his promises to put "the welfare bums back to work," "clean up the mess at Berkeley," and sustain "traditional values." Claiming he was no politician but rather "an ordinary citizen," Reagan easily defeated Brown in the California gubernatorial race. During the campaign, Reagan, like Barry Goldwater and William Buckley, publisher of the *National Review*, blasted Robert Welch, founder of the John Birch Society, but applauded "the Americanism and patriotism" of Birchers, Hodgson indicates. Shortly following the election, the *Houston Post* indicated that Reagan offered "a hope for the future" for those who viewed him as "a conservative with enough mass appeal to win a national election."

In 1968, Reagan, increasingly the favorite of the Republican right, made a late bid for his party's presidential nomination, but eventually backed Richard Nixon, who went on to defeat Hubert Humphrey in the general election. Reagan offered the conservative movement a respectable voice and prevented it from being dismissed as extremist, while his prominence demonstrated how sharply the Republican Party had moved to the right. Reagan himself was hardly inclined to opt for another approach. As massive antiwar protests continued on the University of California's Berkeley campus in the spring of 1969, Reagan warned that order would be restored even "if it takes a bloodbath." Nevertheless his first term as governor was mixed regarding the implementation of conservative principles, as the state legislature remained largely in Democratic hands. He mandated that government hiring be frozen but accepted tax increases to balance the state budget. Reagan won reelection in 1970, maintaining his determination to privatize or localize certain government programs, including the public psychiatric hospital system. Blasting "welfare cheats," he sought a major revision of California's welfare system and, thanks to major budgetary surpluses, delivered popular tax rebates. However, cost-cutting practices triggered a teachers' strike that spread across the state.

After departing from the governor's office, Reagan wrote a syndicated newspaper column, offered political commentary on radio stations across the United States, and returned to the banquet circuit. In a speech before the Executive Club of Chicago on September 26, 1975, Reagan charged that America's ills derived "from a single source," the sensibility that government provided "the answer to our ills." Such a "collectivist, centralizing approach, whatever name or party label it wears, has created our economic problems." Reagan continued, "By taxing and consuming an ever-greater share of the national wealth, it has imposed an intolerable burden of taxation on American citizens." He called for "a systematic transfer of authority and resource to the states—a program of creative federalism for America's third century." Reagan attempted to wrestle the 1976 Republican nomination away from Gerald Ford, who had become president following Nixon's resignation at the height of the Watergate scandal. Narrowly losing his bid for the presidential nomination, Reagan then supported Ford's campaign and blasted "the erosion of freedom that has taken place under Democrat rule in this country, the invasion of private rights, the controls and restrictions on the . . . great free economy that we enjoy." During the administration of Democrat Jimmy Carter, Reagan remained the darling of the New Right, neoconservative intellectuals, and think tanks that charged that democratic excesses endangered the nation and its standing in world affairs. Those forces, like Reagan, urged that social programs be curbed; tax rates reduced, especially for the wealthy and corporations; and the U.S. military beefed up, so that the nation could stand more firmly against the Soviet Union.

Many of their concerns appeared borne out by the doldrums the nation endured by 1979. The Carter administration experienced a malaise that the president acknowledged. The American economy suffered from record-high interest rates and soaring inflation, and U.S. foreign policy foundered mightily, in the face of first Islamic fundamentalism in Iran and then Soviet intervention in Afghanistan. With frustration mounting over the holding of American hostages at the U.S. embassy in Tehran and Soviet incursions in Afghanistan, Carter's popular support slackened. During the summer of 1980, following a failed U.S. military rescue operation in the Iranian desert, the Republican Party selected Reagan as its standard bearer. Then Reagan, like John F. Kennedy twenty years earlier, selected his defeated opponent, George H. W. Bush, who earlier had called Reagan's economic ideas "voodoo economics," as his running mate. The Great Communicator, as Reagan became known, campaigned in support of traditional values, the free market, and a potent America. Reagan also assailed Carter by asking the American people, "Are you better off today than you were four years ago?," pointing to a prime interest rate of over 15 percent, inflation above 12 percent, and unemployment beyond the 7 percent mark. Carter attempted to portray Reagan as an extremist, but following a nationally televised debate in which the telegenic, amiable, but strong-willed former actor deflected the president's criticisms, the Republicans swept into the White House and captured a dozen seats from Democratic senators, including liberal stalwarts George McGovern, Birch Bayh, and Frank Church. Howard Phillips, head of the Conservative Caucus, chortled that this was "the greatest victory for conservatism since the American Revolution." Meanwhile, Reagan appeared to link "capitalism to morality and democracy" in an attempt to strengthen the conservative movement.

Reagan demonstrated the potency of conservatism with a populist flavor while benefiting from the emergence of neoconservative intellectuals, including several former radicals who had become disenchanted with liberalism during the 1960s. The neocons proved distressed by, as they saw it, the overselling of liberal promises through pronouncement of a War on Poverty, the seeking of a Great Society, and the waging of a war of containment in Vietnam. Their discontentment only intensified in the 1970s over such issues as affirmative action, school busing, and détente with the Soviet Union and China. Influenced by the neocons and religious fundamentalists, Reagan drove American conservatism in new directions by melding populism, religiosity, patriotism, and belief in the sacrosanct nature of free enterprise.

Shortly after his inauguration, Reagan became the target of an assassination attempt that left him wounded but seemingly unflustered, as when he told his wife at the hospital, "Honey, I forgot to duck." The near-fatal shot served as one of the early defining moments of Reagan's presidency. His good humor following the shooting that had planted a bullet a mere inch from his heart served Reagan well in the political arena, where he pushed for passage of the Economic Recovery Act. That measure, which cut tax rates across the board, thereby particularly benefiting wealthy Americans and corporations, sailed to easy passage. It demonstrated belief in the supply-side economics supported by the editorial staff of the *Wall Street Journal* and Arthur Laffer from the University of Southern California. Altogether, Reagan's economic policies led to a diminishing of inflation and interest rates but produced record deficits and a massive increase in the national debt. Reaganomics, as the administration's economic approach came to be known, also demanded curtailed social programs. Funding for the Environmental Protection Agency was cut, while public lands in the western United States were opened for private exploration for oil and gas drilling. Regulatory agencies, ranging from the Occupational Safety and Health Administration to the antitrust division of the Department of Justice, lightened their operations. The deregulation of the thrift industry set the stage for massive scandals involving savings and loan institutions, eventually costing taxpayers hundreds of billions of dollars. Another major scandal swirled about the Department of Housing and Urban Development with political appointees allowing contracts to be allocated to Republican supporters of the president. While appointing Sandra Day O'Connor to the U.S. Supreme Court, the first woman to be so honored, Reagan packed the federal judiciary with highly conservative judges, who appeared determined to abridge the more protective rulings afforded criminal defendants, political dissidents, and social pariahs by the Warren Court.

At the same time, Reagan, along with Secretary of Defense Caspar Weinberger, insisted on massive increases for the defense budget. The Reagan administration intensified Cold War rhetoric, with the president denouncing the Soviet Union as "the Evil Empire . . . the focus of evil in the modern world" and demanding a nuclear buildup, insisting on the acquiring of "peace through strength." Reagan backed the Strategic Defense Initiative (SDI), which involved the establishment of a space-based defense system critics decried as "Star Wars," impossible to attain, and certain to reignite the arms race. The supporters of SDI insisted it would work and, equally important, ensure the economic collapse of a struggling Soviet Union as it sought to keep up with its great rival. A controversy brewed following Reagan's flippant declaration to the American people, presented in the midst of a radio microphone test: "I'm pleased to tell you today that I've signed legislation that will outlaw Russia forever. We begin bombing in five minutes." Controversial too was Reagan's championing of so-called Freedom Fighters battling against left-wing forces around the globe; the president again blamed the Soviets for "all the unrest that is going on. If they weren't engaged in this game of dominoes, there wouldn't be any hot spots in the world." The administration provided arms and money to Jonas Savimbi's rebel fighters in Angola, the anti-Soviet mujahadeen in Afghanistan, and the Contras in Nicaragua, all controversial elements in their own right. The CIA funneled weapons, including antiaircraft missiles, and economic assistance to the mujahadeen. The United States opted to send 1,600 marines to Beirut as part of a multinational peacekeeping contingent and to help evacuate members of the Palestinian Liberation Front, but Reagan removed the troops shortly after a massive bombing by Islamic militants left 241 marines dead. The United States provided considerable assistance, including chemical and biological materials, to Iraqi president Saddam Hussein, who was warring with Iran, led by Ayatollah Khomeini. The Reagan administration operated under the assumption that the Iraqi strongman could hold back the tide of Islamic fundamentalism in the Middle East. U.S. policymakers under Reagan also moved to quash revolutionary movements in Central America and the Caribbean, supporting efforts to overthrow the leftist Sandinista regime in Nicaragua, prevent a guerrilla takeover in El Salvador, and oust radical Marxist forces in Grenada. At times this aligned the United States with both democratic and repressive elements as when Reagan's top aides provided military and economic assistance to the Nicaraguan Contras, along with figures ranging from El Salvador's president Jose Napoleon Duarte, once tortured by a right-wing government, to Roberto D'Aubuisson, believed to be the leader of the death squads given to assassinating liberal and radical opponents in El Salvador.

Reagan stood at the height of his popularity as his first term approached its end. Media coverage of the president tended to be highly favorable, with frequent reports of his jaunts to his Rancho del Cielo, situated in the mountains outside Santa Barbara. As Reagan noted, on their ranch he and his wife were able to "put on our boots and old clothes, recharge our batteries, and be reminded of where we had come from." Running on a reelection campaign heralding that it was "morning again in America," Reagan and George H. W. Bush swept to a landslide victory over the Democratic team of former Vice President Walter Mondale and New York congresswoman Geraldine Ferraro. Reagan characteristically responded deftly to the issue of his advancing age, in the midst of a debate with Mondale, declaring, to much laughter, "I will not make age an issue of this campaign. I am not going to exploit, for political purposes, my opponent's youth and inexperience."

Strongly encouraged by his wife Nancy, Reagan began holding summit meetings with Mikhail Gorbachev, the new Soviet premier, which, to the astonishment of many, resulted in promises to discard land-based intermediate and short-range nuclear weapons. Reagan had earlier implored Gorbachev to "tear down this wall," referring to the physical barricade that had divided Berlin since 1961. Notwithstanding movement toward a new era of détente, Reagan's last two years in the Oval Office proved difficult. The Democrats regained control of Congress following the 1986 congressional elections. Wall Street underwent financial readjustments after a boom period during the first half of the decade, and the Reagan Revolution appeared to be ending.

Worse yet, the Iran-Contra scandal presented the possibility that Reagan, like Nixon earlier, might face impeachment proceedings. Congressional hearings revealed that the administration had supported a triangular trade involving the Contras, Iranian arms dealers, and U.S. government officials like National Security Advisor John Poindexter and Colonel Oliver North, backed by CIA director William Casey, often in the face of legislative prohibitions against such activities. However, with many in the nation's capital, including leading Democrats, desirous of sparing the nation another Watergate-like scenario, the Iran-Contra affair faded but left Reagan in a much weaker position for the remainder of his final term in office. In addition, scores of administration officials were convicted of charges pertaining to bribery, corruption, and influence peddling, while many others were compelled to resign because of accusations of such behavior. Reagan, however, remained seemingly immune to the scandals that broke out, compelling Colorado Congresswoman Patricia Schroeder to deem him the "Teflon President." Reagan retained the affection of many Americans, conservative activists foremost among them, until his presidency came to an end. During his farewell address to the nation, Reagan proudly stated, "We've done our part" in carving out "the Reagan Revolution."

Unquestionably Reagan helped to redirect the nation's political orientation and the Republican Party rightward. He emphasized the need to reduce the welfare state, taxes, and regulatory controls. He gave only lip service to the agenda of the Moral Majority regarding abortion and family values, leading Howard Phillips to declare that "the evangelicals were taken to the cleaners." Reagan championed missile defense systems and a hard-line approach to leftist guerrillas and governments, along with a firm anticommunist policy toward the Soviet Union. He also helped to reinstill a sense of pride in America and to cast aside the angst the country endured during much of the 1970s, although that in turn arguably encouraged big power hubris. And while his economic program seemed to dampen inflation and high interest rates, it left behind a debt-laden legacy that would afflict future generations of Americans.

Perhaps already suffering from the Alzheimer's disease that would continue to cripple him, Reagan headed back to California, where he worked on his latest autobiography and readied for the opening of the Ronald Reagan Presidential Library in Simi Valley. He penned an open letter in November 1994 in which he revealed that Alzheimer's was afflicting him. He concluded by acknowledging he was now heading "into the sunset of [his] life," but he knew "that for America there will always be a brighter day ahead." Reagan suffered a debilitating fall in January 2001 that destroyed part of his hip and largely immobilized him. On June 5, 2004, he died of pneumonia at his home in Bel Air. A full presidential state funeral took place four days later, with a service offered at the National Cathedral on June 11, which was attended by many dignitaries, including former British prime minister and longtime ally Margaret Thatcher, Gorbachev, and President George W. Bush. Reagan was buried following a private ceremony involving some 600 individuals, at the Presidential Library in Southern California.

Conclusion

By the early 1980s, William F. Buckley, perhaps the nation's leading right-of-center intellectual, and President Ronald Reagan helped to cement conservative dominance over the nation's political discourse. Buckley helped to keep the conservative flame alive in the 1950s and early 1960s as the McCarthyite phase of the postwar Red Scare waned. He began publication of *The National Review*, which became a highly regarded forum for conservative perspectives, and served as a midwife to the New Right that came to so revere Reagan. When a backlash against supposed liberal excesses occurred amid racial conflagrations in American cities and a stalemated war in Vietnam, Buckley provided intellectual ammunition for politicians ranging from Barry Goldwater to George Wallace and Ronald Reagan. The amiable former actor proved to be the greatest beneficiary of the nation's apparently altered mood, while relying on many of the ideas that Goldwater had offered during his own presidential campaign in 1964. Like Buckley earlier, Goldwater and Reagan called for a restoration of American strength, even supremacy, in the Cold War fight against communist foes, headed by the Soviet Union, which Reagan denounced as "the evil empire." Buckley and Reagan agreed on the need for an aggressive U.S. foreign policy, which included support for forces seeking to oust left-wing and communist regimes or attempting to prevent leftist guerrillas from taking power. The two men also believed that the American welfare state should be curbed, fetters on business operatives reduced, and tax rates lessened, especially for the wealthy and corporations. They were seemingly of one mind about the necessity of rekindling long-held American mores, as they blasted promiscuity, abortion, and a breakdown in law and order. While in office, however, and to the disappointment of many of the most ardent conservatives, Reagan did not push hard for legislation regarding social issues, including constitutional amendments restoring prayer in public schools and prohibiting the burning of the American flag. The personable Reagan still remained the most iconic of all American political figures for most conservatives, while Buckley's reputation among his fellow intellectuals, whether stationed on the right or the left, appeared to ascend during his final years.

Study Questions

1. Explain how William Buckley helped to spark American conservative thought in the 1950s and 1960s.
2. Analyze the roles William Buckley played in creating an organizational framework for American conservatives in the postwar period.
3. Discuss Ronald Reagan's emergence as a significant new figure in American conservatism in the 1950s and 1960s.
4. Explain the ways in which the presidency of Ronald Reagan altered the American political landscape.
5. Analyze how William Buckley and Ronald Reagan were among the two most important figures in the American conservative movement in the postwar period.

Selected Bibliography

Andrew, John A., III. *The Other Side of the Sixties: Young Americans for Freedom and the Rise of Contemporary Conservatism.* Piscataway, NJ: Rutgers University Press, 1997.

Bell, Daniel. *The Radical Right.* Garden City, NY: Doubleday Anchor, 1964.

Brennan, Mary C. *Turning Right in the Sixties: The Conservative Capture of the GOP*. Chapel Hill: University of North Carolina Press, 1997.

Bridges, Linda, and John R. Coyne Jr. *Strictly Right: William F. Buckley Jr. and the American Conservative Movement*. New York: Wiley, 2007.

Buckley, William F. *Cancel Your Own Goddam Subscription: Notes and Asides from National Review*. New York: Basic Books, 2007.

———. *God and Man at Yale: The Superstitions of Academic Freedom*. Washington, DC: Regnery, 1986.

———. *Happy Days Were Here Again: Reflections of a Libertarian Journalist*. New York: Random House, 1993.

———. *Let Us Talk of Many Things: The Collected Speeches*. New York: Basic Books, 2001.

———. *The Unmaking of a Mayor*. New York: Bantam, 1967.

———. *Up from Liberalism*. New York: Bantam, 1969.

Buckley, William F., with L. Brent Bozell. *McCarthy and His Enemies*. Chicago: Regnery, 1954.

Cannon, Lou. *Governor Reagan: His Rise to Power*. New York: Public Affairs, 2003.

———. *President Reagan: The Role of a Lifetime*. New York: Simon and Schuster, 1991.

Crawford, Alan. *Thunder on the Right: The "New Right" and the Politics of Resentment*. New York: Pantheon, 1980.

Dallek, Matthew. *The Right Moment: Ronald Reagan's First Victory and the Decisive Turning in American Politics*. New York: Free Press, 2000.

Diamond, Sara. *Spiritual Warfare: The Politics of the Christian Right*. New York: Guilford Press, 1989.

Diggins, John. *Ronald Reagan: Fate, Freedom and the Making of History*. New York: W.W. Norton, 2007.

———. *Up from Communism: Conservative Odysseys in American Intellectual Development*. New York: Columbia University Press, 1993.

Forster, Arnold, and Benjamin R. Epstein. *Danger on the Right: The Attitudes, Personnel and Influence of the Radical Right and Extreme Conservatives*. New York: Random House, 1964.

Harding, Susan Friend. *The Book of Jerry Falwell: Fundamentalist Language and Politics*. Princeton, NJ: Princeton University Press, 2000.

Hodgson, Godfrey. *The World Turned Right Side Up: A History of the Conservative Ascendancy in America*. New York: Houghton Mifflin, 1996.

Markmann, Charles Lam. *The Buckleys: A Family Expanded*. New York: William Morrow, 1973.

Martin, William. *With God on Our Side: The Rise of the Religious Right in America*. New York: Broadway Books, 1996.

Nash, George H. *The Conservative Intellectual Movement in America: Since 1945*. New York: Basic Books, 1976.

Reagan, Ronald. *An American Life*. New York: Simon and Schuster, 1990.

Reagan, Ronald, with Richard G. Hubler. *Where's the Rest of Me? The Autobiography of Ronald Reagan*. New York: Dell, 1981.

Schaller, Michael. *Reckoning with Reagan: America and Its President in the 1980s*. New York: Oxford University Press, 1994.

Schneider, Gregory L. *Cadres for Conservatism: Young Americans for Freedom and the Rise of the Contemporary Right*. New York: New York University Press, 1998.

———, ed. *Conservatism in America since 1930*. New York: New York University Press, 2003.

Schoenwald, Jonathan M. *A Time for Choosing: The Rise of Modern American Conservatism*. New York: Oxford University Press, 2001.

Steinfels, Peter. *Neo-Conservatives: The Men Who Are Changing American Politics*. New York: Simon and Schuster, 1979.

Viereck, Peter. Review of *God and Man at Yale*. *New York Times Book Review*, November 4, 1951.

Wills, Garry. *Reagan's America: Innocents at Home*. New York: Penguin, 2000.

~

CHAPTER THIRTEEN

Uncharted Territory

America in the Twenty-first Century

In his impressionistic history of the 1990s, *The Best of Times: America in the Clinton Years*, journalist Haynes Johnson predicted that Americans would look back wistfully at the last decade of the twentieth century. Though he found the decade's public discourse sadly distorted by sensationalistic media, Johnson noted that the nation enjoyed peace and prosperity, the latter propelled in large part by new information technologies. Notwithstanding the warnings of many computer experts, the much-anticipated Y2K problem involving massive worldwide software malfunctions failed to materialize as the new millennium arrived. Instead 2000 brought unexpected political developments that signaled an uncertain course for the nation as Americans confronted the first disputed presidential election since 1876. The outcome of the electoral battle between Democratic candidate Vice President Al Gore, and his Republican rival, Texas Governor George W. Bush confirmed public opinion polls that had shown the electorate evenly split between the two men. Though Gore received over 500,000 popular votes more than Bush, the ultimate outcome hinged on hotly contested tallies in Florida; the winner in that state would gain the electoral votes necessary for victory. On December 11, following weeks of uncertainty, the U.S. Supreme Court issued the decision affirming Bush's victory in the Sunshine State.

Despite the contentious circumstances of his victory, Bush demonstrated shortly following his inauguration that he had no intention of pursuing a moderate course. Working with a compliant Republican Congress and greatly influenced by Vice President Richard Cheney, Bush moved quickly to steer major domestic policies to the right. Bush's ideologically rigid conservatism ensured that important constituencies would firmly embrace his presidency, yet all but precluded the realization of his campaign promise of being "a uniter, not a divider." The horrific events of September 11, 2001, introduced new dynamics that radically transformed his presidency and fundamentally changed the direction of the nation. Following terrorist attacks on targets in New York City and Washington, DC, Bush immediately adopted the mantle of wartime president, and his public steadfastness in the weeks after the attacks brought broad public support. Most Americans backed Bush's decision to attack the radical Taliban regime in Afghanistan, which had provided a safe haven for al-Qaeda terrorists, and as early as October, the president's approval ratings reached 90 percent, approximating those that his father had attained after the Gulf War in 1991.

Support for George W. Bush began to waver, however, after he launched an invasion of Saddam Hussein's Iraq in early 2003. In subsequent months, as the stated reasons for the war against Iraq proved unfounded, and as casualties and violence grew under the American occupation, public support for the war eroded. Popular enthusiasm for Bush's strongly conservative domestic agenda had always been problematic, and the president appeared vulnerable as he sought reelection in 2004. After a bitterly fought campaign in which the distinguished military record of his opponent, John F. Kerry, a thrice-wounded Vietnam War combat veteran, was called into question, Bush won a second term, with an increased but still narrow margin of victory. Bush promised to use the "political capital" he had won to push his agenda forward, including his call to partially privatize Social Security, but a series of disastrous moves sorely undercut his efforts. Those included the Bush administration's failure to respond adequately to Hurricane Katrina when it devastated New Orleans and the Louisiana and Mississippi shorelines in August 2005, the mounting casualty figures in Iraq, and an economy that began sputtering before threatening to career into depression in the final months of 2008. Collapsing banking and commercial institutions, a plummeting stock market, soaring numbers of home mortgage foreclosures, and declining employment combined to create a political atmosphere conducive to substantial change, all coinciding with the final stages of that year's presidential race, which pitted the first African American candidate from a major political party against another Vietnam War hero.

Like many of his countrymen, Barack Obama, the offspring of an American mother and a Kenyan father, felt that "on September 11, 2001, the world fractured." A young but promising member of the Illinois Democratic Party, Obama, then serving as a member of his state's general assembly, did not "pretend to understand the stark nihilism that drove the terrorists that day and that drives their brethren still." Nevertheless, Obama was cognizant of the deeper roots of terrorism: the sense of lost dignity and powerlessness that could easily lead to a violent eruption and the corrosiveness of fundamentalist intolerance.

Perhaps he could do so more easily than many other Americans because of his own multiethnic background and his early years spent outside the continental United States, coupled with his drive and ambition to participate in the American dream of equality of opportunity. Indeed, Obama uniquely represented an increasingly ethnically diverse nation, which in the face of unprecedented challenges had to select the best means for maintaining American ideals and traditions while embracing the greater diversity that more and more characterized the nation.

Obama, in the midst of what proved to be a successful campaign for a seat in the U.S. Senate, first gained national attention when he addressed the Democratic National Convention in July 2004. There he offered a withering criticism of George Bush's America, stressing the social and economic inequities that had grown more pronounced during the previous four years. In contrast, he presented a vision of the more equitable, progressive society that Democratic leadership could provide. The differences he described were stark, reflecting the widening ideological divide between the two parties, but the outcome of that year's presidential election revealed much about the Democrats' dilemma. With close to half of the nation voicing serious doubts about the Bush presidency, Democratic candidate Senator John F. Kerry was unable to transform those concerns into electoral victory. President Bush, grounding his campaign on the argument that the terrorist threat could be effectively met only through his policies, was returned to the White House for another four years. His electoral triumph, however, soon proved hollow. During his second term public disenchantment with Bush administration policies grew rapidly and by 2007 it had reached such a level that much of the electorate indicated its receptiveness to a transformative change in national leadership and direction. This widened the parameters of the 2008 presidential election to the extent that former first lady and New York Democratic Senator Hillary Clinton appeared in early 2007 to have an excellent chance of gaining her party's nomination. More surprising, late in the same year, it became increasingly evident that the desire for substantial change was deep and broad enough to support a presidential bid by the young biracial senator from Illinois. By June 2008, Obama, demonstrating surprising electoral strengths, became his party's presumptive nominee, and then faced Republican Senator John McCain in the November election. Both candidates promised change, but Obama's steady performance during the election season, McCain's inability to focus on a single issue that resonated with the American public, and the evident widespread desire to move beyond the Bush era produced a decisive victory for the Democratic candidate, and set the stage for a possible political realignment of historic proportions.

During the early stages of his presidency, Obama had to contend with a welter of issues ranging from the American economy, mired in its deepest recession in over a quarter century, to the soaring cost of health care, which left over 40 million without insurance coverage; plummeting real estate values, stock portfolios, and pension funds; and international crises involving North Korea, Iran, Pakistan, Afghanistan, and other states.

～ GEORGE W. BUSH ～

It was arguably the most dramatic and compelling moment of the relatively new presidency of George W. Bush. On September 14, 2001, with the nation still reeling from the shock of incomprehensible acts of terrorism three days earlier, President Bush arrived in New York City, where he visited the rescue workers who were frantically combing through the still-smoldering wreckage of the World Trade Center. Attempting to address the workers with a bullhorn, Bush was interrupted by shouts of "We can't hear you!" "I can hear you," the president responded forcefully. "The rest of the world hears you, and the people who knocked these buildings down will hear all of us soon!" It was the reassurance that the American public desperately desired, evidence that their president was a man of determination and fortitude who could see the nation safely through an unprecedented disaster. In subsequent days, Bush presented Congress with a rationale for war against the Taliban regime in Afghanistan, and later made his nation's case before the United Nations General Assembly.

George W. Bush takes the presidential oath of office in January 2001 in the aftermath of a hotly disputed election in which his Democratic opponent, Vice President Al Gore (right), won the popular vote but lost the electoral vote. Despite the absence of a popular mandate, Bush governed from the right, pursuing a conservative social agenda. His decision to go to war against Iraq in March 2003 proved highly controversial, seriously undermining his presidency during his second term. (Library of Congress, LC-USZC4-12923)

The attacks on 9/11 altered the contours of the American political land-scape. The Bush presidency began under the lingering cloud of the disputed 2000 election, leaving him without a popular mandate. Many of his con-servative initiatives drew considerable criticism, and his presidency seemed directionless through the late summer of 2001. The events of that terrible September day, however, recast the American political universe, leading to a radical departure in foreign policy and the implementation of an aggressively conservative domestic agenda. For better or worse, the unique circumstances of post-9/11 America provided George W. Bush and conservative ideologues tied to the Republican Party with an unparalleled opportunity to set the nation on a new, controversial course.

Born in New Haven, Connecticut, in July 1946, George W. Bush was one of the earliest members of the baby boom generation and the first of six children born to George Herbert Walker and Barbara Bush. A product of the genteel East Coast establishment, G. H. W. Bush moved his family to Odessa, Texas, in 1948 to pursue a management career with Dresser Industries, an oil field services company. Aspiring to continue the family legacy of public service, Bush ran for a U.S. Senate seat in 1964 but discovered his northeastern roots to be a disadvantage in Texas. Consequently, Bush's political fortunes were delayed until 1966, when he won a congressional seat. G. H. W. Bush later served as CIA director and Republican Party national chairman, but his hopes for significant elective office were not realized until 1981 when he became vice president. Young George, having grown up in Odessa, Midland, and Houston, could lay more authentic claim to populist Texas roots. He soon followed an educational path that took him to two of his father's alma maters, Phillips Andover Academy and Yale University. Evidently oblivious to the political storms sweeping through New Haven and the rest of the nation, Bush gradu-ated in 1968 with an undergraduate degree in history. He gained a prized spot in the Texas Air National Guard, training as fighter pilot. Even before he was officially discharged from the Air Force Reserve, Bush headed east to attend Harvard Business School, emerging in 1975 with a master's degree. He began what he described as his "nomadic period," years characterized by indirection and indulgence in alcohol and, some sources allege, drugs. He gained some needed stability in 1977 when he married Laura Welch, a librarian, and the couple was soon raising twin daughters.

Any early political ambitions were delayed in 1978 when Bush lost a race for a U.S. House seat. Delving into the business world, Bush capitalized on his fam-ily name to gather financial backing for a succession of energy companies, none of which fared especially well. In 1989, Bush organized a group of investors to buy the Texas Rangers baseball team. Five years later Bush challenged popular Democrat Ann Richards for the Texas governorship. Focusing on a few main themes and ignoring Richards's personal jibes, Bush won rather easily. The popular young governor supported legislation for local control of education, welfare reform, harsher penalties for juvenile offenders, and limits on litigation against businesses. Texans voted overwhelmingly in 1998 to reelect the genial governor. Republican Party operatives, noting Bush's popularity even among Texas Democrats and his reputation for moral uprightness, concluded that Bush might do well as a national candidate. Party elders soon traveled to Austin to urge that he run for the presidency and to provide advice on both domestic and international affairs.

Governor of a populous and economically powerful state, Bush was well positioned for the 2000 Republican primaries. A professed born-again Christian since 1985, Bush stressed the primacy of religious faith in his life, winning the support of many socially conservative evangelical Christians. Encountering few serious obstacles, Bush easily won the Republican nomination and named former defense secretary Dick Cheney as his running mate. In the months preceding the election, neither Bush nor his opponent, Vice President Al Gore, was able to galvanize a decisive majority of potential voters. Both were ambiguous as to what their presidency might bring, as Gore promised a continuation of moderately progressive Democratic policies, while Bush proclaimed himself a "compassionate conservative." Polls showed the race tight on election eve—just how tight became evident when the votes were counted. Only after five harrowing weeks of uncertainty, culminating with a 5-4 Supreme Court decision to end the Florida vote count, was it determined that George W. Bush had won that state by the narrowest of margins, which gave Bush a five-vote majority in the Electoral College.

George W. Bush's path to the White House may have been uncertain, but the new president was determined to implement a thoroughly conservative agenda. His foremost domestic priority, an "economic stimulus" package featuring a $1.35 trillion tax cut over eleven years, generated little public enthusiasm, and political opponents challenged it as a payoff to wealthy Republican contributors. Nevertheless, the Republican-dominated Congress complied, passing legislation that reduced taxes for married couples, the estate tax, and marginal rates. Bush's advocacy of government funding for "faith-based initiatives" proved controversial, with critics charging that it violated the Establishment Clause of the First Amendment. Likewise, the Bush administration's proposals for a national energy policy, derived from a secretive task force headed by Vice President Cheney, drew fire from environmentalists alarmed at the administration's readiness to accommodate energy industries. In subsequent months, the Bush administration weakened the enforcement capabilities of the Environmental Protection Agency, introducing reductions of air and water quality standards and justifying the new laxity as part of a "market-driven" and "voluntary" approach to environmental protection.

Long before the events of 9/11, it became evident that Bush intended a radical departure from the internationalist traditions that had long guided U.S. foreign policy. Early in his first term, Bush announced his opposition to the Kyoto Protocol, which established international cooperation to understand and offset the effects of global warming. Bush argued that the proposed treaty was ineffective and would damage the U.S. economy, which he proclaimed as having priority over the global environment. The Bush White House also refused U.S. participation in an international convention banning germ warfare and a treaty to establish an international war crimes court. In late 2001, the Bush administration withdrew from the 1972 Antiballistic Missile Treaty, denouncing it as an irrelevant relic of the Cold War, while advocating the development of a costly, high-tech antimissile defense system. The ideological underpinnings of this new unilateralism could be traced back to the late 1970s, when neoconservatives and "sovereigntist" theorists began to challenge reliance on international institutions, asserting that the United States should reject any international agreement encroaching on its sovereignty. Numerous influential figures in the Bush administration endorsed these perspectives. Bush advanced his controversial agenda in the face of significant criticism because he believed in the conservative principles that underlay his initiatives, and because he understood that the public respected effective and consistent leadership, even if it did not always agree with the specific policies. Contemporary polls affirmed that the public credited Bush with strong leadership capabilities and a fundamental trustworthiness. Many of Bush's critics, however, perceived his vaunted determination and steadfastness as obtuseness and lack of introspection.

Presidential greatness is almost always born out of crisis, and the events of September 11 afforded Bush the opportunity to redefine himself. In the weeks after the disaster he did so, reassuring a shaken nation with his calm demeanor, clear determination, and ease with the role of commander in chief. Once intelligence sources determined that the attackers were part of the al-Qaeda terrorist network in Afghanistan, Bush moved quickly to organize a military response. Bolstered by overwhelming international support, the Bush administration launched air attacks and an invasion of the central Asian nation in early October, successfully routing the Taliban within two months. Though al-Qaeda mastermind Osama bin Laden eluded U.S. forces, the expulsion of the oppressive Taliban regime affirmed the president's resolution.

The new primacy of foreign policy also increased the influence of an elite circle of presidential advisers referred to collectively as the Vulcans. In 1999 Bush had assembled a group of eight Republican advisers with expertise in international affairs. After Bush's election, the best-known among them, including Condoleezza Rice (the group took its name from the Vulcan statue in her native Birmingham, Alabama), Paul Wolfowitz, Richard Armitage, and Richard Perle, together with Vice President Dick Cheney and Defense Secretary Donald Rumsfeld, formulated the policies that comprised what scholars have called Bush's "revolution in American foreign policy." This "hegemonist" perspective, which gained influence in the early 1990s, holds that American predominance in the world is required to secure critical national interests. This view surfaced in a 1992 Pentagon study, commissioned by Cheney and Wolfowitz, which asserted that in the post–Cold War era, the United States should strive to preclude "the emergence of any potential future global competitor." Much of the hegemonists' concern focused on ensuring a continuing supply of energy for the United States, and as early as 2000, Cheney and aide Lewis "Scooter" Libby helped draft a report for the neoconservative Project for a New American Century calling for a takeover of oil-rich Iraq as part of a broader Pax Americana. Bush came to the presidency with little in the way of theoretically based foreign policy assumptions, but the Vulcans' worldview corresponded with his belief that national security demanded military strength and international leadership. Bush proved receptive to the arguments of the "democratic imperialists" like Wolfowitz, who maintained that U.S. national security could be ensured only in a world modeled on the democratic image of the United States.

The transformation of American life in the post-9/11 world proved evident by 2002. Anthrax attacks, shoe bombers, and police-state levels of heightened security at airports and public buildings all fueled continuing anxiety. On October 26 Bush signed the Patriot Act, a sweeping measure authorizing law enforcement agencies to employ wiretaps, detention, and other strong measures to disrupt and thwart terrorism. Against Bush's initial opposition, a new Department of Homeland Security was organized during the fall of 2002, charged with coordinating domestic security activities. Praised for his conduct of the war on terror, Bush succeeded in buttressing Republican margins in Congress in the fall elections. The most startling change, however, took shape in the nation's foreign policy. In his January State of the Union address, Bush foreshadowed the emerging doctrine of preemption, warning that he would not "wait on events" as rogue nations acquired "the world's most dangerous weapons." The president also identified Saddam Hussein's Iraq as part of an "axis of evil" that included Iran and North Korea. Bush repeatedly argued during the next several months that dictators who marshaled weapons of mass destruction (WMDs) and abetted terrorism posed the primary threat to international peace. By September, the doctrine of preemption was clearly articulated in the administration's National Security Strategy, which posited: "Given the goals of rogue states and terrorists, the United States can no longer solely rely on a reactive posture. . . . We cannot let our enemies strike first."

The administration's determination to give priority to toppling Saddam Hussein was unmistakable as of 2002. The rationale for an invasion of Iraq was essentially fourfold. First, many top administration officials, notably Cheney and Wolfowitz, had long advocated ousting the Iraqi dictator and, after 9/11, Bush was receptive to their arguments. Second, Bush and others in the White House believed that the Iraqi strongman was connected to the events of September 11 despite the absence of any significant evidence. Only days after the attacks, Bush told his advisers, "I believe Iraq was involved," and on September 17 he ordered the Pentagon to draw up options for an invasion of Iraq. A third presumption driving the administration's march to war was the belief that Saddam could be easily ousted, given his diminished military capabilities. Finally, it was believed that the removal of Saddam's Baathist regime would permit the implementation of a grand design to establish democratic governments in the Middle East.

Seeking to win international support for the anti-Saddam effort, Bush spoke before the UN General Assembly in September, asserting that the UN faced "a difficult and defining moment" and challenging it to rise to the task. The UN Security Council passed Resolution 1441 in early November, warning of "serious consequences" if Saddam failed to comply with a new inspection regime. Rice, Cheney, and other administration spokespersons regularly underscored the imminent danger that Saddam's regime presented and repeatedly implied that Saddam had some role in 9/11. By early 2003, as American forces gathered in Middle Eastern staging areas, it was evident that the Bush administration intended to proceed with or without UN support or any substantial international military coalition. Secretary of State Colin Powell, who had been skeptical of the Vulcans' views, nevertheless went before the UN Security Council in February to present dire intelligence findings about Iraq's nuclear, chemical, and biological weapons capabilities. By March 2003 the rationale for the war tilted toward the grandiose vision that Bush outlined in a speech at the American Enterprise Institute, a conservative think tank, where he told the audience, "A new regime in Iraq would serve as a dramatic and inspiring example of freedom for other nations in the region." The United States, with the support of Britain and a small "coalition of the willing," went to war against Iraq on March 19.

The defeat of Saddam Hussein's forces required only a brief campaign as the dictator's army offered little effective resistance and seemed to melt away into the civilian population as American forces drove toward Baghdad, capturing the Iraqi capital on April 9. Bush landed on the flight deck of the USS *Abraham Lincoln* in a Navy jet just off the California coast on May 1 and mounted a podium positioned in front of a large banner announcing "Mission Accomplished," where he declared an end to major military operations in Iraq. It proved to be an ill-founded assessment. Though there had been only 138 U.S. deaths in the war prior to May 1, it quickly became evident that the overthrow of Saddam Hussein was the only aspect of the administration's professed designs for Iraq that would be decisively accomplished. There had been little prewar planning for the occupation of Iraq, with most contingencies based on vague, optimistic scenarios offered by Vulcans like Wolfowitz. While most Iraqis seemed gladdened by Saddam's ouster, U.S. occupation forces were not universally greeted with open arms as Wolfowitz had predicted. In the immediate aftermath of Baghdad's fall, the city was swept by days of anarchy as looting, arson, and vandalism rendered much of the metropolitan area's infrastructure unusable. Wolfowitz's assurance that Iraqi oil revenues could be used to fund the occupation proved false. It was soon apparent that American taxpayers would themselves bear the burden. The Defense Department's awarding of no-bid reconstruction and support contracts to companies with close administration ties such as Halliburton, Bechtel, and Kellogg, Brown and Root provoked additional controversy.

More troubling, a broadening insurgency, undertaken by Baathist diehards, disaffected Sunnis, rival sectarian militias, and foreign Islamic radicals, began taking shape during the summer of 2003 and vastly expanded in subsequent months, wreaking havoc on beleaguered Iraqis and inflicting mounting casualties on coalition forces. Administration spokespersons, notably Rumsfeld, having initially denied the existence of an insurgency, later persistently downplayed its extent and effect, an assessment greatly at odds with what Americans could see on the nightly news. U.S. forces finally captured Saddam Hussein in December 2003, but that achievement and his subsequent execution at the order of an Iraqi court seemed to have little effect on events in Iraq. Though the Bush administration adhered to its schedule for the creation of a new Iraqi government, periodic announcements of milestones such as the restoration of Iraqi sovereignty in June 2004 were overshadowed by intense fighting and by the grisly death toll taken by car bombs and improvised explosive devices. Bush nevertheless insisted that the Iraq war was central to winning the war against terrorism and reiterated that U.S. forces would remain "until the job was done." It was an objective that some critics saw as perilously dependent on variables beyond American control: the ability of Iraqis to overcome historical tribal and religious antagonisms, their willingness to adopt habits of mind and practices crucial to a functioning democracy, the capacity of Iraqi security forces to effectively combat the insurgency, and Iranian and Syrian intrigues. The likelihood of favorable outcomes in all of those areas was slim, many military and intelligence experts warned.

Though public opinion reflected majority support for the Iraq war in its early months, serious doubts became evident on the first anniversary of the invasion. Comparisons with the Vietnam War and talk of a new quagmire crept more frequently into the national discourse. Rising U.S. casualties, daily carnage in the streets of Iraqi cities, and allegations of criminally abusive treatment of incarcerated suspects at Abu Ghraib prison in May 2004 all fueled public unease. Several independent policy analysts warned that the American invasion of Iraq, rather than lessening the threat of terrorism, had created a new and unpredictable theater of operations for an unknown number of foreign *jihadis* (radical Islamicist fighters) who entered the country across porous borders. Most of the administration's justifications for the invasion unraveled when a bipartisan Senate Intelligence Committee investigation concluded that CIA intelligence summaries the White House had cited in support of the war were almost universally in error or exaggerated. Contrary to CIA analyses, the Intelligence Committee found, Iraq was not rebuilding its nuclear program, had no chemical or biological weapons, and had "no collaborative relationship" with al-Qaeda. As numerous critics charged the administration with cherry-picking only those intelligence findings that served its purposes, and as administration officials claimed that they had acted in good faith on what turned out to be bad intelligence, the White House turned to emphasizing the importance of removing Saddam from power, arguing that Americans were now safer with the dictator deposed. A year and a half after the war began, it was officially announced that the search for Iraqi WMDs had uncovered no such weapons and that none had likely existed since the early 1990s. U.S. forces halted the search in late 2004.

George W. Bush appeared politically vulnerable as he kicked off his campaign for reelection in 2004. Though Republican support for the president remained high, intense disapproval among Democrats and some independents threatened to offset it. Every setback and misstep in Iraq continued to draw heavy fire from Democratic spokespersons. The president's domestic policies also provoked condemnation from political opponents, who charged Bush with favoring corporate interests over the public in every policy area, including the environment, taxes, and energy. Democrats pointed to the nation's ballooning deficit, which reached a record $413 billion in 2004, arguing that the president's tax cuts and refusal to reduce spending imperiled the nation's economic foundations. Other critics focused on Bush's conservative social agenda, warning that in his readiness to placate the Christian Right, the president would restrict reproductive rights and lower the church-state barrier. When Massachusetts Senator John F. Kerry won the Democratic nomination in July, he took the lead in pounding Bush on these issues. The Bush campaign, guided by political strategist Karl Rove, focused on the president's supposedly superior ability to wage the war on terror, the necessity of establishing a democratic Iraq, and key social issues attractive to the party's conservative base, such as opposition to abortion rights and gay marriage.

Stressing the need for proven, strong leadership and the ambiguous theme of "values," Bush confronted Kerry in one of the most bitterly fought presidential campaigns in U.S. history. Partisans on both sides enlisted political action groups to fund Internet websites and extensive media campaigns dedicated to lambasting the opposition. Kerry, a much-decorated Vietnam combat veteran, was mercilessly attacked by the Republican-backed Swift Boat Veterans for Truth, which challenged the senator's combat record and proclaimed that his decorations were undeserved. Simultaneously, liberal organizations challenged the president's service, or lack thereof, in the Texas Air National Guard. Activist filmmaker Michael Moore produced an acidic quasi-documentary, *Fahrenheit 911*, which pilloried Bush for his ties to the oil industry and the Saudi royal family and for launching an ill-conceived war in Iraq. The 2004 presidential campaign allowed little room for moderation, and the down-to-the-wire finish in November, when Bush won with a 3-million-vote popular majority, reaffirmed the level of political polarization in the nation.

Bush was inaugurated for a second time in January 2005 with historically low approval ratings for a second-term president, and these declined steadily as the months advanced. Though a strengthened Republican majority in Congress afforded Bush the ability to advance his conservative agenda, public support for much of it was lacking. His top priority, the reform of the Social Security system, including the partial privatization of individual accounts, generated little public enthusiasm. Though Bush pushed a long-delayed energy bill through Congress, critics charged that it ignored any significant conservation measures in favor of incentives to increase energy production, primarily through large tax breaks for energy industries. The administration's war on terror, the one policy area in which Bush had consistently gained his highest approval ratings, now produced only problematic results. Though a democratically elected government had assumed power in Afghanistan, both Taliban and al-Qaeda fighters continued to threaten the stability of parts of the country. Meanwhile, events in Iraq suggested that U.S. objectives remained distant. Though elections for a transitional Iraqi government took place as planned in January 2005, the insurgency continued to grow, shifting away from attacking U.S. troops in favor of unleashing devastating car bomb attacks on Iraqi civilians. The U.S. National Intelligence Council concluded that the war had created "a training and recruitment ground and an opportunity for terrorists to enhance their technical skills." A CNN-Gallup *USA Today* poll in September showed 62 percent of those surveyed agreeing that a partial or total U.S. troop withdrawal should commence immediately. With Osama bin Laden still at large and his whereabouts unknown, the public grew increasingly skeptical of the president's repeated assertions that Iraq remained the central front of the war on terror.

A continuing torrent of controversies beset the Bush White House by the fall of 2005. The fiasco following Hurricane Katrina's destruction of New Orleans, the ill-considered Supreme Court nomination of presidential counsel Harriet Miers, scandals involving several high-ranking Republican officeholders, the perjury indictment of Rove deputy I. Lewis Libby, and a major corruption scandal centered on powerful lobbyist Jack Abramoff combined to create what commentators termed a perfect storm of political troubles for the president. Next, 2006 brought little in the way of better news for the Bush White House. Progress in Iraq remained problematic, and at home there was little to cheer the administration other than the Senate's approval of two conservative Supreme Court justices, Samuel Alito and John Roberts. Less than halfway into a second term, the Bush presidency seemed to have lost the clarity of purpose that it demonstrated in the days following 9/11. Democrats capitalized on broad public disaffection with the Iraq War to regain control of both the House and the Senate in the midterm elections in November 2006.

Though Bush quickly accepted the resignation of unpopular defense secretary Donald Rumsfeld, he defiantly rejected the recommendations of the bipartisan Iraq Study Group and, rather than begin U.S. disengagement, ordered a surge of troops into the country. The objective was a reduction of violence prerequisite to an Iraqi political settlement that would stabilize the country. As of late 2008, the conflict had cost the lives of over 4,200 U.S. troops and was costing $10–12 billion a month. Violence in Iraq had diminished significantly, but there remained no clear answer as to when American forces might be reduced or withdrawn, as the nation's political stability remained problematic. During Bush's final months in office, it became clear that his successor would inherit a conflict that defied easy resolution. Equally if not more troubling, the economy began an uncertain slide toward recession as housing prices collapsed and fuel prices unexpectedly spiked to unprecedented levels. In September, with major financial institutions collapsing, the stock market veered erratically, dropping over 700 points in a record plunge as Congress frantically debated a bailout plan for major financial institutions. As the 2008 presidential election and the end of his second term drew near, George Bush confronted some jarring realities. His approval ratings dipped into the low 20s in some polls, reaching depths previously unplumbed since the presidency of Jimmy Carter. Several historians, disregarding the usual courtesy of awaiting the actual end of a presidency before offering judgment, rushed to proclaim Bush the worst president in U.S. history. That hardly boded well for Republican Party presidential candidate John Mc-Cain, who was compelled to distance himself from his own party's sitting president while simultaneously proclaiming himself the most capable practitioner of conservative principles. His task, already difficult because of the electorate's professed desire for significant change, was made all the more challenging when the Democratic party nominated a candidate who not only built a campaign around the theme of change, but who seemed its very personification.

⌢ BARACK OBAMA ⌢

Tall, lanky, and impeccably attired, State Senator Barack Obama spoke in a clear, resonant voice as he delivered the keynote address at the 2004 Democratic Party nominating convention in Boston, Massachusetts. His speech, emphasizing his own biographical tale, was an oratorical version of the American Dream. Speaking "on behalf of the great state of Illinois, crossroads of a nation, land of Lincoln," Obama acknowledged that his presence on the stage was hardly

Though virtually unknown in 2004 when he addressed the National Democratic Convention, Barack Obama won a U.S. Senate seat that year and quickly positioned himself as a major contender for his party's presidential nomination in 2008. By that year, public disaffection with the Bush administration and Republican governance, coupled with a major economic collapse, contributed to the dynamics that led to Obama's election as the nation's first African American president. Some commentators argued that Obama's election signaled the beginning of a new era in national politics. (Courtesy of www.whitehouse.gov)

something that could have been predicted. His grandfather, Obama revealed, served as a domestic servant in Kenya, while his father grew up in a small village where he herded goats and "went to school in a tin-roof shack." However, his grandfather possessed "larger dreams for his son," helping him "to study in a magical place": the United States. America "stood as a beacon of freedom and opportunity" for his father as it had for so many others. The Kenyan scholarship student traveled to Hawaii, where he met Ann Dunham, a transplanted white Kansan in 1960. The couple married in 1961, and their son was born on August 4, 1961, in Honolulu, Hawaii, where both parents were enrolled at the East-West Center of the University of Hawaii in Manoa. They handed him "an African name, Barack, or 'blessed,' believing that in tolerant America your name is no barrier to success." Obama's parents hoped their son could attend the finest schools, and he did exactly that, graduating from Columbia University in 1983 and from Harvard Law School eight years later. Now speaking to the Democratic Party delegates, Obama continued, "I stand here knowing that my story is part of the larger American story, that I owe a debt to all of those who came before me, and that, in no other country on earth, is my story even possible."

His own life story, Obama suggested, demonstrated his nation's greatest strength more than did its tallest buildings, potent military, or enormous economy. The egalitarian principles articulated in Thomas Jefferson's Declaration of Independence, Obama said, exemplified "the true genius of America, a faith in the simple dreams of its people, the insistence on small miracles," such as the ability of parents to "tuck in our children at night and know they are fed and clothed and safe from harm," the right of Americans to "say what we think, write what we think, without hearing a sudden knock on the door," and the opportunity to realize "an idea and start our own business without paying a bribe or hiring somebody's son." And he underscored the expectation that Americans could "participate in the political process without fear of retribution" and have "our votes . . . counted . . . at least, most of the time." More work remained to be done, Obama acknowledged. He referred to laborers from Galesburg, Illinois, whose union jobs at a Maytag factory were being relocated to Mexico. Now those formerly high-paid workers had "to compete with their own children for jobs that pay seven bucks an hour." Obama spoke of a father, about to lose his job and health benefits, whose son required prescription drugs costing $4,500 a month. The Illinois state legislator understood, as did many Americans, that government could not "solve all their problems." Still they recognized that "with just a change in priorities, we can make sure that every child in America has a decent shot at life, and that the doors of opportunity remain open to all."

Referring to Democratic Party presidential nominee John Kerry, Obama insisted that he too "knows it's not enough for just some of us to prosper." For another part of "the American saga" involves "a belief that we are connected as one people. . . . It's that fundamental belief—I am my brother's keeper, I am my sister's keeper—that makes this country work. It's what allows us to pursue our individual dreams, yet still come together as a single American family. 'E pluribus unum.' Out of many, one." Obama dismissed "those who are preparing to divide us, the spin masters and negative ad peddlers who embrace the politics of anything goes." Eloquently, he exclaimed:

> Well, I say to them tonight—there's not a liberal America and a conservative America—there's the United States of America. There's not a black America and white America and Latino America and Asian America; there's the United States of America. The pundits like to slice-and-dice our country into Red States and Blue States; Red States for Republicans, Blue States for Democrats. But I've got news for them, too. We worship an awesome God in the Blue States, and we don't like federal agents poking around our libraries in the Red States. We coach Little League in the Blue States and have gay friends in the Red States. There are patriots who opposed the war in Iraq and patriots who supported it.

Insisting that Kerry and his running mate, Senator John Edwards, promised a politics of hope, not a politics of cynicism, Obama urged the nation to "reclaim its promise."

His parents were Barack Obama Sr., an economist from Kenya, and S. Ann Dunham, a white woman who resided in Honolulu and was a descendant of Jefferson Davis, president of the Confederacy during the Civil War. When their son was two years old, Barack and Ann Obama divorced, with Barack heading for Harvard to obtain a doctorate as a scholarship student before returning to his native land to work as a government economist. Ann subsequently remarried, this time to an Indonesian student at the East-West Center. When her son was six, Ann moved with her husband and son to Jakarta. In that exotic setting, Barack Jr.'s sister Maya was born and Barack was exposed to grinding poverty with beggars appearing "to be everywhere." His regular diet, he remembered, included dog, snake, and grasshopper, and for a pet he had a gibbon. At the age of ten, Obama returned to Hawaii to reside with his grandparents, Stanley and Madelyn Dunham, where he entered the Punahou School, a highly regarded private academy, graduating from there with honors. His father wrote frequently but returned to Hawaii only once for a visit. Obama played basketball during his teenage years, acquiring "an attitude that didn't just have to do with the sport," and he experimented with marijuana and cocaine. As Obama wrote, "Junkie. Pothead. That's where I'd been headed: the final, fatal role of the young would-be black man." But at some point, he relates, "I think I just grew up."

Beginning his undergraduate studies at Occidental College in Los Angeles, Obama encountered a wide diversity of students and faculty, including politically engaged blacks, international students, and Chicanos. Obama jumped at the opportunity to transfer to Columbia University, located in Morningside Heights near Harlem, which intrigued him. New York City was to his liking but the atmosphere seemed fraught with racial tension, which just "flowed freely" with the walls of university's bathrooms containing "blunt correspondence between niggers and kikes." After completing his bachelor's degree in political science and briefly holding positions with the Business International Corporation and the New York Public Interest Research Group, Obama determined to become a community organizer. It was the height of the Reagan era, and Obama believed that change was necessary but must "come from a mobilized grass roots." He ended up in Chicago, where he joined Trinity United Church of Christ and helped a small, religiously based group conduct projects in indigent neighborhoods on the South Side of the city. Spending three years in the Windy City serving as director of the Developing Communities Project, Obama experienced "inner-city despair and inadequate politics and black self-destruction." Hoping to discover more of his heritage, Obama traveled to Kenya in 1989. En route Obama reflected on his "own uneasy status: a Westerner not entirely at home in the West, an African on his way to a land full of strangers." While in Kenya, he learned more about his ancestry, discovering that his grandfather Onyango had once been detained as a purported subversive for several months. Obama's father, Barack, had attended meetings of political dissidents, who agitated for the release of the jailed Kenyan nationalist Jomo Kenyatta.

Obama enrolled at Harvard Law School shortly after returning home. Once again, he excelled academically, graduating magna cum laude and becoming the first African American student to head the *Harvard Law Review*. At times he found the study of law boring and esoteric but at other points he viewed the law as "memory," involving the recording of "a long-running conversation" through which a nation wrestled with its own conscience. Abner Mikva, a former congressman and federal court judge, offered Obama a clerkship, a position that many considered as a prelude to a similar position with the U.S. Supreme Court, but Obama declined the opportunity. While serving as an intern with a corporate law firm in Chicago, he met Michelle Robinson, a graduate of Princeton University and Harvard Law School. They married in 1992 and subsequently had two daughters. The next year, Obama joined a law firm, Davis, Miner, Barnhill & Galland, specializing in civil rights issues. Obama tried voting rights and employment cases, delivered appellate briefs before the U.S. Court of Appeals, assisted with attempts to build mixed-income housing units to supplant public housing projects, and acted as general counsel for community health clinics, social service agencies, and charter schools. He also began teaching constitutional law as a senior lecturer at the University of Chicago. Obama spearheaded a voter registration drive, PROJECT VOTE!, which raised $200,000 for the campaign, placed 150,000 new voters on the rolls, and helped swing Illinois for Democratic Party presidential candidate Bill Clinton in 1992. The following year *Crain's Chicago Business* named Obama, who served on various boards of directors, as one of the city's preeminent young leaders. The year after that, Obama was named president and chairman of the board of directors of the Annenberg Challenge, which championed public school reform. He also received but turned down an offer of a tenured position at the University of Chicago Law School. In 1995 Random House published his memoir, *Dreams from My Father*, in which he wrote of the "audacity of hope," a refrain borrowed from Jeremiah Wright, Obama's minister in Chicago.

The next year the opportunity arose for Obama to run for the state senate in the thirteenth legislative district, which included well-heeled Hyde Park, skirting the University of Chicago, and a series of distressed black communities on the South Side. Following his election, Independent Voters of Illinois/Independent Project Organizations handed him the Best Freshman Legislator Award, while the Campaign for Better Health and Illinois Primary Health Care Association delivered Outstanding Legislator awards to him after his second year as a state senator. Obama helped to pass legislation providing tax credits for indigent families, increasing health coverage, augmenting funding for the prevention of AIDS, transforming Illinois's death penalty statutes, and mandating the videotaping of custodial interrogations of murder suspects. The young legislator also cooperated with U.S. Senator Paul Simon to shape a stringent campaign finance reform measure and he helped to devise welfare reform legislation. Continuing his work for Miner, Barnhill and Galland, P.C., Obama also worked on voting rights litigation and employment law, and represented not-for-profit and community development corporations involved in urban redevelopment projects. In 2000 Obama campaigned for a congressional seat held by Bobby Rush, a four-term representative who had once belonged to the Black Panther Party. Rush easily turned back Obama, who was viewed as not "black enough" and too well heeled during the primary. Obama remained in the state senate, where he served on the Health and Human Services, Judiciary, and Local Government committees; he chaired the Heath and Human Services Committee.

By 2003, Obama's political aspirations reached considerably higher as he envisioned a run for the Democratic Party's nomination for the U.S. Senate, which at the time appeared to be something of a long shot. In the spring of 2004, Obama captured the nomination for a now open U.S. Senate seat, besting six other candidates in the primary, including the man preferred by the city's political machine and labor unions. Ardent volunteers, including many African Americans and white professionals, found something inspirational in the young activist legislator. When asked why he had gone "into something dirty and nasty like politics" despite his "fancy degrees and a professorship," Obama explained, "We've got too much cynicism in this country, and we're all in this together, and government expresses that."

Obama's address at the 2004 Democratic Party national convention resulted in kudos across the ideological spectrum. David Brooks, a former speechwriter for President George W. Bush, termed it "the kind of speech you go to the conventions to hear," while *USA Today* reported that Obama "exploded onto the national scene . . . delivering a rousing keynote address . . . that heralded his arrival as one of his party's fastest rising stars." In Illinois, the Republicans put up Jack Ryan to run against Obama, but a sexual scandal involving Ryan's former wife, television actress Jeri Ryan, led to his departure from the race. Former Chicago Bears football great Mike Ditka, who had coached the Bears to the 1985 Super Bowl title, opted not to undertake a bid to replace outgoing Republican Senator Peter Fitzgerald. That left the Republican Party without a candidate until black, right-wing radio commentator Alan Keyes, a resident of Maryland, agreed to run against Obama. With the polls placing the Democrat nearly fifty points ahead of Keyes as Election Day approached, Keyes opened his campaign bid by condemning gay marriage and abortion and promising to prevail "for God." Obama deflected Keyes's assertion that Jesus would not support him because of his stance on abortion, stating, "I will leave Mr. Keyes to the theological speculations. My job is to focus on the issues that voters care about—jobs, health care, education. . . . I'm not running to be the minister of Illinois. I'm running to be its United States senator." Coinciding with his senatorial campaign, Obama witnessed republication of his 1995 memoir, *Dreams from My Father*. The new preface contained Obama's acknowledgment that he had hoped his story "might speak in some way to the fissures of race that have characterized the American identity, as well as the fluid state of identity—the leaps through time, the collision of cultures—that mark our modern life." He recognized too that in the post-9/11 world "the hardening of lines, the embrace of fundamentalism and tribe, dooms us all."

In a thoughtful and extended article that appeared in the *New Yorker*, William Finnegan discussed how Kirk Dillard, a Republican state senator from the suburbs of Chicago, referred to Obama. Dillard acknowledged, "I knew from the day he walked into this chamber that he was destined for great things. In Republican circles, we've always feared that Barack would become a rock star of American politics." The Republican legislator continued, "Obama is an extraordinary man. His intellect, his charisma. He's to the left of me on gun control, abortion. But he can really work with Republicans." Speaking to a crowd of several hundred in Danville, Obama suggested that his candidacy was predicated on the certainty that "there's a fundamental decency to the American people that can't be denied. If I could tap into that, my election couldn't be denied." Republican senatorial nominee Alan Keyes attacked the buzz surrounding Obama, declaring,

"It's a manufactured, artificial hype like the Wizard of Oz." Obama himself indicated that he was "mistrustful of our celebrity culture. I think it's fickle. What's lasting is the work." On November 4, Obama decisively defeated Keyes, winning 70 percent of the popular vote, thereby becoming the fifth African American to win a seat in the U.S. Senate.

On February 21, 2005, U.S. Senator Barack Obama delivered a speech on the occasion of Representative John Lewis's sixty-fifth birthday. Obama noted that civil rights activists like Lewis had "awakened a nation's conscience," reminding the American people that ordinary citizens could "do extraordinary things," notwithstanding "the fiercest resistance and the most crushing oppression." Today, Obama continued, "we have songs left to sing and bridges left to cross." Courage was needed to point out it was "wrong that one out of every five children is born into poverty" in the world's richest land, and "[we must] do whatever [is] necessary" to afford "our children the care and education they need to live up to their God-given potential." Obama also affirmed that America must provide its veterans with "the very best care." Two months later Obama again underscored the need for the nation to care for its veterans, particularly those who had been injured while serving in harm's way. He proposed an amendment to ensure that those "wounded heroes" would receive free meals and phone service, no matter the bureaucratic entanglements.

That fall, following a trip to Houston where Obama joined with former presidents Bill Clinton and George H. W. Bush in visiting refugees from Hurricane Katrina, he urged again that red tape not be allowed to further victimize those already suffering from the calamity. Obama called for an independent commission to explore "how we could have failed our fellow citizens so badly, and how we will prevent such a failure from ever occurring again." The people of New Orleans, Obama continued, had been "abandoned long ago—to murder and mayhem in their streets; to substandard schools; to dilapidated housing; to inadequate health care; to a pervasive sense of hopelessness." For him, "that is the deeper shame . . . that it has taken a crisis like this one to awaken us to the great divide that continues to fester in our midst." One lesson resulting from Katrina, Obama believed, involved the nation's need for energy independence. In 2005 Obama also served as cosponsor of the Secure America and Orderly Immigration Act. Meanwhile, the success of his second book, *The Audacity of Hope: Thoughts on Reclaiming the American Dream*, enabled Obama to purchase a condominium in Hyde Park, an upscale neighborhood located close to the University of Chicago.

As a senator, Obama was actively involved in substantial international issues, as well as those relating to terrorism. He traveled to Russia, Ukraine, and Azerbaijan with Republican Senator Richard Lugar, to ascertain how successfully the Soviet stockpile of nuclear weapons was being safeguarded. In December

2005, speaking on the Senate floor, Obama discussed the proposed reauthorization of the Patriot Act, which was intended to provide law enforcement officials with the means necessary to track terrorists both inside and outside the United States. As Obama reminded his colleagues, many Americans had complained of violations of civil liberties resulting from implementation of that measure. He stated, "We don't have to settle for a Patriot Act that sacrifices our liberties or our safety—we can have one that secures both." On February 1, 2006, discussing the previous evening's State of the Union address, Obama questioned President Bush's insistence that military commanders would determine when the Iraqi military could replace American soldiers, observing that it was "clear at this point . . . that there is no military solution to the problem, the Sunnis and the Shiites have to decide they want to live together." In 2006 Obama sponsored the Lugar-Obama Bill, providing funding to quash the proliferation of conventional weapons and to prevent the spread of weapons of mass destruction. He also cosponsored the Coburn-Obama Transparency Act to set up an Internet web search engine tracking federal spending.

During his first three years in the U.S. Senate, Obama served on numerous committees, including Foreign Relations, Environment and Public Works, Veterans' Affairs, Health, Education, Labor and Pensions, and Homeland Security and Governmental Affairs. In February 2007, in the midst of considerable speculation, he declared his candidacy for the presidency, with polls quickly placing him in second place, though well behind New York senator Hillary Clinton. Relying on a small donor base, the Obama presidential campaign proved remarkably adept, quickly establishing fund-raising records. Defying political pundits, Obama swept to a succession of victories, including February 2008's Super Tuesday when he swept eleven primaries and caucuses. Previously favored Hillary Clinton fought back, warning that Obama had little appeal to less advantaged whites, was weakened by a dearth of experience, and was largely relying on a single antiwar speech delivered six years earlier. That same spring, his candidacy was briefly threatened by the incessant replay in newscasts of an incendiary sermon by Jeremiah Wright, the long-time pastor of Trinity United Church of Christ in Chicago, which the Obamas attended. Wright's inflammatory and profane denunciation of a racist America was fodder for all Obama opponents, but especially for right-wing pundits, who proclaimed that Obama's continued affiliation with the church confirmed well-disguised radical inclinations. Obama publicly denounced Wright's fiery rhetoric and broke with the church, effectively neutralizing the issue.

Fending off a strong challenge from the Clinton campaign and a barrage of attacks from conservative commentators and media, Obama won the Democratic Party nomination, appearing before 75,000 people gathered in Denver's Mile High Stadium on August 28, 2008, the day following the introduction of

Delaware senator Joe Biden as the presumptive vice presidential nominee, and the anniversary of Martin Luther King's famous speech on the Washington mall some forty-five years before. Pundits accurately acknowledged the historic nature of Obama's candidacy, given the nation's long and troubled racial history. The racial issue was surprisingly inconsequential throughout both the primary and general election campaigns, with most of the criticisms aimed at Obama stressing his alleged lack of experience or his liberal proclivities. Obama's opponent, Republican senator John McCain, confronted difficulties of his own, including a lengthy record as a fiscal conservative and foreign policy hawk, who proudly proclaimed himself a "foot soldier in the Reagan revolution" and one who had wholly backed President George W. Bush "on the transcendent issues, the most important issues of our day." Despite McCain's repeated claim that the surge in Iraq he had supported had staved off military defeat, the second chief objective of that strategy, the establishment of a politically viable Iraqi nation, was as yet unrealized, and McCain was consistently unwilling to project when U.S. forces in that nation might be reduced or withdrawn. Obama skillfully capitalized on McCain's reticence to set a timetable for ending the American military role in Iraq, and consistently reminded audiences that the Iraq war had diverted U.S. military resources away from the more important conflict against the resurgent Taliban in Afghanistan. Shortly after the Republican convention in Minneapolis in early September, where McCain selected little-known Alaskan governor Sarah Palin as his running mate, American financial institutions began to collapse, seriously undermining McCain, who had a longtime record as a champion of deregulation. As the financial crisis expanded, McCain appeared erratic, constantly lurching between positions on that and other issues, while Obama, the far younger candidate whose lack of experience had been cited by both his Democratic and Republican opponents, came across as far steadier and more composed. The increasingly alarming economic debacle, together with Palin's evident lack of knowledge on basic issues and general unpreparedness for the position she sought, weakened McCain's standing in the polls. In comparison, Obama's confident demeanor and careful deliberation strengthened his appeal.

Three weeks before the election, the New Yorker proclaimed its support for Obama, after pointing to the domestic legacy the Bush administration was leaving behind: a national debt that had all but doubled in size, a $500 billion deficit for the upcoming year, slow private sector job growth, 5 million more people slipping into poverty, 7 million more lacking health insurance as premiums doubled, and tax burdens shifted to less affluent Americans. On top of all that, the nation remained mired in complicated wars in Iraq and Afghanistan, having been "manipulated, bullied, and lied" into the first by the Bush administration. The New Yorker condemned McCain's "remorselessly rightward" movement, his "demagogic" demand for additional tax cuts, his inability to address the financial crisis, his constant shifting of positions, and his recent adoption of absolute opposition to abortion. Obama, by contrast, appeared to have seriously studied economic issues, offered "forceful proposals" relating to energy and global warming, and supported progressive judicial appointees. McCain appeared to misunderstand "the messy, open-ended nature" of the Iraq war, whereas Obama, a prescient early critic of the idea of going to war in Iraq, came across as the statesman required to restore America's reputation worldwide and to help rebuild or reconstruct international organizations. The *New Yorker* condemned McCain's readiness "to pander and even lie" on the campaign trail, and his propensity for "contemptuous duplicity" and "meanness," along with his wholly reckless selection of Palin as the Republican Party vice presidential candidate. Whereas McCain was "impulsive, impatient, self-dramatizing, erratic," Obama offered a "transformative message" along with "a sense of pragmatic calm." Obama offered "a formidable intelligence, emotional empathy, self-reflection, balance," and an easy ability to view the world through others' prisms. The election of a cosmopolitan figure like Obama, with his mixed ethnicity, would transform the nation's image and recharge "its spirit at home," while his standing as president would highlight America's long struggle to achieve equality.

The Monday before Election Day, syndicated columnist E. J. Dionne declared that Obama had spawned "a new social movement, new forms of political organizations, and a sense of excitement and possibility" absent from American politics for three decades. The Illinois senator's "post-everything candidacy" particularly appealed to the young, who served as "happy warriors" for their candidate who would, Dionne projected, become "the first truly 21st-century figure in American politics." On November 4, 2008, Barack Hussein Obama easily defeated John McCain in the presidential election, winning almost 53 percent of the vote and 365 electoral votes to 173 for his opponent. Having adopted the "fifty-state strategy" of Democratic Party national chair Howard Dean, Obama won both the expected "blue" or Democratic states in the Northeast and along the West coast, but also flipped ten "red" or Republican states. Cynthia Tucker, a columnist for the *Atlanta Journal-Constitution*, concluded that "tectonic plates have shifted, and the contours of America's cultural landscape look a lot different today than they did before." Katrina van den Heuvel, editor of *The Nation*, wrote that Obama's triumph amounted to "a milestone in America's scarred racial landscape and a victory for the forces of decency, diversity and tolerance." The significance of the moment was perhaps best captured in the televised coverage of Obama's victory speech at Chicago's Grant Park, where a crowd estimated at 250,000 gathered to celebrate an incontestably historic event. No televised image spoke more poignantly that night than that of Jesse Jackson, longtime civil rights activist who had been at Martin Luther King's side when he was murdered in 1968, who stood in the exuberant crowd, tears streaming down his face, as he listened to the first African American president-elect accept his new charge.

The following January, Barack Obama took office as the first African American president of the United States. Retaining a high level of popular support during the first several months of his presidency, Obama confronted a series of potentially grave domestic and international issues. Foremost among these were the sinking American economy, plunging to depths not seen for a full generation or possibly as far back as the Great Depression, and the tenuous state of international relations, as exemplified by anti-American sentiments propounded by the leaders of Iran, Venezuela, and North Korea, as well as continuing concerns about terrorism, poverty, environmental calamities, and global epidemics.

Conclusion

At the beginning of the twenty-first century, the United States appeared to be pulled in different directions. Following the terrorist attacks that occurred on September 11, 2001, the Bush administration determined that the United States should act and stand alone. President Bush quickly embraced a strategy that gave short shrift to international bodies and opinion, and insisted that if the need arose, the U.S. would engage in preemptive action. Such a readiness, in turn, demanded that the United States possess unrivaled military potency, to allow for a go-it-alone approach. In a highly partisan American political universe, Bush's implementation of a starkly ideological domestic agenda ensured support from an overwhelming majority of Republicans but provoked intense opposition from Democrats and increasing numbers of independents, leaving little ground for moderation or compromise. The American public consequently proved deeply divided on almost every significant issue during the early years of the new century. Though Bush maintained throughout his controversial presidency that history would vindicate his policies, initial evaluations in early 2009 were not auspicious. In a C-SPAN–sponsored survey of scholars, George W. Bush was ranked overall as among the ten worst presidents, placing thirty-sixth out of forty-three.

While the Bush administration reflected the influence of ideological conservatives, who pressed for a new "proactive" foreign policy and a lessened role for the national government in economic and social affairs, Barack Obama exemplified another side of twenty-first-century America. The child of an African father and a mother from the American heartland, Obama personified the increasingly diverse makeup of American society, and even reflected the transnational reality of the modern era. In his address before his party's 2004 national convention, Obama denounced those who contributed to the nation's polarization and challenged the assertion that those who disagreed with administration policy were disloyal or un-American. He also challenged the conservative policies that, in the eyes of many Democrats, dismissed the needs of the least powerful and affluent Americans and ignored growing social and economic inequities. Obama's victory in the 2008 presidential race demonstrated a sea change in racial attitudes in the United States. It also promised to usher in a new progressive presidency that would confront unprecedented domestic concerns relating to the economy and global problems of enormous magnitude.

Study Questions

1. How did the events of 9/11 shape the Bush presidency?
2. What was the Bush administration's rationale for the Iraq War? What were the chief criticisms of war opponents?
3. How would you evaluate the presidency of George W. Bush?
4. What were the chief factors that determined the outcome of the 2008 presidential election?
5. Why did many commentators suggest that Barack Obama was a "transformational" individual? What did this suggest for the future of American national politics?

Selected Bibliography

Borosage, Robert, and Katrina Vanden Heuvel. "Progressives in the Obama Moment." *The Nation*, August 13, 2008.

Bruni, Frank. *Ambling into History: The Unlikely Odyssey of George W. Bush*. New York: HarperCollins, 2002.

———. "The Choice." *The New Yorker*, October 13, 2008.

Clarke, Richard A. *Against All Enemies: Inside America's War on Terror*. New York: Free Press, 2004.

Davey, Monica. "Where to Catch a Rising Political Star? Try Illinois." *New York Times*, October 27, 2004.

Dionne, E. J. "The Opening Obama Saw." *Washington Post*, November 3, 2008.

Draper, Robert. *Dead Certain: The Presidency of George W. Bush*. New York: Free Press, 2007.

Frum, David. *The Right Man*. New York: Random House, 2003.

Greenstein, Fred I., ed. *The George W. Bush Presidency: An Early Assessment*. Baltimore, MD: Johns Hopkins University Press, 2003.

Greenwald, Glenn. *A Tragic Legacy: How a Good vs. Evil Mentality Destroyed the Bush Presidency*. New York: Crown, 2008.

Hersh, Seymour M. *Chain of Command: The Road from 9/11 to Abu Ghraib*. New York: HarperCollins, 2004.

Kantor, Jodi. "Teaching Law, Testing Ideas, Obama Stood Slightly Apart." *New York Times*, July 30, 2008.

Kessler, Ronald. *A Matter of Character: Inside the White House of George W. Bush*. New York: Sentinel, 2004.

Kovaleski, Serge. "Obama's Organizing Years, Guiding Others and Finding Himself." *New York Times*, July 7, 2008.

Lacey, Marc. "Illinois Democrat Wins Kenyan Hearts, in a Landslide." *New York Times*, October 25, 2004.

Mann, James. *Rise of the Vulcans: The History of Bush's War Cabinet*. New York: Penguin, 2004.

Mayer, Jane. *The Dark Side: The Inside Story of How the War on Terror Turned into a War on American Ideals*. New York: Doubleday, 2008.

Mendell, David. *Obama: From Promise to Power*. New York: Amistad, 2008.

Obama, Barack. *The Audacity of Hope: Thoughts on Reclaiming the American Dream*. New York: Vintage, 2008.

———. *Dreams from My Father: A Story of Race and Inheritance*. New York: Crown, 1995.

Phillips, Kevin. *American Dynasty: Aristocracy, Fortune and the Politics of Deceit in the House of Bush*. New York: Viking, 2004.

Sabato, Larry J. *Divided States of America: The Slash and Burn Politics of the 2004 Presidential Election*. New York: Longman, 2005.

Savage, Charlie. *Takeover: The Return of the Imperial Presidency and the Subversion of American Democracy*. New York: Little, Brown, 2008.

Scott, Janny. "In Illinois, Obama Proved Pragmatic and Shrewd." *New York Times*, July 30, 2007.

———. "Obama's Account of New York Years Often Differs from What Others Say." *New York Times*, October 30, 2007.

———. "The Story of Obama, Written by Obama." *New York Times*, May 18, 2008.

Singer, Peter. *The President of Good and Evil: The Ethics of George W. Bush*. New York: Dutton, 2004.

Souza, Pete. *The Rise of Barack Obama*. Chicago: Triumph Books, 2008.

Unger, Craig. *American Armageddon: How the Delusions of the Neoconservatives and the Christian Right Triggered the Descent of America—and Still Imperil Our Future*. New York: Scribner, 2008.

Weisberg, Jacob. *The Bush Tragedy*. New York: Random House, 2008.

Wolffe, Richard. *Renegade: The Making of a President*. New York: Crown, 2009.

Woodward, Bob. *Bush at War*. New York: Simon and Schuster, 2002.

———. *Plan of Attack*. New York: Simon and Schuster, 2004.

———. *State of Denial*. New York: Simon and Schuster, 2006.

Index

Note: Page numbers in *italics* designate pages with photos.

~

About the Authors

Blaine T. Browne holds a PhD in history from the University of Oklahoma and has taught at several universities and community colleges. He is currently senior professor of history at Broward College in Fort Lauderdale, Florida, where he teaches U.S. history, history of Western civilization, and twentieth-century world history. In 2006, he was awarded the Children's Opportunity Group Endowed Teaching Chair, and he has served twice as president of the Florida Conference of Historians. In recent years he has authored texts on recent U.S. history, modern world history, and Western civilization.

Robert C. Cottrell recently completed his twenty-fifth year at California State University, Chico, where he serves as professor of history and American studies. He has also taught in London and Puebla, Mexico, and just completed a stint as the Fulbright Program's Distinguished Chair in American History and American Studies at Moscow State University. He has published numerous books, including biographies of radical journalist I. F. Stone, ACLU founder Roger Nash Baldwin, and Negro League pioneer Rube Foster. He has coauthored several volumes with Blaine T. Browne. Among these are *Uncertain Order: The World in the Twentieth Century* and *Modern American Lives: Individuals and Issues in American History Since 1945*.